THE BOUNDARIES OF THE CRIMINAL LAW

The Boundaries of the Criminal Law

Edited by
R.A. DUFF
LINDSAY FARMER
S.E. MARSHALL
MASSIMO RENZO
VICTOR TADROS

OXFORD
UNIVERSITY PRESS

OXFORD
UNIVERSITY PRESS

Great Clarendon Street, Oxford OX2 6DP

Oxford University Press is a department of the University of Oxford.
It furthers the University's objective of excellence in research, scholarship,
and education by publishing worldwide in

Oxford New York

Auckland Cape Town Dar es Salaam Hong Kong Karachi
Kuala Lumpur Madrid Melbourne Mexico City Nairobi
New Delhi Shanghai Taipei Toronto

With offices in

Argentina Austria Brazil Chile Czech Republic France Greece
Guatemala Hungary Italy Japan Poland Portugal Singapore
South Korea Switzerland Thailand Turkey Ukraine Vietnam

Oxford is a registered trade mark of Oxford University Press
in the UK and in certain other countries

Published in the United States
by Oxford University Press Inc., New York

British Library Cataloguing-in-Publication Data

Data available

Library of Congress Cataloging-in-Publication Data

Data available

Typeset by Newgen Imaging Systems (P) Ltd., Chennai, India
Printed and bound by
CPI Group (UK) Ltd, Croydon, CR0 4YY

ISBN 978–0–19–960055–7

3 5 7 9 10 8 6 4 2

Preface

This volume is the first published product of a research project on Criminalization, funded by a grant from the Arts and Humanities Research Council (Grant No 128737). Three further collections of papers from the project's workshops and conference will be published in due course, along with three monographs by members of the project.

We are grateful to the Arts and Humanities Research Council for the grant that made this project possible, and to our own universities for the further material and administrative help that they provided—the University of Stirling and the Stirling Department of Philosophy, the University of Glasgow and the School of Law, the University of Warwick and the School of Law.

Above all, however, we are grateful to the authors who have contributed to this volume, to all those who took part in the workshops and meetings from which this volume has emerged, and in particular to the commentators on the drafts of the papers collected in this volume—Kimberley Brownlee, Erik Claes, Rowan Cruft, Alon Harel, Tatjana Hörnle, Douglas Husak, Susan Mendus, and Andrew Williams. These meetings showed us how fruitful, and enjoyable, this kind of interdisciplinary work can be. We are also extremely grateful to Andrew Cornford for his assistance in preparing the final manuscript and to Christine Kelly for preparing the index.

Antony Duff, Lindsay Farmer, Sandra Marshall,
Massimo Renzo, Victor Tadros

Contents

List of Contributors

Andrew Ashworth is Vinerian Professor of English Law at the University of Oxford, and a Fellow of All Souls College. Among his books are *Principles of Criminal Law* (6th edn, 2009), *Sentencing and Criminal Justice* (5th edn, 2010), and, with Mike Redmayne, *The Criminal Process* (4th edn, 2010).

Markus Dubber is Professor of Law at the University of Toronto Faculty of Law. His publications include *The Police Power: Patriarchy and the Foundations of American Government* (2005), *The Sense of Justice: Empathy in Law and Punishment* (2006), and *Handbook of Comparative Criminal Law* (with Kevin Heller) (Stanford University Press, 2010).

RA Duff was educated at Oxford, and taught for forty years in the Philosophy Department at the University of Stirling. He now also holds a half-time position at the University of Minnesota Law School. He has published books and articles on criminal punishment, on the structure of criminal law, on criminal attempts, and on the criminal trial.

Lindsay Farmer is Professor of Law at the University of Glasgow. He researches and publishes in the areas of criminal law, legal theory, and legal history.

Mireille Hildebrandt is an Associate Professor of Jurisprudence at Erasmus University Rotterdam and a Senior Researcher at the Centre for Law Science Technology and Society at Vrije Universiteit Brussel. Her research interest concerns the nexus of philosophy of (criminal) law and technology, with a focus on the implications of smart environments on the foundations of democracy and the Rule of Law.

SE Marshall is Emeritus Professor of Philosophy at the University of Stirling. Her work is in the overlap between moral, political, and legal philosophy.

Kimmo Nuotio is Professor of Criminal Law and vice-director of the Centre of Excellence in Foundations of European Law and Polity Research, both at the University of Helsinki. He is also the Dean of the Faculty of Law. His research focuses mainly on theoretical issues of criminal law.

Massimo Renzo is Lecturer in Law at the University of York. He works primarily in legal theory and political philosophy. His main research interests are in the philosophical foundations of criminal law, international justice, state legitimacy, and political obligation.

John Stanton-Ife is a senior lecturer in law at King's College London. He has published papers on strict liability, theft and the limits of law. Among his current projects is an examination of the minimum standards for the valid, sexual consent of the severely mentally disordered

Carol Steiker is the Howard & Kathy Aibel Professor of Law at Harvard Law School. Professor Steiker is the author of numerous scholarly works in the fields of criminal law, criminal procedure, and capital punishment. She served as co-author of the Kadish, Schulhofer & Steiker casebook, *Criminal Law and Its Processes* (8th ed. 2007), editor of *Criminal Procedure Stories* (Foundation 2006), and on the Board of Editors of the *Encyclopedia of Crime and Justice* (2nd ed. Macmillan, 2002). In addition to her scholarly work, Professor Steiker has worked on pro bono litigation projects on behalf of indigent criminal defendants and has served as a consultant and an expert witness on issues of criminal justice for non-profit organizations and federal and state legislatures.

Victor Tadros is Professor of Criminal Law and Legal Theory at the University of Warwick, England. He was educated at the University of Oxford and King's College, London and has held previous appointments at the Universities of Aberdeen and Edinburgh. He is in the process of completing a book entitled *The Moral Foundations of Criminal Law*. His books include *Criminal Responsibility* (OUP, 2005) and *The Trial on Trial (3): Towards a Normative Theory of the Criminal Trial* (Hart, 2007. Co-authored with Antony Duff, Lindsay Farmer and Sandra Marshall).

Lucia Zedner is Professor of Criminal Justice, Law Faculty and Corpus Christi College, University of Oxford. Since 2007 she has also held the post of Conjoint Professor at the Faculty of Law, University of New South Wales, Australia where she is a regular visitor. She has also held visiting fellowships at universities in Germany, Israel, America, and Australia. Her publications include *Criminal Justice* (Oxford University Press, 2004), *Crime and Security* (co-edited with Benjamin Goold, Ashgate, 2006), *Security* (Routledge, 2009) and many articles and chapters in the field of criminal justice and security.

1

Introduction: The Boundaries of the Criminal Law

RA Duff, Lindsay Farmer, SE Marshall,
Massimo Renzo, Victor Tadros

This volume of papers is the first published fruit of a four-year project, funded by the Arts and Humanities Research Council, on Criminalization. In this Introduction, we outline the aims of the overall project, and indicate how the papers collected here fit into it.

I   The Question of Criminalization

The project began with an apparently simple question: what should be criminalized? This question about the proper scope of the criminal law is given urgency by two contemporary phenomena. On the one hand, it is often argued that we face a crisis of over criminalization: far too much is criminalized that ought not to be criminal; our criminal law far exceeds its proper boundaries.[1] On the other hand, it is often argued (and governments often seem very ready to believe) that the criminal law should be extended to provide an adequate response to new, or newly disturbing, threats of various kinds. Obvious examples here include the ever-increasing range of offences connected to terrorism,[2] and those concerned with pornography and certain types of

---

[1] See recently D Husak, *Overcriminalization* (Oxford: Oxford University Press, 2007). See also, from different perspectives: A Ashworth, 'Is the Criminal Law a Lost Cause?' (2000) 116 LQR 225; MD Dubber, *Victims in the War Against Crime* (New York: NYU Press, 2002); N Lacey, *The Prisoners' Dilemma: Political Economy and Punishment in Contemporary Societies* (Cambridge: Cambridge University Press, 2008); W Stuntz, 'The Pathological Politics of Criminal Law' (2001) 100 *Michigan Law Review* 506. As we will see later, the 'we' and the 'our' here are problematic: how far is it possible to talk in general terms about the actual or proper scope of 'the criminal law', and how far only more locally of its actual or proper scope in this or that kind of polity?

[2] See, eg Terrorism Act 2000; Terrorism Act 2006.

sexual exploitation.[3] The first kind of argument, which can be offered by people from very different parts of the political spectrum, might appeal to the value of liberty, to the costs (both material and moral) of criminalization and punishment, and to the oppressive kinds of investigation and enforcement that criminalization can bring; while the second kind of argument more typically appeals to the demands of security (of both individuals and the state), and to the rights of potential victims of crime. Between them, these conflicting claims and pressures make it imperative to tackle the general question of what should be criminalized: just what should the criminal law cover?

However, a moment's thought will show how that general question is very far from simple. Some of the ways in which it is far from simple emerge if we ask what it is to criminalize something, and realise the inadequacy of the answer: 'It is to pass a statute defining something as a crime.' Statutory enactment might not even be formally sufficient for criminalization, in polities whose constitutions permit courts to strike down legislation as being unconstitutional, or inconsistent with an authoritative convention such as the European Convention on Human Rights; but even if we sidestep that issue by talking of valid statutes, it is not clear that such statutory enactment is substantively sufficient for criminalization. Suppose, for instance, that possession of a particular kind of drug is statutorily criminal, but that a police force follows a declared policy of not prosecuting the possession of small amounts of that drug.[4] Should we now say that the possession of such quantities of that drug is still criminal, although the law is not enforced; or that such possession has been decriminalized in that part of the country? Or suppose that it is statutorily a crime to assist any suicide; but the head of the prosecution service publishes guidelines concerning the factors to be taken into account when deciding whether or not to prosecute, which, whilst not explicitly declaring that certain kinds of case will never be prosecuted, make it sufficiently clear to would-be assisters the conditions under which they will not be prosecuted.[5]

---

[3] See Criminal Justice and Immigration Act 2008, ss 63–67; Criminal Justice and Licensing (S) Bill, s 34 (creating offence of possession of extreme pornography); Policing and Crime Act 2009, ss 14–21; Prostitution (Public Places) (S) Act 2007 (creating offences related to prostitution and sexual exploitation). A quite different pressure towards an expanding criminal law comes from the need to enforce the ever-expanding range of government regulations covering different aspects of citizens' lives: most of the more than two thousand new offences created in England since 1997 are of this kind.

[4] See, for instance, the Obama administration's instruction on federal prosecution of possession of medical marijuana. See: <http://www.huffingtonpost.com/2009/10/19/new-medical-marijuana-pol_n_325426.html>. See also <http://www.direct.gov.uk/en/YoungPeople/Crime AndJustice/TypesOfCrime/DG_10027693> on UK police procedures. The position is more complicated when the police will confiscate the drug even where they do not prosecute.

[5] See <http://www.cps.gov.uk/publications/prosecution/assisted_suicide_policy.html>. These guidelines were issued by the English Director of Public Prosecutions, as required by the House of

It is hard to resist the conclusion that assisting suicide under those conditions is no longer a crime.

More generally, the familiar distinction between the 'law in the books' and the 'law in action' reminds us that, if what interests us, historically or normatively, is not just the law as it figures in official edicts or declarations, but the law as it impinges on the lives of those who are subject to it; in asking what is or should be criminal we must attend not just to criminal codes or statutes, but to the ways in which such codes or statutes are or are not enforced by police and prosecutors. The importance of this point is not limited to such examples as drug possession and assisted suicide, nor is it obvious that theorists can deal with it by simply saying that statutes should be so formulated that they can be rigorously enforced: that criminal statutes should define as criminal all and only those kinds of conduct that should be prosecuted as crimes, and that prosecutors should then not be able to decide, as a matter of policy, not to prosecute in certain kinds of case. That claim would need to be justified, against the argument that legislatures should sometimes, for the sake of effective protection and prevention, pass criminal statutes that contain over broad definitions of crimes, with the intention that police and prosecutors should exercise a wide discretion in deciding which cases to pursue, so as to prosecute only in those cases that are 'really' criminal, ie that involve the mischief against which the law is aimed.[6] We might have reason to reject such legislative strategies, but we cannot assume in advance that they are always illegitimate: in which case the question of what should be criminalized, as well as that of what is in fact criminalized, cannot be answered in terms simply of criminal statutes.

Even if statutory definition as a crime is sufficient for criminalization in a formal sense, it is clearly not necessary for criminalization either formally or substantively. The most obvious reason why it is not formally necessary is that in common law systems statute law is not the only kind of law: even the law in the books in such systems must include more than the law in the statute books. More interesting is the way in which formal definition as a crime, either by statute or by whatever declarations have formal authority in a common law system, is not necessary for criminalization in a substantive sense. This point can be illustrated by the way in which the European Court of Human Rights has dealt with so-called regulatory offences. When Germany enacted a

---

Lords in *R (Purdy) v DPP* [2009] UKHL 45, in response to cases in which relatives helped intending suicides travel to a 'suicide clinic' in Switzerland. These are intended to help such would-be assisters make informed decisions about what to do—decisions informed by well-grounded predictions about whether they would face prosecution.

[6] See also Carol Steiker's discussion, in this volume, of the use of discretionary mercy as a way of mitigating the problem of over punishment.

regime of *Ordnungswidrigkeiten*,[7] this was portrayed as a matter of decriminalization: kinds of conduct that had fallen under the criminal law as *Straftaten* were now mere *Ordnungswidrigkeiten*, or regulatory infractions, outside the scope of the criminal law.[8] The European Court, however, declared that states could not avoid the protections that the European Convention ascribed to defendants who were charged with 'criminal offences', or who faced 'criminal charges', merely by such a formal reclassification of the violation or the law that defined it. The Court would attend to the nature of the offence, and the nature and severity of the penalty that it could attract, and would be willing to decide that what was formally classified as a non-criminal, regulatory infraction should count substantively as a criminal offence.[9]

One could say, of course, that whilst it is open to the European Court to treat certain kinds of violation *as if* they are criminal offences, and to extend the protections given by Article 6 to defendants charged with such violations, that is not to say that they actually *are* criminal offences. It is notoriously difficult, perhaps impossible, to provide a definition of 'crime' in other than purely formal terms: a crime is that which the law and the courts treat as a crime, in that its perpetrator is liable to be subjected to a criminal process and to criminal punishment; and what counts as a criminal process or criminal punishment is likewise to be defined by the particular legal system. Thus, Gordon argues,

The criminal law is probably, therefore, sufficiently defined as that branch of the law which deals with those acts, attempts and omissions of which the state may take cognisance by prosecution in the criminal courts.[10]

But this formalization merely shifts the problem to another place. If we deny that some legal regulation is criminal, we may also deny that the court, in prosecuting the defendant for breaching the regulation, is acting as a criminal court. Hence, we can see that Gordon's formalization conceals the substantive issues that need to be addressed about the different kinds of legal regulation to which conduct can be subjected. We need to ask which kinds of regulation, backed by what kinds of sanction, should be available to a state, and how, or

---

[7] Gesetz über Ordnungswidrigkeiten (1968/1975).

[8] The European Court noted this claim about decriminalization in *Öztürk v Germany* (1984) 6 EHRR 409. For a useful critical discussion, see T Weigend, 'The Legal and Practical Problems Posed by the Difference between Criminal Law and Administrative Penal Law' (1988) 59 *Revue Internationale de Droit Pénal* 67.

[9] See *Öztürk*, ibid; *Lauko v Slovakia* (2001) 33 EHRR 40; *Engel v Netherlands* (1979–80) 1 EHRR 647. The key protections at stake are those provided for in Art 6 of the European Convention on Human Rights.

[10] GH Gordon, *The Criminal Law of Scotland*, 2nd edn (Edinburgh: W Green, 1978) 15; 3rd edn by MGA Christie (Edinburgh: W Green, 2000) vol I, 7.

on the basis of what kinds of consideration, decisions should be made about which kinds of conduct are to be subjected to which kinds of regulation.

The distinction between crimes and regulatory infractions is just one example of a wider phenomenon—the variety of ways in which the state can regulate, or control, or provide for some kind of formal response to, its citizens' conduct. Other examples include the kinds of civil process that are initiated by individuals seeking damages or injunctions (rather than by prosecutors seeking convictions and punishments); and a wide range of increasingly popular 'hybrid' provisions under which courts make what counts formally as a non-criminal order restraining a person's liberty, but that order has the force and status of criminal law, in that a breach of it is a punishable criminal offence.[11] This phenomenon not only complicates the question about criminalization with which we began; it also forces us to ask whether that is the question with which we should begin. Why, that is, should we ask about criminalization, rather than more generally about what kinds of conduct should be subject to state control? Or, even if we limit our attention to the kinds of control that are initiated by the state, as distinct from the kinds of civil process that are supported by the state but initiated by individuals,[12] why should we ask only about subjection to the regime of the criminal law, rather than about subjection to any of the wide range of possible regulatory regimes? It is worth remembering here that JS Mill's classic formulation of the harm principle referred not to the proper use or scope of the criminal law in particular, but more generally to interference with the liberty of, and to the exercise of power or compulsion over, members of 'a civilized community'.[13]

The force of this meta-question depends on how we should understand the criminal law. If it is best understood simply as one technique amongst others in the state's toolkit for the control of behaviour, differing from other techniques only as saws differ from chisels, then we probably should be asking not about criminalization in particular, but about regulation, or coercive regulation, more generally: we must ask what ends state regulation should serve, and then—as a quasi-technical question—which of the available techniques are likely to be most efficient in serving those ends in different contexts.[14] There

[11] The Anti-Social Behaviour Order remains the clearest example of this kind of provision; for a detailed discussion and critique see Ashworth and Zedner in this volume. One could also note here the provisions for the confiscation of alleged criminal or terrorist assets: see, eg Criminal Justice Act 1988, Pt VI; Drug Trafficking Act 1994, Pt I; Terrorism Act 2000, ss 24–28; Anti-Terrorism, Crime and Security Act 2001, s 1.

[12] But that distinction will also require scrutiny, and justification; note too the range of civil proceedings that may be brought not by private individuals or by corporations, but by governmental agencies.   [13] JS Mill, *On Liberty* (London: Parker, 1859) ch 1, para 9.

[14] See, eg N Lacey, 'Criminal Law as Regulation' in J Braithwaite *et al* (eds), *Regulating Law* (Oxford: Oxford University Press, 2004).

will of course be constraints that limit the state's proper use of its coercive powers, but these too will not be unique to criminal law: they will bear equally on any regulatory regime. If, on the other hand, the criminal law has a distinctive character or distinctive aims of its own; if it is not just one technique among others for regulating behaviour, then it is worth asking our question about the kinds of conduct that should be subjected to this distinctive kind of regulation.

Already, then, our question is becoming yet more complicated. We have to ask what, if anything, is distinctive about criminal law as compared to other types of legal regulation; and the European Court's decisions about what counts as a 'criminal' charge should show us that, if an answer to this question is to do any substantive work in a normative theory of criminal law, it cannot be a purely formal answer—we cannot simply say that criminal law is what the state says is criminal law. If we can offer a substantive answer to this question, we must then recognize that the question about criminalization includes at least three questions. First, what kinds of regulatory regime, what kinds of coercive control of conduct, should be available to a state? Second, what kinds of conduct should be subject to some kind of state control? Third, what kinds of conduct should be subject to the distinctive mode of control that is the criminal law?[15]

Three further sets of complicating factors should also be noted here: one about the nature of the inquiry, and two about its scope.

As to the nature of the inquiry, the key question is how far it can aspire to be universal, and how far it cannot but be relatively local—a question foreshadowed at the very start of this Introduction when we talked about 'our' criminal law, and the crisis of overcriminalization that 'we' supposedly face. We have space here to comment only on three aspects of this large question.

First, the avowed aim with which this project began was to work towards 'a normative theory of criminalization'. Now, to talk in such terms of a 'theory' might imply, first, a neat and coherent systematic structure of goals and principles; we comment below on whether this is something to which we should aspire. But it might also, more relevantly for our present purposes, imply a universal theory about the proper aims and scope of 'the criminal law' as such—of criminal law as it should operate at all times, in all places; and the

---

[15] Even this way of putting the question about criminalization in particular begs at least two questions; for it assumes, first, that it is conduct that is to be criminalized (and not, for instance, character, or condition, or status); and it assumes, second, that the criminal law at least (if not only) aims to control conduct. We say more about the second assumption below, but cannot discuss the first further here: for discussion of the role of conduct as the main ground of criminal liability, see V Tadros, *Criminal Responsibility* (Oxford: Oxford University Press, 2005) chs 1–3; RA Duff, *Answering for Crime* (Oxford: Hart Publishing, 2007) ch 5.

present question is whether that is something to which a normative theorist should aspire. Some clearly have precisely that aspiration: according to Moore, for instance, criminal law is a functional kind, whose essential purpose is to inflict deserved punishment on culpable wrongdoers.[16]

We do not share Moore's metaphysical ambitions, nor his metaphysical confidence. We might also doubt the relationship between moral wrongdoing and political practices implied in his theory. On Moore's account, we begin with the essential aim of criminal law as such—an aim that would by itself mandate the criminalization of every kind of moral wrongdoing; and we then appeal to political theory (in Moore's case to a familiar type of liberal theory) to constrain the scope of the criminal law, and to remove many kinds of wrongdoing from its grasp.[17] But perhaps this puts the moral cart before the political horse, as if criminal law is at root a moral matter, and is then constrained by political principles. An alternative view is that we should instead recognize that the criminal law, as an aspect of the institutional structure of the state, is at root a political matter, ie any account of its proper aims must begin with an account of the proper aims of the state, and of the ways in which a state should deal with and relate to its citizens (since the criminal law is a central aspect of that relationship).

On that view, we cannot ask about the proper aims of criminal law as such, independently of, or prior to, any particular political structure; for an account of those aims must be of the aims that criminal law should serve within a particular kind of polity. Of course, if we could articulate *the* true political theory, *the* right account of the aims and operations of any legitimate state, we could then go on to provide an account of proper aims of the criminal law at all times and in all places; a universal political theory would generate a universal theory of criminal law.[18] If, on the other hand, we should eschew such universalist ambitions, we must content ourselves with a more relativist account of criminal law: an account of what criminal law should be, and should aim to achieve, within this or that more particular type of polity, or within the terms of this or that more particular kind of political theory. The 'we' whose law it is, then, will not be the universal 'we' of humanity (or of rational social beings): it will be the 'we' of some more specific, and local, kind of polity.[19]

Perhaps fortunately, we lack the space to discuss the proper ambitions of political theory further here; we must content ourselves with asking about the

---

[16] MS Moore, *Placing Blame* (Oxford: Oxford University Press, 1997) ch 1.

[17] Ibid, ch 16.

[18] Compare J Braithwaite and P Pettit, *Not Just Deserts: A Republican Theory of Criminal Justice* (Oxford: Oxford University Press, 1990).

[19] This kind of relativism should not undermine confidence in the possibility of rational normative theorizing: see RA Duff, 'Theorizing Criminal Law' (2005) 25 OJLS 353, 363–4.

proper scope and aims of the criminal law within the framework of a particular kind of political theory—within the framework of the kinds of liberalism by which contemporary western democracies are supposedly structured. That is, admittedly, an unhelpfully vague gesture towards a range of different theories, all of which might call themselves 'liberal', and one issue for further work will be that of how far we need to specify a more precise version of liberalism if we are to generate any tolerably precise conclusions about the proper scope of a liberal criminal law or about the factors that should bear on liberal decisions about criminalization. For the time being, however, we need perhaps do no more than cite such values as equality, liberty, and privacy; and note the centrality of citizenship to the ideal of a liberal polity—citizenship to be understood as a matter of equal and mutually respectful participation in the civic enterprise.[20] Our basic question then becomes a question about the kind of criminal law that citizens of a liberal republic could properly create and impose on each other and themselves; about what aims for the criminal law could reflect or be consistent with a mutual recognition of fellow citizenship; about what kinds of conduct the citizens of such a polity could accept should be subjected to the distinctive attentions of the criminal law.

The second issue to be noted here about the nature of the inquiry concerns what is to be taken for granted. The importance of this issue can be seen if we return to the idea that we—at least the 'we' who live in Britain and the USA—face a crisis of overcriminalization. Part of what drives that idea is the extent of the costs (material, human, moral) that criminalization in our existing systems of criminal justice incurs, and the oppressive character of those systems. If the effect of criminalizing a particular type of conduct is that those suspected of engaging in such conduct face a criminal process that gives them no real opportunity to answer to the charge or to defend themselves, and when convicted face imprisonment under oppressive and destructive conditions, we should certainly be very slow to criminalize, and must always ask ourselves whether criminalization is worth such substantial and damaging costs. If, therefore, our question about what should be criminalized is about what should be criminalized in our existing systems of criminal law with the consequences that typically follow in those systems, we might reasonably conclude that our criminal law should be much narrower in scope than it now is.

But our question, as a question in normative legal theory, should not be limited in that way. Instead of asking, 'Given what criminalization actually

---

[20] As this reference to citizenship makes clear, we are here thinking particularly of republican versions of liberalism: for different versions, see, eg R Dagger, *Civic Virtues: Rights, Citizenship, and Republican Liberalism* (New York: Oxford University Press, 1997); P Pettit, *Republicanism: A Theory of Freedom and Government* (Oxford: Oxford University Press, 1997).

involves in our existing systems, what kinds of conduct should be criminalized?', our question must become more thoroughly normative: 'What should be criminalized in a decent system of criminal law that provides an appropriate criminal process and appropriate kinds of punishment?' But in that case a theory of criminalization will have to include, or at least be able to appeal to, a normative theory of the criminal process and a normative theory of punishment. If, for instance (to put a modicum of illustrative flesh on these bare bones), given our best theories of the criminal process and punishment, criminalization would have to imply subjection to the costs and burdens of a full criminal trial,[21] and to imprisonment as the standard mode of punishment, we should favour a very limited criminal law: for we should be slow to subject people to those kinds of burden or oppression.[22] But if, on the other hand, we could envisage a criminal process that was capable of dealing less burdensomely (but still of course justly) with relatively minor kinds of wrong, and modes of punishment far less oppressive and less stigmatic than those that are too often imposed under our current systems; we could also envisage a criminal law of rather wider scope, capturing kinds of wrong for which only such a 'light touch' criminal process would be appropriate.

This, however, leads to the third, related issue to be noted about the nature of our inquiry. A normative theory of criminal law is a normative theory not of some abstract entity, but of a political institution (or set of institutions). It might—indeed, given the manifest failings of all human institutions, it no doubt must—generate a more or less radical critique of our existing institutions; nor can we rule out in advance the possibility that it will show such institutions to be unjustifiable.[23] It must, however, begin with the institutions we have (and this 'we' must, again, be relatively local), with the aims that they could be thought to have, with the values and meanings that they could be taken to embody—however imperfectly. But the institutions we have are neither timeless nor newly minted: they have a history, a long and complicated history, and we must therefore ask how that history bears on our normative theorizing about them.[24] That history includes the history of changing

---

[21] See RA Duff, *et al*, *The Trial on Trial (3): Towards a Normative Theory of the Criminal Trial* (Oxford: Hart Publishing, 2007) ch 6.

[22] Which is not to say that reforms to its scope should consist only in the decriminalization of many currently criminal kinds of conduct; we might still see good reason to criminalize conduct that is not now criminal.

[23] For a recent defence of abolitionism in punishment that might entail abolishing the criminal law as well, see D Boonin, *The Problem of Punishment* (Cambridge: Cambridge University Press, 2008).

[24] See especially Farmer (in this volume); N Lacey, 'Historicising Criminalisation: Conceptual and Empirical Issues' (2009) 72 MLR 936; D Brown, 'History's Challenge to Criminal Law Theory' (2009) 3 *Criminal Law and Philosophy* 271.

conceptions of the criminal law and of its role in society;[25] the history of the changing boundaries and structures of the criminal law and its institutions; and the histories of the wide range of political, economic, and social factors and forces that have helped to determine the particular content of the criminal law.[26]

Were our task the purely interpretative task of trying to explain the ends that our existing institutions either actually serve or are actually designed (by whom?) to serve, or to articulate the values or meanings that actually inform them, their history would of course be crucial: we can understand their present only as emerging from their past. Clearly history, especially history that is both comparative and sociologically informed, can also play at least a modest role, whether cautionary or supportive, in normative theorizing. Minimally, as Herodotus was the first to point out, it can generate a suitable caution in normative theorists: it reminds us that what 'we' do 'here' is not done by others elsewhere, and that what we do here has a history, and was not always thus; what we might take to be unchangeable features of any (civilized) human society turn out to be relatively recent features of certain specific societies. It can also remind us that things are not always what they might appear to be to the incautious or hasty eye—in particular that meanings, functions, and purposes are not always evident, and that the ways in which an institution (or its officials) presents itself do not always give a true picture of its aims or workings. It can also be a source of alternative interpretations: we might find other possible interpretations, other possible aims and values, in the history of an institution. But what is less clear, and more controversial, is the extent to which normative theorizing can break free of the history of the institutions that it theorizes.[27] How far, and on what basis, can a normative theorist legitimately propose aims or meanings for an institution that cannot be grounded in its actual history; how far can a theorist say, 'Whatever purposes this might have served in the past, whatever it might have meant then, *this* is what it should be and do in the future'? We do not propose to try to settle this issue here—partly because it is one on which the editors do not agree amongst themselves—but it should be noted as an important question about the nature of any normative theorizing about our political and legal institutions.

---

[25] Compare Dubber's discussion in this volume.

[26] Including factors that bear on conceptions of wrongdoing that then feed into the criminal law (see Farmer in this volume).

[27] This is distinct from the question of how far such theorizing can break free of its own history—of its own origins in a particular tradition of political, legal, and moral thought. Both questions, however, bear on the general issue of the extent to which normative theorizing must be local rather than universal.

The second complicating factor about the scope of the inquiry to be noted here concerns the structure rather than the scope of the criminal law. If we ask what should be criminalized, we must also ask *how* it is to be criminalized— by which we mean, not the process through which kinds of conduct are to be criminalized or decriminalized (important though such questions are), but the way in which the criminal law is to define offences. A host of new questions now arise: about the internal structure of the criminal law—for instance about the role and utility of such distinctions as those between *actus reus* and *mens rea*, between offences and defences, between justifications and excuses; about the kinds of term in which offences ought to be defined—for instance, about the extent to which definitions should so far as possible be set in purely descriptive terms, or should instead employ a richer normative vocabulary; about the individuation and classification of offences—how far the law should operate with very broad offence definitions and categorizations, or how far with more specific definitions which aim to capture more precise kinds of wrong; and so on. It might seem that such questions are distinct from our central question about the proper scope of the criminal law; for that latter question is about its extent, about the area of ground that this edifice is to cover, whereas the questions about structure noted here are about the internal organization of the building. But we cannot so easily separate questions of extent from questions of internal structure, for at least two reasons.

One obvious reason concerns the extent to which the internal structure of the criminal law should reflect the grounds on which the various types of conduct are criminalized: should the law define (and categorize and individuate) offences in ways that bring out those features in virtue of which the conduct is (judged to be) 'criminalizable'? To illustrate this point, consider two views (each of which is no doubt far too simple as presented here). According to one of these views, the criminal law's definitions of offences should capture the particular kinds of moral wrong that are criminalized. This is a matter both of 'fair labelling',[28] and of transparent communication—the idea that the criminal law should make explicit to citizens not only that something is criminal but also why the conduct for which they are liable to be punished is criminalized. If we see the criminal law as focused on particular kinds of moral wrong, and if such wrongs are to be understood in terms of the rich and particularized vocabulary that characterizes extra-legal moral thought, this would imply that the criminal law's special part should define and distinguish offences in

---

[28] On which see AJ Ashworth, *Principles of Criminal Law*, 6th edn (Oxford: Oxford University Press, 2009) 88–90; J Chalmers and F Leverick, 'Fair Labelling in Criminal Law' (2008) 71 MLR 217. Perhaps what is at stake here, however, is not so much fair labelling as honest or explicit labelling, as it is hard to find anyone who would defend 'unfair labelling'.

similarly rich and particularized ways.[29] The other view appeals rather to the virtues of clarity, certainty, and consistency in the rules that citizens are supposed to obey (and those that courts are to apply): whatever the reasons for criminalizing a certain kind of conduct, what matters about the criminal law's offence definitions is that they should make absolutely clear (even to citizens who do not share the moral values that might inform decisions about criminalization) what they must not do, or may do. This view is likely to lead to a very different style of special part legislation—one that eschews rich moral vocabulary in favour of a more austerely descriptive specification of larger categories of criminal conduct.[30]

A second factor concerns the practicability of criminal law. We might distinguish three stages in deliberations about what to criminalize.[31] The first stage is the 'in principle' stage: what kinds of conduct are in principle 'criminalizable', ie what do we have good reason to criminalize? The second stage concerns, any countervailing principles that may militate, even in principle, against criminalization. Perhaps, for instance, we can see reason to criminalize certain kinds of libel or insult, as wrongful attacks on a person's standing, but we also realize that to do so would constitute an illegitimate infringement of freedom of speech: not because in criminalizing such wrongful libels or insults we would also and inevitably find ourselves criminalizing other kinds of speech that should be protected, but because those very instances of wrongful libel or insult should be protected by the right to freedom of speech.[32]

The third stage concerns the practicability and the costs (material and moral) of actually criminalizing what (in principle) we have reason to criminalize. Here a range of questions arises, including questions of definition. Can we provide a definition of the crime that picks out, with at least tolerable accuracy and specificity, the kind of conduct that is the law's target? Can we provide a definition that is clear enough to be followed and applied by citizens (including lay participants in the criminal process such as jurors and lay magistrates)? Can we provide definitions that are neither grossly over nor

---

[29] See, eg J Horder, 'Rethinking Non-Fatal Offences against the Person' (1994) OJLS 335; J Gardner, 'Rationality and the Rule of Law in Offences against the Person' (1994) 53 CLJ 502. But if we view the realm of moral wrongs in much simpler terms, our understanding of the special part will also be quite different: see L Alexander and KK Ferzan, *Crime and Culpability: A Theory of Criminal Law* (Cambridge: Cambridge University Press, 2009).

[30] See, eg Robinson's Draft Code of Conduct, in PH Robinson, *Structure and Function in Criminal Law* (Oxford: Oxford University Press, 1997); see also PH Robinson and JA Grall, 'Element Analysis in Defining Criminal Liability: The Model Penal Code and Beyond' (1983) 35 *Stanford Law Review* 681.

[31] Compare Schonsheck's 'filters': J Schonsheck, *On Criminalization: An Essay in the Philosophy of the Criminal Law* (Dordrecht: Kluwer, 1994) especially ch 3.

[32] This is one of the contexts in which we might talk of a (legal, if not moral) right to do wrong: compare J Waldron, 'A Right to do Wrong' (1981) 92 *Ethics* 21.

grossly underinclusive? Other issues concern the practicalities and costs of enforcement—including among the costs not only the resources required to investigate and prosecute (and defend), but also such moral costs as the invasions of privacy that effective investigation would require; and the dangers of arbitrary and oppressive uses of discretion if definitions are too vague or too wide. The point here is that, whilst it might be legitimate to begin with the first, 'in principle' stage, we should not talk or think as if that is the only stage with which normative theorists need engage—as if the later stages are matters of technical expertise rather than of normative theory: difficult normative issues are raised at each stage of the discussion, and an adequate normative theory must be able to tackle them all.[33]

The third complicating factor to be noted about the scope of the inquiry concerns a point that is becoming increasingly important—that criminal law is not a purely domestic matter. It is common for theorists to talk, as we have talked so far, about 'the criminal law' as if it is the law of a particular polity, typically of a nation-state,[34] so that issues about criminalization and the enforcement of criminal law are easily represented as issues about the ways in which the state should deal with its citizens. However, recent years have seen significant growth in the scope and importance of both transnational and international criminal law, which requires us to extend, or reframe, the issues about the scope and authority of 'the criminal law'. Thus, for instance, the Freedom, Justice, and Security pillar of the Lisbon Treaty significantly expanded the scope of European criminal law, in both substantive and procedural matters—a trend that is likely to continue after the abolition of the third pillar[35]—whilst the International Criminal Court (along with the various special, ad hoc tribunals that have been created to deal with crimes committed in particular contexts) is giving more substantial form to a body of genuinely

---

[33] This kind of question is addressed by Steiker and by Ashworth and Zedner in this volume.

[34] Although American theorists talk from within a jurisdiction that separates state from federal criminal law, and British theorists from within a jurisdiction that separates English from Scots criminal law, these kinds of distinction do not usually figure in discussions of the proper scope of 'the criminal law'. See further L Farmer, 'Time and Space in Criminal Law' (2010) *New Criminal Law Review* 333.

[35] M Fletcher *et al*, *EU Criminal Law and Justice* (Cheltenham: Edward Elgar, 2008); V Mitsilegas, *EU Criminal Law* (Oxford: Hart Publishing, 2009). This development of transnational criminal law should be distinguished from the role played by such transnational bodies as the European Court of Human Rights: although the European Convention on Human Rights and the European Court of Human Rights do have significant implications for the criminal law (though more for criminal procedure than for the content of the substantive criminal law), this is a matter of national criminal law being subjected to transnational constraints rather than of authentically transnational criminal law.

international criminal law.[36] The questions raised by transnational and international criminal law are not just, or primarily, about the proper content of the criminal law: the crimes defined by such laws could easily be, and typically also are, defined as crimes in the domestic criminal law of individual states. The key questions concern jurisdiction and authority. By what right (by what moral right) do such courts claim jurisdiction over the cases with which, and the defendants with whom, they deal? What grounds the authority (morally or politically, not just legally) of these courts and of the laws that they administer? Should this restrict the kinds of crime for which a person can be held liable at the international level? [37]

In this part we have identified some of the many complexities and ramifications of the apparently simple question about criminalization with which our project began. Some of the further questions and issues identified here figure in the chapters in this volume; others will not be discussed here, but will figure in the further three volumes of papers, or in the three monographs, that will ultimately be published from this project. They are mentioned here simply to clarify some of the background to the project, and to this first set of papers. In the remainder of this Introduction, we will say a little more (in Section II) about our approach to the project, and (in Section III) about how the papers in this volume fit into the project.

II   Towards a Normative Theory of Criminalization

One thing that should have emerged from the discussion in the previous part is that an attempt to work towards a normative theory of criminalization will have different disciplinary dimensions, and must engage with several aspects of criminal law. The latter point will not be discussed further here: we should simply note that a normative theory will need to discuss not just the principles or criteria by reference to which legislatures should decide what kinds of conduct to define as criminal in criminal codes or statutes, but also the aims, principles, and values that should guide the other modes and aspects of criminalization noted above, including the activities of those who enforce (and in enforcing help to define) the criminal law. It will also need to discuss the ways in which crimes should be defined, classified, and individuated; and it

---

[36] See the Rome Statute of the International Criminal Court; and, generally, A Cassese, *International Criminal Law*, 2nd edn (Oxford: Oxford University Press, 2008).

[37] See, eg A Chehtman, 'Citizenship v Territory: Explaining the Scope of the Criminal Law' *New Criminal Law Review* 427. See also the essays in the Special Issue on the Rome Statute of the International Criminal Court (2009) 12 *New Criminal Law Review* issues 3 and 4.

will need either to articulate, or to appeal to, a theory of criminal process and punishment.

As for the disciplinary or interdisciplinary dimensions of the inquiry, its core must clearly lie in practical philosophy, as an attempt—drawing on the resources of moral and political as well as legal philosophy—to articulate and to ground the kinds of consideration that should guide decisions about criminalization. We should note two features of this way of describing the philosophical task. First, it talks in a deliberately vague way of 'considerations', since we should not make any assumptions about the roles to be played by different kinds of reason for or against criminalization—by consequentialist goals that are to be pursued, for instance (in the form of goods to be maximized), or by non-consequentialist principles or constraints that must be respected, or by any other kinds of value. Nor indeed (a point to which we will return shortly) should we assume that we will be able to give a single, coherent account of *the* single set of goals or principles that should govern *all* decisions about criminalization; perhaps we will have to recognize that quite different (and maybe conflicting) considerations will bear on such decisions in different contexts. Second, though our initial question asked directly about what types of conduct should be criminalized, and though a normative inquiry will of course need to discuss particular examples of 'criminalizable' or 'non-criminalizable' conduct, it cannot plausibly aim to produce an exhaustive and exclusive list of 'criminalizable' conduct: the most that we should aim to do is to spell out and justify (and explicate the relationships between) the considerations that should guide decisions about criminalization.

We noted in the previous part that such normative theorizing about criminal law must draw on the resources of both moral and political philosophy.[38] As we also noted, however, it must also draw on the resources of other disciplines: most obviously on criminology for an understanding of how different processes of criminalization actually operate, and on history for an understanding of how we came to have the criminal law we have—and of how debate about criminalization has developed and changed over the years.

The modern philosophical debate about criminalization has been dominated by discussion of the harm principle, as classically formulated by JS Mill:

That principle is, that the sole end for which mankind are warranted, individually or collectively in interfering with the liberty of action of any of their number, is self-protection. That the only purpose for which power can be rightfully exercised over

---

[38] Although the extent to which and the ways in which it will need to draw on moral as distinct from political philosophy will depend on the extent to which and the ways in which the criminal law should be concerned with moral wrongdoing—itself a central issue in the criminalization debate.

any member of a civilized community, against his will, is to prevent harm to others. His own good, either physical or moral, is not a sufficient warrant. He cannot rightfully be compelled to do or forbear because it will be better for him to do so, because it will make him happier, because, in the opinion of others, to do so would be wise, or even right.[39]

We noted earlier that in Mill's hands the harm principle is not about criminalization as such, but about any kind of coercion of members of a civilized community; it is also worth noting that although, at the end of the passage quoted here, he rules out 'it would be right for A to φ' as a good reason for compelling A to φ, his main concern is to rule out paternalist coercion in A's own supposed interests. In the hands of its subsequent advocates (and critics), however, the harm principle has been applied to the criminal law in particular, and has been typically opposed not (or not only) to paternalist legislation or coercion, but to legal moralism—the view that what justifies criminalizing conduct is its moral wrongfulness.

Two further aspects of Mill's formulation are worth noting. First, it does not directly tell us that conduct can only be legitimately criminalized if it causes or threatens to cause harm to others. The most it tells us is that we should criminalize conduct only if by so doing we will prevent harm to others—which in theory leaves open the possibility of criminalizing conduct that is itself harmless if doing so will prevent harm.[40] Typically, however, the principle has been used to justify criminalizing conduct that causes or might lead to harm, and to repudiate the criminalization of conduct that does not cause or threaten harm (to others). Second, the principle seems to offer both a positive reason for criminalizing conduct (that doing so will prevent harm) and a negative constraint on the scope of the criminal law (that we should not criminalize if so doing will not prevent harm). We return to this point below.

The most commonly cited alternative to the harm principle is, as noted above, some form of legal moralism: the view that we should criminalize morally wrongful conduct because of its wrongfulness—though that leaves open the question of whether the point of criminalizing it should be simply to ensure that it is punished, or to prevent it. We say a little more about legal moralism below, but it is worth noting that the two best known debates or controversies about the harm principle did not involve advocates of any straightforward version of legal moralism.

---

[39] JS Mill, *On Liberty* (London: Parker, 1859) ch 1, para 9.

[40] The same is true of Feinberg's formulation of the harm principle: see, eg J Feinberg, *Harm to Others* (New York: Oxford University Press, 1984) 26. That possibility might be actualized if, for instance, the best way to deter actually harmful conduct would be to create a very broad offence that also captured some non-harmful conduct—which is plausibly true of various driving offences such as speeding.

The first of these was the debate between JS Mill and JF Stephen, or more precisely, the vigorous critique of Mill's *On Liberty* mounted by Stephen.[41] Stephen famously insisted that 'criminal law is in the nature of a persecution of the grosser forms of vice', and that vicious conduct is criminalized and punished 'for the sake of gratifying the feeling of hatred—call it revenge, resentment, or what you will—which the contemplation of such conduct excites in healthily constituted minds'.[42] Criminal law gives formal expression, and validation, to those proper moral sentiments: 'the sentence of the law is to the moral sentiment of the public what a seal is to hot wax'.[43] However, this is no simple legal moralism. For Stephen himself held utilitarian beliefs, and therefore believed, if not that only harmful (or harm-threatening) conduct could properly be criminalized, at least that criminalization itself could be justified only if it brought about some consequential good, or averted some evil, sufficient to outweigh its undoubted costs—which is not far from saying that criminalization must prevent harm if it is to be justified.[44] His difference from Mill was thus not about the necessity of harm (or of its prevention) to criminalization: it was partly about (as Stephen saw it) Mill's doomed attempt to mark out an in-principle, 'non-criminalizable' category of purely self-regarding actions, and partly about what kinds of 'harm' are relevant to the criminal law—which also raises the question of what is to count as harm. In both cases he presented a robust defence of the social necessity of forms of coercion in law and public opinion—but in each case he was also careful to insist upon strong practical and theoretical limits on the use of the criminal law, and in particular on the criminalization of vice.

Something similar is true of the second salient controversy a century later, between Lord Devlin and HLA Hart. Devlin's intervention was provoked by the Wolfenden Committee's Report, which recommended, inter alia, that consensual homosexual activity between those over the age of 21 should no longer be criminal, on the grounds that it falls within the realm of private morality that is, 'in brief and crude terms, not the law's business'.[45] If this represented an implicit appeal to Mill and the harm principle, what is striking

[41] JF Stephen, *Liberty, Equality, Fraternity*, 2nd edn (London: Smith, Elder, 1874) (for a contemporary edition see that edited by RJ White (Cambridge: Cambridge University Press, 1967)); see also his *History of the Criminal Law of England* (London: Macmillan, 1883) especially vol II.

[42] *Liberty, Equality, Fraternity* (1967 edn, ibid) 152.

[43] *A History of the Criminal Law of England* (n 41 above) vol II, 81; Cf 'The criminal law stands to the passion of revenge in much the same relation as marriage to the sexual appetite', *General View of the Criminal Law of England*, 1st edn (London: MacMillan, 1863) 99.

[44] *Liberty, Equality, Fraternity* (1967 ed, n 41 above) ch 4.

[45] Sir John Wolfenden, *Report of the Committee on Homosexual Offences and Prostitution* (London: HMSO, 1957) para 61.

is that Devlin's critique also appealed to a version of the harm principle.[46] His claim was not that the criminal law should encompass immoral conduct because of its wrongfulness; it was, rather, that we have reason in principle to criminalize conduct that is widely felt to be wickedly immoral because such conduct, if not criminalized, is liable to harm the very fabric of society. The point here is not to assess the merits or demerits of Devlin's arguments, which provoked vigorous critiques from liberals,[47] but also, later on, some more thoughtful and heavily qualified defences;[48] it is rather to note its reliance on the harm principle, and the fact that the famous debate between him and Hart was not actually about the centrality of the harm principle, but rather about what should count as 'harm', and what kinds of harm could provide reasons for criminalization.

The more general point here is that for a long time the harm principle (especially if the reference to 'others' was dropped) was more or less taken for granted as the central criterion of criminalization: it was accepted, both by theorists engaged in the debates, and implicitly by most who engaged in the public debate, that in order to justify criminalizing any kind of conduct, that conduct must normally be shown to be at least potentially a source of harm— usually to others, though some would also justify paternalistic criminal legislation designed to prevent self-harm. The qualifying 'normally' is needed because there was also wide acceptance of a supplementary 'offence' principle, legitimating the criminalization of conduct that causes grave offence to others, even if such offence would not count as 'harm'.[49] Debate therefore focused on just what should count as, or be meant by 'harm'; what kinds of harm should concern the criminal law; and, increasingly, how 'remote' the prospect of harm could be if it was to provide a good reason for criminalization.

It is also striking, however, that the theorist who did most to explicate the harm principle and give it a tolerably precise meaning was far from an unequivocal proponent of the principle as *the* single principle of criminalization. Not only did Feinberg also make room for an offence principle, and for the

---

[46] P Devlin, *The Enforcement of Morals* (Oxford: Oxford University Press, 1965).

[47] See especially HLA Hart, *Law, Liberty and Morality* (Stanford, Cal: Stanford University Press, 1963); also RM Dworkin, 'Lord Devlin and the Enforcement of Morals' in R Wasserstrom (ed), *Morality and the Law* (Belmont, Cal: Wadsworth, 1971). There is a perceptive discussion of the debate in N Lacey, *A Life of HLA Hart: The Nightmare and the Noble Dream* (Oxford: Oxford University Press, 2004) ch 10.

[48] See, eg G Dworkin, 'Devlin was Right: Law and the Enforcement of Morality' (1999) 40 *William and Mary Law Review* 927.

[49] See especially J Feinberg, *Offense to Others* (New York, Oxford University Press, 1985); but see also Hart, *Law, Liberty and Morality* (n 47 above) 45, on indecent but not immoral behaviour. For useful recent discussions, see AP Simester and A von Hirsch (eds), *Incivilities: Regulating Offensive Behaviour* (Oxford: Hart Publishing, 2006).

criminalization of paternalistic coercion that might not, on balance, harm the person coerced;[50] he also found that he could not simply reject the legal moralist view that the prevention of inherently immoral (but harmless) conduct or of 'free-floating' (and harmless) evils provided good reasons for criminalization. Indeed, he accepted that the prevention of such harmless wrongs always provides *a* reason for criminalization, and was not even confident that it could never provide a *good* reason.[51]

More recently, however, the harm principle has lost its dominant position in the debates, at least among theorists. One of the reasons for this is the revival of legal moralism. In one sense, Feinberg's own version of the harm principle was moralistic, as any plausible version must be: we have good reason to criminalize, not any conduct that causes or might cause a setback to others' welfare interests (the relevant core notion of harmfulness), but only conduct that did so wrongfully.[52] However, wrongfulness figures in the logic of a Feinbergian argument more as a constraint on criminalization than as a positive reason for it: our aim is to prevent harm, but we should not in pursuit of that aim criminalize and punish conduct that, whilst harmful, is not morally wrongful. For true legal moralists, by contrast, the conduct's wrongfulness provides the, or an important part of the, positive reason for criminalizing it. For some legal moralists, we have good reason to criminalize any and every kind of moral wrongdoing—though other principles and considerations should then dissuade us from actually criminalizing many kinds of wrong conduct.[53] For others, only certain kinds of wrong are even in principle appropriate candidates for criminalization.[54] Some might indeed bring the harm principle in again to argue that we have good reason to criminalize wrongful conduct only if it causes or threatens harm;[55] but our interest here is in versions of legal moralism that eschew the harm principle.

Perhaps, however, the revival of legal moralism is explained by, rather than explaining, the demise of the harm principle; perhaps it was one result of a growing sense that the harm principle could not perform the role it was

[50] *Harm to Others* (n 40 above) 78; J Feinberg, *Harm to Self* (New York: Oxford University Press, 1986) chs 18–19.

[51] See J Feinberg, *Harmless Wrongdoing* (New York: Oxford University Press, 1988) especially Conclusion.

[52] *Harm to Others* (n 50 above) chs 1–3. More precisely (see at n 38 above), we have reason to criminalize conduct only if doing so will prevent wrongful harm to others; generally, however, debate focuses on the criminalization of conduct that is itself wrongfully harmful.

[53] See, eg Moore, *Placing Blame* (n 16 above) chs 1, 16.

[54] SE Marshall and RA Duff, 'Criminalization and Sharing Wrongs' (1998) 11 *The Canadian Journal of Law and Jurisprudence* 7–22; RA Duff and SE Marshall, 'Public and Private Wrongs' in J Chalmers, F Leverick, and L Farmer (eds), *Essays in Criminal Law in Honour of Sir Gerald Gordon* (Edinburgh: Edinburgh University Press, 2010); RA Duff, *Answering for Crime* (Oxford: Hart Publishing, 2007) especially ch 6.

[55] A position extensionally equivalent to Feinberg's, though with a distinct logical structure.

supposed to play. Like any would-be master principle it faced two kinds of objection: that it is underinclusive, since it cannot—or cannot without serious distortion—capture kinds of conduct that clearly should be criminalized; and/ or that it is overinclusive, in that it renders 'criminalizable', at least in principle, kinds of conduct that should not be criminalized. Indeed, the two kinds of criticism are closely related: for attempts to avoid the first kind of criticism by stretching the meaning of 'harm', or by weakening the relationship that must obtain between the conduct that is to be criminalized and the harm that is to justify that criminalization, create the danger that the revised principle becomes either vacuous (it can count as 'harmful' any kind of conduct that we see reason to criminalize), or at least vastly overinclusive.[56] Proponents of the first kind of objection might offer examples (admittedly unusual) of wrongful conduct that seems clearly apt for criminalization, but that neither causes nor threatens to cause what orthodox versions of the harm principle can count as 'harm';[57] others argue that focusing on harm distorts our understanding of what it is about certain kinds of wrongdoing that renders them apt for criminalization.[58] Proponents of the second kind of objection point to the ways in which ever wider kinds of 'harm'—ever more remote harms—are cited as grounds for criminalization, with the result that '[c]laims of harm have become so pervasive that the harm principle has become meaningless'.[59]

Legal moralists must, of course, face similar challenges. On the one hand, if they say that every kind of moral wrongdoing is in principle criminalizable, they face the charge of overinclusiveness: surely there are many kinds of even quite serious wrongdoing that are simply, in principle, 'not the law's business'; how then can they limit the scope of the criminal law, if not by appeal to the harm principle, arguing that we should criminalize only harmful wrongs? On the other hand, they also face the charge of underinclusiveness. If we accept some form of distinction between *mala in se*, involving conduct that is wrongful independently of and prior to its legal regulation or prohibition, and *mala*

---

[56] See H Stewart, 'The Limits of the Harm Principle' (2010) 4 *Criminal Law and Philosophy* 17.

[57] See, eg A Ripstein, 'Beyond the Harm Principle' (2006) 34 *Philosophy and Public Affairs* 215; J Gardner and S Shute, 'The Wrongness of Rape' in J Horder (ed), *Oxford Essays in Jurisprudence*, 4th series (Oxford: Oxford University Press, 2000) 193. Gardner and Shute, having explained the wrongness of rape in terms that do not appeal to harm, go on to argue that rape is nonetheless properly criminalized only because it threatens to cause harm. That aspect of their argument, however, is unpersuasive, as Stanton-Ife points out in this volume: if their example of a harmless rape is plausible, and if we agree that rape is properly criminalized because of what it does to the individual victim, it also shows that we cannot ground the law of rape in the harm principle.

[58] See, eg Duff, *Answering for Crime* (n 54 above) ch 6. For a very useful general discussion, see J Stanton-Ife, 'The Limits of Law' in EN Zalta (ed), *Stanford Encyclopedia of Philosophy* (<http://plato.stanford.edu/archives/spr2006/entries/law-limits>).

[59] BE Harcourt, 'The Collapse of the Harm Principle' (1999) 90 *Journal of Criminal Law and Criminology* 109, 113.

prohibita, consisting in conduct that is not wrong prior to or independently of its legal regulation or prohibition;[60] and if we accept that even if many of the increasingly wide range of *mala prohibita* to be found in our existing criminal law should not be criminalized, the criminal law does properly contain some *mala prohibita*: the legal moralist seems to face a problem. If the moral wrongfulness of a type of conduct is to justify its criminalization, that wrongfulness cannot consist simply in the fact that it violates the criminal law; but in what, then, could the wrongfulness of *mala prohibita* consist?[61]

If it becomes clear that neither the harm principle nor an unvarnished legal moralism can provide adequate criteria for decisions about even in-principle criminalization, where should the normative theorist look? One possibility is to look for another master principle, or set of such principles, that will provide a perhaps more complicated but also more adequate account of the proper criteria of criminalization.[62] Another possibility, however, is to accept that we cannot hope to find any such master principle or set of such principles: that different kinds of consideration will be relevant to the criminalization of different kinds of conduct; that these considerations might often conflict in ways that cannot be neatly resolved; and that decisions about criminalization, even at the first 'in principle' stage, can only be made in a piecemeal way that cannot be captured by any neatly structured set of principles.

Two other aspects of the current debate are worth highlighting here. The first reflects the broad scope of Mill's classical formulation of the harm principle—the fact that it concerned not criminal law in particular, but any kind of state (or indeed social or individual) coercion. The prevention of at least certain kinds of harm, and the regulation of at least certain kinds of harmful conduct, do seem to be proper tasks for a liberal state: but that leaves open the question of just how they are to be prevented, or regulated, and certainly does not yet imply that we should do this by means of the criminal law. As we noted earlier,[63] the criminal law could be seen as just one amongst a range of possible ways of regulating or controlling conduct, or of averting or dealing with various kinds of harm: even if the harm principle specifies something that is always a good reason for some kind of coercive intervention, it does not point towards criminal law as the appropriate kind of intervention. A normative

---

[60] But see, eg RL Gray, 'Eliminating the (Absurd) Distinction between *Malum in Se* and *Malum Prohibitum* Crimes' (1995) 73 *Washington University Law Quarterly* 1369.

[61] See DN Husak, '*Malum Prohibitum* and Retributivism' in RA Duff and SP Green (eds), *Defining Crimes: Essays on the Special Part of the Criminal Law* (Oxford: Oxford University Press, 2005) 65; in response see Duff, *Answering for Crime* (n 54 above) chs 4.4, 7.3. See also Farmer's comments on moral wrongs in this volume.

[62] See, eg M Dan-Cohen, 'Defending Dignity' in his *Harmful Thoughts: Essays on Law, Self and Morality* (Princeton, NJ: Princeton University Press, 2002) 150; Ripstein (n 57 above).

[63] See at nn 12–14 above.

theory of criminalization must tackle this question: what makes the criminal law the appropriate kind of measure?[64]

Second, contemporary debate in Britain and the United States has been dominated, and to a degree distorted, by the perceived urgency of the crisis of overcriminalization that these two societies are said to face. In the face of that crisis, and of an apparently ever-expanding criminal law, theorists tend to focus on the question of how that expansion can be constrained or limited: can we find, and if so how can we make efficacious, principles that will set limits on what may be criminalized? Husak's important book has this character: it begins by explaining and justifying the claim that we do face such a crisis, and its two central chapters are then devoted to identifying 'constraints on criminalization'.[65] In similar vein, Carol Steiker's contribution to this volume focuses on the urgent problems raised by 'this era of overcriminalization and the related problem of over punishment',[66] and then looks for ways in which actors other than official legislators can use their discretion to limit the reach or impact of the criminal law. We do not suggest that such efforts are misguided: the criminal law in both the United States and Britain, we have no doubt, does bear far too harshly and oppressively on many people who face conviction and punishment for conduct that should not be criminal at all, or are subjected to punishments that are out of all proportion to any wrongs that they may have committed; in the face of such oppressive harshness, it is imperative to look for ways of mitigating it. But a normative theory of criminalization must have other ambitions than that of responding to our present crises of overcriminalization and overpunishment;[67] for if we are to justify criminal law at all, we must suppose not only that there are legitimate constraints on criminalization, ie reasons why we should *not* criminalize, but also that there are good, positive reasons in favour of criminalizing certain kinds of conduct. It is those reasons that must be central to a normative theory of criminalization, although any plausible theory will also need to attend to considerations that might rather act as constraints on criminalization. Nor should we assume in advance that, whilst a plausible normative theory might well highlight ways in which our existing systems of criminal law are overextensive, criminalizing conduct that should not be criminalized, it will not also show that we ought to extend the criminal law to capture kinds of conduct that are not now criminal.

---

[64] The chapters in this volume by Ashworth and Zedner, Tadros, and Duff all bear on this issue.   [65] Husak, *Overcriminalization* (n 1 above).

[66] C Steiker, 'Criminalization and the Criminal Process: Prudential Mercy as a Limit on Penal Sanctions in an Era of Mass Incarceration', chapter 2 of this volume.

[67] Although Husak identifies overpunishment as the main reason why overcriminalization is objectionable and unjust (n 1 above), we should distinguish the two problems (as Steiker does): there is more significantly wrong with overcriminalization than that it leads to overpunishment.

Both the harm principle and legal moralism, in their more ambitious forms, do of course give such positive reasons for criminalization, and it is surely likely that some version of such principles will need to be part of any adequate normative theory; but what roles they should play, and what other principles or considerations will be relevant, will be central questions for this project.

III   The Boundaries of the Criminal Law

The focus of this volume is on the boundaries of the criminal law. It thus deals in a sense with what can be considered a central question of the project—the question of what normative limits there ought to be on the creation of criminal offences. As we have seen, work on the limits of the criminal law has been dominated by the harm principle. Discussion of that principle figures in this book, but the contributions collected here have a much more varied and broader scope.

First, the book is concerned not only with what principles *ought* to set the boundaries of the criminal law, but also with the question of how those boundaries are in fact being pushed by developments within the criminal law, as well as by other non-criminal or quasi-criminal policies. The first question is addressed in Carol Steiker's contribution. Steiker argues that the dominant discourse between retributivism and social welfare theory about the purposes of punishment inevitably tends toward overpunishment. This is partly due to the current set of political and social arrangements (leading both to differential rates of offending and differential policing in poor and minority communities) and partly to human cognitive biases (which favour the erroneous attribution of criminal offending to dispositional attributes rather than to situational factors). According to Steiker, one way to counter this tendency is by promoting greater discretion to decline punishment on the part of institutional actors throughout the criminal justice process. Steiker's argument amounts to a 'prudential' case for mercy in criminal justice—a case premised not on a new theory of the relationship between justice and mercy, but rather on the predictable failures of existing theories of just punishment.

The question of how new non-criminal (or quasi-criminal) policies are altering the traditional criminal law approach to a range of social problems is tackled by Andrew Ashworth and Lucia Zedner in their contribution. Ashworth and Zedner lament that, while the contemporary debate on criminalization tends to focus exclusively on the problem of overcriminalization, there is a less conspicuous but by no means less pressing problem: the problem of under-criminalization. Ashworth and Zedner critically examine the social, political, and constitutional significance of the proliferation of civil preventive measures and argue that these measures may constitute *undercriminalization* insofar as they exclude appropriate procedural safeguards and other protections for the individual, which would be available if the preventive measures were classified as criminal. When this is the case, instances of undercriminalization pose no less a threat to individual liberty than overcriminalization, as they lead to intrusions upon individual liberty in the name of prevention without due procedural safeguards. Ashworth and Zedner conclude that, while it is certainly true that in many cases preventive measures are to be preferred over traditional criminal law approaches, there are also cases in which criminalization should be preferred.

The question of how the boundaries of the criminal law are being pushed by developments internal to the criminal law, as well as by the creation of other types of policies, is also tackled in Antony Duff's essay. Duff discusses three recent developments that seem to be at odds with the proper role of criminal law as portrayed by a plausible ideal theory (according to which the criminal law's proper role is to define, and to provide for an appropriate formal response to, a range of 'public' wrongs). Two of these developments (the creation of unduly broad criminal offences which capture conduct that cannot plausibly be seen as wrongful; the use of provisions such as Anti-Social Behaviour Orders that attach criminal sanctions to the breach of supposedly civil orders) constitute 'perversions of criminal law', in the sense that they use the criminal law in ways that do not accord with its proper purposes or with the principles appropriate to those purposes. The third (the use of regimes of non-criminal regulation and penalties) is what Duff calls a 'subversion of criminal law', in the sense that it uses non-criminal methods of control and regulation when arguably the criminal law should properly be used.

While Duff and Ashworth and Zedner deal with the question of how the boundaries of the criminal law are being pushed by the developments of non-criminal policies, Mireille Hildebrandt considers the problem of how these boundaries are being pushed by the creation of new technologies. In particular, Hildebrandt examines new profiling technologies that enable law enforcers to predict on a statistical basis which categories of citizen are prone to become involved in what types of criminal behaviour. While this type of risk assessment has been discussed in criminological theory, focusing in particular on the implications for policing and sentencing (see the debate on 'actuarial justice'), Hildebrandt considers the potential impact of these techniques on the process of criminalization. She argues that profiling technologies of this sort seem to 'afford' a criminal justice system that holds citizens responsible not for what they do, but simply for displaying characteristics that match criminal profiles. This raises the important question of whether we may expect the development of new notions of responsibility that justify a kind of pre-crime 'punishment'.

Some of the articles collected in this volume also deal with the more tradi-tional question of the normative principles that ought to be employed in setting the boundaries of the criminal law. Thus Stanton-Ife's, Tadros's, Dubber's, and Farmer's chapters all discuss a range of principles and distinctions that inform our understanding of the scope of the criminal law, and provide posi-tive grounds for creating particular criminal offences. John Stanton-Ife focuses on a particular type of crime that he calls 'horrific crimes'. He argues that neither the harm principle, nor accounts of criminalization grounded on the Kantian maxim that proscribes treating others as mere means, can provide an account of the reasons we have to criminalize these crimes. Horrific crimes are not to be distinguished from regular crimes by appealing to the idea that they involve the setting back of particularly important interests; nor are they to be accounted for by appealing to the idea that they violate particularly important rights. Instead of violating *the rights* of persons, according to Stanton-Ife horrific crimes violate *persons themselves*, in that they involve the crossing of boundaries which play an important role in defining their victims' selfhood.

Victor Tadros's chapter focuses on the distinction between punishment and penalties, and the significance of this distinction for a theory of criminaliza-tion. Tadros illustrates the significant difficulties encountered by retributivist theories in providing adequate restraints on the criminal law, and argues that a better account of the distinction between punishments and penalties can be provided by an alternative, license-based theory of punishment. The license theory claims that, while punishment is imposed on people as a means to pre-vent further wrongdoing by others (provided that the constraint on treating people in that way is lifted because of their wrongdoing), penalties are imposed on certain types of conduct in order to restrict the circumstances in which a person can be treated as a means. Thus punishment involves an intention that the wrongdoer will suffer harm; penalties instead ensure fairness in the dis-tribution of resources. Tadros's chapter explores the implications of this view for the scope of the criminal law, and particularly for the distinction between criminal and civil wrongs.

The distinction between public law and private law is also examined, this time mainly in a historical perspective, in Markus Dubber's contribution. Dubber reconstructs the historical development of criminal law as a part of public law, in order to shed light on the public nature of criminal law, as well as to reflect critically on some contemporary efforts to give greater specificity to the idea of crimes as 'public wrongs'. Dubber accounts for the distinction between crimes and torts by appealing to the idea that the former directly threaten the victim's personhood, while the latter do so only indirectly by diminishing victims' resources for the exercise of their capacity for autonomy. However, punishment also poses a threat to the personhood of those who are subject to it, which is why it should be reserved for the former (more serious) kind of wrongs.

A particular attention to the historical dimension of the study of criminalization also characterizes Lindsay Farmer's chapter. In line with recent developments in the literature on criminal law, Farmer focuses on the concepts of wrong and wrongdoing, rather than on the concept of harm. But while much of the current literature has tended to revolve around the question of what role wrongdoing plays in the public definition and condemnation of criminal behaviour, Farmer argues that this question is too general. In order for the notion of wrongdoing to be of assistance in developing an account of criminalization, it must be framed within a detailed examination of how the wrongness of any particular crime (or group of crimes) manifests itself in different times and places. Farmer's chapter illustrates how the content of the notions of wrongness and wrongdoing has changed over time in relation to different crimes, and concludes that only by paying attention to these changes will we be able to employ these notions usefully to provide a solid ground for an adequate theory of criminalization.

If Dubber's and Farmer's contributions deal with the problems of criminalization in a historical perspective, Kimmo Nuotio's chapter provides a map of the different approaches that these problems have received in the continental debate, focusing in particular on the concept of *Rechtsgut*, which is central in the German-speaking world, and on the Nordic debate. Nuotio considers alternative ways in which the enterprise of developing a theory of criminalization can be understood, and examines different principles that have been employed in different socio-cultural contexts in order to meet the demands that these alternative understandings of criminalization bring with them.

Any attempt to stimulate philosophical discussion in relation to a previously neglected area of investigation will inevitably produce more questions than answers, and this volume is no exception. We hope, however, that the essays collected here will convince the reader that the questions raised are worth being asked. Some of them will be addressed in the following volumes, where our attempt to build up a normative theory of criminalization will take shape; some will no doubt remain unanswered. In any case our effort will have been successful if others will be prompted to deal with them.

2

Criminalization and the Criminal Process: Prudential Mercy as a Limit on Penal Sanctions in an Era of Mass Incarceration

Carol S Steiker*

The question of 'criminalization' is conventionally understood to be a question about the proper contours of conduct subject to criminal sanction. Thus, to the extent that the answer to such a question is directed to any institutions or actors in the world, it is generally taken to be a question directed to legislatures as the drafters of modern penal codes. Indeed, this is precisely the audience that Douglas Husak addresses in his recent book, *Overcriminalization: The Limits of the Criminal Law*,[1] which develops a set of principles for limiting the use of the criminal sanction. Husak argues for narrowing the substantive criminal law on the grounds that the current proliferation and increasing breadth of criminal laws not only threaten the efficacy of criminal law enforcement and its legitimacy in the eyes of the public, but also engender such unfettered official discretion in criminal prosecution as to threaten the central values of the rule of law. Husak's approach has already begun, and will no doubt continue, to generate debate both about the extent of the problem of overcriminalization[2] and about the principles that he develops to do the narrowing work.[3] But no one has really doubted that the audience Husak

* Howard and Kathy Aibel Professor of Law, Harvard Law School.

[1] D Husak, *Overcriminalization: The Limits of the Criminal Law* (Oxford: Oxford University Press, 2008).

[2] DK Brown, 'Democracy and Decriminalization' (2007) 86 *Texas Law Review* 223 (taking issue with Husak's endorsement of the statement that the expansion of the criminal law has moved us 'ever closer to a world in which the law on the books makes everyone a felon'); SW Buell, 'The Upside of Overbreadth' (2008) 83 *New York University Law Review* 1491 (arguing for the value of overbreadth in certain circumstances and cautioning against narrowing the scope of the criminal law in such circumstances).

[3] J Gardner, Review of Husak's *Overcriminalization*, Notre Dame Philosophical Reviews (August 2008) (critiquing Husak's 'internal' and 'external' principles for the constraint of the criminal law); D Scoccia, Review of Husak's *Overcriminalization* (2008) 119 *Ethics* 189 (same).

addresses is the right one; the only question raised about his legislative focus is whether legislators will be at all inclined to listen.[4]

I want to suggest that the audience for concerns about overcriminalization is broader. Legislatures do not wholly determine the contours of the criminal law, nor do individual legislators imagine or hope that they do so. Rather, legislatures know that they cannot foresee all possible applications of prohibitions that they enact and necessarily rely on the decisions of discretionary actors in response to specific circumstances; indeed, sometimes legislatures intentionally craft very broad criminal prohibitions in order to give discretionary actors such as police and prosecutors more powerful tools to combat crime. Thus, the actual shape of the criminal law is cut from the cloth of the substantive law that legislatures enact by the tailoring decisions of discretionary actors that may include police, prosecutors, juries, sentencing judges, parole boards, and executives exercising clemency and pardoning powers. The extent of the various forms of discretion wielded by these actors prevents these officials from viewing themselves as merely faithful agents of the legislature; rather, it is clear that independent judgement of various kinds must be brought to bear. It is therefore worth asking what principles ought to guide *these* actors in their discretionary decision-making.

The question of how discretionary actors should view their roles in demarcating the proper boundaries of criminal sanctions has taken on new urgency in this era of overcriminalization and the related problem of overpunishment. In theory, it is possible to have overcriminalization (too broad a range of conduct subject to potential criminal sanction) without having overpunishment (unnecessary harshness in the actual imposition of punishment). Similarly, one could certainly have overpunishment even in the absence of overcriminalization. However, in recent decades, the two phenomena have tended to travel hand-in-hand. The increase in the number and breadth of criminal laws has coincided with an era of increased harshness in punishment—a breathtaking increase in some parts of the world, most notably the United States. The harshness of punishment has a number of dimensions, including the modes of punishment used (capital, corporal, carceral, financial, etc), the aggregate rate of imprisonment (the harshest sanction currently imposed in most Western democracies), the severity of individual sentences in relationship to the underlying offence, the conditions of incarceration, and the range of offenders subject to criminal sanctions (such as juvenile offenders).[5] By most measures,

---

[4] Gardner (ibid) 7 ('Trying to stem the tide of fatuous law that emanates from our incontinent legislatures, at least in the US and the UK, is a luckless and thankless task.')

[5] JQ Whitman, *Harsh Justice: Criminal Punishment and the Widening Divide Between America and Europe* (Oxford: Oxford University Press, 2003) (exploring differences in the harshness of punishment between the USA and continental Europe over the past two centuries).

the harshness of criminal punishment has increased enormously in recent decades—at least as substantially as the scope of the criminal law—not only in the USA, but also in many other developed countries around the globe. The causes of this increase are debated, but the degree of change cannot be disputed. Moreover, the problems generated by overpunishment are at least as severe as those that flow from overcriminalization. A burgeoning literature now considers the social effects that flow from the criminal justice policies that have produced 'mass incarceration'.[6]

In an era of mass incarceration, with the devastating consequences that such a penal policy entails, it becomes imperative to think about exit strategies. One such strategy would be an appeal to legislatures to limit the scope and/or the harshness of current penal sanctions. Husak's project in *Overcriminalization* of grounding scope limitations in first principles could be viewed as an example of this type of strategy. A different strategy, not inconsistent with the first, would be to seek to slow or reverse the engine of overpunishment by enlisting the potential brake of the 'veto power' over punishment in individual cases that lies in the hands of discretionary actors throughout the criminal process. Such a strategy requires its own first principles—it needs to be grounded in a robust justification for the discretionary veto of legislatively authorized (or even required) punishment (beyond the well-accepted grounds of legislatively unintended consequences or limited resources). Moreover, this justificatory account also needs to be able to identify cases appropriate for robust use of the discretionary veto and distinguish them from inappropriate cases. The attempt to generate such an account necessarily requires engagement with the recent debates among both moral philosophers and lawyers about the role of 'mercy' in criminal justice. I offer a sketch of what might be called a 'prudential' account of mercy, an account that seeks to ground a robust discretionary veto of criminal punishment not in a virtue that stands outside of justice, but rather in the predictable failures of the dominant discourses about the justifying aims of criminal punishment.

Of course, any exit strategy that seeks to rely on discretionary mercy runs into serious 'rule of law' objections—exactly the same kinds of objection about the potential for the misuse of broad discretion that animate some of the concerns about overcriminalization and overpunishment.[7] While there are answers to such objections, these answers depend on contingent facts about our social and political world. Thus, my prudential account of mercy is one that is grounded in particular social conditions rather than timeless first

---

[6] D Weiman, B Western, and M Patillo (eds), *Imprisoning America: The Social Effects of Mass Incarceration* (New York: Russell Sage Foundation, 2004).

[7] Husak (n 1 above) 28 (raising concerns about the selective use of broad criminal sanctions by discretionary officials against unpopular minorities).

principles. It is thus fairly viewed as a second-best account, an account fashioned for the real world of great inequality and penal harshness in which we currently live, rather than for a world of greater equality and parsimony in the use of penal sanctions. What follows is an attempt to explain the need for an exit strategy from current penal practices, to offer an account of prudential mercy, and to respond to powerful objections to such an account.

I Overpunishment and the Need for an Exit Strategy

Is there really a problem that needs addressing? Many within the scholarly community have critiqued the 'punitive turn' in the penal policies of the United States, the United Kingdom, and several other Western democracies.[8] Moreover, this development has raised concerns among such critics that the rest of the West may eventually follow the USA and its punitive cohort.[9] But any claim about over punishment necessarily raises the question of baselines. How do we know how much punishment is the *right* amount? This question is both enormous and enormously difficult, and its resolution is beyond the scope of this chapter.[10] However, it is worth sketching the general grounds for believing that the punitive turn has indeed produced over punishment and that this phenomenon is deeply problematic—at least as problematic as the related phenomenon of overcriminalization. Moreover, to establish the need for an exit strategy, it is also necessary to demonstrate that the problem of overpunishment will not resolve itself without substantial reconfiguration of existing institutions or practices. Thus, I will also sketch the grounds for believing the problem of overpunishment is not merely a temporary and aberrational blip on the screen of criminal justice policy, but rather a durable feature of the criminal justice landscape for the foreseeable future.

[8] S Hallsworth, 'Rethinking the Punitive Turn: Economies of Excess and the Criminology of the Other' (2000) 2 *Punishment and Society* 145.

[9] Compare D Garland, *The Culture of Control: Crime and Social Order in Contemporary Society* (Chicago, Ill: University of Chicago Press, 2001) (arguing that the punitive turn is a feature of late modernity that will affect other liberal democracies), with N Lacey, *The Prisoners' Dilemma: Political Economy and Punishment in Contemporary Democracies* (Cambridge: Cambridge University Press, 2008) (challenging Garland's view on the basis of variations in political economy among liberal democracies).

[10] Indeed, the question of proper punishment proved so difficult that when Congress created the Federal Sentencing Commission to draw up the Federal Sentencing Guidelines, the Commissioners were so stymied by their attempt to reach consensus on the proper punishment for particular offences that they simply agreed to craft Guidelines that would, with only a few exceptions, reproduce the prevailing aggregate federal sentencing rates: S Breyer, 'The Federal Sentencing Guidelines and the Key Compromises upon Which They Rest' (1988) 17 *Hofstra Law Review* 1, 15–18.

A The punitive moment

In the last three to four decades, the United States and a significant (though minority) cohort of other Western democracies have seen enormous, even exponential, increases in their prison populations, as a consequence of both broader criminal liability and harsher sentencing for existing crimes. The USA presents the most extreme example in both relative and absolute terms: currently, approximately 2.3 million people are incarcerated in prisons or jails in the USA, reflecting an incarceration rate of more than 750 per 100,000 residents—the highest reported rate in the world.[11] This current rate of incarceration is the product of several decades of explosive growth: the US prison population is now eight times larger than it was in 1970,[12] and it is projected to continue to grow substantially over the next five years.[13] State expenditures for corrections (over 90 per cent of which flow to prisons, as opposed to community-based supervision) constituted the fastest growing segment of state budgets in the past fiscal year; moreover, these expenditures have grown faster in the past two decades than any other state programme except for Medicaid.[14]

While the most extreme example, the USA is not alone among Western democracies. Without reaching the same absolute heights, a number of other countries have seen similarly large expansions of their prison populations and per capita imprisonment rates over the past few decades. Most of the rest of the English-speaking world—the United Kingdom, Australia, and New Zealand—has seen extremely robust increases in imprisonment rates,[15] with the notable exception of Canada.[16] Similarly, the Netherlands has seen a steady rise in its imprisonment rate since 1975, rivalling the magnitude of the change in the US rate (though starting from a much lower point).[17] Many

---

[11] Bureau of Justice Statistics, *Prison Statistics*, yearly reports, available at <http://www.ojp .usdoj.gov/bjs/prisons.htm>; The Pew Center on the States, 'One in 100: Behind Bars in America 2008' (February 2008), Table A–7 available at <http://www.pewcenteronthestates.org/initiatives _detail.aspx?initiativeID=31336>.

[12] Public Safety Performance, A Project of The Pew Charitable Trusts: 'Public Safety, Public Spending: Forecasting America's Prison Population 2007–2011' (June 2007), at 1 (comparing 1970 prison population of approximately 190,000 to 2005 prison population of approximately 1.5 million), available at <http://www.pewtrusts.org/our_work_report_detail. aspx?id=29967&category=74>.   [13] Ibid, 9.

[14] The Pew Center on the States, 'One in 31: The Long Reach of American Corrections' at 1–2 (March 2009), available at <http://www.pewcenteronthestates.org/report_detail.aspx?id=49382>.

[15] T Lappi-Seppala, 'Trust, Welfare, and Political Culture: Explaining Differences in National Penal Policies' (2008) 37 *Crime and Justice* 313.

[16] CM Webster and AN Doob, 'Punitive Trends and Stable Imprisonment Rates in Canada' (2007) 36 *Crime and Justice* 297.

[17] D Downes, 'Visions of Penal Control in the Netherlands' (2007) 36 *Crime and Justice* 93, 101 (describing how the Dutch imprisonment rate quintupled in the years between 1973 and 2003, though it started at only 20 per 100,000 residents).

other Western European countries have produced more inconsistent fluctu-
ations in their imprisonment rates over the same period, with a significant
number seeing substantial increases during the 1990s.[18]

Why conclude that this sudden, severe shift in penal practices, where it has
occurred, constitutes over punishment, as opposed to an obvious and unre-
markable reaction to changing social conditions, especially rising crime rates
(which rose significantly for several decades across most of Europe and North
America, before declining in the 1990s)? There are several different answers
one can make to this question without attempting to generate an overarch-
ing theory or formula for determining the 'right' level of incarceration. First,
rising crime rates do not appear to provide either a sufficient explanation or
a convincing justification for the shift, because many countries responded to
crime rate rises of similar magnitudes without increases—indeed, in some cases
with significant *decreases*—in their prison populations, without generating
obviously different effects on crime rates. The most startling illustration of this
comparative response to rising crime rates is Michael Tonry's comparison of the
policy reactions of the United States, Germany, and Finland to similar steady
increases in violent crime and homicide rates over the two-plus-decade period
from 1970 to the early 1990s.[19] In the United States, the imprisonment rate
steadily went up; in Finland, the imprisonment rate steadily went down; and in
Germany, the imprisonment rate fluctuated (down, then up, then down again),
while the crime rate curves were substantially similar in all three jurisdictions
over the period studied. This comparison, and many other comparisons that
could be drawn among the numerous countries that faced similar crime spikes,
suggests that rising crime rates do not automatically generate larger prison
populations, nor do larger prison populations necessarily generate lower crime
rates more reliably than other penal policies. Rather, prison rates represent policy *choices* that need further explanation and justification. Of course, one such
justification might lie in the decline in crime brought about by the combined
rehabilitative, incapacitative, and deterrent effect of increased imprisonment.
The extent to which the huge increases in imprisonment in the USA played a
role in the substantial decline in crime that occurred during the 1990s remains
inconclusive—indeed, a matter of intense debate.[20] But even if proven, any

---

[18] M Tonry, 'Punishment Policies and Patterns in Western Countries' in M Tonry and RS Frase,
Sentencing and Sanctions in Western Countries (Oxford: Oxford University Press, 2001) 3, 4.

[19] Ibid, 10–13, figures 1.2, 1.3, and 1.4.

[20] Cf SD Levitt, 'Understanding Why Crime Fell in the 1990s: Four Factors that Explain the
Decline and Six that Do Not' (2004) 111 *Quarterly Journal of Economics* 319 (arguing that incarceration is one of the factors that explain the decline in crime rates in the 1990s), with B Western,
Punishment and Inequality in America (New York: Russell Sage Foundation, 2006) 168–88 (arguing that Levitt and others overestimate the effects of incarceration on crime rates).

effect of imprisonment rates on crime rates must also be balanced against other pernicious effects that increased reliance on imprisonment may entail.

Such other effects may become visible by supplementing comparisons *among* countries with comparisons between a country and its earlier self. The radical nature of the changes in both the rate and the distribution of imprisonment in the United States from 1970 to the present offers grounds for questioning the necessity and wisdom of such changes. For generations before the 1970s, the US imprisonment rate had fluctuated within a relatively narrow range before it exploded in several decades of exponential growth. Moreover, in those earlier generations, the onus of imprisonment did not fall as disproportionately on minority communities. Bill Stuntz has argued that the strong, racially disparate impact of current imprisonment trends, which represents a departure even from the bad old days of the pre-Civil Rights era, provides grounds for radically rethinking current penal policies, so as to empower local and more racially representative communities to weigh the costs and benefits of increased imprisonment for themselves.[21] Bruce Western and others have documented the costs of racially disparate imprisonment policies on minority communities, ranging from labour market effects, to effects on marriage, family life, and the life prospects of future generations.[22]

Racial inequality is only the most obvious of the troubling side effects of the recent punitive turn. Many of the consequences canvassed by Husak in making the case for over criminalization are likewise the products of over-punishment[23]—including the diversion of resources into incarceration that could better be used to address the social problems that contribute to crime;[24] the decline in the legitimacy of the criminal justice system in the eyes of those most burdened by it (and a concomitant decline in their internalization of the criminal law's norms);[25] the ability of prosecutors to use the threat of excessively high sanctions to force defendants to waive their procedural rights and plead guilty without any impartial adjudication of their guilt or the propriety of their punishment;[26] the likelihood of punishment disproportionate to

---

[21] WJ Stuntz, 'Unequal Justice' (2008) 121 *Harvard Law Review* 1969.

[22] Western (n 20 above); Weiman *et al* (n 6 above).   [23] Husak (n 1 above) 12–28.

[24] JJ Donohue III and P Siegelman, 'Allocating Resources among Prisons and Social Programs in the Battle against Crime' (1998) 27 *Journal of Legal Studies* 1 (arguing that resources would be better allocated to social programmes like early childhood education than to prisons).

[25] A Braga *et al* (eds), *Legitimacy and Criminal Justice: A Comparative Perspective* (New York: Russell Sage Foundation, 2007) (exploring the effects of, among other things, the proportionality and distribution of criminal sanctions on the perceived legitimacy of the criminal justice system across legal systems).

[26] DA Dripps, 'Overcriminalization, Discretion, Waiver: A Survey of Possible Exit Stategies' (2005) 109 *Penn State Law Review* 1155 (describing how overcriminalization and overpunishment contribute to plea bargaining).

wrongdoing;[27] and, as noted above, the possibility of selective and discriminatory enforcement. The extent to which each of these pernicious effects has in
fact occurred is an empirical question subject to debate, but the widespread
belief that most if not all of these possible effects have in fact proliferated during the period of the punitive turn is strong evidence of over punishment.

Of course, 'widespread belief' is often wrong. Here, however, the widespread
belief that the punitive turn has produced a litany of pernicious effects reflects
not a popular canard, but rather a broad consensus among scholars from the
disciplines of law, sociology, and criminology. Scholars, too, are not exempt
from mistake, and it is fair to point out that the disciplines of law, sociology,
and criminology tend to produce, in the aggregate, scholars and scholarship
of a politics significantly to the left of prevailing political views—a politics
that may predispose them to reject the policies produced by the punitive turn.
Despite the reasonable caution this caveat may engender, the reliability of the
consensus on overpunishment is bolstered by the fact that even scholars who
doubt whether the expansion of the scope of the criminal law (overcriminalization) is as significant a problem as alleged by its detractors,[28] or who wish
to assert the relative importance of *under*enforcement of the criminal law,[29]
recognize that, when looking 'separately at substantive criminal law and sentencing law',[30] the problem of excessive harshness produced by the punitive
turn cannot be denied.

A different tack to take in evaluating whether current punishment policies
are excessive is to look not at the substance of the policies themselves and
their effects, but rather to the political process that produced the policies in
the first place. As Rachel Barkow crisply explains: 'An alternative method for
evaluating sentencing and incarceration policies is to analyze the institutional
dynamics that produce them. If the political economy that produces sentencing laws suffers from an imbalance or defect of some kind, that could provide
a reason for questioning the sentencing policy itself.'[31] It is clear that the most
significant impact of the punitive turn has been on poor and minority communities and that these are the very communities who are least represented,
both in the legislative sphere, and in the other institutions (police departments,

---

[27] PH Robinson and MJ Cahill, *Law Without Justice: Why the Criminal Law Doesn't Give People
What They Deserve* (Oxford: Oxford University Press, 2005) (criticizing, among other things, disproportionate punishments imposed through harsh sentences that ignore legitimate claims of
blamelessness, such as mandatory minimum penalties and 'three strikes' laws).
[28] Brown (n 2 above) 227 (arguing that 'the reach of criminal statutes has contracted in many
significant, formerly regulated realms').
[29] A Natapoff, 'Underenforcement' (2006) 75 *Fordham Law Review* 1715, 1716 (arguing that
the problem of underenforcement 'has been given short shrift').   [30] Brown (n 2 above) 227.
[31] RE Barkow, 'The Political Market for Criminal Justice' (2008) 104 *Michigan Law Review*
1713, 1714.

prosecutors' offices, courts, parole boards, and chief executive offices) whose discretion shapes the nature and distribution of penal outcomes. As Alexandra Natapoff, a critic of underenforcement, notes: 'Over- and underenforcement are twin symptoms of a deeper democratic weakness of the criminal system: its non-responsiveness to the needs of the poor, racial minorities, and the otherwise politically vulnerable.'[32] Moreover, the process that produces criminal justice policy is not only insufficiently responsive to vulnerable interests; it is also overly responsive to the interests of prosecutors in a way that renders the political process 'pathological', in the words of one observer.[33] Bill Stuntz argues that the existence of prosecutorial discretion creates powerful legislative incentives to broaden the scope of criminal legislation and heighten the severity of penalties in order to lower the costs of successful prosecution of crime. In the absence of robust judicial oversight, which does not currently exist, these institutional incentives create a one-way ratchet towards ever broader and more severe penalties.

While Barkow, Natapoff, and Stuntz identify defects in the political process that lead to overpunishment, other scholars with a more sociological bent have identified a more encompassing cultural shift, called variously a 'culture of control',[34] 'penal populism',[35] and 'governing through crime'.[36] This contrasting school of thought notes changes in the way that crime is portrayed in the media and popular culture, discussed in policy debates, and offered as a frame or lens through which to view other aspects of society. These changes amount to what David Garland calls a new 'cultural formation' that 'we might term the "crime complex" of late modernity'.[37] In Garland's account, this 'crime complex' is characterized by intense and widespread emotional investment in crime by ordinary citizens and the domination in public policy of concerns about crime victims and public safety. Anthony Bottoms, Julian Roberts, and others emphasize the way in which populist influences have shifted toward greater punitiveness and have come to dominate the formation of crime policy, to the displacement of evidence or expertise.[38] Jonathan Simon argues that the irrationally strong and pervasive public fear of crime has led to the proliferation of 'the technologies, discourses, and metaphors of crime and criminal

---

[32] Natapoff (n 29 above) 1719.

[33] WJ Stuntz, 'The Pathological Politics of Criminal Law' (2001) 100 *Michigan Law Review* 505.   [34] Garland (n 9 above).

[35] A Bottoms, 'The Philosophy and Politics of Punishment and Sentencing' in CMV Clarkson and R Morgan (eds), *The Politics of Sentencing Reform* (Oxford: Clarendon Press, 1995); JV Roberts *et al*, *Penal Populism and Public Opinion: Lessons from Five Countries* (Oxford: Oxford University Press, 2003).

[36] J Simon, *Governing Through Crime: How the War on Crime Transformed American Democracy and Created a Culture of Fear* (Oxford: Oxford University Press, 2007).

[37] Garland (n 9 above) 163.   [38] Bottoms (n 35 above); Roberts *et al* (n 35 above).

justice' in the governance institutions outside criminal justice, including 'families, schools, and businesses'.[39]

These various accounts, of both the process and culture variety, of our current penal politics offer powerful grounds to doubt the wisdom of the punitive turn, whatever its effects might be, simply on the basis of its origins in a politics distorted by perverse incentives and irrational fears. Moreover, these accounts also add to the list of pernicious effects of the punitive turn, because the penal practices generated by the punitive turn themselves form a feedback loop further promoting the same perverse incentives and irrational fears that produced them. As Jonathan Simon suggests, current penal policies do not seem to make people feel safer; rather they seem to further fuel 'a culture of fear and control that inevitably lowers the threshold of fear even as it places greater and greater burdens on ordinary Americans'.[40]

B   Impediments to change

How entrenched and enduring are prevailing penal policies in the USA and its punitive cohort? According to some accounts, there is reason to hope that the punitive turn will self-correct. Michael Tonry, drawing on historical literature on long-term crime trends and sociological literature on 'moral panics', argued at the end of the 1990s that the punitive turn in the USA constituted a 'moral panic'—a period in which 'people collectively exaggerate the scale of problems, behave intolerantly, and do things or adopt policies that in less hysterical times would be rejected.'[41] The long historical view taken by Tonry suggested that moral panics are cyclical—generally developing, paradoxically, in periods of declining drug use, or in periods of broad-based public insecurities. Thus, Tonry concluded optimistically: 'If we can recognize [that current crime policy is the product of a moral panic] and take it into account, it ought to be possible to do better.'[42] Presumably, though Tonry did not say so explicitly, even in the absence of conscious recognition of a state of moral panic, the panic should eventually run its course, as other historical panics have done in the history he reviewed—the paradigm example being the Salem witch trials. In late seventeenth-century Massachusetts, nearly two dozen suspected witches were executed over a period of a year or so, but the hysteria soon ran its course, ending with reprieves (for those sentenced to death), discharges (for those held prisoner), and pardons for all persons under suspicion.[43] John

---

[39] Simon (n 36 above) 4–5.   [40] Ibid, 6.
[41] M Tonry, 'Rethinking Unthinkable Punishment Policies in America' (1999) 46 *UCLA Law Review* 1751, 1753.   [42] Ibid, 1789.
[43] Ibid, 1784.

Braithwaite, writing like Tonry at the turn of the millennium, was even more explicitly hopeful that the punitive turn will soon boomerang.[44] Braithwaite asserted that 'we are on the threshold of an era of evidence-based crime prevention',[45] and predicted that in the next twenty years (from 1999), policy makers would turn away from retributive 'get-tough-on-crime' policies towards restorative justice initiatives, in which perpetrator, victim, and other members of the community affected by an offence join in an effort to determine how best to repair the harm caused.[46] More recently, as the US economy and other national economies throughout the world have entered a crisis more serious than any since 1929, criminal justice reformers are renewing hope that the turn around predicted by Tonry and Braithwaite will come to pass, as financial exigencies may require radical slashing of bloated and ever-growing corrections budgets.[47]

Other scholarly commentators are considerably less optimistic about the prospects for substantial change in the foreseeable future. Obviously, those who subscribe to the 'pathological politics' or the 'cultural shift' views described above see little likelihood of change without either substantial reform of the structure of prevailing institutions of criminal justice or some broader cultural shift, which would seem *less* rather than more likely to occur in a time of high financial anxiety and displacement.[48] Moreover, scholars like Jim Whitman, who believes that the roots of American punitiveness lie in long-standing historical differences between the USA and Europe,[49] and scholars like Niki Lacey, who explains penal tolerance and severity in relation to national differences in political economy,[50] would not expect sudden or substantial change in punitive practices, given their roots in essential aspects of the societies that produce them.[51]

I share the scepticism of this latter group, but I wish to explore further the grounds for the 'stickiness' of the punitive turn. Unlike many of these sceptical scholars, my goal is not to tell a fine-grained causal or historical story

---

[44] J Braithwaite, 'A Future where Punishment is Marginalized: Realistic or Utopian?' (1999) 46 *UCLA Law Review* 1727.   [45] Ibid, 1737.

[46] Ibid, 1735–7.

[47] Associated Press, 'Budget Woes Prompt States to Rethink Prison Policies', 10 January 2009; RE Barkow and KM O'Neill, 'Delegating Punitive Power: The Political Economy of Sentencing Commission and Guideline Formation' (2006) 84 *Texas Law Review* 1973 (finding that the high cost of corrections budgets appeared to prompt states to delegate to sentencing commissions power to formulate guidelines to reduce corrections costs by altering imprisonment policies).

[48] B Carey, 'Citizen Enforcers Take Aim', *New York Times*, 7 October 2008 (describing 'strong evidence' that the urge to punish 'hardens in times of crisis and uncertainty, like the current one').

[49] *Harsh Justice* (Oxford: Oxford University Press, 2003).

[50] *The Prisoners' Dilemma* (n 9 above).

[51] Lacey does, however, suggest that there is 'room for policy manoeuvre' in the more punitive market economies: ibid, 170.

about the origins of our penal policies. Rather, I seek to catalogue underlying conditions that currently support prevailing policies, while remaining agnostic on the relative weight of these underlying conditions in any causal account. My goal is to identify stable (or even immutable) social facts and institutional arrangements that stand in the way of any large-scale, near-term retreat from punitiveness. These facts and arrangements generate incentives on the part of various institutional actors and the public at large to maintain harsh penal policies, which in turn are viewed as serving legitimate social functions. The impediments to change that I identify are all part of the American landscape, sometimes uniquely, but many of them exist in part and in varying degrees in other countries as well. I argue that, in the absence of change in these underlying conditions, there is little hope for self-correction of penal policies. Rather, these conditions—which fall into three rough clusters—suggest that we need to think deeply about exit strategies rather than vainly wait for the swing of a pendulum.

1 Social conditions

Harshly punitive policies are easier to promulgate and impose when their burdens are not evenly shared throughout a society, but rather are disproportionately imposed on a disfavoured group or class. The USA and quite a number of other industrial democracies are characterized by great social and economic inequality, an inequality that has grown over the same period that has seen the punitive turn. Minority groups (blacks, Hispanics, and Native Americans, among others, in the USA) are disproportionately represented in an economic underclass that is essentially precluded from participation in the labour market and provided with only a very thin social safety net of public entitlements. Moreover, this underclass is both highly concentrated and highly isolated geographically. Pervasive residential segregation, especially in urban areas, has led to blighted ghettos cut off from jobs and provided with substandard city services, such as housing, education, and transportation, among others. These communities have become social islands having little interaction with the rest of the urban centres that surround them, making it easier for their members to be demonized as a frightening 'other'—a dynamic illustrated by the widely published fears that babies born to crack-addicted mothers would grow up to become a generation of 'super-predators'.[52] These neighbourhoods generate disproportionate criminal offending, and they also make easy targets for relatively cheap and high-impact 'hot spot' policing. Punitive drug

---

[52] M Szalavitz, 'The Demon Seed That Wasn't: Debunking the "Crack Baby" Myth' in *City Limits Monthly*, 1 March 2004 (quoting a paediatric medical researcher to the effect that 'the crack baby is a grotesque media stereotype, not a scientific diagnosis').

interdiction policies have become a popular tool to contain the disorder rampant in such high-crime neighbourhoods. Several generations of high-impact policing and punitive punishment have had devastating impacts on inner-city families and communities, leading to the creation of an apparently permanent urban underclass—thus entrenching and exacerbating incentives to continue the punitive policies that helped to create it. At the same time, decades of explosive growth in the use of imprisonment have also entrenched economic dependence on the jobs generated by the corrections sector, as reflected in the competition among small towns for the placement of new prisons and the power of corrections officers' unions in state and local politics.

2 *Political and legal institutions*

These entrenched incentives to contain the crumbling disorder of the inner city through criminal sanctions will generate more strongly punitive policies to the extent that criminal justice policy is strongly responsive to popular will. What kinds of political and legal institutions are more likely to shape penal policy in response to the interests and fears of 'the median voter' described by political scientists? One arrangement, virtually unique to the USA, is the popular election of local prosecutors (an almost universal practice) and of state judges (the large majority of state judges stand for some sort of election). This arrangement gives local constituencies great power over local law enforcement outcomes and creates powerful incentives for prosecutors and judges to respond quickly and directly to political pressures.[53] Moreover, localities do not generally have to account in their budgets for their share of the financial costs of local charging decisions and sentencing recommendations; rather these costs are born in the USA at the state level, rendering such costs less visible and increasing the incentive of local actors to disregard them. State legislatures, by contrast, do have incentives to lower the costs of prosecution, and one way that they can do this is by passing broader and harsher criminal statutes that give prosecutors more powerful tools for generating cheap and certain convictions through plea bargaining—the 'pathological politics' described by Bill Stuntz. This dynamic is not limited to countries with a strong state/local divide; rather, any country that has seen a substantial increase in the practice of plea bargaining will be subject to some degree to similar pressures.[54] At the level of national politics, 'winner-takes-all' two-party electoral

---

[53] Political scientists studying judicial elections have found evidence that trial judges standing for re-election tend to impose harsher sentences as elections approach: GA Huber and SC Gordon, 'Accountability and Coercion: Is Justice Blind when It Runs for Office?' (2004) 48 *American Journal of Political Science* 247.

[54] M Langer, 'From Legal Transplants to Legal Translations: The Globalization of Plea Bargaining and the Americanization Thesis in Criminal Procedure' (2004) 45 *Harvard*

systems may give more influence to the fears of the median voter than systems of proportional representation with more fractured parties, especially as elections approach and the two parties vie for the 'swing' voter with the easy salience of criminal justice issues.[55]

3   Human cognition and behaviour

The conditions that affect the likelihood that current punitive policies will be moderated or abandoned include not only modes of social organization and structures of political and legal institutions, but also internal aspects of human cognition and motivation. The 'real world' is constituted as much by the way in which people frame, sort, and respond to information about the world as by the world itself. In recent decades, scientists of human cognition and behaviour, including psychologists and neurologists, have developed new insights into human responses to wrongdoing that have implications for the development and maintenance of punishment practices. Two insights in particular warrant attention because of what they suggest about the future of punishment practices in societies characterized by the social and political conditions described above.

The first insight, introduced in 1967,[56] and elaborated at length over the next few decades,[57] is what is widely referred to as the 'fundamental attribution error',[58] sometimes also referred to as 'observer bias' or 'correspondence bias' under the more general rubric of 'correspondent inference theory'.[59] In a variety of experimental settings, researchers observed a strong tendency of subjects to overascribe the observed behaviour of others to dispositional factors (that is, the individual's beliefs, values, or character traits) and to undervalue the influence of situational factors (that is, social and environmental constraints). Although this tendency was widely observed in a variety of contexts among

---

International Law Journal 1 (tracing the growth of plea bargaining in various forms in Germany, France, Italy, and Argentina).

[55] Lacey (n 9 above) 67 (suggesting that 'the volatile force represented by the power of the median voter, who "floats" between the two parties characteristic of majoritarian systems, is correspondingly less, being mediated by credible commitments made during the bargaining process [among multiple political parties forming a coalition government]').

[56] EE Jones and VA Harris, 'The Attribution of Attitudes' (1967) 3 *Journal of Experimental Psychology* 1.

[57] L Ross and RE Nisbett, *The Person and the Situation: Perspectives of Social Psychology* (Philadelphia: Temple University Press, 1991) (fully developing a theory of the influence of situational constraints on human behaviour).

[58] L Ross, 'The Intuitive Psychologist and His Shortcomings: Distortions in the Attribution Process' in L Berkowitz (ed), *Advances in Experimental Social Psychology*, vol 10 (New York: Academic Press, 1977) 173 (coining the term 'fundamental attribution error' to explain the results of a decade of research suggesting that people systematically underestimate situational constraints).   [59] Jones and Harris (n 56 above).

diverse subjects of different ages and across different cultures, its strength varied in ways that suggest that culture and the acculturation process play roles in shaping attribution. The degree of attribution error or bias has been found by a number of studies to be larger in older adults, suggesting the possible role of acculturation in promoting such error.[60] Moreover, the influence of age was found to be stronger in some cultures than others,[61] as was the general level of attribution bias, suggesting that some cultures ('individualistic' ones) may engender more attribution error than others ('collectivist' ones).[62]

These insights regarding the prevalence of attribution error, particularly in individualistic societies, have some implications for the likely future of criminal justice policy in the USA and its punitive cohort. This body of research suggests that both criminal justice policy makers and individual institutional actors making discretionary decisions within the criminal justice system may erroneously attribute criminal offending to dispositional attributes of offenders and fail to accord sufficient weight to situational factors, thus leading to the rejection of appropriate defences or the imposition of inappropriately severe criminal sanctions, at the level of both rule making and rule application. Moreover, the very same individualistic social tendencies that create wide disparities in wealth and social opportunities may exacerbate the distorted perception of the impact of those disparities on the actions of those most constrained by them. This dynamic between culture and attribution in highly individualistic and unequal societies predicts widespread belief in such societies that high rates of criminal offending in impoverished and marginalized communities are attributable to dispositional rather than to situational factors, and that such offending therefore calls for criminal punishment rather than amelioration of societal constraints. Such views represent a source of likely resistance to substantial retrenchment from current punitive policies.

The second insight into human behaviour that is relevant for my purposes is another qualification of the view of human agents as rational actors. Whereas the fundamental attribution error identifies a defect in human cognition by uncovering a systematic bias in the attribution process, research into 'altruistic punishment' qualifies the view that humans predictably act to further their own self-interest. This body of research, undertaken by researchers interested in charting the evolutionary foundations of human cooperation, reveals that

---

[60] Y Chen and F Blanchard-Fields, 'Age Differences in Stages of Attributional Processing' (1997) 12 *Psychology and Aging* 694.

[61] F Blancard-Fields *et al*, 'Cultural Differences in the Relationship between Aging and the Correspondence Bias' (2007) 62 *Journals of Gerontology Series B—Psychological Sciences and Social Sciences* 362.

[62] JG Miller, 'Culture and the Development of Everyday Social Explanation' (1984) 46 *Journal of Personality and Social Psychology* 961.

in a variety of experimental settings people will predictably spend resources to impose punishment on those whom they believe to have acted unfairly, even when such punishment is costly and yields no material gain to the punisher.[63] As with attribution error, this tendency, while widely observed, is not uniform across cultures; rather, it is more widely observed in larger, more complex societies,[64] and it is more likely to be imposed on norm violators who are members of an ethnic, racial, or language 'outgroup'.[65] Moreover, researchers have observed that the imposition of altruistic punishment has neurological correlates. When the brains of subjects were scanned during cooperation experiments, the subjects' observation of unfair behaviour by non-cooperators stimulated heightened activity in brain areas related to emotion as well as cognition,[66] and the subjects' imposition of altruistic punishment activated brain areas associated with the processing of rewards from goal-directed actions.[67]

These behavioural and neurological observations add to the reasons to be sceptical that current punitive trends will reverse themselves. This research suggests the power of underlying human motivations to punish and offers reasons to believe that these motivations are most powerful in exactly the sorts of society in which punitive policies now flourish—large, complex societies with disparate offending and policing of concentrated 'outgroups'. Moreover, this research offers some explanation for the otherwise puzzling willingness of highly punitive societies to allocate enormous resources to corrections, even in the absence of evidence of efficacy. It also suggests that severely tightening budgets may not result in correspondingly large cuts in corrections spending, as predicted by hopeful reformers.

II   Grounding a Theory of Prudential Mercy

Identifying the set of social conditions, institutional structures, and behavioural tendencies that appear to support and entrench current punitive policies may also help us to formulate an exit strategy. These features of our current

---

[63] E Fehr and S Gachter, 'Altruistic Punishment in Humans' (2002) 415 *Nature* 137; J Henrich, 'Costly Punishment across Human Societies' (2006) 312 *Science* 1767.

[64] FW Marlowe *et al*, 'More "Altruistic" Punishment in Larger Societies' (2008) 275 *Proceedings of the Royal Society B—Biological Sciences* 1634.

[65] H Bernhard *et al*, 'Parochial Altruism in Humans' (2006) 442 *Nature* 912.

[66] AG Sanfey *et al*, 'The Neural Basis of Economic Decision-Making in the Ultimatum Game' (2003) 300 *Science* 1755.

[67] Dominique de Quervain *et al*, 'The Neural Basis of Altruistic Punishment' (2004) 305 *Science* 1254.

condition suggest a critique of the dominant justifications for criminal punishment that, if recognized by discretionary actors within the criminal justice system, could present a rationale for the exercise of a robust veto power over legislatively authorized (or even required) punishment. Such a reconceptualization of the role of discretion in the administration of criminal justice offers both a new way to think about the role of 'mercy' in punishment practices and a possible way out of entrenched punitiveness—not only by moderating punishment in individual cases, but ultimately by influencing legislative determinations and public discourse as well.

A Theories of punishment and the punitive moment

Current penal policy is dominated by two major modes of justificatory discourse: retributivism (a deontological theory that justifies the practice of criminal punishment as imposing just deserts on offenders) and social welfare theory (a utilitarian theory that justifies the practice of criminal punishment as increasing social welfare, defined as the aggregate of individual preferences). Each mode, of course, contains within it many disparate strands of discourse, each competing to establish itself as the most normatively attractive version of the larger theory. Moreover, the two general modes of justification clearly compete with each other, starting from distinctive premises and producing sometimes antithetical applications. In the abstract world of theorizing, there is intense rivalry both between these two modes of normative discourse and among the various sub discourses within them. In the less self-reflective world of penal policy making, however, retributivism and social welfare theory coexist with far less antagonism, as both are often invoked simultaneously to support policy initiatives. Indeed, it would be impossible to untangle the influences of the two modes of discourse or to make sense of any policy discussion regarding criminal justice without reference to both of them.

Each of these modes of discourse has contributed to the punitive turn and continues to help maintain current punitive policies because each of these theories is distorted when filtered through the stable set of social conditions, institutional structures, and behavioural tendencies canvassed above. I do not claim that the current crisis of overpunishment is the inevitable result of any embrace of these very general theories of punishment (which, after all, have been around for quite a while and have purchase in many societies with quite different penal policies). Indeed, causation almost certainly runs the other way, too—the social and political conditions and behavioural tendencies that foster punitive practices also promote justificatory discourses to explain and bolster those practices. But we should be cognizant of the way that purposive and justificatory theory itself reinforces and promotes overpunishment because of its inability to insulate itself from the conditions and capacities that constitute the society in which it is deployed. It is common for academics to claim that the cure for defects in penal policy is for policy makers to hew more closely to the demands of the academics' preferred theories. Moral, legal, and economic theorists alike, promoting some version of retributivism or social welfare theory as grounds for penal policy, see themselves as standing outside of politics or a particular social context and offering abstract foundations for the structures of legal institutions and the shape of punitive practices—foundations that while abstract nonetheless yield quite concrete proposals for reform in application.[68] When the discourses of retributivism and social welfare interact with the particulars of a social context, however, they will inevitably be distorted and in predictable ways—in much the same way that the sound of musical instruments can be distorted by heat, cold, and humidity. We thus should be wary of specific normative proposals derived from either theory, or at the very least attentive to the ways in which these theoretical discourses might be distorted by prevailing conditions so as to contribute to the excessive punitiveness of the moment.

At first glance, and to many of its adherents, retributivism appears to offer a promising antidote to excessive punitiveness because it grounds the permissibility of punishment in an account of wrongdoing premised on human autonomy. This account places outside limits on punishment relative to moral desert and it portrays punishment as ultimately vindicating rather than destroying individual autonomy and dignity. Despite this theoretical promise, any attempt to shape the content of criminal sanctions by reference to the concept of 'desert' faces daunting challenges in our current social and legal context. The undisputed criminogenic nature of current social conditions in impoverished and otherwise disadvantaged communities suggests that a penal theory grounded in moral desert needs to generate a very finely calibrated scale that can take account of the impact of social conditions on offender culpability. But the substantive criminal law could not be farther from such a scale; rather, defences or mitigation based on constraints on choice tend to be extremely narrow and crudely 'on/off'. For example, the defence of insanity generally requires an extreme cognitive or volitional impairment; less extreme but still real impairments due to mental defect or illness provide no defence against criminal liability, but are accounted for only sporadically and incompletely through sentencing discretion.[69] Similarly, while the defences of duress and

---

[68] Robinson and Cahill (n 27 above) (offering retributivism as a grounding for criminal justice reforms); L Kaplow and S Shavell, *Fairness versus Welfare* (Cambridge, MA: Harvard University Press, 2002) 294–317 (offering social welfare as a grounding for the criminal law).

[69] The mitigation of punishment for 'diminished' or 'partial' responsibility is a relatively rare doctrine, often limited, when it is allowed at all, to extreme impairments or specific crimes: SJ

self-defence recognize extreme constraints on agency, the more pervasive but less extreme coercive effects of dealing with a violent or gang-dominated street culture are likewise generally ignored in the substantive law.[70]

Partly, the law's narrowness reflects the inherent difficulty of articulating generally applicable rules of liability (or exemption from liability) that can take into account fine gradations of desert. Hence, legislatures tend to delegate the problem of fine-tuning the application of criminal sanctions to prosecutorial charging discretion and judicial sentencing discretion, and in extreme cases, to the fail-safe of executive clemency or pardon. The inability to 'rule-ify' determinations of desert, however, feeds into the 'pathological' political dynamic of crime definition. Legislatures have come to rely more generally on prosecutorial discretion to curtail the overly broad criminal statutes they pass and lower the cost of pursuing convictions. But prosecutors' ability and willingness to use their discretion to make fine-tuned judgements of desert is limited by the same political and social dynamics that promote broad criminal liability. The narrowness of desert-based defences reflects public fears that broad or open-textured exemptions or mitigations will devolve in 'abuse excuses' that will secure the release of too wide a class of dangerous offenders, given the ubiquity of various forms of 'abuse' in the populations most likely to offend. Widespread conditions of extreme social and economic inequality thus generate resistance—by prosecutors as well as the public—to acknowledging the way inequality undermines individual desert by diminishing the opportunity of members of a social underclass to avoid becoming criminals. This resistance to recognizing the effects of inequality on desert is, paradoxically, often defended by recourse to retributivism's respect for human autonomy—to acknowledge the possible effects of social conditions on human agency is to deny the agency of the underprivileged.[71] Fortunately for retributivism, human cognitive bias steps into the breach to offer an alternative account of criminal offending by

Morse, 'Diminished Rationality, Diminished Responsibility' (2003) 1 *Ohio State Journal of Criminal Law* 289 (proposing a formal verdict for reducing punishment in cases of diminished responsibility).

[70] D Rutkowski, 'A Coercion Defense for the Street Gang Criminal: Plugging the Moral Gap in Existing Law' (1999) 10 *Notre Dame Journal of Law Ethics and Public Policy* 137 (arguing that the law should recognize street gang coercion in order to bring criminal liability in line with retributive limits on punishment).

[71] David Dolinko said this best: '[T]he retributivist mind-set encourages legal actors to brush aside qualms about whether the wretched economic, social, and psychological background of many criminals somehow undercuts our right to inflict condign punishment. For if to credit such qualms is to question the criminal's status as a fully responsible individual, then respect for the criminal's very personhood counsels us to reject those qualms and to affirm our deep respect for the offender by refusing to mitigate his punishment no matter how "deprived" his background': D Dolinko, 'Three Mistakes of Retributivism' (1992) 39 *UCLA Law Review* 1623, 1647–8.

the underprivileged that discounts situational constraints on behaviour and emphasizes dispositional explanations for wrongdoing.

Critics of retributivism have decried the 'moral smugness' of retributivism—the belief 'that what we are doing is no regrettable though necessary evil but instead a positive good: respecting persons, doing justice, and generally living up to the most high-minded and Kantian ethical demands'.[72] The burgeoning research on 'altruistic punishment' gives us additional reason to worry about the dominance of emotions like satisfaction and self-righteousness (rather than sadness or doubt) in the imposition of punitive sanctions. The widespread instinct to punish, and the apparent pleasure or reward that the imposition of punishment elicits in the human brain, should make us question whether we give sufficient scrutiny to the grounding or application of justificatory theories that validate our punishment practices. Moreover, the greater incidence observed by researchers of 'altruistic punishments' imposed on members of 'outgroups' gives us further reason to doubt our attributions of deserved punishment in such cases.

Can consequentialist penal theories based on maximizing aggregate social welfare do better at resisting distortion towards overpunishment? One might think that a consequentialist theory of punishment would skew less towards harsh punishment than retributivism. After all, consequentialism counts punishment as an evil 'only to be admitted in as far as it promises to exclude some greater evil' rather than as a virtue in itself.[73] Moreover, there may well be instances, perhaps many, in which the calculation of 'optimal' punishment for consequentialist purposes would lead to punishment less than retributivism would demand. Certainly, rehabilitation as a welfarist goal would tend to promote limits on the most extreme penalties (such as the death penalty, life without parole, or prison sentences of many decades). Finally, social welfare theory has the capacity to respond to the 'bounded rationality' of human agents by discounting irrational preferences that do not in fact promote welfare. Despite these potential safeguards against overpunishment, social welfare theory is as likely to be distorted by prevailing conditions as retributivism, though in different ways.

First, rehabilitation was largely abandoned in the USA, sometimes formally, as a goal of punishment during the decades of exploding incarceration.[74] Sometimes, this abandonment is attributed to the decline of confidence in

---

[72] Ibid, 1625.

[73] Jeremy Bentham, *An Introduction to the Principles of Morals and Legislation* (1781)(Oxford: Clarendon Press, 1996) 158.

[74] For example, Congress explicitly rejected rehabilitation as a goal of incarceration in the 1984 Act that established the Federal Sentencing Commission.

rehabilitative programmes in response to the perceived development of an expert consensus that 'nothing works'.[75] But there is good reason to think that even in the absence of such a perceived consensus, prevailing social conditions would skew the calculus of aggregate social welfare so as to undervalue rehabilitative considerations. Even at times when the rehabilitative ideal was more robustly in play, general deterrence has always been considered a central feature of punishment's contribution to aggregate social welfare. In conditions of great social and economic inequality, however, penal policy makers worry that imprisonment will not act as a sufficiently effective deterrent if those convicted of crimes are accorded benefits or opportunities not available to the most disadvantaged citizens in the society at large. This principle of 'less eligibility' has special power in public discourse regarding criminal punishment in times of increasing or extreme inequality. When the most disadvantaged citizens in the society at large have essentially no prospects for integration into the legal labour force, the principle of less eligibility weighs strongly against robust educational and job training programmes for convicted criminals. Moreover, the tendency to err in attributing criminal offending to dispositional factors rather than situational constraints will lead policy makers and the public alike to further discount the likely benefit of rehabilitative programmes, which generally aim to ameliorate situational constraints (lack of education or job skills, lack of access to counselling or drug treatment) rather than to address dispositional factors (such as disrespect for the law or a taste for crime), which can be checked only coercively through deterrence or incapacitation. While social welfare theorists often adjust their calculations to account for the 'bounded rationality' or cognitive biases of those who are the targets of criminal justice policy initiatives,[76] they are less quick to see how cognitive biases on the part of the deployers of social welfare theory can distort their cost–benefit calculations.[77]

Second, social welfare theory, like all cost–benefit analysis, does a much better job of analysing and aggregating things that can be accurately quantified. Current social and political conditions, however, lead social welfare theory to systematically undervalue the costs of harsh penal policies on criminal defendants. First, traditional cost–benefit analysis tends to quantify costs and benefits

---

[75] C Haney, 'Psychology and the Limits to Prison Pain: Confronting the Coming Crisis in Eighth Amendment Law' (1997) 3 *Psychology, Public Policy and Law* 499 (citing sociologist Robert Martinson's famous conclusion that 'nothing works': 'What Works? Questions and Answers about Prison Reform' (1974) 35 *Public Interest* 22).

[76] R McAdams and TS Ulen, 'Behavioral Criminal law and Economics' (University of Illinois Law and Economics Research Paper No LE0–8–035, November 2008).

[77] '[O]nce criminals are not fully rational, so are not victims, enforcers, and politicians': N Garouopa, 'Behavioral Economic Analysis of Crime: A Critical Review' (2003) 15 *European Journal of Law and Economics* 5, 12; quoted in McAdams & Ulen (ibid) 26.

in monetary terms by gauging how much people would be willing to pay to receive certain benefits or how much people would accept to have certain burdens imposed on them. However, cost–benefit analysis has to account for the so-called 'endowment effect' by which people tend to value more highly a benefit they already possess than one they have yet to obtain (making them less willing to 'sell' an endowment at the same price that they would offer to 'buy' it). In the context of criminal justice policy, the endowment effect makes it difficult to assess the costs and benefits of penal policies accurately in contexts in which large wealth differences (differential endowments) exist between those who are burdened by such policies and those who are benefited, skewing the analysis to undervalue the costs experienced by poor defendants and their families and communities.[78] Moreover, the relative lack of political power of underprivileged communities in general and the class of criminal defendants in particular decreases the likelihood that the full costs of harsh punitive policies will be presented to legislatures,[79] or that prosecutors will face any of the kind of lobbying from regulatory targets that provides information to ordinary administrative agencies in conducting regulatory cost–benefit analysis.[80] These failures of information inevitable skew social welfare theory's assessment of the relative costs and benefits of punitive penal policies.

Finally, social welfare theory rejects what champions of retributivsm often see as its chief virtue—respect for a right *against* punishment that is excessive or undeserved, a right that derives from retributivism's account of individual autonomy. Part of social welfare theory's vulnerability to overpunishment lies in its very thin conception of personhood, which consists only of preferences that are entitled to equal aggregation. Aside from this entitlement, social welfare theory is incompatible with rights discourse; it is unable to generate an *ex ante* limiting principle on permissible criminal sanctions. This vulnerability can be exploited in highly unequal societies, where sanctions are not evenly distributed across social groups, where the political and legal process fails to protect minority interests against excessive criminal sanctions, and where cognitive biases may engender more punitive attitudes than warranted. In such circumstances, the likelihood that the social welfare calculus will fail is much greater, as illustrated by some recent welfarist defences of capital punishment and torture that have implausibly discounted the costs of such practices.[81]

---

[78] DK Brown, 'Cost–Benefit Analysis in Criminal Law' (2004) 92 *California Law Review* 323, 359.   [79] Ibid, 359–60.

[80] Ibid, 361.

[81] C Sunstein and A Vermeule, 'Is Capital Punishment Morally Required? Acts, Omissions, and Life–Life Tradeoffs' (2005) 58 *Stanford Law Review* 703 (answering in the affirmative); EA Posner and A Vermeule, 'Should Coercive Interrogation Be Legal?' (2006) 104 *Michigan Law Review* 671 (answering in the affirmative). But see CS Steiker, 'No, Capital Punishment is Not Morally

Adherents of retributivism or social welfare theory might dismiss the above concerns as simply a statement of the obvious—that social conditions, political and legal institutions, and human biases may distort particular applications of their theories. They might insist that these distortions should not be taken as a reflection on the value of their theories themselves as ways of providing both moral grounding for the criminal law and good guidance on its appropriate contours. My point is not to take issue with retributivism or social welfare consequentialism as theories; I seek here to remain agnostic on the moral foundations of the criminal law. Rather, I mean to suggest that both retributivism and social welfare theory, as discourses deployed in the current world, will tend toward overpunishment, even when policy makers and discretionary institutional actors self-consciously and in all good faith see themselves as trying to promote their appropriate ends. Therefore, it is a mistake to rely on fine-tuning such approaches in order to reverse the punitive turn. A different exit strategy is called for.

B   Prudential mercy

The grounds sketched above for believing that the dominant discourses regarding criminal punishment predictably skew towards overpunishment under prevailing conditions suggests the need for some sort of correction or 'counter-ratchet'. In light of the powerful forces skewing the legislative process, it is worth shifting the focus to the many discretionary actors downstream from the legislature in the criminal justice process and asking how they should conceptualize and exercise their disaggregated power to shape the contours of criminalization and punishment. While these various discretionary actors, such as prosecutors, juries, and sentencing judges, are aware to varying degrees that they possess discretion, they often conceive of that discretion as bounded even when it is not formally confined. For example, prosecutors may think of their charging discretion as properly used to decline prosecution in order to reflect the intentions of the legislature, or in cases in which conviction is too uncertain or costly, or in cases outside current enforcement priorities; they generally do not consider themselves the appropriate audience for more open-ended appeals from defendants or their counsel about the excessive breadth or harshness of particular prohibitions. Juries are often explicitly told to consider only the sufficiency of the evidence in the cases before them; consideration of the appropriateness of the charges or the magnitude of the

Required: Deterrence, Deontology, and the Death Penalty' (2005) 58 *Stanford Law Review* 751 (responding to Sunstein and Vermeule); AA Haque, 'Torture, Terror, and the Inversion of Moral Principle' (2007) 10 *New Criminal Law Review* 613 (responding to Posner and Vermeule).

punishment that will follow from conviction is not encouraged or even generally permitted, despite the fact that jury 'nullification' of criminal charges is essentially unreviewable. Judges in exercising their sentencing discretion, when not controlled by guidelines or mandatory sentencing provisions, explicitly consider the extent to which the legitimate purposes of punishment will be promoted by their choice of sanction; they are unlikely to consider pleas for leniency not couched in terms of promoting the ultimate ends of punishment, as best they can discern them. I argue that these and other discretionary actors should broaden their conceptions of their discretionary powers so as to open themselves to a wider range of considerations that might move them to exercise a veto power over the imposition of punishment in particular cases.

This argument is essentially a claim that officials with discretionary power in the criminal justice system should see themselves as open to appeals for 'mercy' in addition to exercises of discretion of the more quotidian kind described above. For my purposes, exercises of 'merciful' discretion involve leniency based on compassionate concern for the offender, rather than on some more instrumental end. In particular, the mercy that I urge is a self-conscious recognition of the way in which the dominant modes of discourse about punishment predictably skew outcomes toward overpunishment, an openness to doubt whether even our best, good-faith attempts to translate punishment theory into practice will lead us astray, and a willingness therefore to moderate or even forgo otherwise authorized punishment, at least in cases where our doubts are strongest.

The case for grounding mercy in doubt about our capacity to do justice offers a new sort of intervention in the established debate among moral and legal theorists about the role of mercy in criminal justice. This debate, inaugurated by Jeffrie Murphy and Jean Hampton in 1988[82] and accelerating in recent years,[83] concerns whether mercy can be reconciled with the demand for retributive justice, and whether it can play a role as an appropriate value or legal practice even if not reconcilable. Opponents of mercy in criminal justice, like Murphy, see no room for the exercise of merciful discretion in the public sphere of criminal justice (as opposed to family life or private justice), given the duty of public officials to do retributive justice. Proponents of mercy, like Hampton, see the duty to do retributive justice as appropriately offset

[82] JG Murphy and J Hampton, *Forgiveness and Mercy* (Cambridge: Cambridge University Press, 1988).

[83] CS Steiker, 'Tempering or Tampering? Mercy and the Administration of Criminal Justice' in A Sarat and N Hussain (eds), *Forgiveness, Mercy, and Clemency* (Stanford: Stanford University Press, 2007) 16 (surveying approaches to the relationship of mercy to criminal justice); 'Symposium: Questions of Mercy' (2007) 4 *Ohio State Journal of Criminal Law* 321–521 (collection of essays by moral philosophers and legal scholars on the relationship of mercy to criminal justice).

by other incommensurable duties. My case for mercy is simultaneously more modest and more ambitious than the accounts of mercy offered by Hampton and other mercy defenders. It is more modest in that it is a prudential account rooted in the predictable failures of our discourses of justice rather than in an independent set of values that mercy promotes outside of justice; it is more ambitious in that it argues for a place for the exercise of mercy in institutions of criminal justice regardless of which theory or theories of punishment the criminal justice system embraces. Under such a prudential account, mercy neither competes with justice nor tempers it (that is, makes it stronger by altering it); rather, it prevents us from doing *injustice* in the name of justice. But the prudential account remains agnostic between retributivism and social welfare theory; rather, it asserts that both dominant discourses suffer from similar skewing and require some internal counter-ratchet.

It is fair to ask whether it makes sense to call this internal counter-ratchet based on doubt a form of mercy at all. After all, if we are talking about avoiding injustice, we are talking about something individual defendants have a right to demand, whereas mercy is generally conceived of as something for which one begs or pleads and that is bestowed as a matter of grace rather than as a matter of duty. If the concern is that the current legal regime is unjust, on either retributive or welfarist principles, shouldn't we try to make the direct case for its correction from the top (the legislature), rather than call on downstream actors to subvert the regime through discretionary action?[84] The answer to this question is both yes and no. Yes, it is worth attempting to correct faulty applications of punishment theories at the level of legislation. But no, we should realize that legislatures are most susceptible to the pressures that produce overpunishment while least able to attend to individual cases that raise doubts about the policies they enact. By offering a normative account of why such doubts are appropriate, and by empowering individual discretionary actors to act upon them, the cumulative effect of multiple exercises of a discretionary veto offers the best hope for resetting the course of criminal justice policy. In other words, in the arena of criminal justice, the best way to perform the *duty* of ensuring that punishment is not unjustly excessive is to enable *discretionary* acts of dispensation from punishment.

One need not call this invocation of cumulative discretionary authority an invocation of mercy in order to endorse it, but the richly evocative term 'mercy' captures some important aspects of the discretionary authority at issue. It makes psychological sense to describe these discretionary acts as

---

[84] VF Nourse, 'Rethinking Crime Legislation: History and Harshness' (2004) 39 *Tulsa Law Review* 925, 936 (suggesting that criminal law theorists turn their attention to 'specific legislative malfunctions and informational failures').

mercy because they require a conscious setting aside of whatever prevailing accounts of 'justice' would otherwise govern the punishment calculus. From the internal perspective of discretionary actors, what an account of prudential mercy asks of them resembles the voluntary resistance to the demands of justice that ordinary invocations of mercy entail—it feels like the forgoing of what appears to be punishment required by or consistent with prevailing theories of punishment, on the ground that we cannot trust our individual or collective instincts about what any such theory really entails. An analogy might be the directions given to a professional athlete by a training coach who sees that the athlete needs to adjust his or her stride, or serve, or stroke because of the athlete's tendency to veer to one side or the other. The coach will train the athlete to overcompensate, to self-consciously pull in the other direction, even though it doesn't feel natural or 'right' to the athlete. The demands of prudential mercy seek to train discretionary actors to try to counteract a systemic tendency to veer off-course, but it will not necessarily feel, to those actors, like doing justice. Additionally, and still from the internal perspective of discretionary actors, the description of exercising a discretionary veto against punishment as mercy captures an important sense that exercising mercy is a virtue that benefits the mercy-giver as well as the receiver.[85] Premising the exercise of prudential mercy on distrust of our capacity for justice and on fear that we might impose too much punishment works against the smugness and self-righteousness that can attend the imposition of punishment, while reinforcing the recognition of the harms that punishment can wreak on individuals and their families and communities. Religious conceptions of God's mercy emphasized the divine coexistence of perfect judgement with perfect love or mercy. Prudential mercy, however, reminds us that we should not pretend to divine perfection in our judgements, that 'playing God' is a form of hubris that falsely sets us apart from the objects of our judgements. Rather, human mercy needs to be based not on perfection, but on doubt and humility about the finiteness of human judgement, as criminal judgment used to be in more devout times.[86]

C   Merciful discretion in criminal justice institutions

Any defence of mercy in the public sphere must offer an account that can guide the exercise of merciful discretion. After all, it cannot simply be that

[85] Portia in Shakespeare's *The Merchant of Venice* describes mercy as 'twice blessed—it blesseth him that gives and him that takes'.

[86] JA Whitman, *The Origins of Reasonable Doubt: Theological Roots of the Criminal Trial* (New Haven, CT: Yale University Press, 2007) (tracing the concept of reasonable doubt as a theological protection for the souls of Christian jurors).

'anything goes' and that any downward deviations from apparent justice are appropriate exercises of mercy. Rather, a defence of mercy in criminal justice must generate an account that can answer three central questions:

(i) *Who should be empowered to grant mercy?* In the criminal justice system, this question requires consideration of which discretionary institutional actors—police officers, grand juries, prosecutors, trial juries, sentencing judges, executives, parole boards—are the proper institutional *locus* of the exercise of mercy.

(ii) *How should the discretionary powers of these actors be structured so as to permit or encourage them to exercise mercy?* Acceptance of the case for prudential mercy may require restructuring of the discretionary powers of these actors *vis-à-vis* one another.

(iii) What are appropriate reasons for granting mercy, and which reasons are relatively stronger or weaker than others?

To generate a full picture of what prudential mercy should look like across the entire range of institutions of criminal justice in any particular society is obviously a large task, far beyond the scope of this chapter, which has aimed simply to make the moral and practical case for the development of some such practice. However, it is worth sketching how the moral and practical grounds for prudential mercy might lead us to generate the answers to the questions listed above. As for the first question, social inequality and residential segregation suggest that some power of merciful discretion should be located in institutions that are accountable to small locales, even neighbourhoods, which are better able to assess accurately both the situational constraints on offenders within a particular locale and the costs and benefits of punitive penal policies for that locale.[87] The 'pathological politics' of criminal legislation suggests that merciful discretion will be most effectively exercised if it is promoted in actors outside the institutions most prone to pathology (legislatures, prosecutors), such as lay participants or unelected judges. Moreover, actors can be removed from the 'pathological politics' of criminal policy-making temporally as well as functionally, suggesting that executives wielding the clemency power might prove an effective *locus* of merciful discretion.

As for the second question, if lay participants in grand juries or juries look like a promising repository for the power of prudential mercy, we might consider restructuring their relationship to the prosecutor (in the

---

[87] Stuntz, 'Unequal Justice' (n 21 above) 2034–6 (arguing for greater reliance on criminal trials by neighbourhood-based juries); KK Washburn, 'Restoring the Grand Jury' (2008) 76 *Fordham Law Review* 2333 (arguing for neighbourhood-based grand juries).

grand jury) or the judge (in the trial jury) so as to enable them to better exercise that power. Many have already suggested that grand juries be offered legal counsel independent of the prosecutor in order to serve as a true check on the charging function;[88] the promotion of prudential mercy would add support to that recommendation. As for trial juries, while many fear the consequences of permitting defence lawyers to openly appeal for jury nullification,[89] more modest adjustments—such as informing juries of the sentence that the judge may or must impose upon conviction of an offence, or instructing juries that they 'may' rather than 'must' convict upon sufficient proof—would better enable juries to serve as dispensers of appropriate prudential mercy.[90]

As for the third question, prudential mercy accords with conventional accounts of mercy in focusing on features of the wrongdoer's particular circumstances as grounds for merciful dispensation (and not solely on the inability of the decision maker to arrive at an appropriately just punishment). For example, prudential mercy offers obvious grounds for considering social disadvantage as a reason to mitigate or forgo punishment, and suggests that the best institutional actors to undertake such evaluations are those drawn directly from, or politically accountable to, disadvantaged communities. Moreover, the power of cognitive biases suggests that there are grounds in prudential mercy for giving substantial weight to evidence of remorse, repentance, and especially rehabilitation—factors that many supporters and even opponents of mercy find compelling on other grounds.[91] Prudential mercy would privilege such evidence because it tends to call into question the false 'dispositional' accounts of wrongdoing that have skewed the imposition of punitive sanctions.

All of these examples suggest that the *locus* and scope of merciful discretion would track the conditions—social, political, cognitive—that promote over-punishment and ground the case for the exercise of prudential mercy.

---

[88] T Hoffmeister, 'The Grand Jury Legal Advisor: Resurrecting the Grand Jury's Shield' (2008) 98 *Journal of Criminal Law and Criminology* 1171.

[89] AD Leipold, 'Against Jury Nullification' in PH Robinson, K Ferzan, and SP Garvey (eds), *Criminal Law Conversations* (Oxford: Oxford University Press, 2009).

[90] CS Steiker, 'Sculpting the Shape of Nullification through Jury Information and Instruction' in Robinson, Ferzan, and Garvey (ibid).

[91] S Bibas and RA Bierschbach, 'Integrating Remorse and Apology into Criminal Procedure' (2004) 114 *Yale Law Journal* 85; SP Garvey, 'Is It Wrong to Commute Death Row? Retribution, Atonement, and Mercy' (2004) 82 *North Carolina Law Review* 1319; JG Murphy, 'Repentance, Punishment, and Mercy' in *Getting Even: Forgiveness and Its Limits* (Oxford: Oxford University Press, 2003).

III   The Dangers of Discretionary Mercy

To praise mercy (prudential or otherwise) and to call for greater discretionary power for institutional actors to depart from what the legislature may consider just or appropriate punishment runs against the grain of much recent criminal justice reform. The rise of the administrative state has been premised on the value of taming discretionary judgment through democratic accountability and technical expertise.[92] Moreover, concerns about racial discrimination and disparate treatment in the criminal justice system have been at the forefront in discussions of criminal justice reform since the 1960s. Hence, traditional outlets for discretionary mercy (jury nullification, executive pardon, and clemency) have fallen into disfavour and disuse, while discretion-limiting innovations have flourished ('no drop' prosecution policies, mandatory penalties, sentencing guidelines). Any attempt to revive discretionary mercy must address the concerns about accountability, expertise, and discrimination that have prompted the dominant trends in criminal justice reform.

There are two answers to this important concern, of quite different types. The first answer maintains that the call for the exercise of prudential mercy in the criminal justice system is in many ways in accordance with, rather than antithetical to, the values of the administration state. Indeed, the promotion of prudential mercy draws on the same insights as those that govern the general structure of administrative decision-making. Giving multiple actors successive vetoes over potentially dangerous or disruptive interventions (here, the infliction of punishment) is a familiar technique for the *management* of discretion within administrative systems. Reviving discretionary mercy—which is nothing more than a veto exercised by differently configured institutions at different moments—is a way of checking the disproportionate power of some actors in the system (here, primarily legislative and prosecutorial power). Discretion to veto is fundamentally different from discretion to initiate, and it serves a substantial discretion-limiting role. Indeed, the primary hope for a regime of prudential mercy is that it will affect not only or even primarily the individuals whose punishment is mitigated or rejected by discretionary action, but rather the whole class of criminal defendants by disciplining the prosecutorial and legislative choices that are the primary forces in setting penal policy.

The second answer acknowledges that the reinvigoration of discretionary mercy will create new opportunities for—and will in fact yield new cases of—arbitrary and discriminatory imposition of punishment. Given the historic

---

[92]   RE Barkow, 'The Ascent of the Administrative State and the Demise of Mercy' (2008) 121 *Harvard Law Review* 1332.

disadvantage of minority groups, it seems likely that more mercy will flow, as it has in the past, to members of powerful groups, perhaps even in cases of minority victimization.[93] But in response, it must be recognized that mass incarceration has had and will continue to have especially devastating effects on minority groups; indeed, by the turn of the millennium in the USA, 'the risk of imprisonment for black high school dropouts had increased to 60 percent, establishing incarceration as a normal stopping point on the route to midlife'.[94] In the light of the enormous burdens that such a rate of incarceration has placed on poor, minority communities, any strategy that holds the promise of slowing, stopping, or reversing the reliance on mass incarceration as a penal policy seems worth trying. In other words, it may well be preferable, from the perspective of minority communities, to have less punishment but more disparity, than to maintain current punishment levels with less disparity. At some point—and part of the argument of this chapter is that we have reached it—punitive policies are so disabling to minority communities that reducing the impact of such policies might trump other considerations (ie reducing discrimination and disparity) that have long been thought to be paramount.

My call for prudential mercy might prompt an objection from a very different perspective—an objection not to the way in which discretionary mercy might threaten to *undermine* current values (like non-discrimination and accountability), but rather to the way in which discretionary mercy might *entrench* current practices through legitimation. In other words, prudential mercy might not 'go too far'; instead, it might not go far enough. If current reliance on mass incarceration is as devastating as Bruce Western and others suggest,[95] should we not worry that allowing the occasional exemption or mitigation might simply make the general policy more acceptable and quell or diminish the outrage that the policy now generates, at least in some quarters? As Douglas Hay noted about the 'Bloody Code' of eighteenth-century England, in which hundreds of new offences were subject to the death penalty, the widespread exercise of mercy helped to legitimize both the criminal law itself and the larger social order.[96] If the primary exercise of mercy available

---

[93] TF Lawson, ' "Whites Only Tree", Hanging Nooses, No Crime? Limiting the Prosecutorial Veto for Hate Crimes in Louisiana and Across America' (2009) 8 *University of Maryland Law Journal of Race, Religion, Gender and Class* 123 (criticizing the exercise of prosecutorial discretion in the infamous 'Jena 6' case in Louisiana, in which white high school students who hung nooses from a tree that black students sought equal access to were not prosecuted under a state 'hate crimes' statute, but black students who became involved in a violent altercation over the incident were charged with attempted murder).   [94] Western (n 20 above) 30.

[95] Ibid; Weiman *et al* (n 6 above).

[96] D Hay, 'Property, Authority and the Criminal Law' in D Hay *et al* (eds), *Albion's Fatal Tree: Crime and Society in Eighteenth-Century England* (London: Allen Lane, 1975) 17.

passes *de haut en bas* through the pardon power, as it was in eighteenth-century England, then the danger of legitimation through mercy looms larger, since the power to grant mercy remains exclusively the province of the powerful, who are able to invoke the terror of severe sanction and then command gratitude for withholding it. When the potential sites of mercy are many and include lay participants, then the danger of legitimation of the sort Hay describes is less worrisome. Of course, the promotion of any form of institutional change requires wariness about the possible entrenching effects of incremental change, especially of change that takes the form of carving out exceptions rather than mounting more wholesale challenges to disturbing practices.[97] The goal of prudential mercy, however, is not to remain merely incremental and episodic. The hope is that, by empowering multiple and diverse sources of discretionary authority to exercise a veto over punishment, and by offering a normative account of why and when they should do so, the resulting episodic acts of merciful discretion will shape the incentives of prosecutors and legislatures and ultimately alter public discourse regarding penal policy.

IV Conclusion

Should discretionary institutional actors within the criminal justice system think of themselves as possessing the power to grant mercy? Most currently do not, with the likely exception of chief executives who exercise the vestiges of the old divine right of kings to pardon. I argue that they should, at least in a certain sense. The social and political conditions that characterize societies with recent turns towards extreme harsh penal practices predictably distort the dominant discourses about the purposes of punishment so as to skew towards overpunishment. Recognition of this effect should move discretionary actors to approach the exercise of their discretion with greater doubt and discomfort—and therefore with a tendency towards leniency that we would fairly describe as 'merciful'. Why focus on the merciful discretion of individual actors rather than mount a more wholesale assault on the penal policies of highly punitive societies? Because discretion already *exists*, though it is often latent and underutilized, in the criminal justice institutions of these societies. Reviving its use is possible with far fewer radical changes to the institutional structures and penological discourses that now dominate, than would be required under more utopian calls for 'restorative justice'. What can we hope

---

[97] CS Steiker and JM Steiker, 'Should Abolitionists Support Legislative "Reform" of the Death Penalty?' (2002) 63 *Ohio State Law Journal* 417 (addressing issues of legitimation and entrenchment in legal reform movements).

for from the exercise of prudential mercy? It may represent the most plausible exit strategy from the punitive turn of the last several decades. Moreover, it offers an important qualification of our reliance on the discourses of retributivism and social welfare theory in societies, like ours, characterized by severe stratification by race and class. We would do better, both individually and in public discourse, to approach our punishment practices with more of the doubt and discomfort that prudential mercy requires. A different world, one characterized by greater equality, less crime, and less severe punishment, might properly reject a call for officials to exercise greater freedom from rule-of-law constraints. But in the current, harshly punitive world, there can be no justice without mercy.

3

Preventive Orders: A Problem of Undercriminalization?

*Andrew Ashworth and Lucia Zedner**

Introduction

The current criminalization debate is making important strides in developing principled arguments for and against the use of the criminal law, at a time when governments seem to be creating more and more criminal offences. In this chapter, however, we suggest that the contemporary focus on the expanding scope of the criminal law has distracted attention from another significant, related, and contestable development—the proliferation of civil preventive measures. This leads us to question whether not merely overcriminalization but also undercriminalization is a contemporary vice.

The criminal law is one among many possible mechanisms for shaping and controlling behaviour—for example, regulation, licensing, civil laws of tort and contract, town planning, family and housing policies, as well as civil preventive orders. The distinctive method of the criminal law is to declare certain wrongs to be criminal offences, censuring those who commit them by conviction and by state-imposed sanctions. Overcriminalization—creating criminal offences without adequate justification—is problematic insofar as it deprives citizens of liberty that should be theirs, gives considerable power to the state and its agents in matters of stop and search, arrest, prosecution, and punishment, and overextends the penal apparatus of the state. It is because the criminal law is such a powerful condemnatory mechanism that human rights documents such as the European Convention on Human Rights (ECHR) and the International Covenant on Civil and Political Rights provide for extra

* All Souls College and Corpus Christi College, University of Oxford, respectively. Both are members of the Law Faculty and the Centre for Criminology at Oxford. Lucia Zedner is also Conjoint Professor at the Law Faculty, UNSW Sydney. We are grateful to Abigail Bright for her excellent research assistance, to the organizers and participants of the Glasgow and Warwick workshops for their insightful comments, and in particular to Doug Husak for his incisive comments as respondent.

safeguards for citizens who are subject to a criminal charge. Creating civil preventive orders that have no such safeguards and yet are significantly coercive in nature may be an example of undercriminalization in the limited sense that the procedural protections of the criminal law are denied to those subject to them. We will argue that where the conduct in question appears to meet the criteria for criminalization, the state should consider whether the creation of a criminal offence for the relevant behaviour is needed, in which case the appropriate procedural safeguards should apply. Where these criteria are not met and civil preventive orders are appropriate, the coercive elements should be reduced so as to ensure that the use of coercion is an exceptional measure of last resort and that stigmatizing effects are minimized. Our particular interest lies in the growing phenomenon of the civil preventive order, and the possibility that such orders are being used to avoid the proper protections of criminal procedure for what may be severe coercive measures. We suggest that focusing on the territory of the criminal law carries the risk of failing to observe how the parameters of criminalization are defined as much by what occurs *outside* as *within* the criminal law.

Part I below considers the definition of preventive measures and then describes nine families of preventive measure. Part II describes the extent to which the British government has embraced the civil preventive hybrid order (civil orders backed up by penal sanctions for breach) in particular, and examines the political context of this expansion. In Part III we identify the need for a justificatory framework for preventive measures. Part IV embarks on the task of finding such a framework, by examining the endeavours of the European Court of Human Rights to insist on particular conceptions of 'criminal charge' and 'penalty', and also to impose restrictions on purely preventive measures. In Part V we revisit the criminalization debate, and develop four objections to civil preventive hybrid orders that lead us to suggest that they constitute examples of undercriminalization. Part VI sets out our conclusions. The perils of undercriminalization may be less immediately apparent than those of overcriminalization but are no less grave where the result is that disproportionate, ill-defined, and often burdensome intrusions upon individual liberty are imposed in the name of prevention without appropriate procedural safeguards. The nub of our argument is that, whilst overcriminalization is undoubtedly a major problem, instances of undercriminalization are on the rise and that they too pose no small threat to the liberty of the individual. It is not the purpose of this chapter to argue whether or not the current boundaries of the criminal law are drawn in the right place. Still less is it our contention that where procedural protections are inadequate the proper response is simply to criminalize. This chapter does not deny the claim that there is considerable overcriminalization,[1] nor does it call for a more extensive criminal law. It does, however, call for recognition of civil preventive orders as a distinct set of measures in need of special justification and in respect of which appropriate procedural protections should be developed.[2]

I   Mapping Preventive Measures

Two immediate tasks face the cartographer of preventive measures. The first is to identify what it is about the wide variety of measures—using different legal procedural channels, and spanning the seriousness scale from the plotting of terrorist atrocities down to anti-social behaviour—that permits them collectively to be considered preventive. This is tackled in A below, on the question of definition. The second is to distinguish the various families of measures that reside under the collective heading of preventive justice, and in B below we identify nine of these.

A   Definition of preventive measures

What do we mean by the term 'preventive measures'? The essence of these measures is that they involve (i) restrictions on individual liberty of action (ii) in order to prevent harm or a risk of harm and (iii) are backed by threats of coercive sanctions. The first requirement serves to exclude from our analysis many forms of crime-preventive measures that do not impose explicit restrictions on individual liberty of action. Measures of situational crime prevention (eg locks and burglar alarms on buildings, CCTV cameras) cut down the range of likely choices, at least by making some of them less attractive; but they are not the same as excluding an individual from a particular location or part of town, or forbidding a person from associating with or approaching a named individual. Social crime prevention measures lie even further from our discussion here, since they typically involve creating alternative activities or facilities in order to deflect people from the conditions that tend to produce lawbreaking. So, the first element of the term *preventive measure* is that it imposes an explicit limitation on what a named person may lawfully do, usually by forbidding a particular form of conduct,

---

[1] As argued so powerfully by D Husak, *Overcriminalization: The Limits of the Criminal Law* (Oxford: Oxford University Press, 2008).

[2] This chapter only begins this project. Developing a positive definition of preventive justice and a fully-fledged set of principles, values, procedures, and constraints are separate tasks for the future. The authors are undertaking a major study of 'Preventive Justice' generously funded by the AHRC (AHRC reference no: AH/H015655/1).

with or without a particular intention. The fact that many sentences have a preventive purpose (either rehabilitative, deterrent, or incapacitative) does not bring them within the definition, since even though they may impose restrictions aimed at preventing harm or risk of harm (for example the curfew requirement in a community order), a large part of their rationale is punitive. Preventive measures differ because their primary justifying aim is to restrict individual liberty in order to prevent future harm and not to punish wrongdoing (even where the measure is imposed as a consequence of past wrongdoing).

The second element of the measure is to prevent either the occurrence of harm or the risk of harm. One example is an Anti-Social Behaviour Order (ASBO) prohibiting a person from entering the Tyneside Metro railway system, the purpose of which was to reduce *the risk of* vandalism of the railway to which that person was allegedly prone.[3] Some preventive orders are chiefly concerned with the prevention of risk by stopping the person from putting themselves in a position to cause harm, such as Travel Restriction Orders. Others contain prohibitions designed to prevent risk and/or prohibitions aimed at preventing harm, such as ASBOs and Sexual Offences Prevention Orders (SOPOS). Because the preventive measures with which we are concerned are, ostensibly at least, civil orders, they enjoy a licence to restrict liberties in respect of harms or risks of harm that may be too barely specified, remote, or indirect to satisfy the requirements of criminalization (of which more below).

And yet, the third characteristic of preventive measures is that they are backed with the threat of coercive sanctions. The primary example of this is what has come to be known as the civil preventive order: we will analyse the status of such orders below, but the important point here is that breach of their terms constitutes a criminal offence, usually with a maximum sentence of five years' imprisonment. Sanction on breach is clearly an example of criminalization, but the question is whether the whole procedure of imposing the civil order and then prosecuting the breach as a crime may be viewed as a single process. It is this hybrid civil–criminal quality of preventive measures that renders them of particular significance for any debate about criminalization. Sitting on the very margins of the criminal law they can be seen as covertly expanding the scope of punitive sanctions (through their provision of substantial criminal sanctions for breach) and yet they are ostensibly situated in the civil law. They blur the criminal–civil law divide by the device of the two-step

---

[3] *R v Lamb* [2006] 2 Cr App R (S) 11.

civil–criminal procedure they typically employ.[4] The relevance and implications of the most notorious of these measures—the ASBO—has not escaped the attention of criminal lawyers.[5] But as yet little concentrated attention has been given to the larger proliferation of preventive measures.[6] Even if we presume that inchoate liability itself is justifiable—and this has been the subject of intense scrutiny[7]—we need a special justification to go beyond inchoate offences to exercise the preventive functions just outlined. When the exercise of the preventive function does not comply with this special justification, and when the criteria for criminalization are met, then, as we will go on to argue below, it might well constitute an instance of undercriminalization.

B   Families of preventive measures

The next step is to try to identify families of preventive measures, so that the ensuing discussion can be properly targeted. Duff draws a distinction between direct (concrete) endangerment and indirect (abstract) endangerment, and also between explicit and implicit endangerment offences.[8] Those distinctions are taken a little further in the preliminary classification below. Here are nine families:

(i) *Civil preventive hybrid orders aimed at preventing risk only* (risk being understood as preventing persons from putting themselves in a position or place where there is reason to suppose that they might cause harm)—examples would be travel restriction orders, football spectator banning orders, exclusion from licensed premises orders, drinking banning orders, and some ASBOs. These orders may be made without conviction, or at sentence after conviction. Breach of the order is a criminal offence with a maximum sentence of five years' imprisonment.

---

[4] AP Simester and A von Hirsch, 'Regulating Offensive Conduct through Two-Step Prohibitions' in A von Hirsch and AP Simester (eds), *Incivilities: Regulating Offensive Behaviour* (Oxford: Hart Publishing, 2006) 173.

[5] A Ashworth, 'Social Control and "Anti-Social Behaviour": The Subversion of Human Rights?' (2004) 120 LQR 263; P Ramsay, 'What Is Anti-Social Behaviour?' [2004] Crim LR 908; Simester and von Hirsch (ibid).

[6] Though see A Ashworth and L Zedner, 'Defending the Criminal Law: Reflections on the Changing Character of Crime, Procedure, and Sanctions' (2008) 2 *Criminal Law and Philosophy* 21, 35ff.

[7] RA Duff, *Criminal Attempts* (Oxford: Oxford University Press, 1997); B McSherry, 'Expanding the Boundaries of Inchoate Crimes: The Growing Reliance on Preparatory Offences' in B McSherry, A Norrie, and S Bronitt (eds), *Regulating Deviance: The Redirection of Criminalisation and the Futures of Criminal Law* (Oxford: Hart Publishing, 2009) 141.

[8] RA Duff, *Answering for Crime: Responsibility and Liability in the Criminal Law* (Oxford: Hart Publishing, 2007) ch 7.

(ii) *Civil preventive hybrid orders aimed at preventing harm and/or risk of harm*—for example, ASBOs with a direct prohibition such as 'not engaging in any behaviour likely to be threatening, insulting or abusive to others', restraining orders, SOPOs, risk of sexual harm orders, violent crime orders, and serious crime prevention orders. These orders may be made without conviction or at sentence after conviction. Breach of the order is a criminal offence, usually with a maximum sentence of five years' imprisonment.

(iii) *Civil orders aimed at preventing harm and/or risk of harm*—Anti-social Behaviour Injunctions under the Housing Act 1996, section 153A, obtained from the County Court and including such prohibitions as the judge thinks necessary to prevent further such behaviour, and public nuisance proceedings resulting in an injunction to protect the interests of local inhabitants (Local Government Act 1972, section 222). These orders are entirely civil, and breach cannot result in a criminal conviction but will be a contempt of court, for which up to two years' imprisonment is the sanction.

(iv) *Pre-trial orders aimed at preventing risk*—remand in custody, or conditional bail, of people who have been charged and brought before a court; Control Orders (derogating or non-derogating) of people who have not been charged with an offence. Breach of a bail condition is a criminal offence.

(v) *Offences having the prevention of harm as a primary explicit rationale*—for example, attempts, conspiracy, assisting, and encouraging crime (Serious Crime Act 2007, Part 2); the many offences defined in an inchoate mode, such as the Fraud Act 2006 ('making a false representation with intent to make a gain or to cause loss'), whose effect is to push criminal liability even further back, because the offence can be attempted.

(vi) *Offences having the prevention of risk of harm as a primary explicit rationale*—dangerous driving, careless driving, failure to attain health and safety at work standards; what characterizes these offences is that they punish endangerment, whether concrete or abstract, and it is clear on the face of the offence what risks they are concerned with.

(vii) *Offences having the prevention of risk of harm as the primary implicit rationale*—possession offences (knives, guns, equipment for forgery), speeding, drunk driving, offences of belonging to a prohibited organization. These offences are characterized by their criminalization of conduct that might or might not give rise to any actual risk, but where some future and contingent harm is possible. They stand at one stage further back than the offences described in (vi), and are therefore more remote.

(viii) *Criminal court orders aimed at preventing harm and/or risk of harm*—life imprisonment; imprisonment for public protection; extended sentence; disqualification from driving, from being a company director, from working with children; binding over a defendant to keep the peace; a conditional discharge.

(ix) *Licence conditions on release from a sentence of imprisonment*—such orders may include restrictions aimed at preventing harm or the risk of harm, and they are backed by the threat of a coercive sanction (recall to custody). But they probably do not warrant separate examination here.

All nine families can be categorized as preventive measures. Only family (iii) is purely civil in nature: all the others have a link with the criminal law as the sanction for breach, even if some of them are described as civil preventive measures. The focus in this chapter will be on families (i) and (ii), but there will be occasional reference to other forms or families of preventive measure.

II   The Legal Politics of Preventive Justice

Let us begin by listing the civil preventive hybrid measures falling within families (i) and (ii) above to demonstrate the range of these preventive powers:

Anti-social behaviour orders[9]
Travel restriction orders[10]
Foreign travel restriction orders[11]
Football spectator banning orders[12]
Exclusion from licensed premises orders[13]
Drinking banning orders[14]
Serious crime prevention orders[15]
Violent offender orders[16]
Sexual offences prevention orders[17]
Risk of sexual harm orders[18]
Restraining orders[19]
Non-molestation orders[20]

---

[9] Crime and Disorder Act 1998, s 1.   [10] Criminal Justice and Police Act 2001, s 33.
[11] Sexual Offences Act 2003, s 114.   [12] Football Spectators Act 1989, s 14A.
[13] Licensed Premises (Exclusion of Certain Persons) Act 1980, s 1.
[14] Violent Crime Reduction Act 2006, s 1.   [15] Serious Crime Act 2007, s 1.
[16] Criminal Justice and Immigration Act 2008, s 98.
[17] Sexual Offences Act 2003, s 104.   [18] Sexual Offences Act 2003, s 123.
[19] Protection from Harassment Act 1997, s 5.   [20] Family Law Act 1996, s 42A

The Labour government presented these measures as essential sources of protection for citizens, as enhancing the safety and security we all want. But why public protection and concern for victims should result in the vigorous promotion of civil preventive measures in preference to resort to the criminal law is not self-evident. Several possible explanations present themselves, some more clearly legitimate than others. On the more obviously defensible end of the explanatory spectrum sit a group of rationales that speak directly to the limits of the criminal law and, in particular, its limited capacity to tackle certain categories of harm or putative harm. Thus one part of the explanation is *expansionist*: where the conduct in question, although actually or prospectively harmful or offensive, does not amount to a contravention of the existing criminal law (low-level anti-social behaviour is an obvious example here), preventive measures provide a means for state intervention without resort to criminalization. One of the reasons for introducing the ASBO and other civil preventive measures was to expand the net of social control so as to deal with nuisance behaviour that is not an offence (perhaps because single incidents are not considered sufficiently serious) but where recurring acts significantly reduced the quality of life for those living in certain neighbourhoods—examples given at the time were noisy neighbours, youths hanging round on street corners, etc. A related motive was to ensure that victims' interests were given sufficient weight, particularly where their quality of life was blighted by cumulative, continuing low-level anti-social behaviour.[21] This said, in practice the ASBO in particular has sometimes been used to prohibit conduct that is already a criminal offence.

A second impetus for resort to preventive measures was *pragmatic*. The criminal law and criminal process were ill-equipped to deal with a course of conduct or series of omissions that either individually do not amount to a criminal offence (repeated acts of nuisance whether by act or omission) or, if they are crimes, would normally be prosecuted one by one, so that the court would not have a sense of the repetition and persistence of the nuisance. With its focus upon the individual offence, the criminal law has not been thought well suited to the task of dealing with persistence. Prosecuting a single crime (even when others are taken into consideration) might fail to address the aggregate impact or cumulative consequences over time of persistently harmful behaviour as well as the prospective risk of harm posed by the likelihood of its continuance.[22] Attempts have been made to capture courses of conduct within the definition of an offence, for example in respect of stalking under the Protection from Harassment Act 1997, but these have been less than

[21] S Bright and C Bakalis, 'Anti-Social Behaviour: Local Authority Responsibility and the Voice of the Victim' (2003) 62 CLJ 305.
[22] Ashworth, 'Social Control and "Anti-Social Behaviour"' (n 5 above), 264.

satisfactory.[23] Whether sentencing on the basis of a course of conduct (past or prospective) could be formulated in such a way as to resolve this difficulty without introducing the new problem of disproportionality to the present offence(s) remains doubtful at best.

A third and distinct set of possible explanations for the state's resort to preventive measures is broadly *evidential*. In the 1990s there was concern that the hearsay rule meant that prosecutions could only be mounted if the alleged victim were willing to come to court and give evidence. In introducing the ASBO, the government envisaged that council officials would give evidence in the civil proceedings and so there would be no need for the alleged victim to come to court. Although the hearsay rule in criminal proceedings was relaxed in 2003, this use of 'professional witnesses' remains the normal approach, largely because of the fear of and actual witness intimidation. In cases of serious crime or terrorist activity, a further evidential problem is said to be the risk to the safety of intelligence personnel, to security operations, or to their informants (for example in the case of Control Orders).[24] Witness protection remains a significant issue across the criminal justice system, and Part 3 of the Coroners and Justice Act 2009 sets out a new system that respects the rights of both defendants and (potential) witnesses.

More amorphous is a fourth group of explanations that are broadly speaking *political*. Many countries, including England and Wales, have seen a strain of penal populism in government statements and in legislative initiatives that are often presented as measures of public protection.[25] Here it is important to distinguish between the justifications for prevention arising from the demand for substantive protection to stop harms eventuating and those arising from subjective security or what might be called 'the reassurance function'. Whilst reassuring the public is an important role of the state, it is questionable whether reassurance alone is sufficient grounds for adverse interference in the lives of others. Waldron suggests not: 'no doubt the psychological reassurance that people derive from this is a consequential gain from the loss of liberty. But whether it is the sort of gain that should count morally is another question'.[26] In addition to purporting to protect the public, it is notable that, with no apparent irony, some preventive measures also appear to encompass

[23] C Wells, 'Stalking: The Criminal Law Response' [1997] Crim LR 463.

[24] L Zedner, 'Preventive Justice or Pre-Punishment? The Case of Control Orders' (2007) 59 CLP 174, 194.

[25] AE Bottoms, 'The Philosophy and Politics of Punishment and Sentencing' in C Clarkson and R Morgan (eds), *The Politics of Sentencing Reform* (Oxford: Clarendon Press, 1995) 17; J Pratt, *Penal Populism* (London: Routledge, 2007).

[26] J Waldron, 'Security and Liberty: The Image of Balance' (2003) 11 *Journal of Political Philosophy* 191, 209.

a paternalist aim, in that they identify individuals who are at risk of offending and therefore in need of the protection that the order provides. For example, the Foreign Travel Restriction Order introduced by the Sexual Offences Act 2003 imposes travel restrictions upon those identified as being 'at risk' of travelling to jurisdictions where they may offend. The legitimating rationale thus becomes a twofold claim to protect both the public and the offender.

In addition to these political motives, an important spur has been the state's desire to shift the 'prosecutorial' or policing burden onto other bodies or, at least partially, to divest itself of responsibility for crime control. This has been well captured by the responsibilization thesis originated by O'Malley and later developed by Garland.[27] Responsibilization refers to the state's recognition of the limits of its sovereign power to rule, and consequent efforts to shift some of the responsibility for crime control onto individuals, families, communities, and other non-governmental organizations. So, for example, part of the burden of policing is shifted onto local authorities and housing associations in the case of anti-social behaviour; to parents in the case of some measures aimed at young offenders (for example parenting orders and parenting contracts under the Crime and Disorder Act 1998); and to liquor stores in the case of licensing laws. Whereas in other spheres it is arguable that responsibilization tactics were an unproblematic instance of the larger phenomenon of 'governing at a distance' characteristic of Western neo-liberal market economies,[28] in respect of crime control it is arguable that the state devolved its authoritarian role with greater ambivalence.

This ambivalence can be seen in the fact that at the same time, but in quite the opposite direction, some recent preventive measures have arisen from a political desire to retain decision making more closely in the hands of the executive. Thus, running counter to the examples in the previous paragraph, the Home Secretary's power to impose Control Orders under the Prevention of Terrorism Act 2005 retains decision making firmly in the hands of the executive and downgrades judicial scrutiny to *post hoc* ratification of executive decision-making. Control Orders form just a part of a larger raft of counter-terrorist legislation that followed 9/11 and the Madrid and London bombings. This legislation is replete with preventive measures and inchoate offences that target activity remote from commission of the substantive offence or the actual infliction of harm. For example, in a radical temporal

---

[27] P O'Malley, 'Risk and Responsibility' in A Barry, T Osborne, and N Rose (eds), *Foucault and Political Reason: Liberalism, Neo-Liberalism and Rationalities of Government* (London: UCL Press, 1996) 189, 200; D Garland, *The Culture of Control: Crime and Social Order in Contemporary Society* (Oxford: Oxford University Press, 2001) 124–7.

[28] D Osborne and T Gaebler, *Reinventing Government: How the Entrepreneurial Spirit Is Transforming the Public Sector* (New York: Penguin, 1992).

regress from the conventional requirement that to justify criminal liability acts must be 'more than merely preparatory', the Terrorism Act 2006, section 5 criminalizes 'any conduct in preparation' of the commission of acts of terrorism, or assisting another to commit such acts, and attaches a maximum penalty of life imprisonment. This new offence extends further the range of inchoate crimes established by the Terrorism Act 2000 which include widely drafted offences of possession; of providing financial support to a terrorist organization; of omission; and of supporting, belonging to, or wearing the uniform of proscribed organizations.[29] The combined effect of this anti-terrorism legislation is to significantly extend the ambit of inchoate offences within the criminal law. This is contrary to many arguments for restricting inchoate offences: the defendant might not yet be committed to go through with the offence, the defendant might have a change of mind, and police power will be extended unacceptably (especially in combination with adverse inferences from silence under police questioning). Criminalization of activities remote from the actual commission of an act of terrorism is said to be justified by the need to furnish legal grounds for action against individuals at the very earliest stages of preparation.[30] Arguably the political climate post-9/11 has made possible a temporal shift backwards to pre-empt and avert harms before they arise.[31]

Finally, an important question (and perhaps an unanswerable one without further research) is how far the proliferation of civil preventive measures constitutes an instance of *policy transfer*. One possibility suggested by Burney is that the introduction of civil remedies to pursue crime prevention ends was a direct policy transfer from the United States where the use of civil measures

---

[29] An excellent analysis of these offences is provided in V Tadros, 'Justice and Terrorism' (2007) 10 *New Criminal Law Review* 658, 664ff. Further examples analysed in detail by Tadros include: the offence of encouragement of terrorism (Terrorism Act 2006, s 1); possessing an article in circumstances which give rise to a reasonable suspicion that this possession is for a purpose connected with the commission, preparation, or instigation of an act of terrorism (Terrorism Act 2000, s 57); collecting information of a kind likely to be useful to terrorists (Terrorism Act 2000, s 58); having and failing to disclose without lawful excuse information which might be of material assistance in preventing an act of terrorism or apprehending, prosecuting, and convicting another person for the commission, preparation, or instigation of an act of terrorism (Terrorism Act 2000, s 38B); Cf the judgment in *R v G and J* [2009] UKHL 13.

[30] L Zedner, 'Fixing the Future? The Pre-Emptive Turn in Criminal Justice' in McSherry, Norrie, and Bronnit (n 7 above).

[31] A shift widely observed: see, eg A Dershowitz, *Preemption: A Knife That Cuts Both Ways* (New York: WW Norton, 2006); J Mcculloch and B Carlton, 'Preempting Justice: Suppression of Financing of Terrorism and the "War on Terror"' (2006) 17 *Current Issues in Criminal Justice* 397; C Aradau and R Van Munster, 'Governing Terrorism through Risk: Taking Precautions, (Un)Knowing the Future' (2007) 13 *European Journal of International Relations* 89; S Krasmann, 'The Enemy on the Border: Critique of a Programme in Favour of a Preventive State' (2007) 9 *Punishment and Society* 301.

(against gang members, young offenders, nuisance, public order, drug- and alcohol-related offending) was well developed and closely observed by British politicians.[32] Quite another reading is that this is a domestic policy transfer from earlier civil injunctions and remedies to the ASBO and from the ASBO to all those civil preventive orders (Control Orders, Serious Crime Prevention Orders, Violent Offender Orders, etc) that followed in its wake. Such is the symbolic power of the ASBO that Serious Crime Prevention Orders were heralded in the press as 'Super ASBOs' and 'Gangster ASBOs'.[33] Macdonald, referring particularly to the ASBO and the Control Order, identifies not only a governmental willingness to circumvent the criminal law at the very time when the number of criminal offences was rising rapidly, but also a corresponding insistence that the executive can be trusted to employ wide-ranging powers of this kind responsibly.[34]

Whatever the direct cause—and in most cases the likely causes are multiple—it is clear that over the past decade the British state has energetically adopted civil preventive measures as an important means of tackling crime and has shown a striking commitment to ensuring that these measures are actually used.[35] When, for example, after its initial introduction under the Crime and Disorder Act 1998, the ASBO failed to capture the imagination of those expected to deploy it, the British government waged a concerted campaign to ensure that the Order was taken up and used by local authorities and housing associations as part of a larger initiative to tackle local nuisance and disorder.[36] The commitment to prevention is all the greater the more serious the prospective harm. As the Home Office robustly asserted, in respect of Serious Crime Prevention Orders introduced by the Serious Crime Act 2007, 'we are looking to ensure that penalties have the maximum possible impact on preventing future harm from organized criminals'.[37] Maximizing the prevention of harm and protecting the public is a laudable and defensible role of the state. But if it goes hand in hand with provisions drafted so as to avoid traditional procedural safeguards, the costs of any (unproved) increase in security, achieved at the expense of diminishing individual liberty, require careful scrutiny.

---

[32] E Burney, *Making People Behave: Anti-Social Behaviour, Politics and Policy* (Cullompton, Devon: Willan Publishing, 2005) drawing on LG Mazerolle and J Roehl, *Civil Remedies and Crime Prevention* (Cullompton, Devon: Willan Publishing, 1998).

[33] 'Home Office reveals details of "super Asbos"' *The Guardian*, 17 January 2007.

[34] S Macdonald, 'ASBOs and Control Orders: Two Recurring Themes, Two Apparent Contradictions' (2007) 60 *Parliamentary Affairs* 601.

[35] P Ramsay, 'The Theory of Vulnerable Autonomy and the Legitimacy of Civil Preventative Orders' in McSherry, Norrie, and Bronitt (n 7 above) 109.   [36] Burney (n 32 above) 89ff.

[37] Home Office, *New Powers Against Organised and Financial Crime* (Cm 6875, 2006) 11.

III The Need for a Justificatory Framework for Preventive Measures

This brief tour of some of the drivers behind the wider development of preventive measures might tend towards the conclusion that they amount to no more than political expediency. Many are questionable devices, fraught with moral as well as intellectual and practical difficulties.[38] Certainly it is difficult to locate any developed political or jurisprudential justification for the recent surge of preventive measures, set out at the beginning of Part II above. The ostensible rationale for such measures is usually claimed to reside in protecting the public or averting risk of harm, not in past wrongdoing. So obviously desirable and seemingly incontrovertible is the promotion of public safety that preventive measures have not attracted the same justificatory endeavour that is self-evidently necessary in respect of state punishment, nor the same examination of their proper limits. Yet to the extent that preventive measures also impose considerable burdens upon those subject to them (and, at least in the case of the more oppressive measures such as the Control Order, entail pains comparable to those of punishment), they clearly merit this kind of critical scrutiny. Writing in 1998 Steiker observed that the constitutional limits on state action in the name of prevention were barely a topic of debate, still less recognized as a problem worthy of scrutiny: 'Courts and commentators often tend to conclude, too quickly, that if some policy or practice is not "really" punishment, then there is nothing wrong with it'.[39]

Since 9/11 the dearth of attention to the issues raised by the rise of the preventive state has been partially rectified by the voluminous law literature that followed in its wake concerning the exercise of state preventive powers, their legitimate scope and proper exercise in respect of counter-terrorism.[40] If the

---

[38] L Zedner, 'Seeking Security by Eroding Rights: The Side-Stepping of Due Process' in B Goold and L Lazarus (eds), *Security and Human Rights* (Oxford: Hart Publishing, 2007).

[39] C Steiker, 'The Limits of the Preventive State' (1998) 88 *Journal of Criminal Law and Criminology* 771, 777. Though early explorations into preventive justice include HF Del, '"Preventive Justice": Bonds to Keep the Peace and for Good Behavior' (1940) 88 *University of Pennsylvania Law Review* 331; G Williams, 'Preventive Justice and the Rule of Law' (1953) 16 MLR 417.

[40] For example, O Gross, 'Chaos and Rules: Should Responses to Violent Crises Always Be Constitutional?' (2003) 112 *Yale Law Journal* 1011; M Ignatieff, *The Lesser Evil: Political Ethics in an Age of Terror* (Edinburgh: Edinburgh University Press, 2004); B Ackermann, *Before the Next Attack: Preserving Civil Liberties in an Age of Terrorism* (New Haven: Yale University Press, 2006); A Dershowitz, *Preemption: A Knife That Cuts Both Ways* (New York: WW Norton, 2006); O Gross and F Ní Aoláin, *Law in Times of Crisis: Emergency Powers in Theory and Practice* (Cambridge: Cambridge University Press, 2006); A Ashworth, 'Criminal Law, Human Rights and Preventative Justice' in McSherry, Norrie, and Bronitt (n 7 above) 87.

literature concerning the preventive function of the state in respect of the catastrophic risks posed by terrorism is now arguably overdeveloped (or at least overpopulated as a field of enquiry), interest in the state's larger preventive function in respect of lesser risks remains more muted. Steiker's observation that, whilst there is a developed jurisprudence surrounding the proper role and limits of the criminal law, '[i]n contrast, courts and commentators have had much less to say about the related topic of the state not as punisher (and thus, necessarily as investigator and adjudicator of criminal acts) but rather as preventer of crime and disorder generally' remains largely true.[41] It is timely to consider what limits, if any, should be set to the powers that can be taken over the citizen under the twin justifications of the prevention of harm to others and of risk reduction.

Among the writings that have tackled this issue, more questions than answers are to be found. Some, like Slobogin, whilst recognizing the serious constitutional problems inherent in a preventive model, positively welcome its rise as potentially more effective at preventing crime; eliminating 'artificial distinctions between civil and criminal dispositions';[42] and downplaying advertence to blame in favour of the assessment and management of risk. Others regard the preventive state with greater pessimism, as bent upon policies which 'narrow the constitutional protections available to persons accused of posing a threat to society'.[43] Steiker has called, therefore, for urgent discussion of 'whether and to what extent the state's attempt to prevent or prophylactically deter (as opposed to investigate) crime and to incapacitate or treat (as opposed to punish) wrongdoers insulates the state's actions from the limits the law would otherwise place on the investigative/punitive state'.[44] In the name of prevention, and especially since 9/11, states appear all too ready to adopt policies that degrade civil liberties.[45] It is an open question, worthy of further exploration, how far the legal debates around the constitutionality of anti-terrorist measures and the means to their restraint can be carried over by analogy to inform the framing of constraining principles for preventive measures in respect of conventional or domestic crime.[46] Of particular concern for Janus is what he terms 'radical prevention', namely increasing recourse to measures

---

[41] Steiker (n 39 above), 774.

[42] C Slobogin, 'The Civilization of the Criminal Law' (2005) 58 *Vanderbilt Law Review* 121, 165.

[43] EP Richards, 'The Jurisprudence of Prevention: The Right of Societal Self-Defense against Dangerous Individuals' (1989) 16 *Hastings Constitutional Law Quarterly* 329, 392.

[44] Steiker (n 39 above) 806.

[45] E Janus, 'The Preventive State, Terrorists and Sexual Predators: Countering the Threat of a New Outsider Jurisprudence' (2004) 40 *Criminal Law Bulletin* 576.

[46] Gross and Ní Aoláin (n 40 above); D Dyzenhaus, 'Deference, Security, and Human Rights' in Goold and Lazarus (n 38 above); Ashworth, 'Criminal Law, Human Rights and Preventative Justice' (n 40 above) 87.

that seek to intervene where there is a 'propensity' to harm, which operate by substantially curtailing individual liberty before harm occurs, and which undercut the constitutional protections historically offered by the courts. These developments lead Farmer to call for a 'jurisprudence of security',[47] a plea that echoes earlier calls for a 'jurisprudence of prevention'[48] and a 'jurisprudence of dangerousness'.[49] We now turn towards that objective.

IV   Setting Limits to the Preventive State

What is the role of the state in harm prevention? It is an obvious and hardly contestable function of the state to protect its citizens from harms.[50] Two possible rationales for this may be found in social contract theory and in the displacement function. Contractarian authors tend to argue that citizens give up considerable freedom to the state in return for the promise of protection from harm: even if one grants that such a contract can be spelt out, its terms (how much liberty should be sacrificed for what degree of increased security) remain contestable. Another approach also starts from the intuitive assumption that one important and legitimate function of the state is to prevent people from mistreating others, and to safeguard good order and the basic means by which citizens can live good lives. We look to the state for this kind of protection: indeed, it is right that the state should assume this role, since the alternative would be for individuals (victims, their families, protection groups) to 'deal with' those who harm others and disturb the peace, and that would result in lawlessness. The state's role is therefore to perform a kind of 'displacement function', taking measures to deal with these disruptions as a way of pre-empting private vengeance.[51] As with social contract theory, however, this rationale does not indicate the limits to which the state can legitimately go in the exercise of its displacement function.

What principles should guide the state in this task? As Loader observes, 'what matters in a society that is—or wishes to remain or become—a liberal

---

[47] L Farmer, 'The Jurisprudence of Security: The Police Power and the Criminal Law' in MD Dubber and M Valverde (eds), *The New Police Science: The Police Power in Domestic and International Perspective* (Stanford, Cal: Stanford University Press, 2006).   [48] Richards (n 43 above).
[49] C Slobogin, 'A Jurisprudence of Dangerousness' (2003) 98 *Northwestern University Law Review* 1.
[50] L Lazarus, 'Mapping the Right to Security' in Goold and Lazarus (n 38 above) 325; Duff, *Answering for Crime* (n 8 above) 87.
[51] J Gardner, 'Crime: In Proportion and in Perspective' in A Ashworth and M Wasik (eds), *Fundamentals of Sentencing Theory* (Oxford: Oxford University Press, 1998) 31; N MacCormick and D Garland, 'Sovereign States and Vengeful Victims: The Problem of the Right to Punish' in Ashworth and Wasik (ibid) 11.

democracy is not that we control crime but *how* we do so'.[52] Our starting point is that the use of coercion by the state involves a deprivation of the ordinary rights of citizens, which should therefore be kept to a minimum and used only where lesser methods are insufficient. In order to preserve the greatest liberty of subjects, the state should always prefer less intrusive measures. Thus the aim of prevention should chiefly be pursued through educational, family, housing, and town planning policies, and through regulatory mechanisms, such as health and safety regulations, road safety measures, and licensing laws. Reducing the risk of harms should also be pursued through social crime prevention—by organizing activities to take (young) people away from crime—and through situational crime prevention, by making the commission of crimes more difficult (target hardening, opportunity reduction, and security systems) and more observable (design of buildings, urban planning, surveillance mechanisms, and security cameras).

Granted that it is desirable for the state to take measures for the purpose of preventing harm or the risk of harm, the law should intrude as little as possible on individual rights. The primary approach should be through some means other than criminal law, since that is the state's most condemnatory response and should be kept as an instrument of last resort.[53] If we take the example of anti-social behaviour, and leave aside the problems of definition, in principle the response should be an informal mechanism such as an Acceptable Behaviour Contract agreed by the local authority and the individual concerned. The efficacy of such methods should be thoroughly tested. Only if they prove manifestly ineffective should resort be had to a more serious mechanism that invokes the civil courts, depending on the circumstances (not endorsing a principle of escalation, but keeping proportion to the magnitude of the alleged anti-social behaviour). This might be an Anti-social Behaviour Injunction: as outlined in item (ii) in the list in Part I B above, it would contain certain prohibitions, but unlike an ASBO the proceedings would be entirely civil and a breach of the order would be assessed by the County Court judge, applying the contempt of court powers. Those powers are considerable (up to two years' imprisonment), in view of the varying magnitude of anti-social behaviour. Whether this would be sufficient to deal with the problem has not been thoroughly tested, because the British government went quickly for the ASBO. Our concern is that the ASBO accords the defendant fewer rights than on a criminal charge, and yet the result of the civil proceedings is that the defendant is subjected to a detailed and possibly wide-ranging personal criminal code (eg not to enter part of a city; not to use public transport in that city), with a maximum penalty

---

[52] I Loader, 'The Anti-Politics of Crime' (2008) 12 *Theoretical Criminology* 399, 405.
[53] D Husak, 'The Criminal Law as Last Resort' (2004) 24 OJLS 207.

(five years' imprisonment) which is higher than for many criminal offences. This legislation falls foul of the principle of minimum intervention.

These criticisms of the ASBO find their roots in two human rights objections. The first objection arises from the question whether the ASBO is truly a civil measure (as it appears on the face of the legislation) or is in substance criminal.[54] In European human rights law, the Strasbourg Court has developed an 'anti-subversion doctrine', in order to prevent states from dressing up criminal proceedings as if they were civil and thereby avoiding the appropriate safeguards. Thus the Court has insisted that the phrase 'charged with a criminal offence' in Article 6 has an autonomous meaning that transcends national labels. In a long line of decisions since the leading case of *Engel v Netherlands*,[55] three criteria have been developed and applied. The most important is the third—the severity of the restrictions or deprivations flowing from the order that the court can make.[56]

This emphasis on the potential severity of the consequences is in close harmony with the justification for insisting on the extra safeguards. In *Clingham v Royal Borough of Kensington and Chelsea; R (McCann) v Crown Court of Manchester* the House of Lords had to determine whether the proceedings for the making of an ASBO under the Crime and Disorder Act 1998, section 1 are indeed civil, as the Act states, or criminal in substance, as the appellants claimed.[57] The unanimous decision was that the proceedings are civil: no breach of the criminal law need be proved, no criminal conviction results, the Crown Prosecution Service is not involved, and the purpose of the order is preventive. The first two factors are not really relevant, because the question ought to concern the substance of the proceedings rather than their form. Moreover, the House of Lords concluded that the civil standard of proof (on the balance of probabilities) should be applied in such a way as to be sensitive to the 'seriousness of the matters to be proved and the implications of proving them',[58] which in effect means proof beyond reasonable doubt, that is the 'criminal standard'. This demonstrates judicial awareness of conflicting considerations: the

---

[54] For reference to US doctrine on this, see Husak, *Overcriminalization* (n 1 above) 81.

[55] Ibid. For examples, see *Engel v Netherlands* (1979–80) 1 EHRR 647; *Benham v United Kingdom* (1996) 22 EHRR 293; *Ezeh and Connors v United Kingdom* (2002) 35 EHRR 691, and the decisions discussed in B Emmerson, A Ashworth, and A Macdonald, *Human Rights and Criminal Justice*, 2nd edn (London: Sweet & Maxwell, 2007) ch 4.

[56] The last point is emphasized, for example, in para 33 of the judgment in *Garyfallou AEBE v Greece* (1999) 28 EHRR 344.

[57] [2003] 1 AC 787, on which see the notes by S Macdonald (2003) 66 MLR 630 and by C Bakalis [2003] CLJ 583.

[58] Lord Hope of Craighead in *Clingham and McCann* (ibid), para 83; see also Lord Steyn at para 31. Cf the reasoning of the House in the earlier deportation decision in *R v Home Secretary, ex p Khawaja* [1984] 1 AC 74.

law was designed to exert the maximum social control without the 'interference' of the safeguards applicable in criminal cases, yet because it provides for a swingeing sanction for breach by invoking the criminal law with a high maximum penalty, the House of Lords sought the compromise of requiring a high standard of proof. The result of this part of the decision is that these proceedings occupy a position mid way between the civil and the criminal paradigms.[59] The rules of civil evidence apply, so that hearsay evidence can be admitted (in order to address concerns about witness intimidation); but the standard of proof relevant when weighing the evidence is that applicable to criminal cases.[60]

The second human rights objection also derives from an anti-subversion doctrine developed by the Strasbourg Court, this time to prevent any manipulation of the preventive/punitive distinction. Article 7 of the ECHR requires that a criminal law should not operate retroactively (this gives rise to the 'quality of law' test, requiring certainty of definition) and that a penalty should not be increased retrospectively. In order to prevent any unfairness arising from the classification of orders in domestic law, the Court has insisted that the word 'penalty' in Article 7 has an autonomous meaning that transcends national labels:

> To render the protection offered by Article 7 effective, the Court must remain free to go behind appearances and assess for itself whether a particular measure amounts in substance to a 'penalty' within the meaning of this provision.[61]

In the leading case of *Welch v United Kingdom* the applicant challenged an order confiscating his assets under the Drug Trafficking Offences Act 1986.[62] He described it as a penalty and therefore argued that it could not be allowed to have retrospective application. The government argued that the order was not a penalty, since it was partly confiscatory (to remove illegal profits) and partly preventive (preventing the future use of the money in the drug trade). The Court concluded that the elements of the order—including the discretion of the judge to take account of the culpability of the offender in fixing the amount, the 'sweeping' statutory assumptions about the provenance of the money, and the possibility of imprisonment for default—'when considered

---

[59] Considerable variation in court practice on standards of proof was reported prior to the House of Lords decision: S Campbell, *A Review of Anti-Social Behaviour Orders*, Home Office Research Study 236 (London: Home Office, 2002) 49–50.

[60] The same conclusion has been reached in respect of the football banning order, under the Football Spectators Act 1989: the Court of Appeal in *Gough v Chief Constable of Derbyshire* [2002] QB 459 held that the order is essentially preventive but that courts should 'apply an exacting standard of proof that will, in practice, be hard to distinguish from the criminal standard' (Lord Phillips MR, para 66).   [61] *Welch v United Kingdom* (1995) 20 EHRR 247, para 27.

[62] Ibid.

together provide a strong indication of inter alia a regime of punishment'.[63] Mixed though its purposes were, the order was held to have the effect of a penalty, and in consequence it could not be allowed to operate retrospectively, in relation to events prior to the Act.

Challenges were subsequently mounted against the requirement to register as a sex offender, imposed by the Sex Offenders Act 1997. This brings with it an obligation to notify any change of address to the police, among other obligations. The European Commission ruled that this is a preventive order, and not a penalty. It is preventive 'in the sense that the knowledge that a person has been registered with the police may dissuade him from committing further offences'.[64] It was also noted, harking back to *Welch*, that the requirements of registration and notification are far less 'severe' than confiscation of assets—thus recognizing that the severity of the imposition is a key factor.[65] Given that the ASBO has a maximum sentence of five years, is that not in effect a penalty, even though couched in preventive terms? The House of Lords in the *Clingham and McCann* case rejected this argument. Responding to the point that the prohibitions in the order banished the defendant from the area in which he lived, backed up (in the event of breach) by higher penalties than for many criminal offences, Lord Hope of Craighead stated that the wide-ranging restrictions were 'imposed for preventive reasons, not for punishment'.[66] This completely ignores the rationale of the decision in *Welch*, which was that a measure can be punitive in effect even if it is preventive in purpose.[67] Purpose is important but, if the effects of an order are sufficiently burdensome or intrusive (eg liability to imprisonment for up to five years), there comes a point at which they may fairly be held to be punitive, irrespective of purpose. On this basis, since the maximum penalty for breaching an ASBO is more severe than that for many criminal offences, there is a strong argument that the courts should regard the imposition of the order in the earlier civil proceedings as part of the penalty.

This summary of the two anti-subversion devices developed by the Strasbourg Court shows that governments in Europe are not free to manipulate the categories civil/criminal and preventive/punitive as they wish. The Court has taken some steps to ensure that measures that impose significantly punitive burdens on people are classified as criminal and as punitive. In Part V

---

[63] Ibid, para 33.   [64] *Ibbotson v United Kingdom* (1999) 27 EHRR CD 332, 334.

[65] Ibid; see also *Adamson v United Kingdom* (1999) 28 EHRR CD 209.

[66] [2003] 1 AC 787, para 76.

[67] Note 63 above. It is true that the severity of the financial deprivation in *Welch* was considerable and that the prohibitions in *McCann* were restrictive in a less direct way. On the other hand, the Court in *Welch* did take account of the prospect of imprisonment for default, a prospect attached to all ASBOs.

below, we relate these principles to the debate about overcriminalization and undercriminalization, but there remains a further important issue to be discussed here. We have seen that, if a preventive measure is held to be criminal in substance or to impose a penalty, the various procedural rights listed above will be applicable. But what if it is decided that the preventive measure is indeed civil in substance—what rights or restrictions apply to it then?

To this question the answer in European human rights law is relatively undeveloped. The decisions on the definition of 'penalty' reviewed above point to the absence of any non-retrospectivity principle for civil orders—that was the whole point of the litigation. But what about other human rights requirements, relating to deprivation of liberty, restrictions on liberty, and certainty of definition in the prohibitions? Some pointers may be derived from the Strasbourg jurisprudence relating to Article 5(1)(e), which creates an exception to the right to liberty in cases of 'the lawful detention of persons for the prevention of the spreading of infectious diseases, or persons of unsound mind, alcoholics or drug addicts or vagrants'.

In *Witold Litwa v Poland* the Court considered the purpose of Article 5(1) (e) and held that the link between all the categories of person there listed is 'that they may be deprived of their liberty either in order to be given medical treatment or because of considerations dictated by social policy, or on both medical and social grounds'.[68] In this case the applicant had been deprived of liberty for six hours on the ground that he was an alcoholic, and the Court decided that the term 'alcoholic' should be construed to mean anyone 'whose conduct and behaviour under the influence of alcohol pose[s] a threat to public order or themselves', and does not require a medical diagnosis of alcoholism. However, the Court went on to conclude that the Polish authorities had breached Article 5 because they should have used less restrictive methods of responding to the applicant's condition, and deprivation of liberty for six hours was unjustified. In *Enhorn v Sweden* the applicant had the HIV and had transmitted it to another man.[69] The Swedish medical authorities placed him under conditions as to his behaviour, and when he failed to observe those conditions they sought and obtained an order that he be kept in compulsory isolation in a hospital. This order was renewed over a period of five years, although the applicant absconded several times and was in fact detained for about 18 months. He argued that his Article 5 right to liberty had been unjustifiably infringed. The Court held that the essential criteria for exception (e) to Article 5(1) are:

whether the spreading of the infectious disease is dangerous for public health or safety, and whether detention of the person infected is the last resort in order to

---

[68] (2001) 33 EHRR 1267.   [69] (2005) 41 EHRR 643.

prevent the spreading of the disease, because less severe measures have been considered and found to be insufficient to safeguard the public interest. When these criteria are no longer fulfilled, the basis for the deprivation of liberty ceases to exist.[70]

The Court went on to hold that Article 5 had been violated, because 'the compulsory isolation of the applicant was not a last resort' and, since his liberty was at stake, greater attention should have been paid to less restrictive means of protection.

The technique of these two judgments is to approach the difficult task of devising appropriate limits to preventive deprivations of liberty by a procedural route, requiring consideration to be given to certain criteria. Three familiar Strasbourg principles are put to work here—the principle of necessity: that it must be clear that the restrictions are necessary to prevent the harm, the principle of subsidiarity: that less intrusive measures must have been considered and adjudged to be insufficient, and the principle of proportionality: that the measures taken must not be out of proportion to the danger apprehended. It is easy to deride this kind of approach: it is merely procedural, and does not attempt to grapple with the substance (what kind of harm? what degree of risk?); and it relies on broad and malleable concepts that leave room for variable interpretations. On the other hand, this approach led to findings of a violation in both the leading cases, so there are some grounds for believing that the criteria will be applied fairly strictly. This approach suggests that deprivation of liberty for purely preventive purposes may be justifiable *in extremis* and as a last resort, when nothing less will provide adequate public protection. Although the Court was dealing with disease and public protection, the conditions thought appropriate in the *Enhorn* case did respect the individual as a rational agent, and it is thought that a similar analysis could be applied to the circumstances of most civil preventive orders. The strength of the approach is increased by insisting on high standards of evidence on all issues of fact or prediction raised in a particular case.[71]

However, the kinds of civil preventive order on which we are focusing in this chapter tend to involve restrictions on, rather than deprivations of, liberty. We must therefore proceed by way of analogy. Any steps towards justifying such restrictions must surely be premised on (a) a reliable prediction of a high probability of significant risk to the liberties of others, and (b) a judgement that no lesser form of restriction would be adequate to reduce the risk presented by the individual to an acceptable level. These criteria are pregnant with uncertainties and judgements of degree. How reliable must the predictions be? How

---

[70] Ibid, para 44.
[71] For arguments along these lines, see MD Dubber, *The Police Power: Patriarchy and the Foundations of American Government* (New York: Columbia University Press, 2005) Ch 8.

high should the probability of harm be? How serious should the predicted harm be? How high a degree of risk is acceptable, to the extent of allowing less extensive restrictions out of respect for the subject's rights? These are matters for debate, the important point being that the arguments must not only be evidence-based but also show respect for relevant rights. We have recognized that the extra safeguards for criminal cases do not apply here. The right to a fair hearing applies to cases that determine a civil obligation (Article 6 of the ECHR), and there are residual issues of the right to liberty and the right to respect for private life. If we move back from human rights law to general normative argument, then the questions raised earlier in this paragraph must be the focus of debate. All of them involve questions of degree, but that does not mean that no progress can be made.

V   Overcriminalization and Undercriminalization

In his recent monograph, Husak urges the application of restraining principles when decisions on criminalization are being taken.[72] This has a direct relevance to our project, since Husak recognizes that 'the criminal law is appropriately employed not only to reduce harm but also to reduce the *risk of harm*'.[73] He rightly acknowledges that there should be clear limits to the preventive function of the criminal law and argues that overcriminalization arises if the law does not abide by four basic requirements: the 'substantial risk requirement', the 'prevention requirement', the 'consummate harm requirement', and the 'culpability requirement'. These are sophisticated and often complex preconditions and, as Husak is the first to acknowledge, they need further elaboration if they are to provide a working guide to lawmakers. But for present purposes they can be rendered in the following simplified forms: firstly, that an offence is justified only if it is designed to reduce a substantial risk—by which he means both that the harm to be avoided must be not insubstantial, and that the degree of risk that it will occur should be more than insubstantial.[74] Secondly, an offence is justified only if it is likely to be effective in reducing the likelihood of harm occurring. For Husak, offences that fail to specify the harm that is to be significantly reduced contribute to the problem of overcriminalization because they do not permit us to judge whether the state has a sufficient interest in creating the offence, whether the law directly advances its avowed objective, or whether the law is more extensive than is necessary to achieve its purpose.[75] Thirdly, the 'consummate harm

---

[72] Husak, *Overcriminalization* (n 1 above).   [73] Ibid, 159.   [74] Ibid, 162.
[75] Ibid, 164.

requirement' specifies that a crime of risk prevention or an inchoate offence is justified only if it would also be justified to criminalize the consummate offence that 'intentionally and directly causes that very state of affairs'.[76] Fourthly, and finally, the 'culpability requirement' introduces a bar on criminalizing (upon actuarial grounds) mere belonging to a category or group deemed dangerous or risky. Under this constraint only those who bear a sufficient degree of culpability may be criminalized—intention, knowledge, or recklessness all appear as candidates, though Husak leaves open the question of what precise degree of culpability should be required.

These four principles form an essential part of Husak's larger theory of criminalization and together constitute an important framework by which to constrain the proliferation of 'crimes of risk prevention'. The increasing resort to criminalization by governments is without doubt a significant problem: in Britain over 3,000 new offences have been enacted since 1997.[77] But is there a danger that too stringent a delineation of the proper limits of the criminal law may have the unwanted effect of stimulating law-making in alternative procedural channels?[78] It may appear strange to argue that a significant aspect of the criminalization problem is undercriminalization, as well as overcriminalization. Yet if the criminal law is conceived not only in *substantive* terms, as corresponding to particular principles of responsibility and liability for wrongdoing, but also (as argued in Part IV above) in *procedural* terms, as pertaining to and invoking a particular set of procedural practices and, most importantly, protections, it can be argued that recent government initiatives resort to criminal law too little as well as too much.

We should begin by enquiring why liberal theorists are so keen to develop and elaborate principles to restrain criminalization. The answer lies in what the creation of a criminal offence authorizes. It may trigger the exercise of some of the most privatory and condemnatory forms of state power against its citizens: criminalization underpins and makes possible the arrest, interrogation, prosecution, and punishment of citizens by the state. Being found in contravention of the criminal law may result in deprivation of the offender's liberty, even prolonged detention in prison, by way of punishment. In some countries, for the most serious of offences, it may result in death or at least the imposition of a death sentence.[79] It is in recognition of the power that the criminal law bestows upon the state to take such extraordinary actions against its citizens that the safeguards of a fair criminal procedure are brought into play.

---

[76] Ibid, 166.   [77] Ashworth and Zedner, 'Defending the Criminal Law' (n 6 above) 22.
[78] Zedner, 'Seeking Security by Eroding Rights' (n 38 above).
[79] R Hood and C Hoyle, *The Death Penalty: A World-Wide Perspective*, 4th edn (Oxford: Clarendon Press, 2008).

The criminal law can thus be conceived not only as creating the authority to punish but also as calling up a robust set of procedural protections that are regarded as appropriate prerequisites of such extensive powers over citizens' liberty. This is why the Strasbourg Court developed the two anti-subversion doctrines noted in Part IV above, insisting that the Court (and not each state) will decide whether a measure constitutes a 'criminal charge' or constitutes a 'penalty' for the purpose of applying procedural protections. These doctrines are intended to provide fundamental guarantees against arbitrary state conduct and potential misuse of its authority. Procedural protections are 'due' to those who are subject to these kinds of measures, in order to render them predictable, ordered, and fair. The most prominent safeguards applicable to criminal cases under the ECHR are

(a) the presumption of innocence;
(b) the right to be informed of the nature of an accusation;
(c) the right to have adequate facilities for defence;
(d) the right to legal assistance;
(e) the right to confront witnesses;
(f) the right to the free assistance of an interpreter;
(g) the privilege against self-incrimination and right of silence;
(h) the principle of equality of arms;
(i) the right of confidential access to a lawyer;
(j) the right not to be subjected to retroactive criminal laws;
(k) the right to have criminal laws of the necessary quality, ie certainty of definition; and
(l) the right not to be subjected to a higher penalty than was applicable at the time of the conduct.

This list is provided for illustrative purposes: there is room for disagreement about whether or not a particular right should be recognized as 'human' or 'fundamental', but to enter that debate is not a purpose of this chapter.

Conceiving the criminal law as a source of procedural protection as well as the substantive basis for intrusion upon liberty may seem perverse. But these due process protections apply only if the measure is designated criminal, and our argument is that undercriminalization can be said to occur when the state sets out to provide for the exercise of police power against citizens in alternative (non-criminal) procedural channels which are subject only to lesser protections inadequate to constraining an exercise of power of the nature and magnitude involved. The exercise of state power through the criminal law is rightly subject to a whole host of procedural restrictions. When the state pursues its preventive function beyond the criminal law, it is free of those restrictions and so the exercise of state power poses a threat to the citizen's liberty, unless protections more substantial and more systematic than those sketched in Part IV above can be developed. In this sense undercriminalization occurs where the failure to designate a preventive measure as criminal deprives the citizen of what is due to her, in view of the substance of the restrictions on liberty and possible sanctions involved in the ostensibly preventive measure.

Once the criminal law is recognized as a source of procedural protections as well as a source of prohibitions on the conduct of citizens, the danger of undercriminalization can be recognized as well as the danger of overcriminalization. States can misuse the criminal law in two different ways—by creating too many (unjustifiable) criminal offences,[80] and also by dressing up as civil preventive hybrid orders certain measures that restrict liberty or extend the police power without appropriate protections.[81] The crucial issue is then that of classification. The offence of 'doing anything which he is prohibited from doing by an Anti-Social Behaviour Order' is clearly a crime and falls to be justified on the general principles of criminalization.[82] But the contents of that offence (ie the nature and extent of its prohibitions) are the product of earlier, civil proceedings. This leads to the argument, put in Part IV above, that all aspects of the order should be regarded as coupled together and as a single package—in which case the proceedings in which the civil preventive order is imposed should be treated as sufficiently connected to the (possibility of) subsequent criminal proceedings and therefore subject to all the requirements set out above. This was one of the arguments rejected by the House of Lords in the *Clingham and McCann* case,[83] holding that the two parts of the ASBO are properly decoupled, the first stage being treated as civil and the second as criminal—except that their Lordships noted the high maximum penalty and therefore demanded a high standard of proof in the civil proceedings. However, there is much more to civil preventive orders than this, and we may consider four objections to the approach taken by the House of Lords and English law.

First, the 'quality of law' test for criminal offences should be applied to the prohibitions in a civil preventive order. In relation to the ASBO, the Crime and Disorder Act 1998 requires only that the prohibitions be 'necessary for the purpose of protecting persons from further anti-social acts' by the defendant. However, the courts have insisted on an appropriate degree of clarity and certainty in the prohibitions, and (significantly) have justified this by reference to

---

[80] It is worth making the simple point that the proper response to the vice of overcriminalization is not to stop the creation of all new offences—because some new offences might meet the criteria for criminalization—but rather to conduct an audit of all crimes, old and new, with a view to discarding or downgrading those that fail to meet the criteria.

[81] Dubber, *The Police Power* (n 71 above).   [82] Crime and Disorder Act 1998, s 1(10).

[83] Above (nn 57 and 58).

the potential consequences of breach, as argued here. Thus in one case Pitchers J held that, although the proceedings for making the order were civil, 'the actual and potential consequences for the subject of an ASBO make it... particularly important that procedural fairness is scrupulously observed';[84] and in another Hooper LJ stated that a court should always ask itself, before making an order, 'Are the terms of this order so clear that the offender [*sic*] will know precisely what it is that he is prohibited from doing?'[85] These and other decisions indicate that it is the potential consequences of breaching an order—up to five years' imprisonment for an adult, up to two years' detention for a young offender—that have led the courts to impose requirements on civil preventive orders close to, or even identical with, those that should be applied to criminal offences.

Second, the restrictions on liberty included in the prohibitions imposed by civil preventive orders should be more rigorously confined. The courts have attempted to regulate them by holding that the prohibitions taken as a whole must not be disproportionate to the aim being pursued: this may mean that the number and the breadth of the prohibitions should not be too onerous, especially where they involve interference with a right such as the right to respect for private life.[86] However, the statutory test of 'necessity' should be enforced vigorously, and the impact of wide prohibitions on movement scrutinized critically.

The third objection is constitutional—that they involve too great a delegation of rule-making authority. In their analysis of two-step prohibitions, Simester and von Hirsch argue that criminal offences should normally be created as a result of the deliberations of a representative authority (ie the legislature), and that this principle is breached by civil preventive orders for which the court has authority to decide on the prohibitions that go into the order.[87] As they argue, the preventive order 'is a form of criminalization: an *ex ante* criminal prohibition, not an *ex post facto* criminal verdict'.[88] In conferring such wide powers on courts in the Crime and Disorder Act 1998, Parliament has effectively delegated to courts the power to put together a list of specific prohibitions for this defendant (a personal criminal law), with a formidably severe maximum penalty attached to any breach of the order.[89] Parliament itself, then, has given courts authority to behave in this anti-democratic manner. Furthermore, the procedure for making a preventive order fails—certainly in practice—to afford the defendant a sufficient opportunity to contest the

---

[84] *W v Acton Youth Court* [2005] EWHC 954.
[85] *R v Boness* [2006] 1 Cr App R (S) 690, 702.
[86] Ibid; see also *H, Stevens and Lovegrove* [2006] 2 Cr App R (S) 453.
[87] Simester and von Hirsch (n 4 above) 173, 180.   [88] Ibid, 178.
[89] Contrast the perspectives of Macdonald (n 34 above) and of Ramsay (n 35 above) on this.

restrictions on liberty that the court intends to impose. This, added to the fact that there has been no discussion of these particular prohibitions by any organ of the representative democracy, demonstrates what a constitutional anomaly these preventive orders are. It means that courts may impose prohibitions that are remote from the occurrence of any harm. Indeed, the Judicial Studies Board's guidance to judges on the making of ASBOs encourages them to make orders that prevent the risk of harmful behaviour occurring, as by excluding defendants from an area of a city,[90] even though the loss of liberty may be considerable and more than Parliament would find acceptable if legislating.

Fourth, there is a further constitutional objection, not spelt out by Simester and von Hirsch. That is that, even though Parliament has taken a considered decision to remove the sanction of imprisonment from a particular form of behaviour, a court may then prohibit such behaviour as a condition of an ASBO, with the result that a substantial sentence of imprisonment becomes available for breach of the prohibition. Thus, when in 1982 Parliament abolished imprisonment for the offences of begging and of soliciting for prostitution, it was clearly conscious of the fact that some people commit these offences repeatedly; evidently it took the decision that, no matter how often the offences are repeated, the offender should not be liable to imprisonment.[91] Yet this democratic decision can now be subverted by a court if it decides to insert into a preventive order a prohibition on begging or on soliciting. It is doubtful whether the supervisory jurisdiction of the appellate courts over the lower courts constitutes a sufficient constraint on the considerable powers to criminalize and to punish that have thus been bestowed upon magistrates and judges in the name of prevention. It is notable that this apparent legislative gift, if it is that, runs quite counter to another trend observable in respect of counter-terrorist measures where, in the name of protecting the public from the risk of catastrophic harm, the executive has wrested power away from the judiciary. As we observed above, in the case of Control Orders the judicial role has been reduced to *post hoc* ratification of executive decision-making.[92] These two constitutional objections raise questions about the appropriate relationship between the legislature and the judiciary in the framing of preventive measures that might have a significantly restrictive impact on citizens' lives, and might trigger prosecution for an offence with a severe maximum penalty.

---

[90] Judicial Studies Board, *ASBOs: A Guide for the Judiciary,* 3rd edn (2008) at <http://www.jsboard.co.uk>.

[91] Criminal Justice Act 1982, ss 70 and 71; see E Burney, ' "No Spitting": Regulation of Offensive Behaviour in England and Wales' in von Hirsch and Simester (eds), *Incivilities* (n 4 above).

[92] D Bonner, 'Checking the Executive? Detention without Trial, Control Orders, Due Process and Human Rights' (2006) 12 *European Public Law* 45.

VI   Conclusion

In this chapter we have noted that the distinction between criminal charges and civil preventive orders is difficult to determine precisely, but that in European human rights law an effort has been made to generate a workable distinction that recognizes the significance of severe sanctions in indicating that a measure should be classified as criminal. We also noted the different implications of classification: whereas those charged with a criminal offence may expect to have the safeguards of a considerable number of rights, the position of a person against whom a civil preventive order is sought is procedurally inferior, with a few scattered and still developing rights. This points to one reason for our concern about the use of civil preventive orders—that the prohibitions contained in them can involve extensive restrictions on liberty, yet neither principled limits nor any legal restrictions are well developed. Moreover, the typical hybrid or two-step civil preventive order is enforced through a criminal offence that is surely unintelligible in terms of the current criminalization debate. How can the justifications for a crime of 'doing anything that is prohibited by an Anti-Social Behaviour Order' be assessed without considering how the content of such prohibitions is determined and what they are in a particular case?

Our argument has been that fresh scrutiny should be given to the civil preventive orders listed at the beginning of Part II, and particularly to the civil preventive hybrid orders.[93] In our view, greater attention should be paid to the substance of these measures and less to their current legal form. If the target of a civil preventive measure is a significant wrong or social harm, as is the case with many uses of the ASBO, then, in the interests of both the alleged perpetrator and the victim, consideration should be given to defining and criminalizing the behaviour as such. Determining what is and what is not suitable for criminalization should be subject to the principles elaborated by Husak and discussed in Part V above. Where conduct accords with these principles, criminalization would ensure that those deemed to present a risk of such offending could rely on the appropriate safeguards, which is particularly important if imprisonment is a possible penalty on breach. If on the other hand the target of a preventive measure is not thought sufficiently significant and fails to satisfy Husak's principles, it should remain as a preventive measure but without the swingeing penalty for non-compliance that exists as part of the present hybrid or two-step prohibitions. Efforts would need to be made

---

[93] Britain's coalition government announced a review of the ASBO and related measures on 28 July 2010.

to develop a positive definition of preventive measures, and a legal structure which retains some coercive force, but which does not run afoul of the four objections set out above—insufficient certainty, overextensive restrictions on liberty, no opportunity to contest restrictions, and circumvention of existing legal limitations. Developing a framework for preventive justice would not be a simple endeavour, but it is an urgent one. As we have explained, the existing legal form of civil preventive hybrid measures can be more coercive than many criminal offences, yet they are imposed without the protections that adhere to criminalization, and that is simply unacceptable.

4

Perversions and Subversions of
Criminal Law

RA Duff

This chapter is concerned with the clash between ideal theory and actual practice. It takes as its starting point three aspects of English criminal law that appear inconsistent with a plausible normative theory of criminal law; these are discussed in Part II.[1] From the perspective of that ideal theory, such provisions count as perversions or subversions of criminal law: but can we sustain that ideal point of view as anything more than an 'academic' (in its pejorative sense) exercise? That will be the topic of Part III: can normative theorists insist on the authority of ideal theory, and argue that we must condemn and seek to abolish such provisions; or should they recognize that, given the changing world in which the criminal law must operate, some such developments are practically and morally inevitable, and that theory must be adapted to make room for them? As a necessary prelude to that discussion, however, Part I will briefly sketch the normative theory on which I will rely.

I An Ideal of Criminal Law

The criminal law deals in wrongs—in wrongs that count as 'public' wrongs in the sense that they are the proper concern of all citizens in virtue of their

---

[1] Examples of the abuse of criminal law are all too common: for useful introductions to the wider issues, see (on English law) IH Dennis, 'The Critical Condition of Criminal Law' (1997) 50 CLP 213 and AJ Ashworth, 'Is the Criminal Law a Lost Cause?' (2000) 116 LQR 225; (on American law) W Stuntz, 'The Pathological Politics of Criminal Law' (2001) 100 *Michigan Law Review* 506; DA Dripps, 'Terror and Tolerance: Criminal Justice for the New Age of Anxiety' (2003) 1 *Ohio State Journal of Criminal Law* 9; D Husak, *Overcriminalization* (Oxford: Oxford University Press, 2007) ch 1.

shared membership of the polity.[2] The sanctions it imposes on offenders are not merely taxes, or morally neutral penalties for breaches of the rules:[3] they are punishments, which express the polity's condemnation of the offender's conduct as a wrong. The convictions that precede and legitimize those punishments do not merely record the fact that the defendant broke a rule and so is eligible for punishment: they condemn the defendant as a proven wrongdoer. The substantive criminal law that defines the offences for which people are tried, convicted, and punished does not merely promulgate sanction-backed rules, or Austinian commands backed by threats: it purports to define wrongs that merit the condemnation and punishment for which it provides. Some of those wrongs, so-called *mala in se*, are wrong independently of any legal regulation; others, the so-called *mala prohibita*, are wrong as breaches of legal regulations that are themselves justified as serving some aspect of the common good: but what is legitimately defined as a crime must constitute a wrong that merits the polity's condemnation.[4]

Such claims about the character of criminal law are, clearly, normative rather than purely descriptive: they do not claim, for instance, that what offenders actually suffer in our prisons can be plausibly portrayed as censure-expressing burdens appropriate to their crimes; or that the trials to which defendants are actually subjected in our courts (or, more often, not subjected, given the prevalence of bargained 'guilty' pleas) can plausibly be portrayed as processes that ground a communication of justified censure to convicted defendants; or that everything which our laws actually define as criminal is, or is thought to be, a wrong that merits public condemnation. But they are not normative claims based in pure *a priori* speculation, or moral thought detached from the actual legal world (which some would call moral fantasy): they are based on central aspects of our actual systems of criminal justice, as rational reconstructions of those practices in terms of their own rhetoric, doctrines, and logic; they articulate what the criminal law must in its own terms purport to be as a distinctive mode of legal regulation, and the normative goals and standards in terms of which it must be appraised and criticized.

To say that the criminal law is concerned with wrongs (with moral wrongs) is to espouse some form of Legal Moralism. Just as we can distinguish 'negative' from 'positive' versions of retributivism in penal theory, we can distinguish

---

[2] On the sense of 'public' in play here, see SE Marshall and RA Duff, 'Criminalization and Sharing Wrongs' (1998) 11 *Canadian Journal of Law and Jurisprudence* 7.

[3] On the distinction between punishments and penalties, see classically J Feinberg, 'The Expressive Function of Punishment' in *Doing and Deserving* (Princeton, NJ: Princeton University Press, 1970) 95.

[4] See further RA Duff, *Answering for Crime* (Oxford: Hart Publishing, 2007) especially chs 2, 4, and 6.

'negative' from 'positive' forms of Legal Moralism. For the negative Legal Moralist, wrongdoing is a necessary condition of criminal liability and punishment. We should not criminalize conduct that is not in some relevant way morally wrongful, nor impose criminal liability on those who are not morally culpable, but the wrongfulness of the conduct and the culpability of its agent do not give us positive reason to criminalize it: the practice's 'general justifying aim' does not include ensuring the conviction and punishment of the morally guilty.[5] For the positive Legal Moralist, by contrast, the moral wrongfulness of the conduct and its agent's culpability give us positive reason to criminalize it: a central purpose of criminal law as a distinctive mode of legal regulation is to define, and provide for the formal condemnation and punishment of, various kinds of wrongdoing. Some Legal Moralists of this type hold that we have good reason to criminalize any and every kind of culpable wrongdoing— although we will also find other and stronger reasons that militate against such an extensive criminal law[6]—others set limits on the kinds of wrongdoing that are even in principle the criminal law's business, arguing that some wrongs are 'private' matters in which the criminal law and the polity have no proper interest.[7]

The disagreements between positive and negative Legal Moralists, and between different forms of positive Legal Moralism, are not about morality; they might indeed agree about what kinds of action constitute culpable moral wrongs. Their disagreement is grounded in political rather than in moral theory, since it concerns the proper aims and responsibilities of the state: is it the proper business of the state, or of the polity in whose name the state acts, to condemn moral wrongdoings? If so, does the state have a proper interest in every kind of moral wrong, or only in a more limited range of 'public' wrongs? We cannot answer such questions without a normative account of the state, and of its dealings with its citizens; but that simply reminds us that a theory of criminal law, as a theory of the proper aims and workings of this central institution of the state, must rest on a political theory of the state, as well as on a moral theory of wrongdoing and culpability.

Positive and negative Legal Moralists agree that the criminal law should not subject to criminal convictions and punishments those who have done no culpable wrong. They differ about, inter alia, whether the wrongfulness of conduct gives us good reason to criminalize it—rather than subjecting it to some other mode of legal regulation, or leaving it outside the law's scope altogether.

---

[5] On 'general justifying aims', see HLA Hart, *Punishment and Responsibility* (Oxford: Oxford University Press, 1968) ch 1. For a plausible form of negative Legal Moralism, see Husak (n 1 above) ch 2.
[6] See, eg MS Moore, *Placing Blame: A Theory of Criminal Law* (Oxford: Oxford University Press, 1997) especially chs 1, 16, and 18.　　　　　　　　　[7] See Duff (n 4 above) ch 6.

For a positive Legal Moralist, at least part of the point of criminal law as a distinctive mode of legal regulation is to focus on, to make salient, wrongdoing (of the relevant kind): even if we could regulate it more efficiently by other means, even if bringing it within the criminal law is likely to be consequentially unproductive, we still have reason to criminalize it—to mark it and to respond to it as a public wrong. My own position is a modest form of positive Legal Moralism, and some of the issues to be discussed later are really issues only for positive Legal Moralists: the question that they raise is not whether we can justifiably criminalize actions that are not morally wrongful, but whether we can justifiably use means other than the criminal law to deal with kinds of wrong that were traditionally thought to be the proper business of the criminal law. However, other issues to be discussed later concern both positive and negative Legal Moralists, since they have to do with the criminalization of conduct that cannot be plausibly portrayed as culpably wrongful.

A normative theorist must attend not just to the scope and content of the criminal law, but whom it addresses, in whose name, in what tones. It speaks of wrongs, but to whom does it speak, and in what voice? The best answer for a liberal democracy is that the law addresses us as citizens, in our voice, as a common law. It is not the voice of a sovereign whose commands (whether backed by authority or by threats) we must obey; it is part of the apparatus through which we define and structure the civic enterprise of our shared polity. It must express values that are our values as members of the polity, to identify and condemn what we can recognize as wrongs in terms of those shared values; it must be a voice in which we speak to each other, to ourselves, as citizens.[8] In attaching sanctions to what it defines as crimes, it may also aim to deter from such conduct those who are insufficiently moved by its normative claims.[9] It also gives the police authority to intervene to prevent crime: any who do not refrain from criminal conduct because it is wrongful might still be prevented, by vigilant policing, from successfully engaging in it. Such preventive and deterrent functions are, however, secondary to the criminal law's primary functions: to declare the public wrongfulness of certain types of conduct, and to provide for an appropriate formal, public response to such wrongs.

Central to that formal, public response is the criminal trial. The criminal trial is not simply a procedure for determining the truth of a charge, or deciding whether a defendant is eligible for punishment. It is an attempt to engage the defendant, as a responsible citizen, in a rational process that calls her to

---

[8] Cf R Cotterrell, *Law's Community* (Oxford: Oxford University Press, 1995) ch 11, on 'community' models of law.

[9] See, eg A von Hirsch, *Censure and Sanctions* (Oxford: Oxford University Press, 1993). Cf RA Duff, *Punishment, Communication and Community* (New York: Oxford University Press, 2001) ch 3.

answer to the charge, and to answer for her commission of the crime if it is proved. She is expected to attend her trial and respond formally to the charge (although given the Presumption of Innocence, that response need be only a plea of 'not guilty'); but if the prosecution proves that she committed the offence, she must then either offer a defence, an exculpatory answer for her criminal conduct, or accept the condemnation of her conduct as a public wrong that a conviction expresses. The trial is a process of calling to account, which summons a citizen to answer what she should recognize as a legitimate (even if mistaken) charge of public wrongdoing, and holds her to account for that wrong if it is proved against her.[10]

The criminal law, in both its substantive and its procedural dimensions, is thus addressed primarily to us as citizens of the polity whose law it is. It speaks to us of what we owe to each other as fellow citizens: what we owe not just by way of refraining from conduct it defines as criminal, but also by way of answering to each other, through the trial process, for such public wrongs as we commit—and indeed what we owe by way of calling each other thus to answer, since to call another to answer is to recognize and respect his civic status.

This completes my sketch of a liberal ideal of what criminal law ought to be, if it is to be true to the aims and values that are internal to it as a distinctive legal institution. It requires far more explanation than it can receive here; but it will gain credibility if it can offer a plausible account of why we should be disturbed by the provisions to be discussed in Part II. All actual systems of criminal justice fall well short of that ideal; but normative theorists will claim that we must criticize such failings, and seek to reform our actual systems in such a way that they approach closer to the ideal. The question will be whether such claims are still cogent.

II   Perverting and Subverting the Criminal Law

The criminal law is perverted when it is used for purposes that are not proper to it, or in ways that violate the values which should structure it; it is subverted when conduct that should be dealt with by the criminal law is dealt with by other modes of legal control. Perversions must concern both positive and negative Legal Moralists; subversions must concern positive Legal Moralists, but need not disturb negative Legal Moralists—at least, not *qua* subversions.

---

[10] For a fuller explanation of this account of criminal trials, see RA Duff *et al*, *The Trial on Trial (3): Towards a Normative Theory of the Criminal Trial* (Oxford: Hart Publishing, 2007).

In this part I offer recent examples of both defects. The examples are, I believe, not merely individual aberrations: they are symptomatic of broader trends in criminal law policy that present serious challenges to anyone who takes penal justice seriously.

A Criminalizing the non-wrongful

My first example illustrates two perversions of criminal law: criminalizing conduct that cannot plausibly be portrayed as wrong, and laying an unjust burden on the defendant.[11]

Section 57(1) of the Terrorism Act 2000 defines an offence of 'Possession for Terrorist Purposes'.

A person commits an offence if he possesses an article in circumstances which give rise to a reasonable suspicion that his possession is for a purpose connected with the commission, preparation or instigation of an act of terrorism.[12]

'Possession with intent' offences are easier to justify than offences of mere possession,[13] but an obvious objection to this offence is that it is both vague and broad. It is unclear what 'for a purpose connected with . . .' should mean;[14] but on any reading the section stretches criminal liability well beyond the realms not only of completed substantive crimes but also of attempts to commit such crimes. That is not, however, the objection that concerns me here: it is surely wrongful, in a way that concerns all citizens, to acquire items with the intention of using them to commit a crime; we have *some* principled reason to criminalize such possession. But while the section's title talks of such 'possession with intent', the offence definition itself talks only of possession that 'give[s] rise to a reasonable suspicion'; it is hard to see *that* as wrongful, since a reasonable suspicion that *p* is true is wholly consistent with *p* not in fact being the case.

Perhaps we sometimes have a duty to avoid acting in ways that would create a reasonable suspicion in the minds of others that we have a criminal purpose.[15] Some crimes consist in *deliberately* creating anxiety or fear, or a

---

[11] We should distinguish misguided law (criminalizing conduct that the legislator misguidedly thinks wrong) from perverted law (criminalizing conduct that the legislator does not believe to be wrong): V Tadros and S Tierney, 'The Presumption of Innocence and the Human Rights Act' (2004) 67 MLR 402.

[12] See also s 58: collecting or possessing 'information of a kind likely to be useful' to terrorists.

[13] See generally MD Dubber, 'Policing Possession: The War on Crime and the End of Criminal Law' (2001) 91 *Journal of Criminal Law and Criminology* 829.

[14] But see *Zafir et al* [2008] EWCA Crim 184, for a restrictive reading of that phrase.

[15] Thanks to Andrew Williams for pressing this point.

suspicion that the agent intends to commit a crime.[16] Perhaps we also some-times do wrong if we act in a way that gives rise to such suspicion even without intending to arouse it: criminal assault, for instance, can consist in acting in a way that causes another to apprehend immediate personal violence, being reckless as to whether such apprehension is caused.[17] There are questions about what makes suspicion 'reasonable', but such offences as these are quite differ-ent from the offence defined in section 57. They involve something more active than mere possession, which arouses suspicion or fear of immediate harm; and they involve conduct that the agent could be expected to realize might arouse such suspicion, and therefore should see that he had reason to avoid. Furthermore, the mischief at which such offences are aimed is precisely the fear or anxiety that the conduct arouses, not the crime whose commission is suspected. Section 57, by contrast, is aimed at the terrorist activity for which the possessor of the article is suspected to be preparing. Thus even if conduct that arouses suspicion that a crime is intended is sometimes a public wrong that we have reason to criminalize, we cannot say this of the kind of possession that section 57 criminalizes.

To show that this offence is illegitimate, it is not enough to show that the conduct that it criminalizes could not plausibly be thought to be pre-legally wrongful. For the criminal law contains many so-called *mala prohibita*, of which precisely that is true; but it is no part of my argument that *mala pro-hibita* are for that reason perversions of criminal law. If we define *mala pro-hibita* as consisting in conduct that is not wrongful prior to the law that criminalizes it,[18] it is of course impossible to show that any *mala prohibita* could be consistent with even negative Legal Moralism; but if we define them more appropriately, as consisting in conduct that is not wrongful prior to its legal regulation, we can justify some such offences. To justify them, we must first show that we have good reason to create a legal regulation that prohibits the conduct in question, by showing that such a regulation serves some aspect of the common good in a way that does not unreasonably burden those sub-ject to it. Second, we must show that once the regulation is in place, conduct that violates it is wrongful, in a way that merits formal condemnation as a

[16] For example, Offences Against the Person Act 1861, s 16 (threats to kill); Criminal Damage Act 1971, s 2 (threats to damage property); Public Order Act 1986, s 38 (contaminating or interfer-ing with goods, or making it appear that they have been contaminated or interfered with, intending to cause alarm, anxiety, or economic loss). See also Criminal Law Act 1977, s 51 (bomb hoaxes).

[17] D Ormerod, *Smith and Hogan Criminal Law*, 12th edn (Oxford: Oxford University Press, 2008) 584–5, 588. Compare too (more controversially) Public Order Act 1986, s 5: causing 'har-assment, alarm or distress'.

[18] A common definition: see, eg WR LaFave, *Criminal Law*, 4th edn (St Paul, Minn: West Group, 2003) 36. Cf Husak (n 1 above) 104–5: conduct that 'is not wrongful prior to or independ-ent of law'.

public wrong: by arguing, for instance, that anyone who breaks the regulation thereby refuses to accept his fair share of a burden that it was reasonable to impose on him (along with other citizens) for the sake of some aspect of the common good.[19]

Even if this kind of argument could justify some *mala prohibita*, it cannot justify section 57. It makes sense to tell citizens that they should accept certain modest burdens (those imposed by road traffic rules, for instance), for the sake of the common good; but it makes no sense to tell them that they must not possess items in circumstances that give rise to reasonable suspicion that their possession is for a terrorist purpose, or to define such possession as a public wrong.

However, I have only partially described section 57; for section 57(2) provides that it is a 'defence' for someone charged under this section 'to prove that his possession of the article was not for a purpose connected with . . . terrorism'.[20] Furthermore, whilst it might seem grossly onerous to require the defendant to 'prove' that his intentions were unrelated to terrorism, section 118(2) provides that the defence is made out if he 'adduces evidence which is sufficient to raise an issue with respect to the matter . . . unless the prosecution proves beyond reasonable doubt' that his possession was for terrorist purposes. The burden laid on the defendant is therefore actually evidential, not persuasive, and section 57 might then not seem so unreasonable. What is criminalized is not merely possession that creates a reasonable suspicion, but possession for terrorist purposes, which is a plausible public wrong. The only difference between this crime and 'standard' crimes is that the issue of the defendant's intention, which is normally a *mens rea* matter to be proved *ab initio* by the prosecution, is shifted to the category of defences, laying an evidential burden on the defendant; but it will surely not be hard for an innocent person to adduce evidence of the innocence of his intentions sufficient at least to create a reasonable doubt ('raise an issue') about the matter.

Such shifts of probative burden are common in contemporary criminal law, and are often seen as devices that avoid the injustice of strict criminal liability (liability without proof of fault), whilst meeting the practical concerns to do with ease, cost, or possibility of proof that motivate strict liability offences: the fault-free defendant must take on an additional probative burden, but can

---

[19] Cf SP Green, 'Why it's a Crime to Tear the Tag off a Mattress: Over-Criminalization and the Moral Content of Regulatory Offenses' (1997) 46 *Emory Law Journal* 1533; Duff, *Answering for Crime* (n 4 above) chs 4.4, 7.3. For criticism, see Husak (ibid) 103–19.

[20] Section 57(3) lays a similar burden on the defendant in relation to possession: given proof that an article was within his house, or on the same premises as himself, 'the court may assume that [he] possessed the article, unless he proves that he did not know of its presence on the premises or that he had no control over it'.

avoid liability by adducing evidence of his innocence.[21] Tempting though the device might be for legislators, however, it still constitutes a perversion of criminal law, since it constitutes an abuse of the normative distinction between offences and defences.

The presumption of innocence does not require the prosecution to prove, *ab initio*, every fact that bears on the defendant's guilt. The prosecution must prove all the elements of the offence—for instance that *D* intentionally wounded *V*; but this does not amount to conclusive proof of guilt, since *D* could still have a defence—that, for instance, she wounded *V* in self-defence, or under exculpatory duress. However, if the prosecution discharges its persuasive burden in relation to the elements of the offence, a probative burden shifts onto the defendant: to avoid conviction, she must adduce evidence of a defence which suffices, if not rebutted, to create a reasonable doubt about her guilt.[22] We can make normative sense of this procedural structure by thinking about what it is reasonable to expect citizens to answer for in a criminal court, on pain of conviction and punishment if they cannot offer an exculpatory answer. They can be expected to answer for what we can call 'presumptive wrongs'—conduct that the court can properly conclude or presume to have constituted a culpable public wrong in the absence of an exculpatory explanation for it:[23] if the prosecution proves that the defendant committed such a deed, it is reasonable to expect her to offer evidence that her conduct was not wrongful (a justification) or not culpable (an excuse) if she is to avoid conviction. But they cannot reasonably be expected to answer for conduct that warrants no such presumption or conclusion, by offering evidence of its innocence. That is why the presumption of innocence is interpreted as (normally) requiring the prosecution to prove *mens rea* as well as *actus reus*:[24] proof that, for instance, my action caused harm to another person does not normally by itself warrant any presumption of culpable wrongdoing, in the absence of proof that I caused that harm intentionally, or recklessly, or at least negligently.

A defendant is expected to answer *to* the charge, but given the Presumption of Innocence that answer need only be a formal plea of 'not guilty': he can then remain silent, challenging the prosecution to prove that he committed the offence charged; there is nothing yet *for* which he must answer. If the prosecution proves

---

[21] On such offences see AJ Ashworth and M Blake, 'The Presumption of Innocence in English Criminal Law' [1996] Crim LR 306.

[22] On the normative significance of the offence–defence distinction, see G Fletcher, *Rethinking Criminal Law* (Boston, Mass: Little, Brown, 1978) chs 7, 9–10; J Gardner, 'Fletcher on Offences and Defences' (2004) 39 *Tulsa Law Review* 817; V Tadros, *Criminal Responsibility* (Oxford: Oxford University Press, 2005) ch 4; Duff, *Answering for Crime* (n 4 above) ch 9.

[23] See Duff (ibid) 217–24; also Tadros (ibid) 108–15.

[24] See famously *Woolmington v DPP* [1935] AC 462, 481.

only that he committed the *actus reus* of the crime charged, he normally still has nothing to answer for: an *actus reus* does not itself constitute a presumptive wrong for which the defendant can legitimately be condemned if he cannot offer an exculpatory explanation. Only when the prosecution has proved the commission of what can properly count as a presumptive wrong is it reasonable to shift the probative burden onto the defendant: to require him to answer for his conduct either by offering a defence for which he can offer some supporting evidence, or to accept conviction as a wrongdoer. The definition of any crime should therefore specify something that could legitimately be classed as a public wrong for which the perpetrator should have to answer in a criminal court.

We can now see why section 57 is inconsistent with the Presumption of Innocence: possessing articles in circumstances that create even a reasonable suspicion that their possession is for a purpose connected to terrorism is not something for which citizens should have to answer in criminal court on pain of being convicted if they cannot offer an exculpatory answer.[25] There may be contexts in which it is legitimate to require the defendant to adduce evidence of lack of *mens rea*: for instance, when the activity in which she is engaged creates such material or moral dangers that she can reasonably be expected to bear an extra burden of care, and when the actualization of that danger can be said to constitute a presumptive wrong for which she should have to answer.[26] We cannot, however, count the mere possession of articles under circumstances that create a reasonable suspicion of terrorist purposes as an activity of that kind, or plausibly portray it as a presumptive wrong: to define the offence so broadly, and to require the defendant to offer evidence of the innocence of his intentions, must count as a perversion of criminal law.

B Anti-Social Behaviour Orders

My second example concerns both the perversion and the subversion of criminal law, but in relation to harms and wrongs rather less serious than those involved in terrorism.

English criminal law contains various offences that deal with offensive conduct: it is, for instance, an offence to engage in 'disorderly' conduct 'within the hearing or sight of a person likely to be caused harassment, alarm or distress thereby', or to breach a 'warning notice' about the level of noise one makes in one's house at night.[27] Now there are familiar questions about whether or to

---

[25] See also Tadros and Tierney (n 11 above); V Tadros, 'Rethinking the Presumption of Innocence' (2007) 1 *Criminal Law and Philosophy* 193.

[26] See Duff, *Answering for Crime* (n 4 above) 242–52.

[27] See Public Order Act 1986, s 5; Noise Act 1996, ss 2–4.

what extent the criminal law should capture offensive conduct—conduct that causes annoyance, irritation, or even distress, but that does not have a substantial enough impact on others' interests to count as harmful.[28] It is arguably appropriate, in principle, to treat some such conduct as a public wrong that merits a formal, albeit proportionately mild, response of censure and punishment; but that is not the issue here. My concern here is with a particular way in which English governments have tried to deal (or to appear to deal) more effectively with 'anti-social' behaviour, by a provision that creates a disturbing hybrid of civil and criminal law—the Anti-Social Behaviour Order (ASBO).[29]

A local authority or chief police officer can apply to a court for an ASBO. The applicant must prove that the person has acted 'in an anti-social manner', that 'caused or was likely to cause harassment, alarm or distress', and that an order is 'necessary' to protect others against further anti-social acts. Although the criminal standard of proof 'beyond reasonable doubt' must be satisfied, the proceedings are civil, not criminal;[30] and although what must be proved is the *actus reus* of an offence under section 5 of the Public Order Act 1986, there need be no proof of *mens rea* for that offence. If the court accepts the applicant's claims, what follows is not a criminal conviction and punishment: instead, the court can impose a variety of restrictions on the person (including restrictions on his movements), in order to prevent the repetition of the anti-social behaviour. Those restrictions may exclude the person from what would otherwise be lawful activities (for instance from entering a particular housing estate or shopping mall); and since they are not punishments, they are not constrained by demands of proportionality to a past offence. The breach of an ASBO is a criminal offence, punishable by up to five years' imprisonment; but what the person is (formally) convicted and punished for is not anti-social behaviour of a kind that already constituted an offence, but the breach of the ASBO, which might itself involve no anti-social behaviour.

Now it is true that 'anti-social' behaviour of various kinds is a serious social problem: in some areas it can make life nearly intolerable, and there are familiar difficulties (especially in finding witnesses willing to testify in a criminal court) in using the criminal law to deal with it directly. The attractions of ASBOs for local authorities and police forces, and for those who suffer from serious, persistent, anti-social conduct, are therefore obvious (leaving aside

---

[28] See generally A von Hirsch and AP Simester (eds), *Incivilities: Regulating Offensive Behaviour* (Oxford: Hart Publishing, 2006); also J Feinberg, *Offense to Others* (New York: Oxford University Press, 1985).

[29] Crime and Disorder Act 1998, ss 1–4. See AJ Ashworth, 'Social Control and "Anti-Social Behaviour": The Subversion of Human Rights?' (2004) 120 LQR 263; Ashworth and Zedner in this volume; von Hirsch and Simester (ibid).

[30] *R (McCann) v Crown Court of Manchester* [2003] 1 AC 787.

here the question of whether ASBOs are actually effective). We must also recognize, however, that these provisions constitute an abuse of criminal law.

First, the civil process of applications for, and the making of, ASBOs is not one in which an alleged misbehaver is called to answer for his conduct; nor is he formally given the chance to offer an exculpatory answer, for instance by arguing 'that his conduct was reasonable'—a defence allowed to someone who is criminally charged under the Public Order Act.[31] It might be said that this cannot constitute an abuse of criminal law, since it is not a criminal process. However, ASBOs are intimately bound up with criminal law: what justifies an ASBO is the person's previous criminal conduct, and the ASBO itself amounts to an individualized criminal law, by making it an offence for this person to enter this housing estate or that shopping mall, for instance. Furthermore, if we are to treat each other, including those of us who engage in anti-social behaviour, as responsible citizens, the appropriate way to respond to such behaviour is to call perpetrators to answer for it, and to censure and punish them for it if they cannot offer an exculpatory answer. If we have to deal with someone who is not a responsible agent—for instance with someone who is so mentally disordered that she cannot be held responsible for her actions—we may treat the fact of past criminal conduct as evidence that we must subject her to some kind of restriction in order to prevent her from harming others (or herself) in the future.[32] But the justification of such purely preventive treatment depends essentially on her lack of responsibility—on the fact that she cannot be held to account for what she has done; if we are dealing with a responsible agent, we subvert criminal law by treating her past criminal conduct not as something for which she should be called to answer, but as evidence of a need for preventive restrictions on her future conduct.

Second, ASBOs subvert criminal law in that they impose what might be quite oppressive restrictions (including, for instance, exclusion from the housing estate where one lived) which are neither justified nor justifiable as punishments. Some kinds of exclusion can be justified as punishments: temporary exclusion from a shopping mall could be an appropriate sentence for a shoplifter, and temporary exclusion from football matches an appropriate sentence for a football hooligan. Such punishments must be justified as proportionate responses to the offender's past wrongs, however, whereas ASBOs have a purely preventive rationale. Apart from the fact that this removes a principled constraint on their possible harshness, we should object that, like other preventive or incapacitative measures, they fail to treat those subjected to them as

---

[31] Public Order Act 1986, s 5(3)(c); ss 5(3)(a)–(b) also allow 'defences' that are open to the same objection as s 57 of the Terrorism Act 2000 (Part II A of this chapter, above).

[32] See, eg the provisions in Parts II–III of the Mental Health Act 1983.

responsible agents. The criminal law addresses us as responsible agents: it reminds us what we have normally conclusive reason not to do, and intervenes coercively only if we fail to act as those reasons require. An ASBO, by contrast, whilst it does address the person on whom it is imposed as a responsible agent in that it requires him (rather than forcing him) to abide by the restrictions it contains, does not treat him as a responsible agent in relation to his potential anti-social behaviour; it simply excludes him from the contexts in which he might misbehave. We might be justified in excluding from an activity for which a licence is properly required someone who has shown that she cannot be trusted to engage in it safely or appropriately: we can ban unsafe or unfit drivers from driving, dishonest or incompetent doctors from practising medicine, fraudulent lawyers or directors from practising law or directing companies, on the grounds that by their misconduct they have lost the right to engage in this dangerous activity which is not essential to a human life.[33] But exclusion from the housing estate on which one lived, or from a shopping mall, cannot be thus normatively rationalized as exclusion from a specialized or especially risky activity for which a licence is properly required; it is exclusion from a central aspect of normal life. We may also impose restrictions on people who cannot help presenting a threat to others' safety or well-being: for instance, we may quarantine one suffering a dangerously infectious disease,[34] who cannot help endangering others if he goes out in the world. But an ASBO is not imposed to prevent misconduct that the person would be unable to avoid for himself; it is imposed precisely to deny him the opportunity to decide for himself how to behave—which is to fail to treat him as a responsible agent.

Third, the punishment imposed on one who breaches an ASBO is imposed, formally, for that breach—not for any criminally anti-social behaviour in which she might have engaged before or after the ASBO was imposed. However, there will be the inevitable suspicion that what really determines the sentence is the underlying anti-social behaviour, even though that is not something that was formally proved as a criminal offence, and the 'defendant' has no chance to make a case for exculpation or mitigation; and while we can make good normative sense of 'breach sanctions' (further punishments imposed for failure to carry out the requirements of an initial punishment),[35] it is harder to make such sense of punishments that are formally inflicted for

---

[33] There is much more to be said about such exclusions and disqualifications: see A von Hirsch and M Wasik, 'Civil Disqualifications Attending Conviction' (1997) 56 CLJ 599.

[34] See, eg the provisions in the Public Health (Control of Disease Act) 1984.

[35] Though there are important problems here too, including the application of proportionality requirements to breach sanctions, and the question whether we can avoid using imprisonment as the final sanction.

the breach of a non-criminal, supposedly non-punitive order whose imposition did not even require proof of criminal guilt.

The provisions for ASBOs thus constitute a subversion of criminal law, in that they use a non-criminal procedure and supposedly non-penal restrictions to deal with conduct that, if it does constitute a public wrong, should instead be dealt with through the criminal law; and a perversion of criminal law, in that they impose criminal conviction and punishment on those who break the supposedly non-criminal orders that are imposed. Finally, however, we should note that a kind of provision that in some ways resembles an ASBO can be legitimate—an injunction that formally directs the person on whom it is imposed not to engage in a specified kind of criminally wrongful conduct. If the precise meaning of the criminal law is unclear or might be misunderstood; if, for instance, it might not be clear (to this person) just what kind of conduct counts as criminally anti-social, then a court could issue an injunction that enjoins the person from engaging in specified types of anti-social behaviour.[36] The difference between such injunctions and ASBOs is that the injunction prohibits conduct which itself constitutes a 'criminalizable' wrong; so long as what someone who breaches the injunction is convicted and punished for is the wrong that she thereby commits, this constitutes a legitimate specification, rather than perversion or subversion, of the criminal law.

To object to ASBOs is not to deny that anti-social behaviour is often a serious problem for its victims. It is to say that if we are to wield the criminal law in this context, we should use it properly—to define relevant public wrongs, and to call to account those who commit them; and that we should wield the criminal law to respond to such wrongdoing. We might add that, as with so many problems to which politicians see criminal law as an (apparent) quick fix, real solutions to the problems of anti-social behaviour can be found in non-criminal measures to address their causes.

(A provision structurally very similar to the ASBO is the kind of control order that can be imposed on someone suspected of involvement in terrorist activities,[37] as being necessary to protect the public against terrorism. Such orders raise similar issues about the subversion or perversion of criminal law (the breach of a control order is a criminal offence), although the threat against

---

[36] Compare the provisions in the Anti-Social Behaviour Act 2003, s 13; Protection from Harassment Act 1997, s 3; Environmental Protection Act 1990, ss 79–80; Noise Act 1996, ss 1–4: see RA Duff and SE Marshall, 'How Offensive Can You Get?' in von Hirsch and Simester (n 28 above) 57, 82–5.

[37] Prevention of Terrorism Act 2005: see L Zedner, 'Securing Liberty in the Face of Terror: Reflections from Criminal Justice' (2005) 32 *Journal of Law and Society* 507, and 'Preventive Justice or Pre-Punishment? The Case of Control Orders' (2007) 60 CLP 174; V Tadros, 'Justice and Terrorism' (2007) 10 *New Criminal Law Review* 658; Ashworth and Zedner in this volume.

which they are directed is dramatically greater than that of anti-social behaviour. They also raise distinct issues about the normative character of terrorism: how far should it be understood as criminal activity, and how far as something more like an act of war?)

C   Crimes and regulatory offences

English criminal law includes a number of offences that other systems do not classify as 'crimes'. Many so-called 'regulatory' offences, concerning business activities and health and safety matters, as well as various traffic offences, are formally distinguished from 'crimes' in some legal systems (and informally distinguished from 'real' crimes by many who deal with English law). The Model Penal Code (§1.04) distinguishes crimes from violations—offences for which the penalty can be no more than a fine, or forfeiture or 'other civil penalty', and conviction for which does not have the effects of a criminal conviction. Other legal systems draw an even sharper distinction between two categories of penalizable conduct: the German category of *Ordnungswidrigkeiten* exemplifies this possibility.

The 1968 Gesetz über Ordnungswidrigkeiten transferred various types of offence (among them many road traffic offences) from the criminal law to a regulatory regime: what had been crimes (*Straftaten*) became regulatory infractions (*Ordnungswidrigkeiten*); financial sanctions that had been fines (*Geldstrafen*) became administrative penalties (*Geldbussen*).[38] The main distinguishing features of *Ordnungswidrigkeiten* are, first, that they do not attract the formal condemnation that attaches to crimes.[39] Second, *Ordnungswidrigkeiten* can be penalized only by administrative fines, which are formally distinct from criminal fines.[40] Third, although the alleged 'offender' can formally object to the *Geldbusse*, in which case the matter is decided in a criminal court, the procedure is simpler than that of a criminal trial: neither defendant nor prosecutor need attend, evidence can be taken in writing, and the rules of evidence are relaxed.[41]

This is an obviously tempting strategy of formal 'decriminalization' for governments that are concerned to find more economically efficient ways of

---

[38] For a useful critical discussion, see T Weigend, 'The Legal and Practical Problems Posed by the Difference between Criminal Law and Administrative Penal Law' (1988) 59 *Revue Internationale de Droit Pénal* 67.   [39] See Gesetz über Ordnungswidrigkeiten, s 1; Weigend (ibid) 71–2.

[40] However, someone who wilfully fails to pay a *Geldbusse* can be imprisoned for up to six weeks (OWiG, s 96). In the case of serious and persistent breaches of the road traffic regulations, the offender can also be disqualified from driving for up to three months (Strassenverkehrsesetz (1982), s 25).   [41] See Weigend (n 38 above) 80–81.

regulating various kinds of risky conduct.[42] Since being required to pay an administrative penalty is not a criminal conviction that condemns the 'offender' as a wrongdoer (since it is 'non-stigmatic'), we need not build in so many safeguards against 'convicting' the innocent; we need not insist on a requirement of 'fault' that shows the person to have been culpable, and might impose strict liability with a clear(er) conscience; and we need not make provision for the expensive procedural paraphernalia of a criminal trial (with the attendant risk of not securing convictions against 'offenders' who can afford adept defence lawyers).[43] Furthermore, this is not a perversion of the criminal law, in the way that imposing strict criminal liability may be: it does not involve condemning as a wrongdoer someone who has not been proved culpable.[44]

Should we see it, however, simply as a sensible regulatory device, withdrawing criminal law from areas in which our proper aims are better served by such a non-criminal regime; or as a subversion of criminal law that excludes from criminal law kinds of conduct that should be seen and treated as criminal? To see the force of this question, imagine a suggestion that, in order to reduce the difficulties that rape prosecutions notoriously involve, and to increase the law's efficacy by increasing the rate of 'convictions', we should turn rape from a criminal into a regulatory *Ordnungswidrigkeit*. There would of course be pragmatic objections to this: if only financial penalties could be imposed, the law would be unacceptably ineffective either as a deterrent or as enabling preventive incapacitation. But there would be deeper objections: that what rape requires, by way of an official response, is not simply a financial penalty whose sole aim is to dissuade, but condemnation as a serious public wrong; that the rapist should not be subject only to a discreet official process to determine a breach of the rules and the penalty for that breach, but should be called publicly to answer for his crime at a criminal trial; and that he should suffer not a penalty, but a punishment that condemns his deed. *Ordnungswidrigkeiten* are not marked, addressed, or condemned as wrongs: that is precisely what distinguishes them from crimes. Sometimes, however, it is important to mark a type of conduct as a public wrong that should be condemned, and whose perpetrator should be called to public account—which is to say that it should be a matter for criminal law, rather than for non-criminal regulation. In deciding

---

[42] As the European Court noted in *Öztürk v Germany* (1984) 6 EHRR 409: see also *Lauko v Slovakia* (2001) 33 EHRR 40. In both cases the Court had to decide whether someone accused of an *Ordnungswidrigkeit* is facing 'a criminal charge'. If he is, the process is a criminal process, and he is entitled to the protections of Art 6 of the ECHR.

[43] See I Ayres and J Braithwaite, *Responsive Regulation: Transcending the Deregulation Debate* (Oxford: Oxford University Press, 1992); A Ogus and C Abbot, 'Sanctions for Pollution: Do We Have the Right Regime?' (2002) 14 *Journal of Environmental Law* 283.

[44] Which is not to say that strict criminal liability always perverts the criminal law: see AP Simester (ed), *Appraising Strict Liability* (Oxford: Oxford University Press, 2005).

whether we should create a distinct, non-criminal category of *Ordnungs-widrigkeiten* (and if so, what kinds of conduct it should capture) we must therefore ask not merely whether this would make for a more efficient regulatory regime, but whether the kinds of conduct that are to be regulated should be marked, treated, and condemned as wrongs.

Regulatory offences may often be so defined that they capture conduct that is not always harmful, dangerous, or culpable. But very often (if they are sensibly formulated) the conduct that they capture will also be both harmful or dangerous and culpable; it will expose others to a risk of harm that they should not have to suffer, and reflect a lack of the care that we owe to each other when we engage in potentially harmful activities. Those wrongful endangerments will also often be plausibly classed as public wrongs—wrongs that properly concern us all as citizens; indeed, since they often involve general dangers that are not focused on particular victims, they might seem even more obviously 'public' wrongs than are attacks on individual victims. This might suggest that it is a subversion of criminal law to subject the perpetrators of such wrongs to a regime of regulatory penalties, rather than calling them to account in a criminal court, but that would be too hasty: to subject conduct to a criminal rather than a non-criminal mode of regulation is to make its wrongfulness salient—to focus on it as a wrong; we must ask whether and when that is how we should formally respond to public wrongs.

The question whether we are to subject potentially harmful conduct to a criminal or to a non-criminal mode of regulation also matters from the point of view of those who engage in it. One worry from their point of view is that, while a shift to non-criminal regulation removes the threat of criminal stigmatization, it also removes some of the protections that criminal law provides: 'offences' might be defined broadly, without substantial fault elements; there might be a higher risk of being penalized when legally or morally 'innocent'. The European Court took the severity of the potential penalty to be crucial in deciding whether a procedure should count as 'criminal':[45] the harsher the potential penalty, the greater the need for the protections provided by Article 6. But there is more to it than that: we must ask about the terms in which the state should address its citizens when it seeks to regulate their conduct, and whether the tones of criminal law, speaking of wrongs that are to be condemned, are more appropriate than those of a regulatory regime that speaks only of rules and of penalties for their breach.

(I have assumed that the aims of a regulatory regime are preventive: its penalties serve as deterrents; the provisions for disqualification that it may also involve serve an incapacitative role. That is how such regimes are typically

---

[45] See *Öztürk* (n 42 above); *Engel v Netherlands* (1979–80) 1 EHRR 647; n 42 above.

understood, but there is a different possibility: a regime that attaches financial burdens to breaches of its regulations might be understood as compensatory, rather than preventive. The prohibited conduct is typically harmful, and the payments exacted from those who engage in it go towards the costs of repairing those harms. Rather than trying to allocate the cost of each instance of harm to its agent, the overall costs are distributed, justly and efficiently, among all those who engage in such conduct. This again raises the issue of whether our response to public wrongs should focus on their wrongness.[46])

In this Part I have discussed three ways in which the law's dealings with (potentially) criminal conduct can diverge from the normative conception of criminal law sketched in Part I. Some of these dealings count, given that conception, as perversions of criminal law: they use criminal law in ways inconsistent with that conception, to criminalize conduct that cannot be plausibly portrayed as a public wrong. Others count, from that perspective, as subversions of criminal law: instead of using the criminal law to respond to conduct that constitutes a public wrong, we use other legal devices to control and regulate it. The question now is: how should normative theorists of criminal law (if they have sympathy with that conception of criminal law) respond to such divergences?

III Theory and Practice

Normative theory must not simply aim to align itself with actual practice, of course: practice, the theorist can properly insist, is answerable to and assessed in the light of normative theory. But theorists cannot simply ignore actual practice and the ways in which it changes: we must ask whether it is still possible, in the light of changing practices and the circumstances under which they change, to maintain the demands of our preferred normative theory as demands that hold good not just in an imagined and better world, but in the world in which we live, and for that reason to condemn such perversions and subversions as those described in Part II.

There is much to be said—but not here—about the origins of the kinds of change noted in Part II, and about the perceived threats or problems to which they are rationalized as responses; but how should normative theorists who have sympathy with the version of Legal Moralism sketched in Part I respond? We need to consider separately those changes that mark what I have called perversions of criminal law, and those that rather constitute subversions: in the former case the criminal law is used improperly—to impose liability, for

---

46 Thanks to Victor Tadros for pressing this suggestion; see further at n 51 below.

instance, without proof of what could plausibly be portrayed as culpable wrongdoing; in the latter, conduct that amounts (or could be seen to amount) to a public wrong is dealt with by non-criminal modes of control or regulation—by preventive orders, or by a non-criminal regime of administrative rules and penalties. Perversions of criminal law challenge both positive and negative Legal Moralists: they violate the principle, which both assert, that proven culpable wrongdoing is a necessary condition of criminal liability. Subversions, by contrast, do not as such challenge negative Legal Moralists, whose claims concern only ways in which criminal law should *not* be used; subversions of criminal law do not involve the use, and therefore cannot involve the misuse, of criminal law.[47] Subversions do, however, challenge positive Legal Moralists, who claim that criminalization is an appropriate response to public wrongdoing: for these provisions replace criminal law by other modes of regulation or control.

Negative and positive Legal Moralists should agree, I think, in condemning perversions of criminal law, and insist that practice is answerable here to normative theory. The criminal law is a distinctive institution, which purports to mark culpable public wrongdoing as wrong, and condemns those who commit it: if it is worth maintaining such an institution, for other than purely instrumental reasons, it should be maintained precisely as such an institution, ie as one that is focused on culpable wrongdoing. If instead we criminalize conduct that cannot plausibly be portrayed as publicly wrongful, or impose criminal liability without appropriate proof of fault, we unjustly condemn and punish as culpable wrongdoers those who are not, and whom we do not believe to be, culpable wrongdoers. Such provisions could of course gradually lead either to a change in our conception of criminal law (we cease to understand it as concerned with culpable wrongdoing), or to a firmer distinction between 'real' crimes and 'quasi-criminal', 'non-stigmatic' offences:[48] perversions can become subversions. Whether such developments should be welcome is our next question; but the point so far is that, insofar as we purport to maintain a system of *criminal* law, we should apply it only to what can plausibly be portrayed as public wrongdoing, and hold criminally liable only those who culpably commit such wrongs. We should therefore reject the kinds of criminal provision described in Parts II A and II B above.

---

[47] This is not to say that negative Legal Moralists should happily accept the kinds of subversion of criminal law sketched in Part II; but any objections they may have cannot be grounded in their Legal Moralism.

[48] See, eg *Warner v Metropolitan Police Commissioner* [1969] 2 AC 256, 272; FB Sayre, 'Public Welfare Offenses' (1933) 33 *Columbia Law Review* 55, 70–75. For critical discussion, see AP Simester, 'Is Strict Liability Always Wrong?' in Simester (n 44 above) 21, 37–41; Weigend (n 38 above).

It might be said that this fails to take seriously the problems to which the 'perversions' noted above were responses: that a criminal law that satisfies the demands of Legal Moralism (negative or positive) is simply inadequate to deal with the threat of terrorism, or with the real problems of anti-social behaviour. I am sure that in one way that is absolutely true: we cannot look to criminal law, as both kinds of Legal Moralism portray it, to be effective in preventing terrorism or anti-social behaviour. But that is because criminal law can generally play only a limited role in preventing harm or danger: one error in so much contemporary penal rhetoric is to portray criminalization as a solution to an ever wider range of social ills. Once we grasp the distinctive character of criminal law, we can also see more clearly the limitations on what an institution of that kind can be expected to achieve; but if we see value in maintaining such an institution, we should maintain it as such an institution, and seek other ways of addressing problems with which it cannot deal.

This leads us from perversions to subversions, and from the question of what the criminal law should be to that of what role it should play in our polities. It leads us away from criminal law theory as narrowly conceived, towards larger issues in legal and political theory—which is where any adequate theorizing about criminal law must be led.

A positive Legal Moralist must hold that we have reason to criminalize any public wrong: any such wrong is our collective business; we have reason to call its perpetrator to answer for it and to censure him as a wrongdoer. That is not yet to say, however, that we have conclusive reason to do so: quite apart from the fact that the costs, both material and moral, of enforcing the criminalization of a public wrong might be so great, and the chances of doing it justly and effectively so small, that we should not on balance seek to criminalize it, we might have two other kinds of reason for not criminalizing a public wrong.

First, some public wrongs are too trivial to justify the attention of the criminal law: even if a better system of criminal justice than our own was able to provide appropriately modest, non-oppressive procedures and punishments for minor offences,[49] some wrongs are too minor to warrant even that much formal attention. For just one example, there are kinds of incivility that we may display to each other in public places (barging rudely along a crowded street, for instance) that constitute civic wrongs, and that merit comment from others, but that it would be absurd to think of criminalizing; that is why any sane system of criminal law recognizes a *de minimis* principle.[50]

---

[49] Compare, for instance, the system of 'prosecutor fines' (see P Duff, 'The Prosecutor Fine' (1994) 14 OJLS 565); s 51 of the Criminal Proceedings etc (Reform) (Scotland) Act 2007.

[50] Such a principle can operate as a constraint both on legislation, and on the criminal process: legislatures should not criminalize types of conduct that are only trivially wrong; prosecutors should not prosecute, and courts should not convict, utterly trivial wrongs even if they fit the

Wrongs that fall under a *de minimis* constraint on criminalization are typically trivial in two ways: they do not have a serious enough impact on others to count as harmful; and they display only a relatively minor kind of moral fault. Second, however, there might be kinds of public wrong that cause or threaten serious harm, but that we should not criminalize because it is more important to ensure that the harm is repaired or paid for, and to allocate the costs of such repair or compensation justly, than to call those who cause it to public, criminal account; and, perhaps, because criminalizing the conduct would hinder the attempt to allocate its costs fairly—if, for instance, those who caused the harm would then be less likely to admit their responsibility for it. In such cases we would see reason to prefer something more like a civil-law than a criminal-law response. Rather than defining the harmful or dangerous conduct as a criminally punishable wrong, the law specifies the kind of conduct that will render its agent liable to pay for the harm that it causes or might cause; the aim of any legal proceedings is to determine that kind of civil, rather than criminal, liability. Those proceedings could be the familiar kind of civil suit in which the plaintiff who has suffered harm sues the alleged harm-causer for damages; or the polity could collectively pursue harm-causers to make them pay; or the law could make all who engage in specified types of dangerous conduct liable to pay, whether their particular conduct caused harm or not, so that the cost of the harm caused by such conduct is spread among all those who engage in it.[51] This kind of compensatory, rather than punitive, response might be especially appropriate when the harm involved is significant, but agents' fault is typically quite minor—as when, for instance, the harm is caused through (non-gross) negligence rather than recklessly or intentionally.

The distinctions between criminal and civil responses to harmful conduct in our existing legal systems are of course far less clear and sharp than the previous paragraph suggested. For one thing, a civil process whose formal aim is to assign responsibility for harm, and liability to pay reparation or compensation for it, is also a process in which culpable harm-causers are called to account for what they have done; and although a verdict for the plaintiff does not in itself constitute a formal condemnation of the defendant as a wrongdoer, it often carries such an implication, at least in the eyes of participants and the public. For another, provisions such as those for punitive damages in civil

---

formal definition of an offence. On the latter possibility see Model Penal Code §2.12; DN Husak, '*De Minimis*' in RA Duff and SP Green (eds), *Philosophical Foundations of Criminal Law* (Oxford: Oxford University Press, forthcoming).

[51] See text to which n 46 above relates for this way of understanding and structuring a system of regulatory penalties.

cases,[52] or for compensation orders in criminal cases,[53] combine aspects of criminal and civil processes. For present purposes, however, the relevant point is that we may sometimes see good reason to focus on allocating the costs of repairing harm, rather than on prosecuting and punishing wrongdoers, in our formal response to public wrongs. Some would argue that our focus should *always* be on repairing harms rather than on punishing wrongs—that is the mantra of advocates of one kind of restorative justice.[54] Legal Moralists can agree that this is sometimes an appropriate focus; they need not demand that we always make the wrongfulness of public wrongdoing our primary focus in responding to it. They will insist, however, that sometimes we should make wrongfulness salient: that we must sometimes seek to hold wrongdoers to public account for their wrongdoing through a criminal process that condemns and punishes them. The force of that insistence is most clearly visible in the case of the serious wrongs that form the familiar core of criminal *mala in se*: whatever else we do in response to murder, or rape, or other serious attacks on citizens and their vital interests, we should seek to call the perpetrators of such wrongs to public, criminal account.[55] We owe this, we might say, not just to the victims of such crimes, as a matter of responding appropriately to the wrongs they have suffered, and to ourselves, as a matter of being true to the values that we collectively profess, but also to the wrongdoers: for to treat another as a fellow member of a normative community is to be ready, inter alia, to hold her to account for the serious wrongs that she commits.

This highlights one central question about criminalization: which kinds of public wrong are such that we should make their wrongfulness salient in our formal responses to them; and which are such that we can properly either ignore them as too trivial for the criminal law, or focus on the need to repair such harm as was caused (and to allocate the cost of such repair) rather than on calling the wrongdoers to answer for their wrongdoing?[56] That is not, however, quite the question that is raised by the provisions described in Part II as subversions of criminal law: for the key point about those provisions is that their

---

[52] See D Markel, 'Retributive Damages: A Theory of Punitive Damages as Intermediate Sanction' (2009) 94 *Cornell University Law Review* 239; 'How Should Punitive Damages Work?' (2009) 157 *University of Pennsylvania Law Review* 1383.

[53] See N Walker and N Padfield, *Sentencing: Theory, Law and Practice*, 2nd edn (London: Butterworths, 1996) 245–50.

[54] See, eg L Walgrave, 'Restoration and Punishment: On Favourable Similarities and Fortunate Differences' in G Maxwell and A Morris (eds), *Restoring Justice for Juveniles* (Oxford: Hart Publishing, 2001) 17.

[55] See N Jareborg, 'Criminalization as Last Resort (*Ultima Ratio*)' (2005) 2 *Ohio State Journal of Criminal Law* 521; also RA Duff, 'Restoration and Retribution' in A von Hirsch *et al* (eds), *Restorative Justice and Criminal Justice: Competing or Reconcilable Paradigms?* (Oxford: Hart Publishing, 2003) 43.

[56] The question is especially relevant in the context of corporate liability.

direct aim is to regulate and control behaviour. ASBOs, and the kinds of regulation whose breach attracts a non-criminal, administrative penalty, require those to whom they apply to behave in certain ways, and attach sanctions to failures to obey those requirements; they purport to offer those to whom they apply reasons to act as they require. By contrast, a civil or quasi-civil system of compensation or damages, whilst it might in fact or by design also serve to guide conduct, is not explicitly conduct-guiding. The question raised by ASBOs and *Ordnungswidrigkeiten* is then the question of the conditions under which and the terms in which it is proper for a polity to impose such sanction-backed requirements on its citizens.

The objection that such provisions subvert criminal law does not rest on the claim that the kinds of conduct that they aim to control should not be subject to legal regulation or sanction. It rests, rather, on the claim that a polity should deal honestly with its citizens: in particular, the reasons it offers them for behaving in a certain way should match the reasons that justify both the attempt to persuade them to behave in that way and the imposition of sanctions on those who do not behave in that way. The criminal law, as sketched in Part I, is in this sense an honest institution: in defining certain types of action as public wrongs, it declares that we should refrain from such actions because they are wrong; and it is the wrongfulness of those actions that justifies the convictions and punishments to which their perpetrators are liable. By contrast, neither ASBOs nor a regime of *Ordnungswidrigkeiten* are in this sense honest.

An ASBO is directed ultimately against anti-social conduct that does indeed constitute a public wrong; but it does not treat that conduct as a public wrong, or its agent as a responsible citizen, since it does not call the agent to answer for it through a criminal process. Instead, it treats the alleged previous anti-social behaviour as evidence of the need for preventive constraints which could be justified only if their subject lacked control over his anti-social behaviour;[57] and it then imposes criminal liability for the breach of those constraints, although that cannot plausibly be portrayed as a public wrong. The only reason the court could give the person for obeying the restrictions imposed by the ASBO is, roughly, 'we cannot trust you to behave properly, and are therefore imposing restrictions to limit the temptations to or opportunities for misconduct'. But the only proper way to justify such restrictions on a responsible citizen is to justify them as proportionate punishments for a public wrong for which she is called to answer through an appropriate criminal process—which ASBO hearings signally fail to do.

---

[57] See at n 34 above.

A regulatory regime like that of *Ordnungswidrigkeiten* does not fail in the same way to treat those whose conduct it governs as responsible agents, but there is a mismatch between the reasons that justify its regulations and its response to breaches of them. If its regulations are justified, they must either prohibit conduct that is directly harmful or dangerous in ways that properly concern the polity; or require conduct that is necessary to protect some aspect of the common good, or to the functioning of an institution that serves the common good. In the former case the prohibited conduct constitutes a *malum in se*; in the latter case, failure to obey the regulations constitutes a *malum prohibitum*.[58] We thus have reason to censure those who culpably violate such regulations: for even if their actions do not directly harm or endanger others, they refuse to accept a regulatory burden that is legitimately required of them for the sake of the common good. This then gives us reason to criminalize such violations: to define them as public wrongs, and to provide for those who commit them to be called to public and criminal account. But that is not what a regulatory regime does. By removing such violations from the criminal law, it fails to mark them as public wrongs: hence the common complaint that corporations whose harmful activities are subject only to non-criminal regulation are not called to account, as they should be, as wrongdoers.[59] Furthermore, it fails to address those whom it penalizes in the appropriate terms, by appealing to the reasons that justify its rules and its penalties. It does not speak to them of what they should do for the safety of citizens or to protect the polity's common good; it does not call them to account for the commission of the wrongs that they commit in violating the rules, or censure them as wrongdoers; rather, it treats them simply as self-interested agents whose conduct can be controlled by the provision of prudential deterrents.[60] To put the point succinctly, we can justifiably impose requirements of this kind only if they serve the public, common good; we can justifiably penalize breaches of such requirements only if those breaches constitute public wrongs; but we then owe it to those who violate the regulations to treat their violations precisely as public wrongs for which they must be called to answer through a criminal process.

If we take a fairly simple consequentialist approach, and ask what kinds of measure might be most economically effective in dealing with terrorism, with anti-social behaviour, or with conduct (including corporate conduct) that we need to regulate for the sake of public health, safety, or convenience, we might

---

[58] The complexities of the distinction between *mala in se* and *mala prohibita* need not concern us here; see at nn 18–19 above, and the references in n 19.

[59] Complaints that partly motivated the campaign for an offence of corporate manslaughter: see J Gobert, 'The Corporate Manslaughter and Corporate Homicide Act 2007: Thirteen Years in the Making but Was It Worth the Wait?' (2008) 71 MLR 413.

[60] See further Duff, *Punishment, Communication and Community* (n 9 above) chs 2.4, 3.2.

see merit in the kinds of measure discussed in Part II (though I have not discussed the extent to which such measures are in fact effective or efficient). If we expect the criminal law to play a major role in dealing with such problems, we might also see merit in the extensions of its scope that I described in Part II as perversions, or look to replace it by other, non-criminal measures (those described above as subversions) when it is shown not to be effective. But if we instead see the criminal law, as I suggested in Part I we should see it, as an institution which defines a range of public wrongs and provides for those who commit such wrongs to be called to answer for them; if we understand the modest but still significant role that such an institution can play in a liberal republic, we can then see why we should not pervert the criminal law by criminalizing conduct that does not constitute a public wrong, or by requiring citizens to answer, on pain of conviction and punishment, for conduct that does not constitute a presumptive public wrong. We can also then see why we should not subvert it by subjecting those who commit or might commit such public wrongs to non-criminal modes of regulation or control that fail to address them as responsible citizens.[61]

[61] Thanks for helpful comments are due to Alice Ristroph, Andrew Williams, the co-editors of this book, and the participants in workshops at Rutgers and Warwick at which earlier versions of this paper were given.

5

Proactive Forensic Profiling: Proactive Criminalization?

Mireille Hildebrandt

With the aid of your precog mutants, you've boldly and successfully abolished the post-crime punitive system of jails and fines. As we all realize, punishment was never much of a deterrent, and could scarcely have afforded comfort to a victim already dead.[1]

I Introduction

In his short story 'The Minority Report', science fiction author Philip K Dick has one of his main characters suggest that a pre-emptive strike of pre-crime 'punishment' should comfort the victim, claiming that the life of the victim is more important than an individual human subject's ability to develop her moral agency.[2] This pointedly confronts us with the dilemma of the criminalization of future behaviours. If criminal intelligence is capable of predicting who will most probably commit a murder, should we *punish* the culprit before she can perform the act? The reader might object that in such a case the suspect cannot be punished, as punishment cannot refer to future action: so long as a person has not performed the action her behaviour cannot be qualified as wrongful and thus cannot be liable to punitive intervention. The right term would be something like a preventive measure, such as detention, therapy, or any kind of physical intervention that would rule out the criminal act that has

---

[1] Philip K Dick, 'The Minority Report' in *The Collected Stories of Philip K Dick*, vol 4 (New York, NY: Citadel, 2002) 71.

[2] The story was written in 1956; in 2002 a film was released based on the book, directed by Steven Spielberg. On the film see CD Bond, 'Law as Cinematic Apparatus: Image, Textuality, and Representational Anxiety in Spielberg's *Minority Report*' (2006) 37 *Cumberland Law Review* 25. For information on related technologies see <http://www.technovelgy.com/ct/content.asp?Bnum=690>.

been predicted. I invite the reader, however, to imagine that having been categorized as a person that will commit a crime at some point in the future could indeed lead to an accusation of wrongfulness and culpability. Contrary to our present common sense, this wrongfulness would inhere in the fact that a person *will* violate the criminal law, and this future violation would also imply guilt. That we now think this to be nonsensical is no guarantee that epistemic changes triggered by novel computing infrastructures could not instigate an entirely different concept of what it means to punish a person.

In this chapter I will explore the implications of this thought experiment, suggesting that proactive forensic profiling could extend the boundaries of the criminal law in a way that surreptitiously erodes the very meaning of punishment as we understand it today. Such an exercise may sharpen our awareness of the achievements of the legal protection offered at present by the criminal law and confront us with the extent to which we take this protection for granted. Building on findings within the field of profiling practices I will argue that new ways of knowledge construction will challenge the logic of the criminal law. They may counter our expectations, first, that the criminal law responds to past rather than future events, and second, that the criminal law concerns actions rather than biological or behavioural characteristics. Those who prefer to think of the central tenets of criminal law as moral or conventional maxims that are independent of socio-technical infrastructure, could find my argument a tiring exercise. They may not be interested in the technicalities of what has been called 'knowledge discovery in databases' (KDD). However, if (as has been argued by a number of legal scholars) the epistemic shift generated by the digital revolution has serious implications for the meaning of law, this would also concern the meaning of punishment. To understand these implications we need to come to terms with the technologies that trigger them. This chapter thus offers a tentative exploration of the implications of emerging socio-technical infrastructures of knowledge production for the scope of the criminal law.

After a brief discussion of the meaning of terms like criminal and forensic profiling, I undertake an analysis of proactive forensic profiling as producing novel types of knowledge claims that are highly relevant for proactive criminalization. I will argue that these knowledge claims, typical of actuarial justice, are an affordance of the socio-technical infrastructure of profiling technologies. The novelty of KDD relates to its focus on effective prediction *without* the need to understand or explain the patterns it uncovers. This brings in the issue of human autonomy in relation to causal determination and freedom of the will: what does it mean that profiling technologies are capable of 'predicting' our future behaviours? Rejecting both determinacy and *in*determinacy as problematic Cartesian viewpoints,

I embrace the *under*determinacy of human agents as situated, embodied subjects, and investigate how such underdeterminacy relates to profiling and to the boundaries of criminalization in the present legal framework. In Part VIII will argue that the knowledge claims generated by profiling techniques can restrict human freedom if they profile people as *correlated objects*, whereas they can also enlarge human freedom if they allow people to become aware of the profiles they match. People can realize their potential as *correlatable subjects*, capable of resisting the correlations they are presented with. Returning to the main point of this chapter, I will conclude that the issue of whether human agents are treated as correlated objects or as correlatable subjects is not just a matter of moral philosophy, but of engaging in the design of the architecture of proactive forensic profiling.

II   Criminal and Forensic Profiling

Criminal profiling has a relatively long history. It usually refers to the process of inferring the behavioural characteristics of an unknown offender from events related to specific crimes, often (though not always) serious violent crimes such as serial murder or rape.[3] Criminal profiling has been a tool, produced mainly by psychologists, to aid police and justice authorities in their investigation of a crime *that has been committed*. Criminal profiling is, in this sense as part of 'crime investigation' or 'crime analysis', a type of retroactive forensic profiling.[4]

Forensic profiling encompasses both retroactive and proactive profiling. Recently, it has incorporated the use of advanced mathematical techniques that allow sophisticated data processing, for instance, biometric profiling (fingerprints and DNA templates), various types of technologically mediated monitoring and surveillance (CCTV, RFID tracking[5]), and financial profiling to detect money laundering, which is often undertaken by the financial institutions that have a duty to report suspicious transactions. Automated profiling technologies provide what is referred to as 'criminal intelligence', meaning that they provide knowledge and information not related to a particular case, but rather to types of cases or offenders and to trends (patterns) in developments relevant to security and crime prevention. Such profiling produces an actuarial

---

[3]   RN Kocsic, *Criminal Profiling: Principles and Practice* (New Jersey: Humana Press, 2006) 3.

[4]   Z Geradts and P Sommer, *Forensic Profiling, FIDIS deliverable 6.7c* (2008), available at <http://www.fidis.net>, last downloaded on 24 July 2009; O Ribaux *et al*, 'The Contribution of Forensic Sciences to Crime Analysis and Investigation: Forensic Intelligence' (2006) 156 *Forensic Science International* 171.

[5]   CCTV stands for closed-circuit television, RFID stands for radio frequency identification.

type of knowledge, shifting the attention from retroactive to proactive profiling. Within the context of this chapter I will focus on the implications of proactive forensic profiling for the criminalization of *future* behaviours based on present *characteristics* that match proactive forensic profiles. While retroactive forensic profiling refers to the traditional focus of forensic expertise to be used in a court of law, I will broaden the scope of analysis to include all forms of profiling that are used in the context of security: criminal investigation, intelligence, surveillance, and risk analysis. So, while retroactive forensic profiling is restricted to the investigation of a particular crime that has already been committed, proactive forensic profiling targets the less well defined field of potential security threats that may or may not qualify as criminal actions. The fuzzy borders between intelligence for (inter)national security, crime investigation, and criminal intelligence require a broad concept of proactive forensic profiling in order to prevent missing out on pertinent and highly relevant developments in the shadow of crime-related profiling.

III   Proactive Forensic Profiling

A   Organic, human, and computerized pattern recognition

Profiling has been defined as *pattern recognition*. This has been described as a crucial capacity of *all* organisms, allowing them to anticipate events and behaviours in their environment. The idea that pattern recognition is pertinent for autonomous systems has been discussed extensively in the cognitive sciences.[6] Profiling is a discriminate characteristic of life since it allows adaptation in changing circumstances, enabling life forms to anticipate the behaviours of their environment, which is necessary to survive. In fact, the recognition of profiling as a crucial sign of life has introduced the idea of context awareness to the field of artificial intelligence (AI) as a precondition for machine learning.[7]

---

[6] R Franz, 'Herbert Simon: Artificial Intelligence as a Framework for Understanding Intuition' (2003) 24 *Journal of Economic Psychology* 265; E Goldberg, 'The Wisdom Paradox' in HR Moody (ed), *Aging* (Thousand Oaks, Cal: Sage, 2006) 103.

[7] FJ Varela and P Bourgine (eds), *Towards a Practice of Autonomous Systems: Proceedings of the First European Conference on Artificial Life* (Cambridge, Mass: MIT Press, 1992). My own position mostly conforms to that of Varela, rejecting the model of mental representation for human cognition, involving a critique of symbol processing as the model for AI, building on Searle's connectionism and Varela's situated, embodied enaction as more refined tools to explicate cognition. On the need for embodiment see HL Dreyfus, *What Computers Still Can't Do: A Critique of Artificial Reason* (Cambridge, Mass: MIT Press, 1992); D Ihde, *Bodies in Technology* (Minneapolis, Minn: University of Minnesota Press, 2002).

Profiling in this broad sense is not a new phenomenon. People are continuously profiling each other and their social, organizational, and physical environment. They are permanently generalizing behaviours or traits of others in order to avoid the cognitive overload of having to pay attention to each and every aspect of each and every event at all times. Stereotyping, categorizing, and profiling are necessary to build tacit expectations of how others will behave, *and* of how we think that others profile us.[8] In fact, we are always—tacitly—profiling (reading) how others profile (read) us, engaging in *a double anticipation* or *double hermeneutic* that is a precondition for meaningful action.[9] If I have no idea how my actions will be interpreted by others and how others will respond to them, my actions will lose their meaning. One of the hallmarks of the criminal law is that I should know in advance which of my behaviours falls within its scope, so that I can anticipate how others will interpret my actions.

One of the questions raised by proactive forensic profiling practices is how they will affect the ability to engage in this double anticipation, since people may not be aware of how they are being profiled, creating a tension with the principle of legality. Imagine that I behave in a way that is profiled as presenting a high risk for a criminal career in embezzlement, and imagine that displaying such a risk profile is criminalized. If I have no access to knowing which of my behavioural data match such profiles I cannot anticipate how I am being profiled and I cannot seek to change my behaviour to avoid violating the criminal law. From a security perspective this may be seen as a good thing: because I don't know which of my current behaviours 'betrays' my future behaviour I cannot hide them and get away without being recognized as a potential risk.

B   Knowledge discovery in databases and the end of theory

In the case of computer-mediated profiling, the use of mathematical data-mining techniques enables software to detect patterns invisible to the naked human eye. Unexpected correlations between different data *emerge* as a result of data-mining operations, presenting novel insights that can be highly relevant for organizations (like the criminal justice system) that have to survive in a fast-changing environment. What makes profiling such an interesting technology is its capacity to uncover correlations that were not anticipated. The correlations that are confirmed by data mining need not be

---

[8]   F Schauer, *Profiles, Probabilities, and Stereotypes* (Cambridge, Mass: Harvard University Press, 2003).

[9]   M Hildebrandt, BJ Koops, and E De Vries (eds), *Where Idem-Identity Meets Ipse-Identity: Conceptual Explorations, FIDIS deliverable 7.14a* (2008), available at <http://www.fidis.net>, last downloaded 24 July 2009.

hypothesized by the researcher; they are not necessarily the starting point of the investigation: instead, they are often its result.[10] Indeed, profiling can provide hypotheses about future events, while the ongoing process of matching the resulting profiles with new data allows for continuous refinements of these hypotheses. Such hypotheses do not supply causes or reasons, they are merely statistical correlations. Unless further research is done to explain their causal or semantic background, they imply nothing but a stochastic relation. Anderson in fact claims that the construction of theories about the causes or reasons for certain events will soon be a redundant exercise.[11] The speed and reliability of computerized pattern recognition turns the explanation or the justification of behaviours into a difficult and unnecessary undertaking. Their predictive value may *give reason* for specific measures and—in as far as these measures are built into the software—the emerging correlations can even be said to *'cause'* certain interventions. Thus, while the correlations are meaningless in themselves, they will often *acquire* meaning and impact on the decision making of those who use profiling technologies.

If, for example, DNA databanks contained the DNA materials of all citizens charged with a criminal offence, the genetic make-up of the persons involved could be linked with their criminal records. Group profiles could emerge, indicating that specific combinations of genes correlate with specific types of crime (violent, impulsive, calculated, complex, white collar, etc). If a new suspect's DNA is then found to match a high-risk profile of the type of crime she is charged with, this will impact on the case. Note that the group profile contains no information about the reasons for or causes of the crimes that are predicted, but can nonetheless start functioning as a reason, or even cause, for criminal policies. The predictive knowledge produced by these databanks might be used to argue for national databases containing the DNA materials of all citizens, which would allow prediction of criminal careers at an early stage. At some point in the future this could trigger an argument for proactive 'punishment' in the case where a person's DNA matches a high-risk profile for serious crime. Though such proactive criminalization may sound like science fiction, the example of the UK DNA database demonstrates the extent to which national governments are experimenting with infrastructures that afford this type of data mining, notwithstanding the decisions of the

---

[10] B Custers, *The Power of Knowledge: Ethical, Legal, and Technological Aspects of Data Mining and Group Profiling in Epidemiology* (Nijmegen: Wolf Legal Publishers, 2004).

[11] C Anderson, 'The End of Theory: The Data Deluge Makes the Scientific Method Obsolete' (2008) 16 *Wired Magazine* 7.

European Court of Human Rights.[12] Similarly, the introduction of indeterminate measures like 'imprisonment for public protection' (IPP) and 'extended sentence for public protection' (EPP) in the UK's Criminal Justice Act 2003 indicates that we are already on the verge of what some would like to believe is merely science fiction.[13]

One of the problems of profiling is the difficulty of coming to terms with the technical intricacies of the process of data mining.[14] To understand the implications of proactive forensic profiling, however, we must comprehend the logic on which it builds. To understand this I will introduce the concepts of (1) indirect individual profiling,[15] and (2) non-distributive profiling.[16]

Data mining infers patterns from the data of one particular person (individual profiling) or from a large group of people (group profiling). An example of individual profiling is the profiling of keystroke behaviour, which uncovers individual typing patterns that can function like a person's signature. An

---

[12] On 13 February 2009 the website of the UK Home Office stated:

DNA samples obtained for analysis from the collection of DNA at crime scenes and from samples taken from individuals in police custody can be held in the national DNA database. The UK's database is the largest of any country: 5.2% of the UK population is on the database compared with 0.5% in the USA... By the end of 2005 over 3.4 million DNA profiles were held on the database—the profiles of the majority of the known active offender population. (Now archived at <http://webarchive.nationalarchives.gov.uk/20070305103538/http://homeoffice.gov.uk/science-research/using-science/>

In 2008 the European Court of Human Rights ruled that:

the blanket and indiscriminate nature of the powers of retention of the fingerprints, cellular samples and DNA profiles of persons suspected but not convicted of offences, as applied in the case of the present applicants, fails to strike a fair balance between the competing public and private interests... Accordingly, the retention at issue constitutes disproportionate interference with the applicants' right to respect for private life and cannot be regarded as necessary in a democratic society. (*S and Marper v United Kingdom* (2009) 48 EHRR 50, para 125)

Note that the Court is not explicitly against keeping samples of those convicted of offences, and note that the discussion is about DNA samples, which provide much more information than DNA templates. At this moment (11 June 2010) this information has been removed from the website of the Home Office. Even the archived version, kept by the National Archives, has been cleansed.

[13] Criminal Justice Act 2003, ss 225, 226, and 228. Cf P Ramsay, 'The Insecurity State' in M Hildebrandt, A Makinwa, and A Oehmichen (eds), *Controlling Security in a Culture of Fear* (The Hague: Boom, forthcoming).

[14] Profiling involves the construction as well as the application of profiles. Construction takes place via the process of KDD, which consists of five interrelated steps: collection and aggregation of machine-readable data, data mining, interpretation of the results, and application of the profiles to test and refine the profiles found. Construction and application are inextricably bound up. Data mining is the process of running algorithms through a database to uncover hidden patterns. For an overview of the technical process and its social and legal implications, see M Hildebrandt and S Gutwirth (eds), *Profiling the European Citizen: Cross-disciplinary Perspectives* (Dordrecht: Springer, 2008).

[15] D-O Jaquet-Chiffelle, 'Reply: Direct and Indirect Profiling in the Light of Virtual Persons' in Hildebrandt and Gutwirth (ibid) 55–63.

[16] Custers (n 10 above); A Vedder, 'KDD: The Challenge to Individualism' (1999) *Ethics and Information Technology* 275.

example of group profiling would be the profiling of a person's keystroke behaviour in relation to the onset of Parkinson's disease, in order to detect early signs of Parkinson's in people not yet affected by the more serious symptoms.[17] In the case of group profiling the correlations concern a *category* of people and because the correlations are statistical the group profile will often present an average risk that is valid for the group as a whole, but not necessarily for the individual members of the group. The profile is *non-distributive* within the relevant population.[18] This is a well-known problem in epidemiology: though a certain event or feature increases the risk of developing a specific disease in a population, one cannot be sure to what extent this increases the risk for each individual. In law this gap, between statistical averages at the level of a population and their application to an individual case, generates problems of causation. For instance, if an employee sues his employer after contracting lung cancer, the employer could claim that the cancer might well have been caused by the smoking habits of the employee. Applying a group profile to an individual person is called *indirect individual profiling*, because it applies a group profile inferred from other people's data to an individual person. Although a non-distributive profile may not be valid for any individual, it can be tempting to apply it in this way.

If non-distributive group profiles are used in a retroactive forensic context, further inquiry should decide whether an individual in fact deserves the status of suspect or—in the case of a trial—offender. Proactive forensic profiling involves the construction of group profiles that target a refined categorization of citizens in order to detect potential criminals, terrorists, or illegal immigrants. For instance, surveillance measures could be taken that monitor unemployed people, black persons, males of Arabic descent, or people living in specific neighbourhoods, because statistics indicate that their chances of becoming involved in criminal behaviour are significantly higher than other categories of citizen. Again, further inquiry is needed before acting upon the statistics, and the literature on racial profiling confirms that categorization can easily turn into stigmatization, which can 'normalize' people into the types of behaviour

---

[17] PC Cattin, *Biometric Authentication System Using Human Gait* (2002) 104, PhD thesis available at <http://e-collection.ethbib.ethz.ch/eserv/eth:25753/eth-25753-02.pdf>, last downloaded 24 July 2009.

[18] An example of a distributive group profile is the category of bachelors, who all share the characteristic of not being married (tautological or analytical group profiles). Another example of a distributive profile is the category of people who all have the same chance of contracting a specific disease. This must not be confused with a group profile that indicates the average probability of members of the group contracting a specific disease; though on average the chance may be 56 per cent, the chance will differ for different members. This means that the group profile is non-distributive.

that fits the profiles they match. Harcourt provides an extended argument of how such profiling generates a bias in both policing and sentencing.[19]

IV   Actuarial Justice as an Affordance of Profiling Technologies

Profiling seems to 'afford' a criminal justice system that holds citizens responsible for displaying characteristics that match criminal profiles. To argue my point I will first discuss the concept of 'affordance', which is crucial here, since it is capable of bridging the gap between technological infrastructures and human action.

The term 'affordance' (as a noun) was coined by James Gibson.[20] He defines an affordance in terms of the reciprocity between an organism and an environment:[21]

The affordances of the environment are what it offers the animal, what it provides or furnishes, either for good or ill . . . [By this I mean] something that refers to both the environment and the animal in a way that no existing term does. It implies the complementarity of the animal and the environment.

An affordance relates to the fact that technologies *afford* certain behaviours that would otherwise have been impossible, or *do not afford* certain behaviours that were available before the technology was in place. In other work I have called this the constitutive and regulative normativity of technologies.[22] For instance, the steam engine 'afforded' the development of the railway system, allowing people to move from one place to another in less time, creating a variety of behaviours that were simply not possible without the railway

---

[19] BE Harcourt, *Against Prediction: Profiling, Policing, and Punishing in an Actuarial Age* (Chicago, Ill: University of Chicago Press, 2006) makes a rather technical argument, partly based on law and economics, that (1) racial profiling—in the sense of targeting minorities that are calculated as likely to commit more crimes—does not take into account the comparative elasticity of the choices made by those targeted and those not targeted, meaning that the statistics are distorted and do not prove what they claim to prove; (2) targeting subgroups that are calculated to commit more offences leads to disproportionate policing and detention of such subgroups, compared to the distribution of offending in the entire population, and that this produces the social cost of self-fulfilling effects; and (3) using actuarial models to target minorities that are calculated to offend more often reshapes our conception of justice, shifting from individual desert to actuarial risk assessment.

[20] J Gibson, *The Ecological Approach to Visual Perception* (Hillsdale, NJ: Lawrence Erlbaum Associates, 1986) ch 8.   [21] Ibid, 27.

[22] M Hildebrandt, 'Legal and Technological Normativity: More (and Less) than Twin Sisters' (2008) 12 *TECHNÉ* 169; M Hildebrandt, 'Ambient Intelligence, Criminal Liability and Democracy' (2008) 2 *Criminal Law and Philosophy* 163.

system, and thereby changing our sense of time and space. A speed bump, on the other hand, does *not* afford speeding, since speeding over the bump will seriously damage one's car. This is not to say that technologies *cause* these behaviours, but rather that they constitute or regulate them. In general terms a technology may trigger one behaviour rather than another.[23] More precisely, a behaviour may be an affordance of a technology, as it is made possible by that technology.

The concept of affordance implies a relative and relational understanding of both the human person and technological devices. First, whatever is an affordance for one organism, need not be an affordance for another: the play of light that allows visual perception is not an affordance for a bat, but it is for us; the play of sound that allows perception by means of echo is not an affordance for us, but it is for a bat.[24] Second, whatever is an affordance of one type of technology, for instance the technology of the written or printed script,[25] need not be an affordance of another type of technology, like the digital.[26] The added value of the concept of affordance is that it bridges, or rather leaves aside, the Cartesian division of reality into a material (objective) and a mental (subjective) world. Instead of thinking in terms of deterministic physical physics and voluntaristic psychological mental states, it understands the relationship between an organism and its environment in terms of what Gibson calls ecological physics, pinpointing the fact that the properties of an object are to be measured relative to an observer (an organism):[27]

An important fact about the affordances of the environment is that they are in a sense objective, real, and physical, unlike values and meanings, which are often supposed to be subjective, phenomenal, and mental. But, actually, an affordance is neither an objective property nor a subjective property: or it is both if you like. An affordance cuts across the dichotomy of subjective–objective and helps us to understand its inadequacy. It is equally a fact of the environment and a fact of behavior. It is both physical and psychical, yet neither. An affordance points both ways, to the environment and to the observer.

Gibson relates his concept to earlier concepts, like Kurt Lewin's concept of *Aufforderungscharakter*, and suggests that an environment or an object—whether natural or artifical—basically invites certain kinds of behaviour and inhibits others. Spectacles invite the person who needs them to look through them,

---

[23] P Lévy, *Les Technologies de l'Intelligence: L'Avenir de la Pensée à l'Ère Informatique* (Paris: La Découverte, 1990).

[24] T Nagel, 'What is It Like to be a Bat?' (1974) 83 *Philosophical Review* 435.

[25] J Goody and I Watt, 'The Consequences of Literacy' (1963) 5 *Comparative Studies in Society and History* 304; W Ong, *Orality and Literacy: The Technologizing of the Word* (New York, NY: Methuen, 1982); E Eisenstein, *The Printing Revolution in Early Modern Europe*, 2nd edn (Cambridge: Cambridge University Press, 2005).   [26] Lévy (n 23 above).

[27] Gibson (n 20 above) 129.

affording her the pleasure of restored vision. A speed bump invites slow driving; its affordance is a reduction of speeding. A green traffic light invites one
onto the street, a red one inhibits crossing. One could say that the coordination and regulation of safe driving at a public crossroads is an affordance of
traffic lights (and other socio-technical constructs).[28] The fact that technologies have certain affordances for a human person, while technological infrastructures have certain affordances for human society, explains the normative
impact of technologies (not to be confused with the moral evaluation of such
an impact). As Ihde contends: 'If we humans "invent" technologies; then
reciprocally, our technologies re-shape our lifeworlds and thus invent us within
these worlds as well.'[29] Technologies codetermine our behaviour patterns.

Profiling technologies afford the visibility of patterns not visible to the
naked human eye. They also afford a more precise calculation of risks and
threats to public safety, something not available to the computing powers of
the human brain. I am not suggesting that profiling technologies can predict
the future in any great detail and I do not intend to denounce the human
capacity to imagine (and thus cocreate) the future. I am merely establishing
the fact that computer-mediated actuarial techniques allow an unprecedented
calculation of risk. My point is modest but nonetheless pertinent: proactive
forensic profiling affords proactive criminalization.

A sidestep may illustrate this point. Felix Stalder has described privacy as an
affordance of the printing press.[30] He convincingly argues that the proliferation of printed texts, especially the proliferation of identical texts (multiple
copies of the same book), facilitated the move from reading in public and
aloud, to private and silent reading. According to Stalder, the possibility of
private ownership of relatively large collections of books 'triggered' the development of privacy as we understand it today. He raises the question whether
the digital age has a similar affordance, or—on the contrary—inhibits or even
prohibits the opacity of personal identity that was generated by the printing
press.

The example of privacy demonstrates the urgency of rethinking the relationship between technological infrastructures and legal tenets. Many privacy
advocates have declared the 'end of privacy', due to the increasing and often
invisible visibility created by data recording and data processing. Legal scholars

---

[28] These constructs (traffic lights, speed bumps, demarcations on the street, road signs) are
devices that embody legal and social norms: inviting/enforcing or inhibiting/precluding certain
types of behaviour.

[29] D Ihde, *Ironic Technics* (Copenhagen: Automatic Press VIP, 2008) vi.

[30] Though he does not use the term 'affordance': F Stalder, 'The Failure of Privacy Enhancing
Technologies (PETs) and the Voiding of Privacy' (2002) 7 *Sociological Research Online* 2, section 2,
available at <http://www.socresonline.org.uk/7/2/stalder.html>, last downloaded 24 July 2009.

like Lessig have emphasized the enormous impact of digital technologies on the legal protection of privacy, fair use in intellectual property, and freedom of speech, arguing that technologies are competing with legal instruments in the regulation of social life.[31] Katsh and Collins and Skover, in turn, have described how modern law depends on the printing press, envisioning vast changes in the legal landscape, for instance with regard to the legal force of precedent, with the onset of electronic media.[32] As I have argued elsewhere, to sustain the practice of privacy we may have to design the affordance into the technological infrastructure that could otherwise erase our privacy.[33]

V   Actuarial Prediction and Human Autonomy

The problem of proactive forensic profiling could be that in order to aid justice authorities in providing security, the legislature or even the courts could resort to a type of criminalization that does not concern intentionally or culpably wrongful actions, but behaviours that are indicative of a certain risk to society or parts thereof. Inspired by 'The Minority Report', I will describe this as proactive punishment.[34] Within criminology the tendency to criminalize behaviours that are indicative of risk rather than those that have actually caused harm has been termed actuarial justice.[35] The term 'actuarial' is especially pertinent for our subject because it relates to the mathematical models used by insurance companies. Insurance is supposed to spread individual risk by turning it into a population risk (in the statistical sense of the word), thus distributing the population's risk evenly over the entire population (while rewarding the insurance company for the risk it takes). Insurance companies are thus assumed to provide *security* when *safety* is lost: we might not be safe from natural disaster or burglary but we are secure in being compensated in monetary terms. Criminal justice systems may be tempted to opt for a similar anticipation of risk: since we are never sure who will offend, we target those that are calculated to present the biggest risk of becoming offenders, thus presumably reducing the risk that they will actually cause harm.

[31] L Lessig, *Code and Other Laws of Cyberspace* (New York, NY: Basic Books, 1999).
[32] ME Katsh, *The Electronic Media and the Transformation of Law* (Oxford: Oxford University Press, 1989) and *Law in a Digital World* (Oxford: Oxford University Press 1995); RKL Collins and DM Skover, 'Paratexts' (1992) 44 *Stanford Law Review* 509.
[33] M Hildebrandt, 'A Vision of Ambient Law' in R Brownsword and K Yeun (eds), *Regulating Technologies* (Oxford: Hart, 208) 175.
[34] Dick (n 1 above), though the story does not speak of proactive punishment, but of pre-crime punitive detention.
[35] M Feeley and J Simon, 'Actuarial Justice: The Emerging New Criminal Law' in D Nelken (ed), *Futures of Criminology* (London: Sage, 1994) 173.

The actuarial tendencies in contemporary criminal justice systems manifest themselves in targeted surveillance and perhaps in statutory or tacit sentencing policies.[36] However, the possibility of calculating future risks of criminal behaviours could eventually impact on criminalization: if the punishment of behaviour that matched proactive forensic profiles would actually reduce the harm caused, a utilitarian approach could justify the criminalization of such behaviour. Imagine, for instance, that the characteristics summed up in Hare's checklist of psychopathology are calculated to correlate with an increased risk of violent criminal behaviour.[37] I suggest that we should face up to the possibility of a future legislator proactively criminalizing behaviour that matches these characteristics, so as to 'punish' the onset of criminal behaviour instead of waiting for more serious harm to occur, even if this goes against all of our present moral intuitions. The emerging technological infrastructure of tomorrow's society seems to afford a further—perhaps non-moral—intuition, potentially reducing individual behaviour to an instance of transpersonal patterns. Over and against the Cartesian subject that is constituted on the basis of independent rational deliberation, profiling technologies disclose the extent to which our behaviour correlates with that of others.[38] They unveil a heteronomous subject rather than the autonomous agent we like to think we are. To resist the knowledge claims of profiling technologies we may have to move beyond moral grounds that build on a voluntarist conception of the human subject.

Insofar as proactive forensic profiling builds on the categorization of citizens to detect future criminal behaviour, it seems to contradict the logic of the criminal law. Criminal justice—today—is a response to past events, requiring an action that precedes punishment. If we agree with Duff that punishment aims to communicate censure with regard to a crime that has been committed,[39] proactive punishment raises the issue of whether punishment makes sense as communicating censure of future criminal behaviour. Today, the criminal trial affords holding a person accountable for harm caused, reinforcing the normative authority of the legal norm that this person violated; actually this already connects past (the crime), present (the punishment), and future (the normative

---

[36] Harcourt (n 19 above).

[37] R Hare, *The Psychopathy Checklist—Revised*, 2nd edn (Toronto: Multihealth Systems, 2003); I Zinger and AE Forth, 'Psychopathy and Canadian Criminal Proceedings: The Potential for Human Rights Abuses' (1998) 40 *Canadian Journal of Criminology* 237.

[38] W Schreurs and M Hildebrandt, '*Cogitas Ergo Sum*: The Role of Data Protection Law and Non-Discrimination Law in Group Profiling in the Private Sphere' in Hildebrandt and Gutwirth (n 14 above).

[39] RA Duff, *Punishment, Communication, and Community* (Oxford: Oxford University Press, 2001).

force of the law).[40] In this sense punishment is always proactive, because it aims to initiate a learning process with those punished (special prevention) as well as with those who share jurisdiction (general prevention). In this chapter, however, I have been referring to proactive punishment as a punitive intervention before harm is caused, or substantive legal norms are violated, based on actuarial calculations that imply a high risk of such harm and/or violation. Could such proactive punishment be a more effective way of communicating censure of future behaviours? This is an interesting question that confronts us with the meaning of censure. If censure means simply ruling out future behaviour, for instance by detaining a person, the aspect of communication is lost, since communication implies a measure of reciprocity. If communicating censure means that a person is addressed as an agent who can act in various ways, appealing to her *not* to act in a way that violates the criminal law, then proactive punishment makes no sense. This is not an appeal to a person's agency but a straightforward restriction of her actions.

This touches on issues of freedom, causality, voluntarism, determinism, and compatibilism which are central to the issue of criminalization. If we are not free to act as we wish—within certain constraints—criminalization makes no sense. Adherents to determinism and especially adherents to compatibilism tend to refute this position.[41] They basically claim that every event—including our moral intuition—is causally determined. If this is so then acting on knowledge about future events is itself determined: it cannot make a difference because there was no other way to act, and so the assumption that we have a measure of freedom does not matter for the criminal law. Of course, compatibilism runs amok where it suggests that having knowledge of how we are being determined would suddenly create the freedom it denies.[42] Acting on such knowledge cannot be more than being caused by specific brain states (that have been caused by a great many other factors), thus adding to the chain of causally related events.

The problem with voluntarism is that it separates a realm of causally related material events (the Cartesian *res extensa*) from a realm of mental acts that are free from causal influences (the Cartesian *res cogitans*), though they may have a

---

[40] M Hildebrandt, 'Trial and "Fair Trial": From Peer to Subject to Citizen' in RA Duff *et al* (eds), *The Trial on Trial (2): Judgment and Calling to Account* (Oxford: Hart, 2006) 15.

[41] For example, S Smilansky, 'Determinism and Prepunishment: the Radical Nature of Compatibilism' (2007) 67 *Analysis* 347.

[42] This is why Morse's elegant rendering of compatibilism still does not convince me. He seems to suggest that determinism at the micro-level of brain states does not challenge the law's common sense, meaning that we have a measure of freedom when engaging in practical reason: SJ Morse, 'Determinism and the Death of Folk Psychology: Two Challenges to Responsibility from Neuroscience' (2008) 9 *Minnesota Journal of Law Science and Technology* 1.

causal impact on the material world.[43] Whereas determinism seems to follow this Cartesian framework after having discarded the realm of the *res cogitans*, voluntarism seems to endorse the idea of a disembodied, ahistorical Cartesian *ego*. Following the extensive critique of the Cartesian dichotomy by authors who take a relational, embodied, and situated view of the subject,[44] I would argue that as a human agent I *am* a body (*Leib*) and *have* a body (*Körper*) thrown into an *Umwelt* and a *Welt* that *shape* and *signify* me, while I also *shape* and *signify* them. Autonomy, in this perspective, is always relative and relational. This moves us from a monopolistic usage of the language of causality to the language of mutual constitution, which of course does not preclude the attribution of causality. This position also means that knowledge about future events can actually impact on those events, creating a measure of freedom that is absent if we cannot anticipate what may probably or will certainly happen. It brings the kind of knowledge produced by profiling software back into the realm of knowledge that can create freedom, without suggesting that it *necessarily* creates freedom. It also directs our attention to the issue of *whose* freedom is enlarged: that of the profiler or that of the profiled (or both)? If the profiled person becomes aware of how she is being profiled, she can engage the double anticipation mentioned above. If she remains in the dark about how forensic profiles may impact on her life, she is in chains.

VI   Criteria for Criminalization in the Present Legal Framework

In a constitutional democracy criminalization does two things: (1) it constitutes the competence to punish (*ius puniendi*), and (2) it restricts this competence to what has in fact been criminalized (*lex certa*). Criminalization thus both *constitutes* and *limits* the competence to punish; it turns the contingent *power* to punish (which may be unlimited) into a legal *competence* (which is conditional). This provides tools to a government to exercise the *ius puniendi*, while providing protection to citizens to contest the application of the criminal law in a court of law. This means that an important criterion for criminalization is that it should indeed constitute the competence to punish in a manner that restricts arbitrary or unlimited exercise of the *ius puniendi*. This

---

[43] I use the term 'Cartesian' to depict a way of thinking that is usually traced back to Descartes, without claiming that this is an accurate description of Descartes' own position.

[44] For example, FJ Varela, E Thompson, and E Rosch, *The Embodied Mind: Cognitive Science and Human Experience* (Cambridge, Mass: MIT Press, 1991); NK Hayles, *How We Became Posthuman: Virtual Bodies in Cybernetics, Literature, and Informatics* (Chicago, Ill: University of Chicago Press, 1999).

criterion relates to the idea of moderate government within political theory; as a condition for criminalization it is part of the framework of constitutional democracy as a historical artefact (and is not a logical or universal characteristic of punitive intervention).[45]

Let us now see how criminalization in fact restricts the competence to punish. First, it allows a citizen to claim that she did not perform the criminal action (*actus reus*). Second, it allows a citizen to argue that the incriminated behaviour does not fall within the scope of a particular criminal act, meaning that even if her behaviour were undesirable or morally wrong she cannot be punished for it under the principle of legality. This protective dimension of criminalization is then extended by the requirements of fault, wrongfulness, and culpability (*mens rea*). Whereas the wrongfulness of an act relates to the act and not to the person who committed the act, culpability concerns only the offender. If an action falls within the scope of a specific offence, the absence of wrongfulness or culpability can lead to the action not being punishable after all. Thus these requirements further restrict the application of the criminal law and, as conditions for punishment, they provide further protection to citizens.[46]

This legal framework was introduced by Abelard in his *Ethics* or *Scito te ipsum* in the twelfth century,[47] writing against the background of old Germanic legal traditions that were more in tune with the 'grammar' of oral cultures. His ideas went against the grain of the old Germanic laws, especially as regards the emphasis he put on intention. However, as the hallmark of sin in the context of Christian doctrine, intention has been a necessary condition for punishment ever since Gratian and the canonists followed Abelard's emphasis on the subjective dimension of a crime.[48] Nevertheless, according to Abelard, intention in itself cannot be sufficient cause for punishment. Suggesting that only

---

[45] I am following the relational conception of law, advocated by 't Hart and Foqué. Building on Montesquieu and Beccaria, the main point is that crime control and due process are not conceptualized as competing objectives, but as two sides of the same coin. It means that any legal competence that is attributed must incorporate the possibility of its exercise being contested: R Foqué and AC 't Hart, *Instrumentaliteit en Rechtsbescherming* (Arnhem: Gouda Quint, 1990).

[46] In civil law systems a person must be charged with having performed an *action*, describing in detail which behaviour is at stake. A defendant can argue that she did not perform this action (a defence against the evidence provided by the prosecution) or she can claim that it does not fall within the scope of the particular criminal offence that was charged (a defence against the qualification attributed by the prosecution). After the charge is found proven and the behaviour qualified as an offence, the defendant can claim that her behaviour was nevertheless not wrongful, constituting a defence of justification. After this the defendant can argue that she cannot be blamed, a defence of non-culpability.

[47] P Abelard, DE Luscombe (ed), *Peter Abelard's Ethics* (Oxford: Clarendon Press, 1974).

[48] HJ Berman, *Law and Revolution: The Formation of the Western Legal Tradition* (Cambridge, Mass: Harvard University Press, 1983) 187.

God can see into a man's mind, Abelard answered the question 'Why works of sin are punished rather than sin itself?'[49] by stating that 'men do not judge the hidden, but the apparent, nor do they consider the guilt of a fault so much as the performance of a deed'.[50] This sounds very much like the law of an oral culture, which depends on face-to-face communication and direct observation. However, while in oral cultures the act that warrants punitive intervention is a sufficient condition for revenge, Abelard introduces an extra condition for the use of the *ius puniendi*, namely the mental state of the offender, restricting the scope of the criminal law in comparison to that of punitive intervention between peers. In addition, he further restricts the *ius puniendi* by suggesting that intention can only be established by looking at the performance of the deed, since we cannot look inside a person's mind.[51]

The prominence of intention or—more generally—*mens rea* as a precondition of punishment can be related to the development of a new socio-technical infrastructure of information and communication in the late Middle Ages. The technology of the script introduced a distantiation and a delay that affords private reflection in a novel manner, paving the way for private deliberation and the constitution of conscious intention as something that precedes the performance of a deed. In other words, the separation of an action from the intention to act may well be an affordance of writing, reinforced by the printing press. This separation is connected to the fact that intentions are often attributed after the fact, 'read' into the act, thus initiating the anticipation of which intentions will be attributed to the performance of which acts. It may be this anticipation that—in the end—triggers conscious intention as something that comes in before the act and is capable of constraining action. Though spoken language already initiates this loop of reflection on past actions, enabling 'pre-flection' on future acts, the script and the printing press facilitate a much more extended separation of action, reflection, and intention. Thus, while the introduction of intention as a precondition of punishment fits the age of the scribe, more detailed elaborations on *mens rea* awaited the age of the printed text. In fact, we may expect the printing press to invite a further constitution and exploration of the self as a domain of linear sequential reasoning typical of the written text. If all this makes sense, then we should also expect the transformation of the socio-technical infrastructures of communication and information to afford novel ways of defining what counts as an object of criminalization.

---

[49] Abelard (n 47 above), 39.   [50] Ibid, 41.

[51] Note that this further restriction is not followed by the canonists. Their emphasis on individual intention eventually leads to the use of torture to force those under suspicion to disclose what is on their mind (confession). See Berman (n 48 above).

VII   Proactive 'Punishment', Correlated Objects, and Correlatable Subjects

If profiling technologies are a precondition of the criminalization of behaviour that merely matches criminal profiles, we need to anticipate how such criminalization would impact on contemporary conditions for criminalization, and to what extent this would go against the grain of what we hold to be constitutive for criminalization in a constitutional democracy. Criminalization of future behaviour seems to violate the requirement of an action, while criminalization of specific biological or behavioural characteristics that match high-risk profiles seems also to violate the requirement of culpability. Equally, it is difficult to understand how the fact that one's machine-readable characteristics match high-risk criminal profiles implicates wrongfulness. What is wrongful about being the sort of person that might develop into an offender? Should we be called to account for not having reconstructed our self into a person with more promising machine-readable characteristics?

Given the recognition that constitutional democracy is a historical artefact, we can acknowledge the constitutive role of the technological infrastructure of the written and printed word in the architecture of the rule of law as the framework of modern democracies. This implies that, insofar as specific conditions of criminalization emerged as affordances of writing and the printing press, we must confront the question of the extent to which proactive forensic profiling affords similar conditions. This will depend on the design of the technology and how it is woven into the social fabric of the collective it coconstitutes and coregulates. On this basis I will now analyse which common-sense assumptions are challenged by proactive forensic profiling and whether this can either undermine or further develop the protective dimension inherent in the type of criminalization afforded by the socio-technical infrastructure of the printing press.

In what follows I will first discuss how the use of non-distributive group profiles to target individuals with proactive punishment if their data match a criminal profile would overdetermine their future behaviour, turning human subjects into *correlated objects*. In this case a citizen is subjected to correlations between her data shadow and patterns detected in large databases. I will argue that even if profiling technologies afford such proactive interventions, we should resist them, because they build on two presumptions: that future behaviour is entirely determined by the past, and that we should act on the results of actuarial technologies that do not even claim to predict the future. Second, I will discuss how the use of profiling technologies challenges the epistemology of the self-transparent sovereign subject, triggering awareness of the relational and interdependent nature of human agency by demonstrating the extent to which we are all *correlatable subjects*. Profiling practices confront a person with the fact that her data shadow can be correlated in numerous ways, depending on which data are recorded, which database was used, and which algorithms were used to mine the data. Profiling then becomes a subversive technique, potentially disclosing uncomfortable knowledge about how our behaviour correlates with behaviour patterns we do not want to be associated with. This could allow us to anticipate which criminal profiles match our behaviour, allowing us to mend our ways or contest the application of such profiles in a court of law. This argument depends on a measure of visibility: if I am not aware of the profiles until I am seized for proactive punishment there is no way I can anticipate how my behaviour will be interpreted.

A   The human subject as a correlated object

Proactive forensic profiling could develop into a technique that makes visible what is at present invisible to the naked human eye, for instance by disclosing correlations between keystroke behaviours, behaviours of the human brain, psychopathology, and specific types of criminal career. Though this may sound fantastic, funding is being invested in this type of research, with a view to creating a pathway towards refined group profiling that connects biometric behavioural profiling, sophisticated profiling of the electromagnetic wave patterns of the brain in action, data mining of clinical psychological and psychiatric databases, and data mining of the aggregated records of crime investigation. The complexity involved would be an insurmountable obstacle to further analysis by the human mind, but the exponential increase in computing power of interconnected computer systems allows algorithms to take into account an unprecedented amount of correlatable variables.

Imagine that your own keystroke behaviour matches a profile that is indicative of repressed impulsive conduct that has a high chance of erupting at some point into a totally 'unexpected' violent attack on a close friend.[52] Imagine that your keystroke behaviour is found to match a profile that is indicative of a manipulative personality with an inclination to persistent deception that most often develops into fraudulent and corrupt behaviour. Let us assume that the phrase 'is indicative of' means that 94 per cent of the individuals with your type of keystroke behaviour have been convicted for the crimes that correlate with the profile. One can easily imagine that such statistics would warrant

---

[52] Unexpected by yourself and your friend(s), but 'expected' by profiling technologies that compare your brain states to those of other people who suddenly—and perhaps secretly—kill another person (either a close friend or a complete stranger).

extensive monitoring of your behaviour, in order to prevent you from actually committing these crimes. This would be open to a number of objections, but I will not deal with them all here, as my question is the more limited one of whether such statistics could ever legitimate proactive punishment, violating contemporary criteria for criminalization.

Could the potential victims of your future behaviour claim that the state is obligated to impose some form of proactive punishment? Could one argue that you should be punished for negligence, since your characteristics display a dangerousness you should have avoided? Is it possible to change your behavioural biometrics and other biological features? Or must we rearticulate the meaning of punishment and stop arguing that it involves an appeal to human agency, acknowledging that punishment is merely an instrument to protect society from the potentially dangerous behaviour of its members? Does the emerging socio-technical architecture demonstrate that the idea of censure is an outdated attempt to legitimize a practice that follows its own utilitarian logic anyway—taking sides perhaps with Foucault, Deleuze, and Cohen against the Enlightenment discourse on the emancipatory function of the criminal law that somehow hides the micro-physics of an emerging society of control?[53]

Two objections can be raised against the idea that the proliferation of actuarial techniques nourished by profiling technologies could *legitimate* proactive punishment. Taken together these objections can be articulated as the fact that proactive punishment overdetermines the human subject, mistaking her for a stable object. In using the verb 'overdetermines' I mean two things. First, proactive punishment would presume that human behaviour is causally determined in a mechanical way, leaving no room for indeterminate spontaneous discontinuities. Proactive punishment would imply that profiling technologies would disclose a kind of transparency of human agents that is in line with Cartesian dreams of a sovereign subject having unmediated access to itself, though this time the transparency concerns other selves. It would deny the unpredictability of creative invention, of what Deleuze and Lévy have called actualization,[54] of what Arendt has called natality, and of what Butler called the constitutive opacity of the self.[55] It would take for granted that today's

[53] M Foucault, *Discipline and Punish: The Birth of the Prison* (New York, NY: Random House, 1975); G Deleuze, 'Postscript on the Societies of Control' (1992) 59 *October* 3; S Cohen, *Visions of Social Control* (Cambridge: Polity Press, 1985).

[54] G Deleuze, *Difference and Repetition* (New York, NY: Continuum, 2005); P Lévy, 'Sur les Chemins du Virtuel' (1997), available at <http://hypermedia.univ-paris8.fr/pierre/virtuel/virt0.htm>, last downloaded 24 July 2009; *Becoming Virtual: Reality in the Digital Age* (New York, NY: Plenum Trade, 1998).

[55] H Arendt, *The Human Condition* (Chicago, Ill: University of Chicago Press, 1958); J Butler, *Giving an Account of Oneself* (New York, NY: Fordham University Press, 2005).

correlations will hold in the future. In that sense, I contend, proactive punishment would be based on a serious misunderstanding of the nature of profiling technologies. Proactive forensic profiling generates profiles of correlated subjects, but these fixed correlated subjects are snapshots. They are objectifications that will change as time goes by. They depend on what events have been translated in which ways into machine-readable data, on how they have been aggregated, on which databases have been fused, what algorithms have been used, and how the resulting patterns have been interpreted and applied. Other data, other aggregates, other algorithms, and other interpretations will make a difference to how a person is correlated. This is not to say that our knowledge is finite even though reality is fully determined, which would presume the possibility of a partition between reality and knowledge of reality (dividing tasks between ontological and epistemological undertakings). It is rather to acknowledge a fatal and inherent element of discontinuity that implies a measure of indeterminacy that is best captured in the idea that the coconstitution of an individual and her environment is *under*determined. The concept of underdeterminacy builds on reality as a matter of becoming instead of being, in the static sense of the word, on the ephemeral nature of reality as something we cannot define or presume, as something that happens to us as we fit in.

Second, in saying that proactive punishment overdetermines the human subject, I mean that proactive punishment could generate what it presumes, actively determining people to behave in certain ways, because alternatives would simply be ruled out. In particular, if a person is not aware of how she is being profiled, she cannot anticipate or contest the way she has been correlated. In being treated *as if* she has the characteristics that are part of the non-distributive group profile she matches, she might end up being normalized into the profile—a phenomenon not unlike Merton's self-fulfilling prophecy and Foucault's discourse on the normalizing powers of disciplinary practices.[56] In a discussion of the use of profiling technologies for commercial purposes Lessig notes:[57]

When the system seems to know what you want better and earlier than you do, how can you know where these desires really come from?...Profiles will begin to normalise the population from which the norm is drawn. The observing will affect the observed. The system watches what you do; it fits you into a pattern; the pattern is then fed back to you in the form of options set by the pattern; the options reinforce the patterns; the cycle begins again.

---

[56] Robert Merton's self-fulfilling prophecy builds on the so-called Thomas Theorem ('if men define situations as real, they are real in their consequences'): RK Merton, 'The Thomas Theorem and the Matthew Effect' (1995) 74 *Social Forces* 379–424; Foucault (n 53 above).

[57] *Code* (n 31 above) 154.

Treating a person on the basis of a particular stereotype, categorization, or profile implies that you do not know how she would have acted if treated otherwise. This goes for everyday profiling (stereotyping), but it also goes for proactive punishment. In preventing people from acting dangerously, proactive punishment would also prevent them from developing their agency. The problem is not even that the state sometimes interferes with individual freedom in order to protect the individual freedom of others. This protection, based on the monopoly of violence, is constitutive for the modern state. The problem is the extent to which proactive punishment would interfere with the construction of human agency. The point is not that the state should refrain from punishment, but the question is how we should moderate its *ius puniendi*. Giving in to proactive punishment would introduce an unbounded type of criminalization that is ready to intervene any time the stochastics predict a match with a high-risk profile. The type of criminalization afforded by proactive forensic profiling consists not only of the criminalization of a person's match with specific profiles. Since these profiles will be continuously updated, the law could simply refer to any profile that describes a high risk of violent, fraudulent, corrupt, or other behaviour that is deemed to violate the current societal order. It may be similar in many ways to regulatory offences that do not cause harm, but are thought to create a risk for the administrative framework of the modern welfare and/or security state. One of the problems of this type of criminalization is the rigidity of the statutory norms that try to anticipate a risk within fixed parameters. Other than these regulatory offences, the criminalization of future behaviour based on proactive profiling could refer to parameters determined dynamically by the profiles as they are inferred. Though this may be more effective than using fixed parameters, legal certainty and the principle of legality seem to lose their meaning here.

B   The human subject as a correlatable human

In taking seriously the notion of an affordance, we must refrain from suggesting that proactive forensic profiling will necessarily *cause* a policy of proactive punishment. Though the socio-technical infrastructure of criminal intelligence may come to afford such punishment, its actualization will depend on many other factors. One of these is that profiling affords us the perception of the human subject as a correlatable human,[58] rather than as a correlated

---

[58] M Hildebrandt, 'Profiles and Correlatable Humans' in N Stehr (ed), *Who Owns Knowledge? Knowledge and the Law* (New Brunswick, NJ: Transaction Books, 2008) 265; S Gutwirth and P De Hert, 'Regulating Profiling in a Democratic Constitutional State' in Hildebrandt and Gutwirth, (n 14 above) 271.

object. While the latter could invite a policy of proactive punishment, treating a person as a correlatable human invites the idea of an underdetermined future; of treating a person as if she can be 'the kind of person who will not commit murder even if a profile she matches suggests otherwise'. The mere fact that—as indicated above—a person's data shadow can be correlated in numerous ways, depending on how and which behaviours and events are translated into machine-readable data and profiles, presents us with a plurality of potentially correlated objects. These different correlated objects will probably contradict each other, presenting us with radically different 'kinds' of person, depending on alternative group profiles that can be inferred and applied to the targeted individual. I am not suggesting that anything goes here or that any type of profile can be inferred based on the same events being translated into machine-readable data. I am merely proposing that a diversity of patterns can be read into the raw materials of data mining, and that this diversity coconstitutes our freedom. It compares to what Ihde has called the *multistability* of technologies,[59] meaning that a technology's affordances are always multiple, and the way that they end up being integrated into our way of life depends on how we engage with them. In a deterministic understanding of reality this engagement is also determined—of course—but if we follow the perspective of an *under*determined, coconstituted reality it matters how we engage with our technologies and we should make the effort to figure out which is 'the difference that makes a difference'.

The criminalization of future behaviour based on the machine-readable behavioural and biological characteristics of a person is problematic because it would turn human subjects into correlated objects, denying their status as correlatable humans, thus also negating their freedom. It suggests that, after being found to correlate with a high-risk profile for—for instance—murder, a person can be treated as if she will indeed become a murderer. The correlation is petrified and used as a stamp to qualify a person as fitting the relevant group profile. Though the profile only relates to correlations between data translating past events, it would be used to determine the future—both by predicting the future as if it were entirely determined, and by actually deciding on the future of the person that would be punished.

If, on the other hand, we could find ways of communicating to a person what types of profile match her behaviour or characteristics, providing her with a range of correlated objects that indicate how she fits different group profiles, this could actually enlarge her freedom to behave in one way or another. In becoming aware of the fact that her behaviour matches profiles of corruption, she might come to look in a set of mirrors that allow her to

---

[59] *Bodies in Technology* (n 7 above).

anticipate how others profile her. If she is aware of the fact that actually engaging in corruption will meet with censure in the form of punishment, then these mirrors allow her to anticipate the censure, inviting her to mend her ways, or to remonstrate. She could remonstrate against her behavioural characteristics being profiled as indicative of future corruption, seeking correlations with other profiles, or she could remonstrate against the fact that these profiles qualify certain future behaviours as corruption: challenging whether what she is expected to do should 'count' as corruption. Finding ways to communicate how a person's behaviour matches predictive forensic profiles would open novel pathways, giving a person the possibility of experimenting in order to figure out how her behaviour is interpreted in the process of proactive forensic profiling.[60]

VIII   Conclusions

In this chapter I have explored the relationship between proactive forensic profiling and proactive punishment. The main point is that the central legal tenets that constitute and restrict the state's competence to punish may be an affordance of a specific socio-technical infrastructure. Requirements like *actus reus*, wrongfulness, and *mens rea*—introduced in the twelfth century by Pierre Abelard in his *Ethics* or *Scito te ipsum*—fit the distantiation, delay, and hesitation afforded by writing, compared to orality. Facing the novel socio-technical infrastructure of proactive profiling raises the question of the extent to which these requirements will survive, and the related question how we should design these novel architectures of knowledge production in a way that sustains the possibility of reflection, intention, and calling a person to account for actions performed.

Avoiding problematic Cartesian fantasies of a voluntaristic mentalism as well as a deterministic empiricism, I have argued that profiling technologies build on the *under*determined nature of human action. They demonstrate how our behaviours correlate in numerous ways with those of others, without thereby providing certainty about the future. They deliver probabilities or even plausibilities, but they do not rule out novel possibilities not disclosed by the logic of high-tech computations. As information theory philosopher Ciborra

---

[60] Finding ways to communicate how a person's behaviour matches predictive forensic profiles is not an easy task, for a number of reasons. Apart from the security aspect the problem resides in the fact that the socio-technical infrastructure does not accommodate such transparency. See M Hildebrandt (ed), *Behavioural Biometric Profiling and Transparency Enhancing Tools. FIDIS deliverable 7.12* (2009) Brussels, available at <http://www.fidis.net>, for an interdisciplinary approach to transparency rights in the case of behavioural biometric profiling.

has saliently described in his *Duality of Risk*, the risk of actuarial risk analysis is that 'what is "real" is what technology is able to define and represent',[61] generating a new type of ignorance concerning risks that are not part of the equation. Alternative correlations—undetected by proactive profiling—are thus cause for concern, but are also cause for celebration. They form the niches of creative freedom that are preconditional both for calling a person to account where she violated the criminal law and for contesting the proactive criminal profile that one is calculated to match.

Instead of rejecting proactive forensic profiling, therefore, I think we should take it seriously on its own grounds, thereby rejecting proactive punishment as incompatible with the knowledge claims inherent in profiling. At the same time, we should not turn a blind eye to the fact that the architecture of proactive forensic profiling could indeed afford a form of proactive criminalization. This requires us—criminal law philosophers, criminal lawyers, legislators, police, computer scientists, and citizens—to engage actively in the process of designing and organizing forensic profiling in a way that allows citizens to become aware of the profiles they match, in order to change their ways and/or to contest a profile's application.

---

[61] C Ciborra, *Digital Technologies and the Duality of Risk* (2004), ESRC Centre of Analysis of Risk and Regulation, London School of Economics, Discussion Paper No 27 at 16.

6

Horrific Crime[*]

John Stanton-Ife[†]

Some crimes are horrific. At any rate, in the media and in popular discussion it is common to hear certain criminal activity described in this way or—what seems to be equivalent—as horrendous or horrible. In two random episodes of the BBC programme *Crimewatch UK*, the terms were used to describe a gang attack with sledgehammers on two security guards, a hammer attack by a man to the head of his former girlfriend causing her brain damage, and the rape and strangulation of a 9-year-old boy.[1] On the day I type this, the news bulletins report that a man has been charged with the murder of a woman who was found in a street with one of her hands cut off.[2] These adjectives also occur to one inevitably when reading the facts of some reported criminal law cases. Consider two examples. In the first the driver of a heavy goods vehicle attempted to transport 60 illegal immigrants into the United Kingdom via the seaport of Dover. The vehicle's container, not having been designed to transport human beings, had only one vent through which oxygen could get in. The driver had shut the vent so that no noise would be audible from outside the container, and it remained shut for over five hours of the journey. When the lorry's container was inspected upon arrival at Dover,

* I am grateful to the volume editors and to the organizers of the two excellent weekend conferences at the Universities of Glasgow and Warwick at which an ancestor of this paper was discussed. I benefited from the input of all participants, especially Erik Claes, my commentator on both occasions. I presented a related paper at a Law School Staff Seminar at King's College, London, and thank all participants, especially Dennis Baker, Aileen McColgan, and Alan Norrie. Written comments late in the day from Antony Duff and Grant Lamond were most helpful.

† King's College, London.

1 Broadcast on BBC 1 on 2 September 2009 and 12 November 2009. CM Shafer and M Frye in their much cited paper 'Rape and Respect' also speak of the 'rage and *horror* feminists express about [rape]'. The paper may be found in M Vetterling-Braggin, FA Elliston, and J English (eds), *Feminism and Philosophy* (Totowa, NJ: Littlefield, Adams, 1977) 333, 334 (emphasis added).

2 <http://news.bbc.co.uk/1/hi/england/london/8372020.stm> (downloaded 22 November 2009).

2 of the 60 people inside were still alive: the other 58 had suffocated to death.[3] In the second case S1 and S2 had agreed with P1 and P2 that they would jointly attack a certain victim. S1 and S2 believed that the agreement they had reached amounted to giving the victim a severe beating and perhaps 'kneecapping' him, that is shooting bullets into his kneecaps in order to paralyse him. In the event there was no kneecapping because P1 and P2 deliberately killed the victim by slitting his throat.[4] The fate of the victim evokes a feeling of horror, as indeed would the fate S1 and S2 wrongly believed was in store for him. In this case, the people-trafficking case, and the other cases drawn from the television and news reports, we perceive the destruction and damage to the victims, together with the attitudes of the defendants, as horrific. Moreover, as well as individual cases that evoke reactions of horror, it seems appropriate to group together certain kinds of activity and identify certain crimes themselves as generally horrific. It is intuitively plausible to suggest that murder, torture, rape, and maiming are quite generally horrific.[5]

I doubt whether anyone would want to deny anything that I have said so far. However, even if it seems fitting to label certain crimes as horrific in the ways described above, the idea has not to my knowledge been considered worthy of theoretical attention. Maybe the reason for that is not far to seek. For murder, torture, rape, and maiming all cause untold *harm*. Obviously they do. They are therefore, one might say, the easiest of easy cases for the best known theory of criminalization, based on the harm principle, which gives pride of place to the notion of harm in accounting for criminal wrongs. According to proponents of the harm principle, we should centrally be concerned to criminalize harmful conduct and, in any case, should never criminalize conduct that is not harmful. While these crimes are of course devastating to their victims, one might accordingly say they are banal from a theoretical point of view. Perhaps our collective psychological feelings that some crimes are horrific is indicative simply of our sense of the *magnitude* of the harm; horrific crimes in other words are really serious crimes. If so, it is hardly a surprise that the idea of the horrific has been passed by as an area of theoretical attention for the criminal lawyer: the features making the qualitative difference to what is and what is not rightly thought criminal would still need to be identified entirely independently of any notion of moral horror. Moreover, while I am not aware of any criminal law theorist hitherto seeking to get any mileage out of the

---

[3] *R v Wacker* [2002] EWCA Crim 1944; [2003] 4 All ER 295.

[4] *R v Gamble* [1989] NI 268. See the discussion in AP Simester and GR Sullivan, *Criminal Law: Theory and Doctrine*, 3rd edn (Oxford: Hart, 2007) 224–5.

[5] There may be various difficulties fixing the scope of these offences *qua* 'horrific crimes' that I cannot go into here. For example, is euthanasia at the competent request of a suffering adult best understood as horrific but justified, on the one hand, or not horrific in the first place?

notion of horrific crime, one of the best known theorists of the criminal law, Lord Patrick Devlin, did try to get such mileage out of a kind of psychological reaction that may seem rather similar: the idea of crimes that evoke *disgust*.[6] But many commentators, myself included, believe Devlin's arguments were decidedly unsuccessful.[7] Why should the idea of crimes-that-evoke-horror succeed where Devlin's crimes-that-evoke-disgust failed?

I will have something to say about these questions in what follows. My main aim is to try to secure a hearing for the idea of the horrific as a notion that is worthy of the attention of the criminal lawyer concerned with the conditions for legitimate criminalization. Notwithstanding the objections raised above I will also be suggesting that horrific crime, despite the considerable harm it typically leaves in its wake, is not the easiest of easy categories for the harm principle. On the contrary: I believe it reveals the essential irrelevance of the harm principle to our understanding of the legitimate criminalization of conduct of the sort.

I The Morally Horrific

Coming to an understanding of the idea of the horrific in relation to the criminal law is made considerably easier by work already done by two philosophers on the idea of the 'morally horrific'. The philosophers in question are Robert Merrihew Adams and Marilyn McCord Adams.[8] It was, indeed, only after reading their work that it started to strike me how common it is to hear certain crimes described in popular discussion as horrific and to wonder whether this was evidence of some distinct moral fact of potential importance to the question of legitimate criminalization. As I will explain, part of what these authors say about the morally horrific applies straightforwardly to the criminal context, while other parts require some adaptation. My debt to these authors will be obvious in what follows.

I will come to the significance of the word 'morally' in 'morally horrific' below. But it is first important to sideline a potentially fatal obstacle to my plan to borrow from these authors. The problem lies in the fact that both are avowedly theistic writers. Endorsing their accounts lock, stock, and barrel would entail endorsing certain theistic premises and that is a consequence I wish to

---

[6] P Devlin, *The Enforcement of Morals* (Oxford: Oxford University Press, 1965).

[7] Stanton-Ife, 'Limits of the Law' in E Zalta (ed), *Stanford Encyclopaedia of Philosophy* (2006) <http://plato.stanford.edu/entries/law-limits/>, especially the section entitled 'Legal Moralism'.

[8] Merrihew Adams, *Finite and Infinite Goods* (Oxford: Oxford University Press, 1999); McCord Adams, 'Horrendous Evils and the Goodness of God' in Adams and Adams, *The Problem of Evil* (Oxford: Oxford University Press, 1990) 209.

avoid. I am presupposing by contrast that any account of criminalization we should wish to adopt must be religiously agnostic. It should require no commitment to any specific religious creed, nor for that matter any commitment to atheism. Fortunately, as it turns out, we do not need to endorse the entirety of what the authors say about moral horror to benefit from a key part of their analysis. They use the notion of the morally horrific in a way that allows it to be excised without loss of coherence from their theological concerns. In their hands it is a datum for theological interpretation, not a result of that interpretation.[9] While they believe the data making up the notion of the horrific is best interpreted theologically, they do not claim that such data cannot be interpreted non-theologically. A secular interpretation of the horrific remains a possibility as far as they are concerned, one that might or might not conflict with their own. I will be suggesting that the notion can indeed be given the sort of secular interpretation and grounding that it needs for our purposes. To be sure, care will be needed to avoid reliance on any unobvious aspect of the authors' thinking that only a religious believer of any stripe could maintain, but as just indicated this should prove more straightforward than it may at first have looked. I will focus mainly on the work of Merrihew Adams. His concern with moral philosophy makes his work more easily adaptable for our purposes than that of McCord Adams, which is concerned primarily with the theological problem of evil, though I will touch in places on her work too. What follows will of necessity be programmatic and will leave many stones unturned.

A   Horrific crime: sceptical challenges

I shall now try to block out the notion of the morally horrific in a way that shows its significance to theories of criminalization. I will begin the account by way of response to some potential objections, two of them already mentioned or hinted at, to the bare possibility of finding theoretical, criminal-law significance in the notion of horrific wrongs or horrific crimes. We began by observing that some crimes evoke feelings of horror. That is plainly true but so what? One might be sceptical in at least three ways of the possibility that the notion of 'horrific crime' could have any theoretical significance. First, while it is no doubt true that such feelings or reactions will often or usually relate to matters of the deepest seriousness, is not the theoretical idea itself trivial? As already mentioned, is the designation of something as 'horrific' nothing more than a way of saying something is wrong in an emphatic way: that is, that it is *very* wrong? Second, are such feelings not bound to be too subjective and variable to have any theoretical utility? Third, though horrific things happen

---

[9] The phrasing is taken from Merrihew Adams (ibid) 121.

to people, it might be argued, the idea is not well suited to the criminal law context because the horror that can befall persons need in no way imply that human agency of any sort is responsible, as is true of the destruction that follows a tsunami. Criminal law, unlike natural disasters, is by contrast concerned with harms and wrongs resulting from human agency.

It is easiest to start with the second of these possible objections. If sentiments that some crimes are thus-and-so pick out nothing more than a set of (varying) subjective reactions, they cannot play any useful theoretical function in debates about legitimate criminalization, so the objection goes. Lord Devlin's account of legitimate criminalization was plagued by this difficulty. Devlin's views were constructed in opposition to accounts of the limits of legitimate criminalization based on the harm principle of John Stuart Mill and HLA Hart.[10] While not disagreeing with Mill and Hart on the importance of harm to criminalization, Devlin understood the idea of harm very differently to those authors. Unlike them, Devlin thought one could legitimately criminalize behaviour in order to prevent the putative harm to a society caused by the flouting of its morality. In particular, he thought, the widespread evincing of the emotion of disgust on the part of a specified community is a mark of the limits of societal tolerance, and itself sufficient to furnish a good reason for the imposition of criminal sanctions against those who indulged in the behaviour that occasioned the disgust.[11] There are many problems with this view. One is that what evokes disgust across a population may be a most inaccurate guide to what is morally wrong or blameworthy or bad. Communities can label and have labelled 'disgusting' certain activity that is not morally wrong and that might even be morally admirable. Loving interracial and homosexual relationships are obvious examples. Devlin's main example, indeed, was homosexual sex between consenting adults in the United Kingdom of the 1950s, the criminalization of which was (I take it) straightforwardly unjust, however many people found it disgusting at that time.

Is one bound to fall into the same trap in trying to stress the significance of reactions of moral horror? It has to be admitted that, so long as one focuses on the reactions of horror themselves and on these alone, one is. In principle a widespread feeling that something is horrific could be directed unjustly at an inappropriate target in the same way that a widespread feeling that something is disgusting could be and has been. This, however, should not lead us to abandon the notion of the horrific. It should rather remind us that caution is in order in constructing an account of it. One has to allow for the possibility that the feeling that some activity is horrific might not support any conclusion that the activity is appropriately stigmatized or criminalized.

---

[10] Devlin (n 6 above) 102–39.   [11] Ibid, 17.

If one is to trust such feelings one has to be able to give good grounds for the reasonableness of reposing that trust and be open to the possibility that a given reaction that 'X is horrific' might be mistaken. Merrihew Adams is clear that his notion of the morally horrific is not to be taken as a subjective notion:

It is important ... that the feeling of horror will not be taken to constitute, in itself, the sort of moral fact ... I am seeking to understand. It is rather to be taken as a sign-post to an objective fact that is independent of it ... The feeling can be mistaken. We may hope that sometimes it will be reasonable to trust it ... [12]

The psychological fact that we react to, say, murder and rape with feelings of horror is not in itself the key. These reactions point beyond themselves to something objective and independent of them. In claiming that we should attend to the notion of the horrific in crime, I am not claiming that the feelings are themselves the crucial notion; rather, they are signposts to that notion. Answering the question what it is that these reactions point to, just where the signposts direct us, is too large a task to be undertaken adequately here. But roughly speaking the answer is this. These reactions are tracking *intrinsic value*. What horrifies us is what has happened to something intrinsi-cally valuable. It is tempting here to focus on what has happened to something *sacred*, rather than what has happened to something of intrinsic value. Ronald Dworkin puts the idea of sanctity at the heart of his account of the morality and legitimate regulation of abortion and euthanasia.[13] In his view people across the political and moral spectrum broadly agree that human life is sacred, but disagree on how to interpret these ideas. He understands sanctity in terms of varying kinds of investment. A religious person might see the sanctity of human life in terms of divine investment in that life, while an atheist might see the sanctity or intrinsic value of human life in terms of the investment of a natural process of evolution. Another sort of invest-ment stressed by Dworkin is the investment of human creativity in the origin or development of another's life.[14] As Dworkin understands it, then, the sacred can be understood as a religious notion, but it need not be. Deploying Dworkin's, or some other notion unrestricted to religious contexts, is poten-tially an option. But interesting as it would be to explore the idea in the present context, I nevertheless do not propose to do that and therefore will not pause to consider the plausibility of Dworkin's 'investment model' of sanc-tity. The historical connection of the sacred with the religious is simply too

---

[12] Merrihew Adams (n 8 above) 106.
[13] R Dworkin, *Life's Dominion: An Argument About Abortion, Euthanasia, and Individual Freedom* (New York, NY: Knopf, 1993).   [14] Ibid, 82–4.

strong, I believe, to allay any suspicion that the idea, if adopted, is ultimately, if implicitly, religious in nature.[15]

Alternatively, in a Kantian vein, one could identify the horrific in terms of what happens to *rational nature*.[16] Here the stumbling block is not one of any unwelcome associations the idea of rational natures may or may not have. It is rather that rational nature is too restrictive an idea to capture the full scope of what I believe underlies our reactions when we take certain criminal behaviour to be horrific. Horrific crimes can be committed against non-human animals and very severely mentally impaired human beings and it is most unlikely that the explanation for this can lie with any violation of their rational nature. The broader idea of a violation of intrinsic value promises, with more development, to accommodate such cases and perhaps also the possibility of certain environmental crimes. Be that as it may, the essential point is that, to be worth its theoretical salt, the idea of horrific crime must not rest simply with a set of psychological reactions, but must be conceived in terms of what underlies those reactions. One must seek a theoretical account against which to test the trustworthiness of such intuitions.

Rather than focus on the evocation of the horrific, then, we must focus on the *appropriate* evocation of the horrific. This brings us to the first source of scepticism about the notion of the horrific mentioned above. Could it be that the popular description of a crime as 'horrific' captures nothing more than the quantitative idea that the underlying wrong is really serious? That is, a given crime is horrific just when it is *very* wrong? Wrong in spades? If that is to be the conclusion it would suggest, as I have already noted, that there is nothing to be gained from a theoretical point of view in attending to the notion. If we need to pick out the negative qualitative dimension of the criminalized behaviour in which we are interested entirely independently of the idea of the horrific, only then to add the idea for emphasis or rhetorical effect, nothing significant will have been achieved. However, as I will now try to explain, I believe the idea is much more interesting than that. It is not merely a way of emphasizing other factors to be independently identified. Its interest is based on the idea, advanced by Merrihew Adams, that the morally horrific is more to be conceived as a species of the *bad* than as a species of the *wrong*.[17] It is of course more familiar to us to distinguish the right from the good than to distinguish the wrong from the bad. But it is natural enough to ask how the negative pair are related just as it is in relation to the positive pair. Again, very little can be

---

[15] Cf Raimond Gaita's remarks on why he prefers to speak of the preciousness of individuals, rather than the sacredness of individuals: *A Common Humanity: Thinking about Love and Truth and Justice* (London: Routledge, 2000) xxiv.

[16] I Kant, HJ Paton (trans), *Groundwork of the Metaphysics of Morals* (London: Hutchinson, 1969).   [17] Merrihew Adams (n 8 above) 105.

said about this vast topic here. Is the right prior to the good or vice versa? Is the wrong prior to the bad or vice versa? Are rightness/wrongness and goodness/badness rather coeval? How strong a distinction should one draw between the pairs? I take it that however strongly or weakly one draws these contrasts, the right and the wrong pertain to questions of obligations and rights. They concern what, in TM Scanlon's phrase 'we owe to each other'.[18] 'Without a context of social requirements,' Merrihew Adams says, 'murder and torture would not have the property I think is wrongness; but they would still be bad, and specifically horrible.'[19] Possibly that goes too far, but it is clear that murder and torture are bad—horrible—in a primitive way that is not reducible to the social categories of right and wrong.

If the horrific is more a facet of the bad than of the wrong, it seems unlikely that it can be understood uninterestingly as the 'very wrong', and the second source of scepticism about the morally horrific could accordingly be safely ignored. However, it may well seem puzzling to say right at the outset that that which appropriately evokes feelings of moral horror is not or not primarily a species of the wrong. After all, we earlier identified murder, rape, maiming, and torture as paradigmatically horrific. It would surely be crazy to say these things are not wrong! It would indeed, so it is important to stress that they *are* all wrong. The claim is that the horror they evoke has *more* to do with their badness than their (undoubted) wrongness, although the two will inevitably be heavily entangled.

The difference between the wrong and the bad emerges clearly when one realizes that wrongness is not sufficient for the appropriate evocation of moral horror.[20] It is here that we see most clearly that 'horrific' is not to be equated with 'seriously wrong'. Vandalism, theft, and assault are not typically horrific, although they are wrong. To say, however, that except in special circumstances these crimes are not horrific is not to say that they are not serious. Gangs that clone credit cards can profit from their dishonesty, and so can tax evaders from theirs; sometimes outrageously so. The fraud engaged in by a Bernard Madoff can be on a vast scale. But these actions and their profits are not horrific. Unlike a rape, murder, or maiming, it does not reach to the core of a person, however damaging to his or her interests. It is therefore a mistake to suggest, as our imagined objector did, that the notion of the horrific adds nothing to the idea of wrongness but a stress on the degree of wrongness. Horrific crime is not synonymous with serious crime. Even if all horrific crime is serious, not all serious crime is horrific. The first of the *Crimewatch UK* episodes that we mentioned in the opening paragraph also featured a £40 million heist

---

[18] TM Scanlon, *What We Owe to Each Other* (Princeton, NJ: Princeton University Press, 1998).
[19] Merrihew Adams (n 8 above) 105.   [20] Ibid.

carried out on a London jeweller; it was notable that the elsewhere liberally used adjective 'horrific' was not deployed in that context.

Can one also say that wrongness is not *necessary* for the appropriate evocation of moral horror? Merrihew Adams believes so because, he suggests, one can reasonably believe that an action is morally horrific without believing it is wrong. Some cases of euthanasia or mercy killing, he believes, meet this description. Certainly both the causation of death and the fact that one is the agent of the death of others understandably evoke horror, even if one thinks one is doing the right thing. Amputating the limb of another is also horrific, even if any alternative would be fatal to them.[21] However, it could be that while these cases reasonably evoke horror they do not appropriately evoke *moral* horror. As already touched on, not all that is horrific is morally horrific, as the example of the tsunami shows. But this is not an issue that we need to settle here.

We can put aside two of the sceptical challenges with which we began the section. The notion of horrific crime does not collapse into a ragbag of disconnected subjective responses to certain conduct; for it is the appropriate evocation of moral horror that is significant. And to describe a crime as horrific is not simply to emphasize the seriousness of the crime: it is to point beyond its wrong-making features to its bad-making features. The third objection floated at the beginning of the section was that the idea of the horrific is inappropriate to the context of crime because it need not implicate human agency at all. It is indeed correct that the horrific involves no essential reference to human agency, but this shows, not that the notion is inappropriate to the criminal context, but rather that horrific crime involves a subset of the category of the horrific, a (large) subset that does implicate human agency. Horrific crime, as we will now see, should focus on the idea of a violation.

B   Horrific violations

As just noted, to make the case for a theoretically interesting notion of horrific crime and to have some theoretical resources with which to test individual intuitions that particular conduct is horrific, more will need to be said. One aspect of the Merrihew Adams account is especially promising. He identifies as a subset of the category of the horrific the notion of a horrific *violation*.[22] Here the concern is specifically with what is caused by human agency and so moves us in the right direction for criminal law purposes. It is focused on destruction, damage, and (in some circumstances) the crossing of the will

---

[21] Cf the comment at n 5 above.   [22] Merrihew Adams (n 8 above) 107–12.

of another. The criterion of a horrific violation is made up of two necessary conditions, both of which he says must be satisfied for the label to apply:

(1) An act that violates a person must *attack* the person. Its foreseeable effects must be so damaging to the person, or so contrary to her (actual or presumed) will, that fully intending them, in the absence of reason to believe them necessary for the prevention of greater harm to her, would constitute *hostility* toward the person. I do not mean that the effects must be in fact foreseen, or fully intended, by the agent, though full intention aggravates the violative character of the act.

(2) A person is not violated by every act that harms her interests or crosses her will. A violation is an act that attacks the person *seriously* and *directly*. Most (but not all) violations of a person will assault her body. Acts that mainly damage a person's possessions, what she *has* as distinct from what she *is*, will typically not violate *her*, even if they are quite hostile to her interests. This second condition is the point on which I find it hardest to attain generality and precision at once. I think we must sometimes rely on our sense of moral horror to determine which acts attack a person seriously and directly enough to violate her.[23]

I will comment first on condition (1). There is rather a lot to the three sentences that make it up and it is not clear just what Merrihew Adams means to convey by it. For there seem to be two accounts of what the necessary condition for a violation in (1) amounts to, not just one. The headline claim, so to speak, is that a violation *must* involve an *attack*. Merrihew Adams also later refers to (1) as 'the hostility condition' suggesting that a violation *must* involve hostility.[24] However, the final sentence of (1) seems clearly to suggest that neither an attack nor hostility is actually necessary for there to have been a violation. It implies a distinction between two kinds of violation, what we might call a 'basic violation' and an 'aggravated violation'. The general idea is that there is an event that (objectively speaking) is very damaging to a person or very much contrary to her will, whether or not the 'violator' in fact aims at the damage to the victim or the crossing of her will. Given such damage or such a will-crossing, the violator's full intention will aggravate the violation into a *hostile* violation, subject to the absence of conditions of necessity as in (say) the case of a doctor who amputates a leg to save a life. I take it that by 'fully intending' Merrihew Adams means intending in the sense of an aim or a purpose, as opposed to what is sometimes called the 'oblique' sense of intention *qua* foresight that one's action will cause harm as a side effect of one's aim or purpose. So a 'basic' violation might involve recklessness or negligence on the part of the violator whose aim or purpose is not to damage the person or cross her will, while an 'aggravated' (hostile) violation will involve an intention *qua* such an aim or purpose. However, 'attacking' someone surely implies

---

[23] Ibid, 108. The emphases are in the original.   [24] Ibid.

intention in the sense of aim or purpose, not in the sense of mere foresight that he might be damaged.

I therefore think the thrust of (1), taken as a whole, is at odds with an understanding of it that insists a violation must involve an attack and must involve hostility: for only an aggravated violation does those things. This raises the question which view is to be preferred. Should we restrict the idea of a violation only to cases where there is an attack, an intention (*qua* aim or purpose) to damage, or should we understand it more widely as leaving room for damage and certain will-crossings that are or should have been foreseen, and that are reckless or negligent rather than purposeful? In my view, it is the latter view that should be preferred. For it seems to me highly plausible that at least some cases of recklessness or negligence can be horrific violations of others. The people-trafficking case we cited in the opening paragraph—*R v Wacker* in which the lorry driver's gross negligence led to the suffocation to death of 58 illegal immigrants—is an example.[25] It strikes me that the notion of a horrific violation must leave some room for *endangerments* as well as attacks, although that will require further specification that I cannot attempt here. Some endangerments may be horrific violations of other people.[26] Though cases of horrific violations involving endangerments rather than attacks might turn out to be relatively rare (and more would need to be said about this), I do not think one should insist that an attack is a necessary condition of a violation.

The second condition suggests that horrific violations will usually have an impact on the body. The central notion, though, seems more broadly to involve *the self*, the self and the body taken as an integral whole. This is true in all of the paradigmatic cases we have considered of murder, rape, torture, and maiming. It also draws our attention perhaps to the key to what is distinctive of horrific crime. Horrific crimes violate *their victims* as opposed to violating their *victim's rights or interests*. One can of course speak of a right not to be raped or a right not be murdered, and there are many contexts in which doing so will be both legitimate and necessary: one should not be driven to any rigid dualism between people and their rights. But what is crucial here is the sense

---

[25] Consider another example cited in a recent Law Commission report:

D is in the process of stealing V's car. V leaps on the bonnet to deter D from driving off. D accelerates to 100 miles per hour and continues at that speed. Eventually V's grip loosens and V falls off the car. The fall kills V. D claims he did not intend to kill V or to cause V serious injury but was simply determined to escape come what may (Law Commission, *Murder, Manslaughter and Infanticide* (Law Com No 304, 2006) 57)

Some might wish to insist that this is really a case of intention even in the absence of aim or purpose. I'll not enter into that question here, but whatever one thinks about that, this is a case of horrific crime.

[26] The distinction between attacks and endangerments is due to RA Duff, *Answering for Crime: Responsibility and Liability in Criminal Law* (Oxford: Hart, 2007) 147–74.

in which rape or murder victims have had *more* than their rights violated, they have *themselves* been violated.

It would be useful to analyse in detail all the general cases of horrific crime we have mentioned, as well as a number of the specific ones. In particular, it will be important at some stage to examine the cases of murder, torture, and maiming as well as the offences in English law of 'gross negligence manslaughter' and of corporate manslaughter in order to deepen our understanding of the notion of horrific crime.[27] Rather than attempt all of that here, I will focus in the second part of the chapter on only one of the paradigm cases of horrific crime, namely rape, touching only occasionally in passing on the other cases. Another point has obvious significance to the criminal law. McCord Adams, in her account of the morally horrific (or horrendous), stresses *participation* in horrors as calling for a special kind of response.[28] While one's first and most natural concern is with victims of moral horror, there is a large question regarding the ramifications for *perpetrators* of their participation in horrific crimes. McCord Adams's rendering of the notion of moral horror is a little more precisely stated than Merrihew Adams's account, which leaves a bit more to intuitive understanding. According to the former, one's participation in moral horror, be that as victim or perpetrator, gives one a *prima facie* reason to doubt that one's life is a great good to one. Interesting as it would be to explore this proposal and its clear implications for the victims and perpetrators of crime, I will assume in what follows the slightly more intuitively drawn account of Merrihew Adams.

II The Moral Structure and Criminalization of Rape

Nobody seriously doubts that rape is wrong or that it ought to be criminalized. But there has been considerable controversy over why, in both cases, that should be. The aim of this part will be to suggest that rape is illuminatingly viewed as a horrific crime. In order to try to establish this it will be useful to compare this proposal with an account of a different sort that is presented in the impressive, wide-ranging, and thought-provoking argument of John Gardner and Stephen Shute.[29]

---

[27] Cf Corporate Manslaughter and Corporate Homicide Act 2007.

[28] McCord Adams (n 8 above) 211.

[29] J Gardner and S Shute, 'The Wrongness of Rape' in J Horder (ed), *Oxford Essays in Jurisprudence*, 4th series (Oxford: Oxford University Press, 2000) 193–217. The paper is reproduced without change in J Gardner, *Offences and Defences* (Oxford: Oxford University Press, 2008) 1, from which all citations here are taken. See also Gardner's comments on the paper in 'Reply to Critics' in the same volume, 241–5.

Gardner and Shute are proponents of the harm principle. They believe that among the necessary conditions for legitimate criminalization in general are the presence of a wrong and the prevention of harm. Their view in a nutshell is that the explanation for the clear legitimacy of criminalizing rape is (1) that rape is wrong because it is the treatment of another as a mere means or, as they more often put it, the sheer use of another,[30] and (2) it would be harmful not to criminalize all cases of rape, even if, as they claim, not all cases of rape are themselves harmful.[31] The second of these issues will not be addressed until the final part of this chapter, entitled 'Harm and the Harm Principle'. It is the first of the authors' claims I now propose to examine.

The Kantian 'sheer use' principle is one of the most famous ideas in the history of moral philosophy. But it is not the first answer that comes to mind when asking why rape is wrong. The initially most obvious explanation of why rape is wrong is that what is done to the victim is something to which she (or sometimes he) does not consent. As Carolyn Shafer and Marilyn Frye say, 'the wrongness of rape rests with the matter of the woman's consent.'[32] Why, then, do Gardner and Shute reject consent as the key to the explanation of the wrongness of rape? Apparently, for three reasons. First, they think consent does not explain the particularity or distinctiveness of the wrongness of rape. Second, it does not explain the seriousness or gravity of rape. Third, as we have mentioned, there is in their view a better account of the wrongness of rape, namely that it is the sheer use of another. We will come to the third point presently. The first two points are encapsulated in the authors' own words in the following passage:

Why should [rape] be a *separate* entry on Feinberg's short list of crimes which nobody should decriminalize? Consent does not give the answer, since many other wrongs prohibited by the criminal law, such as vandalism, theft, and assault, might equally be defined in terms of absence of consent. Why are these not all handily collapsed into one crime of 'doing to another that to which they do not consent'? Why aren't they not all just one and the same wrong? You may still think that the answer is obvious: rape is a worse violation than mere vandalism, theft and assault. True enough. But in what respect, in what dimension, is rape worse? Wherein does its 'worseness' lie? What exactly, in other words, is wrong with rape?[33]

---

[30] Ibid, 16.   [31] Ibid, 29.

[32] Shafer and Frye (n 1 above) 334. As indicated in the text, I am not assuming that all victims of rape are women. Statistically, that is indeed emphatically the case and that to be sure is something that thinking about rape must reflect: see J Temkin and B Krahé, *Sexual Assault and the Justice Gap: A Question of Attitude* (Oxford: Hart, 2008) 11. Some believe that male victims of rape should be *seen as* women. For scepticism about the claim that men inhabit sexual roles as 'honorary women' in certain circumstances, see L Green, 'Pornographies' (2000) 8 *Journal of Political Philosophy* 27, 32–5. Whatever the better view on this, one must surely be aware of a range of features of victims: gender, sex, age, the potential presence of varying kinds of mental disorder, and so on.

[33] Gardner and Shute (n 29 above) 3.

If 'consent' is the answer to the question why rape is wrong, Gardner and Shute believe, we would neither be able to explain why rape is a wrong distinct from vandalism, theft, and assault, nor why rape is more serious than those wrongs. Against this, though, could one not respond immediately that accounting for all four offences in terms of a lack of consent does not preclude explaining what is distinctive about each, since each refers to different background interests? Such a response, I think, would indeed be on the right lines. But Gardner's and Shute's argument helpfully raises the question of whether we should see consent as functioning in essentially the same way throughout the criminal law; a point to which I will return. In my view, distinguishing the nature and gravity of rape from vandalism, theft, and assault is to be done by recognizing that rape is a horrific crime and the others are not. Doing so, moreover, does not involve marginalizing the role of consent in an account of the wrongness of rape. But before returning to that argument, let us look in more detail at the account proposed by Gardner and Shute of the role of consent in accounting for the wrongness of rape, and at how they tackle their own questions.

A   The particularity of rape

As we have seen, Gardner and Shute propose that rape is wrong because it treats the victim as a mere means. How, then, does this proposal meet the criteria that they claim cannot be met by an account of the wrongness of rape based on consent, namely of explaining the particularity or distinctiveness of rape and its gravity? They do not answer these questions explicitly, presumably because they take the answers to be contained in their account as it unfolds. Let us take the question of distinctiveness first. At first sight it is a little puzzling how the distinctiveness of the wrong of rape is to be explained by the claim that it involves the sheer use of another. For the authors themselves assert that prostitution and pornography *also* involve the sheer use of another.[34] Of course if it is true that the wrong of rape is the same as the putative wrong of prostitution and pornography, the wrongness of rape would not be distinct in the sense of *unique*, but would still be perfectly distinct, one might argue, from the wrongness of vandalism, theft, assault, and so on. However, the authors would not want to rest the matter there, since they also claim that there are clear differences in how others should treat users of prostitutes and consumers of pornography on the one hand and rapists on the other. In many cases of prostitution and pornography, the authors rightly observe, there is strong reason to doubt the genuineness of any apparent consent given by sex workers and models. However, as they also observe, again plausibly,

---

[34] Ibid, 15–16.

one should not conclude on the other hand that there is no such thing as valid consent in pornography and prostitution.[35] And it is this latter case of prostitution and pornography, where all consents are genuine, that is relevant here: these activities, they argue, should be tolerated, not criminalized. In other words, even if prostitution and pornography involve the sheer use of another just as rape does, they should *not* be treated in the same way as rape. Gardner and Shute are not then arguing for the radical conclusion that users of sex workers and consumers of pornography (where all consents are genuine) should be treated as seriously as rapists. Rape is to be distinguished from (consensual) prostitution and pornography, notwithstanding that all three in their view instantiate the same wrong of sheer use. (Consensual) prostitution and pornography involve the *licensed* sheer use of another, as they put it, and rape the *unlicensed* sheer use of another.[36] The former pair of cases are to be protected, as the authors also put it, by a '*right of sexual autonomy*', while rape is not.[37]

But have they not simply made a show of expelling consent from the front door only to bring it back in by the back door? Has not sheer use simply dropped out of the picture when we come to the question of how the rapist, on the one hand, and the consumer of pornography and user of sex workers on the other hand, are to be treated by third parties and legislators? The authors will readily agree that consent/licence ultimately plays an important practical role in their argument, as we saw in the previous paragraph, but presumably they will claim it is important to see how that conclusion is derived. They will say, I imagine, that the role of licence/consent in their 'right of sexual autonomy' is not derived from any premise that the wrongness of rape lies in the fact that what is done to the victim is something to which she does not consent. What then do the authors mean by the right to sexual autonomy?

The right, as the authors understand it, appears to be compounded of two elements: the right to personal autonomy and a right to be regarded as a moral agent.[38] By the value of personal autonomy I take them to be endorsing the Razian account of the value of being an author of one's own life, of having and choosing between an adequate range of valuable options.[39] But if that is right, it is of no help to the authors, given their claim that prostitution and pornography are systematically wrongful and abusive. The value of personal

---

[35] Ibid, 19.   [36] Ibid, 21.   [37] Ibid.   [38] Ibid, 20.

[39] J Raz, *The Morality of Freedom* (Oxford: Clarendon Press, 1988). Though the authors do not cite Raz explicitly at this stage of their argument, his account is elsewhere endorsed by them in their essay (ibid, 4). It is true that Raz argues that one should not use coercion against a bad option if it is not harmful. But the authors do not repeat this argument, and I believe it is in any case problematic in the context of the general account of personal autonomy: see Stanton-Ife (n 7 above), particularly the section entitled 'A Perfectionist Harm Principle'.

autonomy is restricted to choice among *valuable* options on Raz's account. It does not come into play in a choice between valuable and valueless options. What of the second element making up the authors' right of sexual autonomy? This is the right persons have that others 'regard *them as moral agents* capable of understanding their own value and making up their own minds about their relationships with others'.[40] This surely proves far too much. It seems as it stands to stretch to *any* choice agents might make about their relationships with others. After all, rapists, while they must be punished, must yet be treated (in the authors' phrases) 'as people', and 'as moral agents', and 'as beings with value other than use-value'.[41] But nothing is more obviously true than that they enjoy not the slightest latitude to engage in rape: in short, that others must regard consumers of pornography and users of sex workers as moral agents does not explain why they should be tolerated if the authors are right to claim that what they do shares the essential wrongfulness of rape.

I agree with the authors that one should not criminalize users of sex workers and consumers of pornography in cases where all consents are genuine, whereas rape is obviously to be criminalized. But I strongly suspect that the reason for this takes us back to where we started the argument, to the claim the authors rejected: that rape is wrong, at least in significant measure, because it does to another that to which she does not consent. Reasserting this claim makes it again obvious why the criminal law should treat rapists so differently from users of sex workers and consumers of pornography where consents are genuine, something that became puzzling thanks to the suggestion that we focus on the sheer use of another as the wrong of rape. The proposal that rape is wrong because it treats the victim as a mere means runs into trouble when it attempts to account for the difference between how rapists, on the one hand, should be treated by the criminal law, and how those who engage in consensual prostitution and pornography should be, on the other.

B The gravity of rape

How does the proposal meet the second criterion that the authors claim cannot be met by an account of the wrongness of rape based on consent: can it explain the gravity of rape? Though we have focused so far on a comparison between rape and prostitution and pornography, the authors' initial question was in terms of how one distinguishes rape from offences such as vandalism, theft, and assault. Plainly none of these offences is as serious as rape. But are the authors right that this is because the wrongness of rape is to be explained in terms of the sheer use of another? I think not. Consider for example an

---

[40] Gardner and Shute (n 29 above) 20.   [41] Ibid.

assault, in the sense involving a battery. Imagine someone who, fleeing from the police, is heading for a park wall, planning to jump over it and escape. He first steps onto a park bench, then onto the shoulder of the startled woman sitting on the bench minding her own business, and finally vaults over the wall. In doing so, he treats the bench as a mere means and he treats the woman as a mere means. In fact he treats *the woman* as a bench, or better, a stepladder. But though he commits an assault and sheerly uses the woman, he does nothing nearly so grave as he would do if he raped her. There is, in short, nothing about the notion of sheer use that implies that it must be *very* serious.

C   The wrongness of rape as the sheer use of another

As for the authors' claim that consent does not give the answer to the question why rape is wrong, because there is a better account in terms of the sheer use of another, that too is, I believe, mistaken. An adequate examination of the Kantian principle cannot be undertaken here. However, there seem to be plenty of possible counter-examples to the claim that rape is wrong because it is the sheer use of another. There are many potential cases in which a rape has taken place, with all that implies in terms of seriousness and stigma, but the victim has not been *sheerly* used, has not been treated as a *mere* means. Consider first cases in which the rapist does not believe that the victim consents. Many films contain dubious scenes in which men force themselves on resisting women, only for the woman's resistance to dissolve and transform into enthusiastic participation.[42] This can express or encourage the belief that the woman's non-consent is merely a temporary obstacle which it is in her interests that the man should overcome. Alternatively, imagine a gay man who forcibly penetrates a heterosexual male friend on the grounds that the latter is repressed and is denying his own true sexuality, and must be shown this for his own good; or a heterosexual man setting out to 'save' a lesbian woman by proving to her, against her protestations, that she will enjoy sex with a man and never look back. In these cases the rapist, while knowing that the victim does not consent, believes (perversely of course) that he is acting in her or his interests. There are also, of course, cases in which the rapist does not have knowledge of a lack of consent, but in which his beliefs are unreasonably held. Unreasonable beliefs in consent may well include the rapist's belief that he is merely acting as his companion would desire. An extreme and perhaps merely hypothetical example is given by Richard Tur. Adonis, as Tur names the character in his example,

---

[42] For example, *The Postman Always Rings Twice* (1981).

strongly believes that he is irresistible to women. Thus, believing that no woman could say no to him, Adonis has sexual intercourse with a non-consenting woman, but such is the strength of his belief that he misinterprets her resistance and does not register her protests. Adonis honestly believes that the woman consented.[43]

There are also much discussed cases in which a third party suggests to the rapist that the woman is consenting and her protestations of non-consent are part of an elaborate game she enjoys playing,[44] or where a man believes that the woman consents because her sexy dressing can only be an invitation to him ('I was the only man there'). Slightly different are cases in which there is no belief in consent. This might include cases of date rape in which a man penetrates a heavily intoxicated woman without taking any steps to establish whether she consents to his continuing to touch her or to moving on to penetrative sex: he hopes that she consents and would certainly stop if he knew that she did not, but he does not trouble in any way to find out. Whatever else is wrong with one's actions, one does not use another as a mere means if one believes oneself to be acting in that person's interest, even if the belief is unreasonable. In these cases the victim has not been used as mere means nor been sheerly used— certainly not if the words 'mere' or 'sheerly' are actually supposed to carry anything akin to their ordinary meaning.[45]

In short, the authors do not sufficiently justify their removal of consent from centre stage in accounting for the wrongness of rape. Rape is a horrific crime. It is contrary to the will of the victim. It violates the body and the self of the victim. Moreover, an account can be given of *why* consent is of such significance in the sexual domain. Criminal lawyers often talk about consent as if it must play the same role throughout the criminal law. However, there appear to be considerations making consent important in the sexual domain in a way that will not necessarily carry over to other contexts. The self is formed against a backdrop of social structures. In significant part through the internalization

---

[43] R Tur, 'Subjectivism and Objectivism' in S Shute, J Gardner, and J Horder (eds), *Action and Value in the Criminal Law* (Oxford: Oxford University Press, 1996) 213, 220.

[44] *DPP v Morgan* [1976] AC 182. The defendants who gave an account along these lines were not believed, but the decision supported the proposition that an honest belief in consent, however unreasonable, was sufficient for an acquittal. This is of course no longer the legal position in England and Wales: see Sexual Offences Act 2003, s 1.

[45] I am assuming that the idea of using another as a mere means turns in large measure, if not entirely, on the attitudes of the user. At one point Gardner and Shute (n 29 above) 24, suggest that they understand using or treating another as a mere means as an objective notion that does not turn on how 'the user' sees the person he is using. I explore this further in 'Kant, Kantianism and the Wrongness of Rape' (in progress). It is interesting to note that some Kantians believe that Kant's Principle of Humanity on which Gardner and Shute rely would be best understood if the reference in it to treating as mere means were to be dropped or placed securely in the background: see A Wood, *Kantian Ethics* (Cambridge: Cambridge University Press, 2008) 87.

of such structures, children come to understand themselves as selves.[46] The idea of boundaries, notably in the sexual domain, plays an indispensable role in the forming of the self, for example through understandings of the appropriateness of touching and viewing. Very young children are quite literally incapable of giving valid consent to sexual touching. As they get older some, before others, will start to have the same understanding—be able in principle to give the same tokens of consent—as adult human beings, but there might yet be good grounds for the criminal law to refuse to acknowledge the legal legitimacy of such consent before a certain age is reached. But there comes a point for the vast majority of persons at which the boundaries of selves are understood sufficiently well.

The social structures through which boundaries are largely learned can of course change, be that after centuries or within a single generation. Like conventions in general they are contingent. Some, like the proscription of sexually touching children below a certain age, are now as a matter of sociological fact very widespread, if not universal. But the age at which someone is 'marriageable', for example, has varied considerably over history (Lady Margaret Beaufort gave birth to the future Henry VII when she was just 13 years old).[47] As we have already observed, these social structures can be unjust and can be perpetuated over many generations. Lord Devlin's account was marred by his willingness to accord too much authority to such conventional structures.[48] Again, as already noted, at many times and in many places homosexual and interracial sex have been other examples of such structurally unjust proscribed boundaries. In short, conventional, boundary-imposing sexual structures can be just or unjust. The interesting point is that we do not think that the question whether someone has been sexually violated turns purely and simply on the question of the justice of the conventional, boundary-imposing proscription. In a society in which homosexual and interracial sex is persecuted, we do not say in general that such sex violates anyone. We *do*, however, take one party to have been violated even in such a society if he does *not consent*. And we might well think that a polygamous marriage within a polygamous society is an unjust arrangement to the many women married to the one man, and that it is objectionable as such. However, where sexual intercourse is validly consented to in such an

---

[46] In this and the next paragraph I take myself to be largely recounting (and endorsing) Merrihew Adams' account: (n 8 above) 108–10. Since I've changed some wording and the order of presentation, and added the odd qualification or illustration, something may have been lost in translation.

[47] C Erickson, *Brief Lives of the English Monarchs* (London: Constable, 2003) 189–90.

[48] Devlin (n 6 above), eg 114.

arrangement, there is no *violation* of selfhood. Consent retains its power through these conventional variations. Even in hippy free-love cultures where members are permitted, indeed encouraged, to experiment widely with multiple partners and a variety of sexual practices, consent keeps its force and non-consensual sex remains a horrific violation.

Consent, then, is important to the understanding of the wrongness of rape. It is violative because it involves the crossing of the will and it involves a direct violation of the victim's body and selfhood. It is the crossing of boundaries that are partly definitive of the self. Typically it is also damaging to the victim, a point we pick up in the next part. We also see clearly why rape is *grave*. It is readily distinguished from vandalism, assault, and theft because it violates persons *themselves* while vandalism, assault, and theft violate the *rights* of persons. Gardner and Shute pushed consent away from centre stage in accounting for the wrongness of rape because rape, they saw, has got to be differently and more gravely wrong than vandalism, assault, and theft. I have argued that they then took a step in the wrong direction by assimilating the wrongness of rape to the putative wrongness of consensual prostitution and pornography, and introducing what I believe to be a red herring wrapped in the sheer use principle. The question they pose, however, does nicely expose a danger in criminal law thinking. We think in terms of rights, obligations, and deontological categories, like the sheer use principle. But the gravity of rape is also in part a function of its badness, rather than its wrongness.

III Harm and the Harm Principle

I would like to close with a brief consideration of the harm principle. Attention to the notion of horrific crime should make us suspect that the harm principle has no useful role to play in debates about the criminalization of crimes of that sort. Gardner's and Shute's essay also has as a major aim the vindication of the harm principle (and though there are, of course, other versions of the harm principle, I will stick primarily to theirs). They wish to vindicate the harm principle against what might be thought a damaging counter-example from the context of rape. The counter-example in question is described by the authors as the 'pure case of rape':

A victim may be forever oblivious to the fact that she was raped, if say, she was drugged or drunk to the point of unconsciousness when the rape was committed, and the rapist wore a condom ... Then we have a victim of rape whose life is not changed for the worse, or at all, by the rape ... Indeed the story has no prospective dimension for the victim, except possibly a hangover in the morning; otherwise the victim's life goes on exactly as before. Not even, for that matter, a prospective dimension for others, who might be put in fear of midnight rape by tales of soporific victims taken unawares. Remember in our example the incident never comes to light at all.[49]

The worry for those who, like Gardner and Shute, wish to support the harm principle is this. There is absolutely no doubt that their undiscoverable, 'pure case' is one of rape, that it involves a wrong, and that there is nothing illegitimate about its criminalization. But it looks like it might be harmless, or at least harmless in the restricted sense of harm that proponents of the harm principle need. So, if harm is to be held a necessary condition for legitimate criminalization, we seem to have a damaging counter-example. For we surely cannot stomach the conclusion that it would be *wrong in principle* to criminalize such a rape, even if one might say—since undiscoverability is one of its features—that it might be pointless to do so if somehow the case was not already covered by existing rape laws. The authors' way of dealing with this example is to accept that it is a case of harmless rape, but to claim, first that harm is irrelevant to the question of wrongness, and second that the case, initial appearances to the contrary, ultimately jumps the hurdle to legitimate criminalization set up by the harm principle.

Let us take the second of these points first, since it can be dealt with more briefly. While the 'pure case' is harmless, it does not follow, say the authors, that a failure to criminalize it would also be harmless. 'It is enough', they say, 'to meet the demands of the harm principle that, if the action were not criminalized, *that* would be harmful.' 'This test', they add, 'is passed by the pure case of rape with flying colours.'[50] But how exactly would it be harmful if the pure case were not criminalized? I cannot myself see a satisfactory response. Gardner and Shute answer that people's rights to sexual autonomy would more often be violated.[51] For this consideration to support their argument the harm would need to be caused specifically by the legislator's omission. If there were somehow a loophole such that rape laws did not cover the pure case but otherwise covered all the cases they should, the authors' claim is that the legislator must close the loophole, on pain of causing more harm by way of more violations of sexual autonomy. There would of course be no relevant resulting harm in Gardner's and Shute's sense if failing to close the loophole led to actual, undiscovered, pure cases of rape. It is, after all, their own claim that such cases are harmless. Perhaps the idea is that potential rapists would (irrationally) take encouragement from the existence of the loophole and carry out rapes they would not otherwise attempt, even though a successful attempt

---

[49] Gardner and Shute (n 29 above) 5.   [50] Ibid, 29.   [51] Ibid, 30.

would be beyond the law because undiscoverable, and a failed attempt would already be covered by the existing law. I am not sure if sufficient sense can be made of this suggestion, but surely if the harm principle hangs on this it hangs on a thin thread indeed.

For all that, I do not doubt that proponents of the harm principle could come up with some other story to show that this case is criminalized consistently with its demands. But we should question the motivation for doing so in the first place. For there is a deeper consideration that should put us off thinking in terms of the harm principle here at all. Harm is a protean notion containing many potential meanings of importance to the criminal law; too many to capture in a restricted formula such as the harm principle. Developing this point brings us back to the first claim that the authors made, that their pure case itself is not harmful. Let us backtrack a moment. Is it plausible to conclude with the authors that their 'pure case' is in itself harmless? In their view, because the life of the victim goes on exactly as before, because her life prospects are not set back, because her capacity to choose amongst an adequate range of valuable options is not affected, she is not harmed. It will be useful to give this conception of harm a label. Let us call it *prospect-harm*. It is clearly of very great moral importance. But can it by itself account for the importance of harm?

Must harm, in other words, be understood as restricted to such prospect-harm only? Could one not say that the victim of the pure case *is* harmed because her interest in sexual integrity is set back by virtue of having undergone sex to which she did not consent? Of course, she does not know this at the time and does not discover it subsequently, but it remains true of her that her sexual integrity has been set back, notwithstanding her lack of knowledge: does that not harm her?[52] Alternatively, could one not say that the victim of the pure case suffers a *dignitary harm*? Dignitary harms are 'the indiginities that an actor A inflicts upon S by manifesting that he has so little regard for S that he is ready to abridge S's legitimate interests in order to aggrandize himself.'[53] Again, S's ignorance of what has taken place does not here preclude the harm. These are stipulated senses of harm, of course, but so is Gardner's and Shute's. All three pick out factors of genuine moral significance and none of the three is obviously unnatural as an ordinary-language understanding of harm. Presumably the reason Gardner and Shute restrict 'harm' to prospect-harm is theoretical. It ties harm to the value of autonomy in order, inter alia, that autonomy can constrain legislation in general and criminalization in particular. It

---

[52] D Archard, 'The Wrong of Rape' (2007) 57 *Philosophical Quarterly* 374.
[53] P Westen, *The Logic of Consent: The Diversity and Deceptiveness of Consent as a Defence to Criminal Conduct* (Aldershot: Ashgate, 2004) 149.

can thereby block the criminalization of certain harmless immoralities, or paternalist measures, so the thought goes. But in doing so it is bypassing matters of moral importance to precisely the context of criminalization.

Leaving aside the untypical 'pure case' of rape, one can buttress this point by observing that there is *another* sense of harm, of considerable practical importance to rape, which is not captured in the authors' notion of prospect-harm. This we might call *experiential harm*. Experiential harm (unlike prospect-harm, which points to those objective factors that affect the presence or adequacy of one's valuable options or one's ability to choose between them) concerns what a life feels like from the inside. Though there can be cases in which there is no experiential harm suffered as a result of a rape (as the 'pure case' establishes), the typical case of rape is followed by considerable experiential suffering. Such suffering of rape victims, even if not invariably present, is part and parcel of the horror of rape. An understanding of the character of a victim's attendant and consequent suffering is indispensable, I believe, to our understanding of the wrongness, badness, and gravity of rape.[54] The testimony of victims must remain a very strong consideration in our understanding of the wrongness, badness, and gravity of rape. This fits naturally into the idea that horrific violations typically involve damage. There might in some exceptional cases be reasons not to take some victim testimony at face value—some victims blame themselves, for example, for what has happened to them.[55] But our sense of the horrific must in general be informed by testimony of how certain suffering feels from the inside. In an interesting recent monograph, Jamie Mayerfeld develops a focus on 'suffering in the psychological sense, because [he wants] to claim that this particular phenomenon has towering moral significance in its own right, and that we have a powerful duty to stop and prevent it'.[56] Rape would be a good case study for his thesis. While one must not make the utilitarian mistake of *reducing* all harm to psychological feelings, one must also not make the mistake of forgetting the importance of psychological suffering. Gardner and Shute rightly identify the importance of what I called 'prospect-

---

[54] See, eg J Saward, *Rape: My Story* (London: Pan Books, 1991); J Jordan, *Serial Survivors: Women's Narratives of Surviving Rape* (Sydney: Federation Press, 2008). McCord Adams (n 8 above, 211) stresses the importance of how things seem from the inside to accounts of our understanding of the horrific. Gardner and Shute have a further argument for their conclusion that the experiences of victims are irrelevant to the wrongness of rape: (n 29 above) 6–7. The argument is similar to Judith Jarvis Thomson's argument from 'belief-mediated distress' in *The Realm of Rights* (Cambridge, Mass: Harvard University Press, 1990) 250ff. Thomson's argument, however, is effectively criticized by Alan Wertheimer in *Consent to Sexual Relations* (Cambridge: Cambridge University Press, 2003) 98–9.

[55] Temkin and Krahé (n 32 above) 38 and references therein.

[56] J Mayerfeld, *Suffering and Moral Responsibility* (Oxford: Oxford University Press, 1999) 11–12.

harm'. But harm cannot be confined to this notion. Someone who suffers psychologically after a rape might or might not be affected in terms of her ability to choose between an adequate range of valuable options. Often, of course, such psychological suffering might damage her capacity for the sort of autonomous life Gardner and Shute are rightly concerned should be protected. But it need not. The rape victim might *just suffer* while her life otherwise goes on as before. Attempting to prevent such suffering is very much the business of the criminal law.

It is not implausible, then, to say that the pure case of rape *does* harm the victim in the sense of a dignitary harm or in the sense of a setback to her interest in sexual integrity; and the more typical case of a suffering-inducing rape usually causes experiential harm. The lesson of this necessary profusion of senses of harm is not that we should adopt a new, broader harm principle (it would anyway be much *too* broad for the liking of traditional supporters of the principle). It is rather that one must focus carefully on the moral character of anything that is to be considered apt for criminalization, without any artificially truncated, technical sense of harm to distort our thinking. It is common to distinguish between crimes that are *mala in se* and crimes that are *mala prohibita*. The latter presuppose legal regulation whose breach constitutes an offence and are not our present concern. *Mala in se* crimes are wrong in a way that does not presuppose prior legal regulation in the same way. I have been trying to urge attention to a further division within *mala in se* crimes, between those that are horrific and those that are not. The guiding thought is that some crimes—horrific crimes—violate persons while others do not violate persons themselves, they violate their rights.

In suggesting that it is otiose to insist that the terms of the harm principle be met in the case of horrific crimes like rape, I have sided with the legal moralist against the proponent of the harm principle. I do not mean, however, to endorse any form of legal moralism that states boldly that a moral wrong is a sufficient reason for criminalization. It is not: there are many more hurdles for the legal moralist to get over. Most obviously, not any and every moral wrong or evil is a candidate for criminalization, an obviously large topic that requires a full and separate treatment. Moroever, where there is reason to criminalize a moral wrong, detailed attention will always be needed to questions such as: will criminalization be self-defeating? Will it have undesirable side effects? Will it deflect resources away from a point at which they are needed more? And so on.[57] The ultimate judgement in such cases may yet be that criminali-

---

[57] A little more is said on this in Stanton-Ife (n 7 above), especially in the brief section entitled 'Means–Ends Limits'.

zation is unjustified. For all that, it is high time to loosen the unhelpful grip of the harm principle on our understanding of criminalization.

IV   Conclusion

In the second half of this chapter, I observed that Gardner and Shute had posed two good questions. First, how are we to understand rape as a wrong distinct from other wrongs like vandalism, theft, and assault? Second, how are we to account for the greater seriousness of rape than these other crimes? I have argued that their own proposal in response to both questions—that rape is wrong because it is the sheer use of another—itself answers neither of them. The answer to both, I believe, is that vandalism, theft, and assault are not *horrific* crimes, while rape is. Vandalism, theft, and assault violate *the rights* of persons, rape violates these people them*selves*. In understanding the idea of horrific crime one should, I believe, begin with common psychological reactions to what we find horrific, excluding those psychological reactions for which human agency bears no responsibility, and then ask how far we can trust such reactions. We should test the intuitive reactions against an understanding of horrific violations which accounts for them in terms of destruction, damage, or the crossing of the will of the victim in a way that impacts directly on the victim's selfhood. To reject 'consent' as the answer to why rape is wrong and why it is so grave is, I believe, to sell its moral importance short. For sexual consent is central to selfhood. A further salutary lesson that emerges is that the importance of consent should not be conceived of as a constant from one offence to the next. One needs to examine its importance separately in different cases: one size is unlikely to fit all. Consent might not turn out to have the importance it has in rape when attention shifts, say, to murder or maiming. There is a tendency in criminal law thinking, encouraged by the harm principle, to try to account for crimes in general in terms of interests. This, to be sure, has been illuminating in many contexts. However, it can also have the effect of shoehorning all crimes into one box, with the result that we fail to see how best to explain the gravity of some crimes; horrific crimes in particular. One should not conceive of the victims of crime in all *mala in se* offences as simply those whose interests have been violated. Victims of horrific crimes have been violated themselves.

7

Criminalization and Regulation

*Victor Tadros**

I Introduction

What ought to be the scope of the criminal law? The most familiar way to approach this question is to consider what moral constraints there might be on the decision whether to criminalize some conduct. It is not permissible to criminalize a particular type of conduct, it might be argued, unless that conduct is harmful, or it is publicly wrongful, or it is deserving of punishment, or some combination of these. Answers of this kind are likely to be highly indeterminate. The best efforts to produce principled constraints on the criminal law, even were they endorsed by policy makers, might do little to constrain its expansive and expanding scope. Even if we think that there are many constraining principles and each must be satisfied for criminalization to be permissible, our principles would warrant the criminalization of many things that we do not wish to see criminalized.[1]

There is another approach to the question of the scope of the criminal law that is both less familiar and less well developed. It is comparative. We investigate whether criminalization is permissible given the alternatives available to us. We ought to criminalize some conduct only if doing so is permissible

* Forerunners of this paper were given at the Centre for Criminology, University of Oxford, Osgoode Hall Law School, York University, and at the workshop in Warwick. Thanks to my audiences on all three occasions for probing questions. Particular thanks go to Susan Dimock, my respondent at Osgoode Hall and to Alon Harel, my respondent at Warwick. Thanks also to Octavio Ferraz, Danny Priel, Massimo Renzo, Prince Saprai, and François Tanguay-Renaud for detailed comments.

[1] A range of constraints that must be mutually satisfied is recommended by D Husak in *Overcriminalization* (Oxford: Oxford University Press, 2007). Husak's book is the most sophisticated treatment of criminalization to date. But it has been suggested that even Husak's set of constraints would do relatively little to constrain the scope of the criminal law. See V Tadros, 'The Architecture of Criminalization' (2009) 28 *Criminal Justice Ethics* 74 and J Gardner's review of Husak's book, *Notre Dame Philosophical Reviews* (August 2008).

given the other possible things that we could do in response to that conduct, including nothing. We might conclude that, although some conduct is harmful, publicly wrongful, and in principle deserving of punishment, we ought not to criminalize it because this is a disproportionate response to the conduct we are concerned with.[2] It is disproportionate because some less draconian alternative is available to us.

My aim in this chapter is to make some progress with this approach to criminalization by comparing criminalization of some conduct with civil regulation of the same conduct. By civil regulation I mean laws introduced by the state that impose some kind of liability on those who breach the regulation, but which are not criminal. Private wrongs, such as torts and breaches of contract, count as one kind of civil regulation. Private law typically regulates conduct by requiring citizens to compensate the person who has been harmed in the breaching of the relevant regulation. In order to claim compensation, the individual harmed must bring an action against the individual who has harmed her.

Another kind of civil regulation is less distinct from the criminal law. We distinguish between criminal offences and 'regulatory' offences, though the law in England and Wales (at least) does not distinguish formally between the two. The latter, it is sometimes said, are not *truly* criminal. Here we are concerned with a set of regulations which, if they are breached, render the person breaching them liable to pay a fine. But the fine is considered to be a penalty rather than a punishment.

In setting up this comparison we will need to know something more about the distinctive mark or marks of a true criminal offence. What makes an offence truly criminal as opposed to merely regulatory? As our investigation is normative, how we decide that question depends upon our theory of the criminal law and punishment. What is it that criminal law does that regulatory offences do not do? I will aim to make best sense of that distinction by drawing on what I think is the most plausible theory of punishment. I will then show why we might sometimes have reason to use the criminal law: where civil regulation is not good enough.

II Condemnation, Punishment, and the Scope of the Criminal Law

There are three things that might be thought distinctive of the criminal law. One is that criminal convictions are said to have a condemnatory function that civil regulations lack. When a person is convicted of a criminal offence he

---

[2] I will clarify the conception of proportionality at work here in the conclusions of this chapter.

is condemned for what he has done. Breach of a civil regulation does not warrant condemnation. A second feature of the criminal law that plausibly makes it distinctive is that criminal convictions, unlike civil regulations, warrant punishment of the offender. Those who breach civil regulations are liable to bear some cost for what they have done, of course, but they are not liable to be punished. A third mark of the criminal law is the process which one must go through to warrant criminal conviction. Criminal convictions are warranted only if a high standard of proof has been met and a range of other procedural protections, which have a role both in protecting people from wrongful convictions and in ensuring that their rights of participation are fully protected, is present in criminal trials.

It is natural to think of the third of these features of the criminal law as dependent on the other two. The first two features are the two central functions of the criminal law. The third provides a constraint on the exercise of those functions. It is because the criminal law is concerned with condemnation and punishment that we ought only to convict people of criminal offences if they have been subject to an adequate process. The process will be adequate only if it gives people proper protection against wrongful conviction as well as providing them with proper opportunities to answer the charge that is made against them. In contrast, in the case of civil regulation condemnation and punishment are not involved, so procedural protections against the imposition of liability, though still important, may be weaker.

Both of the central functions of the criminal law are important ones for a state to carry out. We have good reason to condemn some people for their wrongful conduct and we have good reason to punish people for what they have done. In principle at least, we could set up institutions that do one or the other of these things but not both. We might develop condemnatory institutions that do not punish or punitive institutions that do not condemn. And we could have two sets of laws: condemnatory laws and punitive laws that regulate and are administered by these two institutions. We could then ask what the scope of these different sets of laws should be and what procedures should apply to them. Perhaps one set might be broader than the other, or perhaps they might intersect. Why do we have a single institution that performs these two functions?

A Public wrongs, condemnation, and punishment

For some philosophers of the criminal law, the justification of condemnation and punishment are very closely related. Expressivists, who believe that punishment is justified because of its communicative potential, will argue that the grounds for condemnation are inevitably the grounds for punishment as the two practices are intimately related to each other. Retributivists, who argue that punishment is warranted to ensure that wrongdoers get what they deserve, might also believe this. Those who deserve to suffer, they will argue, are also those who deserve publicly to be condemned.

These views about punishment bring with them a certain degree of pressure to expand the criminal law in some respects at least. There are many morally wrongful actions that we do not criminalize. But if the institution of punishment is justified for its condemnatory potential, or to give people what they deserve, we will naturally ask why we ought not to punish people for these actions. These philosophers will need arguments against expanding the criminal law in these ways.

Legal moralists, such as Michael Moore, think that there *are* good reasons in favour of punishing all wrongdoers, although these reasons may be defeated by various epistemic, pragmatic, and moral considerations. There may be doubts about what is morally wrong, and we ought to err on the side of caution; and even if we are certain that some conduct is morally wrong, criminalizing that conduct, if the law is to be enforced, might be very expensive. Also, expanding the law might restrict autonomy too much.[3]

Others attempt to stem the potential tide of criminalization at the first stage, arguing that there is no reason in favour of the criminalization of particular kinds of wrongful conduct. There are some actions which are wrong, but not *publicly* wrong, it has been argued. These actions might merit condemnation by someone, these scholars argue, but they ought not to be condemned by the state in the name of the citizens of the polity. Wrongdoers may be responsible for committing these wrongs, but they are not responsible *to the state* for committing them.[4]

We can perhaps make some progress in this latter way, but our progress is, I think, limited. Here's how we can make some progress. There might be wrongs that people commit but which the state has no interest in at all. Perhaps we can say about these wrongs that they are none of the state's business. It has no role in condemning them, nor in punishing people for perpetrating them. We might think that adultery is a good example of this.[5] Adultery is plausibly at least sometimes wrong, perhaps even seriously wrong, but it is not a wrong that the state has any interest in. We have no right to condemn people *publicly* for committing adultery. For this is a private rather than a public matter.

---

[3] M Moore, *Placing Blame* (Oxford: Oxford University Press, 1997) pt III.

[4] See, eg SE Marshall and RA Duff, 'Criminalization and Sharing Wrongs' (1998) 11 *Canadian Journal of Law and Jurisprudence* 7; RA Duff, *Answering for Crime* (Oxford: Hart Publishing, 2007); and Husak (n 1 above) 135–7.   [5] See Duff (ibid) 144–5.

I might owe an obligation to my partner not to cheat on her if I have promised not to do so and she trusts me to be faithful. Perhaps I owe that obligation to others as well, say to my children. These people can rightly hold me responsible for my adulterous actions. But I do not owe that obligation to the state and I cannot be held responsible by the state for adultery. That is so even if adultery is seriously wrongful, if it is a serious breach of trust which is psychologically crushing to my partner.

I'm not sure whether this is true, but at least it is plausible. But it is not a very good account of the scope of the *criminal* law in particular. We should already have been alerted to the problem by the fact that, if there are reasons of this kind not to criminalize adultery, those reasons seem to count equally against the civil regulation of adultery. Because adultery is not the business of the state, neither do we think that we should regulate adultery through private law. If a person is not answerable to the state for committing adultery, we do not think that the state should legally regulate adultery at all. This concern applies quite generally. Anything that the state is justified in prohibiting, whether through criminal or civil law, is a public wrong.

Assuming that what the state has done is just, the regulations that are created by the state, both civil and criminal, will normally create obligations on citizens. It is morally wrong to breach any just regulation that creates an obligation on citizens to abide by it. Furthermore, if a regulation is just, it inevitably follows that it is in the interests of the state as a whole that the regulation is adhered to. Only in adhering to just regulations will justice be served. From that it follows that breach of the regulation is not only wrong but also that it is *publicly* wrong. It is a wrong that the state must take an interest in, for were it not rightfully to take an interest in that conduct what business would the state have had in regulating it in the first place? If that is true, what argument can be advanced for the claim that it is not in principle permissible to condemn citizens for breaching civil regulations?

Those defending the idea of public wrongs as a mark of the criminal law in particular face the difficult task of showing that, even though the imposition of civil public regulations on our conduct is just, we are not answerable to the public, in principle, for breaching those regulations. I do not see how this can be done. Were we able to show that we are answerable only to each other as private citizens for breach of private law, we would also show that private law ought to be abolished. If conduct is justly regulated by the state we are responsible to the state for adhering to those regulations.

Now, it might be objected that citizens do not have an obligation to abide by civil regulations. Rather, they have an obligation to pay the appropriate cost if they breach the regulation. On this model, civil regulations amount to conditional permissions to act. A person is permitted to breach the regulation as long as he or she is willing to bear the cost laid down by the law. In other words, civil regulations price conduct rather than prohibiting it.

But even if this is the best way to understand some civil regulations it does not seem plausible as a general model of civil regulations. Civil regulations typically create obligations on citizens to do what the regulation requires. They do not merely price conduct—they prohibit it. The state imposes obligations on us not to breach our contracts, nor to defame or negligently harm each other. The law does not declare to us that we may breach these regulations if we wish to, so long as we are willing to pay the costs.

We might ask why this should be the case. Why should we not regard civil law as pricing rather than prohibiting conduct? A brief and incomplete answer is that justice is normally better served if everyone adheres to civil regulations rather than breaching them and paying compensation. Being compensated for being harmed is not normally fully satisfactory to the person harmed. One reason why is that a person who breaches a just regulation is not normally required to pay the full cost that they and others impose on us by breaching the regulation. Often, breaches of the regulations are not discovered and even if they are their effects are ameliorated by a range of expensive social services. Those who breach the regulations, and who are discovered, are not typically expected to cover all of these costs through the liability that they incur.

But why should we not make it so? Why not make those who breach the regulations pay the full costs that would make the person harmed indifferent about the fact that they had been harmed? Could we not develop the civil law to ensure that full compensation is paid? And if we did that could we not regard the civil law as pricing rather than as prohibiting conduct? I doubt that it would be just to do that. We can be expected to bear some of the costs of the harmful conduct of our fellow citizens, even the harms that they wrongfully cause. We should expect that people will sometimes make unwise choices and we should not expect people to bear the full costs of those choices.[6] If they cannot be expected to bear these costs, someone else will be required to bear them. And if the regulations are just this suggests that breach of a regulation may impose costs and duties on others: costs and duties that they would prefer not to bear. It follows from this that people ought not to breach civil regulations. For in doing so they impose on us an obligation to bear or contribute to the losses that are caused by breach. And we will prefer not to have these costs and obligations. Contrary to what HLA Hart thought,[7] then, we cannot

---

[6] For further discussion of limits on the internalization of choice-sensitive costs, see SV Schiffrin, 'Egalitarianism, Choice-Sensitivity, and Accommodation' in RJ Wallace *et al* (eds), *Reason and Value: Themes in the Moral Philosophy of Joseph Raz* (Oxford: Oxford University Press, 2004).

[7] *Punishment and Responsibility*, 2nd edn (Oxford: Oxford University Press, 2008) 6.

distinguish crimes from other regulations on the grounds that crimes prohibit. Both crimes and civil regulations prohibit.

If this is right, there seems very good reason to think that, in principle at least, the state is justified in condemning the breach of *any* state regulation that citizens are supposed to abide by, be that regulation civil or criminal. It follows that, if we accept an expressivist or a retributivist view of punishment, there is a strong reason to punish people for breaching the civil law. Even more, as expressivists and retributivists tend to think that the state has a strong reason, or perhaps even a duty, to condemn wrongful conduct or to give people what they deserve through punishment, punishing people for civil wrongs is not only warranted, it is justified or perhaps even required.

Of course, expressivists and retributivists might argue that we ought not to condemn offenders through the civil law for other reasons, most obviously because the procedural protections which provide us with a high degree of confidence that condemnation is appropriate are absent in the civil law. But that only reinforces the point that there would be good reason to criminalize much of the conduct regulated by the civil law. By criminalizing the conduct we would require prosecution of that conduct in a criminal trial. And we would then ensure that the conditions under which we can properly condemn people for their wrongful conduct are met. That would allow us to meet our obligation to condemn them.

A question for expressivists and retributivists, then, is why may we not incorporate the whole of the civil law into the criminal law? I do not say that these theorists cannot answer this question, but that is the difficult question which they face. Since I do not share their view of punishment I will not ex plore this any further. My own view of punishment is different. I believe that punishment is justified only if it has instrumental benefits, most obviously that it can reduce crime. I agree that the criminal law has a condemnatory function, but I do not think that punishment is primarily justified by the obligation to condemn offenders.

What role can the condemnatory function of the criminal law play in a theory of criminalization, in that case? Surely the condemnatory function of the state has some significance in determining what we ought to criminalize? I think that it does, but it makes only a modest contribution to that investigation. There might be some actions that the state has a strong duty to condemn. Even if we were to abolish punishment, perhaps we should retain condemnatory institutions that would provide opportunities to make people accountable for committing these wrongs. We might do this in order to ensure that the victims of these wrongs appreciate that they are important to us, and that their rights must be respected. Or we might do it to help to guide people in their private responses to wrongdoing, to help to ensure that they do not over or underreact to wrongdoing.

But although I think that it is true that we have strong reasons to condemn some wrongdoers I doubt that these reasons are very important in an investigation of the appropriate limits of the criminal law, for I do not think that there are very strong reasons to condemn offenders for wrongdoing that is not very serious. Were we not to publicly condemn people for theft of £100, for example, we would not fail in a very important duty, just as we do not fail to perform a very important duty by failing publicly to condemn people for breach of a contract to build a wall. These things are wrong, and the victims have had their rights violated. There is some reason for the state publicly to acknowledge this. But the reason is not very compelling. Were there no further reasons to criminalize the conduct, given the expense of criminalization and the burdens it imposes, our desire to condemn the conduct publicly would be insufficiently strong to warrant criminalization.

In deciding whether theft or breach of contract should be criminalized we should not focus on the obligation to condemn these things. Even if we have such an obligation it is not very powerful. We should rather focus on whether we wish to punish people for perpetrating these wrongs. If punishment provides good reason to criminalize these things then we will create the conditions under which they can be condemned; we will prosecute the person in a criminal court with all of the procedural protections that are required before it is permissible to punish the person. But it is punishment that ought to guide us in determining what to criminalize, not the obligation to condemn.

B The centrality of punishment to criminalization

If the state's duty to condemn wrongful conduct is not very important in a theory of criminalization, then, we would do better to focus on the other function of the criminal law: the punishment of offenders.[8] This will raise more difficult issues, though, as the justification of punishment is heavily contested. The way in which punishment figures in a theory of criminalization depends on what the right justification of punishment is.[9] I have already suggested that two theories of punishment, expressivism and retributivism, will create significant pressure to expand the scope of the criminal law to occupy areas that are currently left to be regulated by the civil law.

I now want to focus on an alternative justification of punishment, one that I endorse, which focuses on its instrumental effects. The most important positive effect that the criminal law might have is that it will tend to deter people from committing criminal offences. It might do this by issuing threats to

---

[8] See also Husak (n 1 above) ch 2.II.
[9] For further discussion why this is so, see Tadros (n 1 above).

people, threats that it carries out through punishment. On this view, it is not a good thing, and indeed it is a bad thing, that the offender is made to suffer through punishment. But doing that bad thing might be justified by the good effects that it has.

It is often thought that focusing on the instrumental benefits that punishment might bring is best explained by consequentialism as a general moral theory. Because many people reject consequentialism they reject instrumentalism as well. But instrumentalism and consequentialism are not importantly related. Consequentialism is a comprehensive moral theory which claims that the rightness and wrongness of an action are determined entirely by the consequences it has. Instrumentalists think that punishment is justified by the good consequences that it has, but they may also believe that the consequences of an action are not *all* that matters to its rightness or wrongness; and that suggests that a theory of punishment might be both instrumentalist and non-consequentialist.

Non-consequentialist instrumentalists will try to show that punishment has its central justification in virtue of the good consequences that punishment brings, and that pursuing these good consequences is not wrong. They will do this by showing that punishing people for these reasons is consistent with the best understanding of the set of principles and duties governing what it is right and wrong to do. These principles and duties are not to be endorsed simply because of the consequences that would result from abiding by them. The way in which the consequences are brought about, the rights that people have, and the extent to which bringing them about is fair to each person taken individually might also be important in determining what these principles and duties are.

One familiar way to go about exploring whether it is permissible to punish people on instrumental grounds is to explore the relationship between punishment and self-defence. There is good reason to draw this parallel. Self-defence is typically justified on instrumentalist grounds. We are permitted to defend ourselves against wrongful attacks in order to protect ourselves, but not in order to give our attackers what they deserve. If that is right, harming the attacker is instrumentally valuable rather than intrinsically valuable. But most of the philosophical writing on self-defence is in the non-consequentialist tradition, recognizing the importance of protecting the rights that people have, or ensuring that harms are distributed fairly according to non-consequentialist principles.

The main objection that is raised to this approach to punishment is that, in punishing offenders in order to deter other people, the offender is harmed as a means to the good of others.[10] Non-consequentialists typically argue that there is a constraint on harming a person as a means, what we might call the *means principle*. Punishing people for reasons of deterrence, it is sometimes argued, would violate the means principle.

There are two responses to this objection. One, which is by far the most familiar response, aims to show that deterrence does not always harm a person as a means to the good of others.[11] This approach builds on the permissibility of making and carrying out threats against particular individuals. If we threaten a person that if she harms us we will harm her in return, we do not use her as a means. To threaten a person, at least if we are honest in making that threat, involves forming a conditional intention to carry out the threat. Carrying out the threat, it is argued, does not violate the means principle: it merely executes an intention that was justly formed. And if it was just to form the intention to harm under certain conditions, it is just to execute the intention if the conditions are met.

The challenge for this approach is to show that the justification of carrying out a threat follows from the justification of making that threat, which is no easy task.[12] We might think that the main reason to carry out the threat is to ensure that other people recognize that our threats are not idle, enhancing the extent to which we are protected from them. But if that is the right explanation why we ought to carry out the threats that we make, we must also accept that in carrying out the threat we harm the person we punish as a means to avert harms that others might cause us in the future. Some answers have been suggested to this problem. They mainly focus on the possibility that we might automatically carry out the threat. That response is innovative but not, I think, wholly convincing.

Another response, one that is more promising, explores the idea that the means principle is not absolute, and that its limits are governed by other important principles. The aim is to show that punishment is warranted as an exception to the means principle. The aim, on this approach, is to identify a source of exceptions to the means principle and show that punishment can be justified on the same basis.

To see that there are some exceptions to the means principle, consider the following example. Suppose that I hire a hit man who is about to kill you. He

[10] See RA Duff, *Punishment, Communication and Community* (Oxford: Oxford University Press, 2001) 16–19.

[11] See W Quinn, 'The Right to Threaten and the Right to Punish' in his *Morality and Action* (Cambridge: Cambridge University Press, 1993) and A Ellis, 'A Deterrence Theory of Punishment' (2003) 53 *Philosophical Quarterly* 337.

[12] See especially D Farrell, 'On Threats and Punishments' (1989) 15 *Social Theory and Practice* 125.

is pointing a gun at you and will kill you unless you use me as a shield to protect yourself. Assuredly, it would not be wrong for you to use me (but not an innocent bystander) as a shield in this case. Nonetheless, if you do use me as a shield, you use me as a means to prevent yourself from being harmed. This seems a plausible exception to the means principle.

Obviously enough the example of the hit man is a long way away from our punishment practices. There are a number of objections that would need to be addressed to show that they are also an exception to the means principle. For example, in the hit man case you avert an immediate threat that I am responsible for creating. In punishment, in contrast, we avert threats that the offender is not responsible for creating, and that are not even in existence. Furthermore, the threat posed by the hit man is imminent whereas punishment addresses potential threats that are not yet in existence. I will not attempt to address these concerns here, though I think they can be satisfactorily overcome.[13]

Whether punishment provides an exception to the means principle depends on the other principles that govern the permissibility of harm. From a non-consequentialist perspective, three things might be regarded as important in securing the plausibility of general deterrence as part of the justification of punishment:

(i) People have an adequate opportunity to avoid suffering punishment given adherence to the rule of law and other principles of criminal law, as well as a rigorous system of trials that protects people against wrongful convictions. With these protections in place it is easier to justify an exception to the means principle.

(ii) Breaching the law only renders offenders liable to suffer proportionately to their crime, so citizens are given adequate protection against being made to suffer extensively, even given the opportunity citizens have to avoid punishment.

(iii) The punishment of offenders prevents others suffering a burden that is comparable to that suffered by the offenders who are punished and which they would not otherwise have an opportunity to avoid. So, were it not for the fact that offenders are punished, someone else would suffer without adequate protection against that suffering.

Rather than defending these ideas further, which I will do at length elsewhere, I want to show that, if this is the right view about punishment, it will have important implications for the scope of the criminal law.

---

[13] See V Tadros, *The Moral Foundations of Criminal Law* (Oxford: Oxford University Press, forthcoming).

This view of punishment provides us with an unfamiliar but plausible account of the distinction between punishment and penalties. By far the most familiar view of the distinction between punishment and penalties is that punishment has an expressive quality that penalties lack. Punishment communicates censure in a way that penalties do not, it is thought.[14] I doubt, though, that punishment must have this communicative aspect to it. We can impose suffering on people to deter other people without intending to communicate condemnation for that person's wrongdoing. Also, punishment is not distinctive from civil penalties in imposing suffering on people. A person might also suffer as a result of having penalties imposed on them. Fines that are imposed only in order to compensate the victims may make the person who is liable to pay them suffer.

But penalties are not *aimed* at making the offender suffer. Punishment aims at the suffering of wrongdoers to deter others. It is, in that case, an example of something bad that it is aimed at. Furthermore it is aimed at averting acts of other would-be criminals who might be deterred by punishing offenders. Hence, when we punish an offender we harm that offender as a means to avert threats that others might pose. Penalties, in contrast, are aimed at redistributing benefits and burdens. Penalties are aimed at ensuring that the costs of breaching regulations are borne by those who breach rather than those that suffer from the breach. In other words, penalties aim at redistribution of the costs of the breach of regulations whereas punishment aims to reduce the instances of breach by making those who breach the regulations suffer. Hence, punishment makes people suffer as a means to avert threats that the offender is not responsible for creating. Penalties do not do this.

That is why we will be especially concerned about the scope of the criminal law. When we create a criminal offence we expand the range of conduct that will make a person liable to be harmed as a means to avert threats that the person is not responsible for creating. The broader the scope of the criminal law, the more likely it is that people will breach it. In consequence, by expanding the scope of the criminal law we provide less protection to people against being liable to be harmed as a means in this way. If we think that it is important to protect ourselves from being harmed as a means, we will wish to restrict the scope of the criminal law. For we will know that, even if the criminal law is very clear and is known to us, we might be tempted to breach it, and that will render us liable to be harmed as a means for the good of others.[15]

---

[14] Influential in the acceptance of this idea is J Feinberg, 'The Expressive Function of Punishment' in his *Doing and Deserving* (Princeton, NJ: Princeton University Press, 1970).

[15] I consider this further in 'A Human Right to a Fair Criminal Law?' in J Chalmers, L Farmer, and F Leverick (eds), *Essays in Criminal Law in Honour of Sir Gerald Gordon* (Edinburgh: Edinburgh University Press, forthcoming).

This contrasts with the expansion of legal regulations in general. From our discussion of civil regulations, we can see that there are good reasons to be concerned at the expansion of state power in general. The state has the ability to control areas of our lives, restricting our autonomy. If I am right that regulations typically prohibit conduct, a concern with liberty, autonomy, and so forth should lead us to scrutinize the limits of state regulation in general, and not those of the criminal law in particular. Furthermore, if we breach the civil law we are made liable to suffer and if the fines are high enough we might suffer a great deal.

But in expanding the *criminal* law the state expands the range of conditions under which a person is liable to be punished. And that involves an expansion of the range of circumstances in which a person is liable to be harmed as a means to avert threats that the person is not responsible for creating. We have good reason to be sceptical about the scope of the criminal law in particular, and over and above the expansion of state regulation in general, because we have good reason to protect our moral status as ends. Civil law may harm us, perhaps as much or even more than the criminal law does. But it does not aim at our suffering and it harms us only to rectify the harm that we have caused.

III Compensation Schemes

As punishment involves intentionally harming others, we might wonder whether it is justified at all. There are, no doubt, exceptions to the means principle, and punishment is plausibly one of those exceptions. But whether it is permissible to impose punishment on others depends on the other things that we could do to meet the threats that we face. In order to work out whether it is permissible to punish a person for an action we will want to know that punishment is a proportional response to the threat of harm. And in order to know whether it is a proportional response we need to consider the other things that we could do to avert or ameliorate those harms. I will return to this issue in the conclusions. My question in this part makes an important contribution to that investigation: how bad would things be were we not to punish people?

A The role of compensation

One thing that we could do were we to abolish punishment is to require wrong-doers to compensate victims for the harm that they have suffered. The possibility of compensation has played a role in discussions of criminalization. Doug Husak, for example, explores the idea that it is permissible to criminalize some conduct only if victims of that conduct cannot be expected to accept compensation for the harm they have suffered in some depth.[16] Compensation might be thought second-best to averting the harm: we ameliorate or counter-balance the harm a person suffers rather than avoiding it altogether. But if the burdens that victims of the breach of a regulation suffer from being harmed and compensated are modest perhaps we could expect them to accept compensation, even at some cost to themselves. We could justify this on the grounds that the alternative is to punish offenders, which involves aiming at their harm as a means to avert threats posed by others.

Furthermore, we could increase the amount of compensation that wrong-doers owe to victims to take into consideration the fact that it is worse to be harmed and restored to health than it is to be healthy all along. It is typically only if a person is just as well off as they would have been had they not been harmed, *all things considered*, that they have received full compensation.

A rule of thumb to test whether compensation is adequate might be to consider whether the person compensated, if she is reasonable about it, is indifferent about the fact that she has been harmed or whether she regrets the fact. The scope of the criminal law is determined by considering the nature of the harms that victims of some conduct would suffer to see whether compensation (most plausibly monetary compensation) ought to be accepted by the victim if it were available. Could money make a reasonable person indifferent to the fact that she has been harmed? This approach plausibly leaves some work for the criminal law to do. For we cannot expect victims of some kinds of wrong to be indifferent about having been wronged, however much they receive in compensation. A person who is murdered obviously cannot be sufficiently compensated to ensure that he is as well off as he would have been had he not been murdered. And given the effects of rape, perhaps this is true of rape as well.

But this approach to criminalization would render the criminal law implausibly narrow, I think. There are many wrongs for which, if the person is compensated sufficiently, they might be made *better* off than they would have been had they not been wronged. For example, it might be painful, frightening, and demeaning to be assaulted. But if a person has quite limited opportunities in life a large sum of money will probably be sufficient compensation for assault, especially if no permanent injury is caused. If the sum was big enough, the person might well look back and think that it was a good thing that they had been assaulted given the compensation they received. And even if that is not true of assault, it is certainly true of theft.

---

[16] (Note 1 above) 184–7. Ultimately he rejects the approach that I take here on the grounds of the expressive function of the criminal law that I considered above.

It might be argued that the principle that crimes must be incapable of being adequately compensated can justify retaining a criminal law beyond this narrow core. It might be argued that the effects of being a victim of wrongdoing are incommensurable with the good of receiving more wealth, and that makes it impossible to compensate a person for being a victim of wrongdoing. But if that is true it is also true of civil wrongs. The effects of breach of contract, of defamation, and of tort are no different in this respect from the effects of crime. So this idea cannot plausibly make more than a modest contribution to determining the scope of the criminal law.

Alternatively, it might be argued that we should attend not only to whether the direct victims can be compensated, but also to collateral effects of decriminalization. For example, Husak suggests that were theft decriminalized the population at large would be anxious that their possessions would be more likely to be stolen. Perhaps any increased fear that might come about through decriminalization of theft would be difficult to compensate.

There are two responses to this. First, as Husak recognizes, it might make the principle under consideration more or less redundant. People are afraid of losing their jobs, of injury in the workplace, of having contracts breached, and of being defamed. So if we could take into account anxiety, the principle that we can only criminalize that which cannot be compensated for loses much of its force. And second, if it is true that anxiety is difficult to compensate, this is true because of the practicalities of compensating people for anxiety rather than because a person cannot be compensated for the anxiety they feel. A large sum of money will surely compensate a person for feeling anxious about having a smaller sum stolen!

This last point suggests that the right way to understand the significance of compensation for criminalization is by investigating the comparative advantages and disadvantages of punishment and compensation in practice. Punishing a person for wrongdoing might be warranted, not because it is impossible to compensate the person for suffering the wrong in principle, but rather because it will be much too difficult to require the wrongdoer to compensate the victim in practice. We might be permitted to harm some offenders as a means of reducing the rate of offending because the alternative—providing compensation to victims—will be too difficult and costly to administer. That this is the right view is obvious enough: why should we think that we have done enough to protect victims of wrongdoing from suffering harm by showing that they could be expected to accept compensation were they to receive it? It must also matter that they will in fact receive it. What matters, then, is how effective our compensation schemes might be and what burdens they will impose on people in order to make them effective.

This approach is relatively familiar from the law and economics movement. However, those in that movement tend to have a more utilitarian approach than the one that I adopt here. They typically think that the central value to determine whether we should use tort law or the criminal law is efficiency, and they have rightly been criticized for that. Wealth and efficiency are subservient to, and must take their place within a comprehensive conception of justice.[17] A non-consequentialist, instrumentalist approach will be less reductive about the set of values and principles that ought to drive us in making comparisons between different schemes. It will be outlined in the light of principles that determine what justice requires.

B   Compensation schemes

In order to make further progress with our comparative approach we will need to know a little bit more about how compensation schemes might work. Our main focus when we think about compensation tends to be private law. But private law is not the only way that we could ensure that victims of wrongdoing are adequately compensated by wrongdoers. We could also do that by creating regulatory offences which penalize those who breach the regulations. Funds gathered in this way could be distributed to those who suffer as a consequence of wrongdoing. Regulatory offences are non-criminal in that they are not aimed at making offenders suffer, which I have suggested is the hallmark of punishment. Rather, offenders are required to bear a fair proportion of the costs of breaches of the regulations.

Regulatory offences rather than private law will provide my main alternative to the criminal law, both because they are closer to criminal law, and so are more likely to provide some of the benefits that are claimed for the criminal law, and also because regulatory schemes are often preferable to private law.

Why might we choose a scheme of civil regulation over a private law scheme? Here are three reasons. First, regulatory offences do not require private citizens to bring actions against those that harm them, and we thus make it less burdensome on them to mitigate the harm that they have suffered. Those who suffer from breach of a regulation might well prefer a scheme that never requires them to bear the costs of bringing an action over being compensated for the time, effort, and expense of doing so at a later stage.

It might be easier to ensure that those breaching the regulations shoulder a fair burden of the costs of investigation, prosecution, and enforcement through a scheme of civil regulations than it is in private law. Private law has

---

[17] See especially R Dworkin, *A Matter of Principle* (Oxford: Oxford University Press, 1985) pt 4.

the disadvantage that those harmed through breach of a regulation are asked to bear some risk in putting resources into the investigation. There is a risk that the courts, in error, will fail to attribute liability to the person who breached the regulation, and the person harmed will suffer not only the impact of the breach of the regulation, but also the costs that they have put into supporting a failed action. A regulation scheme will be more effective in ensuring that these costs are distributed fairly amongst complainants and those held liable.

Second, through regulatory offences, we might distribute the costs of the conduct regulated more fairly amongst those who breach the regulations. In particular, regulatory schemes are more effective than private law schemes in reducing the impact of luck both on those who breach the regulations and those who suffer through breach. Private law requires that the burden suffered as a result of any particular breach of a regulation is shared between the parties concerned. The harm caused by a particular breach, which may be very large, must be borne by a small number of people: either the defendant pays, or the plaintiff bears the cost, or the cost is distributed between the two. By creating a regulatory offence, we might ensure that costs of breach of the regulations are spread more evenly between those people that breach the regulations, reducing the role of causation in determining the extent of liability. In that way, we might reduce the impact of outcome luck.

Many philosophers of private law, of course, think that there are strong moral reasons to require people to compensate others fully for the harms that they cause. They think that morality or justice requires liability to track causation.[18] It is at least difficult to defend the extreme implications of this view where neither of the parties is seriously at fault for causing the harm.[19] Whether causation should play some role or no role at all in determining the degree of liability, we can control its impact through regulation schemes in a way that is very difficult to control through private law.

Also, regulatory schemes make it easier to ensure that whether those harmed by the regulated conduct are compensated is less sensitive to luck. Compensation might be provided to victims of breach where the person who breached the regulation cannot be found, or where that person has insufficient funds to pay, or where the person breaching the regulation was not at fault. Requiring those who are found to have breached the regulations to pay extra may help to achieve this result.

Finally, it might be easier to discover the total harm caused by the conduct to be regulated than it is to discover the contribution that each person makes

---

[18] See, eg T Honoré, 'Responsibility and Luck: The Moral Basis of Strict Liability' in his *Responsibility and Fault* (Oxford: Hart, 1999).

[19] See especially J Waldron, 'Moments of Carelessness and Massive Loss' in DG Owen (ed), *The Philosophical Foundations of Tort Law* (Oxford: Oxford University Press, 1995).

to that harm. For example, in the area of environmental harms, the harm caused by each agent who breaches an environmental regulation may be much more difficult to quantify than the damage suffered overall by breaches of that regulation. Regulatory schemes have the advantage that they do not necessarily require investigation of the causal contribution of any agent in order to impose liability.[20]

With respect to any such scheme, there is also the possibility that part of the costs of breach will be borne by the taxpayer rather than by those who breach the regulations or the victims of breach. That might occur directly, through taxation being paid into a compensation scheme, or indirectly through provision of subsidized or free health care and other features of the welfare state.

Private law, then, might be thought problematic both in the way that it distributes resources and the extent to which the distribution of resources is governed by the state. If it is justified to retain schemes of private law, this will probably be for reasons of efficiency. Whilst the costs of actions in private law may themselves be expensive, by imposing costs for harms that a person causes, private law makes it easier to determine the extent of each person's liability: each person must pay for what they have done. And in this way, individual citizens can easily mimic the decisions that would be achieved through legal action without resorting to the courts. When private regulations are breached, then, the parties themselves can often resolve disputes in the shadow of the law.

Once causation of harm is dropped as a marker of the quantity of liability, it will be much more difficult to know what a person who has breached a regulation ought to pay. Hence, distribution of resources must be achieved through some bureaucratic enterprise that will be expensive to administer. In other words, we might be willing to tolerate tying liability to causation, even though this gives a greater role to outcome luck than is ideal, because it allows disputes to be resolved without recourse to bureaucracy.

Furthermore, insurance might do the same kind of job as the regulatory scheme in reducing the influence of outcome luck even if we retain private law. It might reduce the effects of luck in a way that is more efficient than a regulatory scheme. And it might do so in a way that protects autonomy more effectively in that people can choose whether or not to insure. Whether such a scheme is just is to be determined by standards set by regulatory schemes. We should think of regulatory schemes as being morally primary, in a sense, then. Were it not for efficiency considerations, they would distribute resources more fairly, and we should depart from fairness only if the bureaucratic costs

---

[20] See R Cooter and A Porat, 'Total Liability for Excessive Harm' (2007) 36 *Journal of Legal Studies* 63.

of fairness turn out to be too high or the restrictions on autonomy turn out to be too great. Regulation, then, is the main moral alternative to criminal law. Private law is a default institution.[21]

IV   Comparing Criminal and Civil Regulations

Given this account of them, how might regulatory offences compare to the criminal law? To what extent ought we to prefer civil regulations to criminal regulations? Some people might believe that punishment is so awful a violation of rights that we ought always to prefer compensation schemes to punishment. We ought to prefer them even if they are not very effective in providing compensation in fact. If this is true, we have grounds to abolish the criminal law altogether and to rely entirely on compensation. Compensation may sometimes be inadequate, it might be argued, but punishment is so awful that we ought not to use it to ameliorate these inadequacies.[22]

But, given the right level of institutional protection against being punished, I do not believe that punishment is always worse than requiring compensation. Compensation schemes will have serious disadvantages, and sometimes the great majority will be better off if we criminalize some conduct rather than requiring wrongdoers to compensate their victims for the harms they cause. Let us explore the merits and problems of compensation schemes in more depth.

A   How the costs are distributed

Although compensation schemes do not aim at harming individuals, we might think, they do involve harming those individuals intentionally. They take property from those individuals, and that harms them, or so it might be argued. Although this is true, we might also think that the fair redistribution of resources ought not to be considered a violation of the means principle. We do not do a person a relevant kind of harm, if indeed we can be said to harm them at all, by taking property away from them to which they are not entitled. No-one, I think, would object to our requiring negligent drivers to compensate their victims on the grounds that this harms the negligent driver

---

[21] In the context of tort, which is the most obvious but not the only context to which this applies, this idea is explored, though in a fairly mystical way, in C Schroeder, 'Causation, Compensation, and Moral Responsibility' in Owen (n 19 above).

[22] See D Boonin, *The Problem of Punishment* (Cambridge: Cambridge University Press, 2008) ch 5 for a defence of this view.

as a means. For even if it is true that compensation in a way harms a person as a means, they are only harmed as a means to avert or ameliorate a threat or harm that the person is negligent in creating. This is one reason to prefer compensation schemes to criminalization.

For this reason, we need not provide the full range of protections that we provide to people in the criminal law to plaintiffs in civil cases. As we are not harming people as a means to avert threats created by others, but only to avert threats wrongfully caused by themselves, we will be less concerned to protect them from being harmed than we are for the criminal accused.

Not only that, there are good reasons why we would want to relax the protections that we provide in civil schemes when compared with the criminal law. The reason is this. Suppose that we regulate some harmful form of conduct through a civil scheme. A number of people are harmed by the conduct and we will wish to compensate them. But not all of the wrongdoers will be held liable for imposing the harms they cause. If we wish to provide full compensation to each person harmed we will need to raise enough revenue to compensate victims of wrongdoing even if we cannot hold the person who has harmed them liable. We could do this through taxation or by imposing heavier fines on those who breach the regulations.

The more that we relax procedural protections provided to people in civil law the greater the pool of people who contribute to compensating those who are harmed by the relevant conduct. By relaxing the standards of liability we therefore reduce the amount that must be paid by each person who breaches the regulations without imposing any extra burden either on those harmed or on the taxpayer.

In relaxing the standards of liability we reduce the protections that people have against being held liable. But we also reduce the burden on each person who is held liable. And it may be in the interests of each person to have a greater risk of being held liable imposed on them but with a reduced quantity of liability. In this way, we tend to distribute costs of breach of the regulation to people who had an opportunity to avoid bearing those costs. Neither the taxpayer nor the victim needs to foot the bill. And we can justify this on the grounds that otherwise either the victim or the taxpayer would have to bear a cost which it would be impossible, or at least very difficult, for them to avoid.

But if we do reduce the protections available in civil procedure to some degree we also limit the opportunity that people have to avoid bearing these costs. Even if regulations are announced in advance, it might be difficult and costly to avoid liability if the regulation operates under strict liability and if evidential standards are below the criminal standard. How can this reduction in protection be justified? It may be justified because it is the only way of ensuring that persons held liable do not bear the additional burden of compensating victims of other people's conduct.[23] Hence, civil regulations might be thought a compromise between two extremes. At one extreme we could distribute the costs to all citizens through general taxation or to victims by not providing them with full compensation. Or we could provide maximum protection against being held liable by imposing a very high cost on those who are held liable. These extremes will often be unattractive, and we will prefer our regulations to occupy some middle ground.

The question that must now be faced is why this kind of analysis is not available in the case of the criminal law. In the criminal case, could we not also reduce the protections available in order to distribute burdens more effectively? Let us focus on punishment. It is *possible* to distribute the burden of punishment more broadly by reducing protections to each person, assuming that general deterrence provides the main justification for punishment. I have suggested that the theory of punishment I favour will impose some restrictions on the magnitude of punishment it is right to impose on offenders. But, of course, we could always punish *less* than this maximum. For, on my view, although (as I will indicate in a moment) proportionality is important in the justification of punishment, there is no duty to punish in proportion to the gravity of the crime.

One way in which we could reduce the burden that each wrongdoer faces would be by increasing the number of people held criminally liable. Suppose that there is a particular deterrent effect that we currently achieve. We could achieve the same deterrent effect by reducing protections provided to each person and at the same time reducing the severity of the punishment. Reducing the severity of the punishment would reduce the deterrent effect to a degree, but this could be compensated for by the extra deterrent effect of making it more likely that a wrongdoer will be convicted. If we were to do that we would effectively share the burden of deterrence more widely amongst people who are convicted.

Of course, only some people who are convicted are wrongdoers, so we increase the risk to each citizen that they will be wrongfully convicted. And hence we increase the risk that the citizen will be used in a way that is difficult and costly for them to avoid. A system that does this reduces the control that each person has over being used as a means. As people have good reason to value having control over whether they are used as a means, we have good reason to reject this system.

---

[23] Stephen Perry notes that strict liability in tort law is normally defended by libertarians, who claim that one must bear the full benefits and the full costs of one's actions. See 'Risk, Harm, and Responsibility' in Owen (n 19 above), 339–45. Perry rightly notes that this implausibly assumes that bringing about harm is a one way street rather than an interaction between two people. The argument here shows that those concerned with distributive justice might also favour strict liability on grounds different to those Perry identifies: grounds that avoid his objection.

And that reason is even stronger when it is the state, rather than a private individual, that would treat them as a means.[24] We would prefer to keep control over our status as ends in ourselves, particularly when our status is eroded by the state, even if greater burdens are in consequence imposed on those people who voluntarily violate the law and are convicted of a criminal offence.

In other words, we have powerful reason to ensure that our status as an end is protected by ensuring that it is eroded only when we have a proper opportunity to avoid that erosion. That is so even though people who do not avoid being treated in that way each suffer a greater burden in consequence. We are willing to distribute suffering more narrowly and at a greater cost to each person in order to do more to protect our status as ends in ourselves.

Because these restrictions on punishment are just, the criminal justice system is also able to condemn offenders for what they have done. Assuming that the criminal law is properly restricted, the procedural guarantees that are required to protect people from being punished ensure that we do not convict offenders without a high degree of confidence that they have perpetrated a wrong. And that also creates the conditions under which offenders can be condemned. This helps us to answer an earlier question: the question why we have a single institution both to condemn and to punish. The answer is that similar procedural guarantees are required for the just performance of each of these functions. It therefore makes sense to have a single institution performing both tasks.

B   The possibility of compensation and the scope of the criminal law

Suppose that we wish to ameliorate the harm caused by some form of conduct. How do we decide whether to use the criminal law or the civil law? One important issue to guide us, that we have been focusing on so far, is the way in which costs are distributed amongst those who we hold liable in the two systems. When it comes to distributing the burden amongst those who breach the regulation, civil standards do this more broadly than criminal standards; and criminal standards employ those who break the law as a means to prevent future harms. These might seem to be powerful reasons in favour of the civil law over the criminal law.

To see this more clearly, consider a form of conduct, v, which causes harm to others. We could attempt to deter people from v or we could attempt to compensate people who are harmed when others v. It is plausible that supplementing a compensation scheme by criminalizing the conduct will reduce the

---

[24] See also T Nagel, *Equality and Partiality* (Oxford: Oxford University Press, 1991) 142–3.

instances of *v*. But the cost that is borne to achieve this reduction is high for a small number of people. Not only will they be harmed, they will be harmed as a means for the good of others.

Were we not to criminalize the conduct we can expect there to be more victims of *v*, and more people who *v* will then be required to pay compensation. A scheme of civil regulation such as the one I outlined above would require them to pay, not only for the damage that they cause, but a proportion of the overall damage caused by breaches of the regulation and the costs of running the scheme. If we do not wish the burden of these breaches to fall on victims of the conduct or on taxpayers, that cost may be high, depending on how easy it is to hold people liable for breach of the regulation. And the easier we make it to hold people liable for breach of the regulation the greater the risk that some people who are held liable have not *v*.

This suggests that even if full compensation were available, in both principle and practice we would have a strong reason to reduce the instances of *v* so that fewer people had to compensate others for their conduct. We will wish to protect people from having to pay high levels of compensation without great protection against suffering this burden. That creates pressure to criminalize, even if we recognize that criminalization imposes a very high cost on those who are punished.

Now, it might be argued that criminalization on these grounds would be unfair. For the burden that would be faced by the criminals—condemnation and punishment—would be much graver than the burden that would otherwise be faced by any individual were we to rely entirely on the civil scheme. We would prefer to assign a smaller burden to a larger number of people than to reduce the number of people who suffer a burden but increase the magnitude of the burden suffered by the smaller group. That, we might argue, is so even if the overall magnitude of the burden is less in the latter case.

This is the kind of argument that is often raised against utilitarians. Suppose that we must distribute some burden amongst people. If we could either distribute it to a smaller number of people who will suffer intensely, or to a larger number of people who will suffer less, we will often prefer the latter. And we will prefer the latter even if the number of people in the latter case is sufficiently large that the overall magnitude of the burden is greater if we choose to distribute the burden to the larger number rather than the smaller.[25]

That is plausible enough. But there is also an important feature of the case we are discussing that distinguishes it from other cases in which we distribute

[25] See, eg TM Scanlon, *What We Owe to Each Other* (Cambridge, Mass: Harvard University Press, 1998) 234–5. I doubt that we should take as extreme a view as Scanlon does about the significance of the number of people suffering the smaller burden, particularly if the burden is not very small.

benefits and burdens. The smaller group of people who are punished have been given an excellent opportunity to avoid the burden that they suffer. All they have to do to avoid being punished is to conform to the requirements of the criminal law. And if the criminal law is clearly stated and prohibits only actions which the person has no strong reason to perform, avoiding punishment comes at a minimal cost. In contrast, if we rely solely on the civil scheme it is much more difficult for the larger number to avoid liability, for reasons I noted above. We have less reason to complain of suffering in order to prevent the suffering of others if we have been given plenty of protection against suffering. And perhaps the most important way in which we give people protection against suffering is by providing them with a straightforward opportunity to avoid suffering which does not impose heavy costs on them.[26]

This suggests that, depending on how effective the criminal law is in deterring people, we might prefer to supplement criminal schemes with civil schemes even if full compensation might otherwise be provided to those who are victims of the conduct that we are regulating. We might use the criminal law, not in order to ensure that the victims receive adequate protection (we could do that by ensuring that those held liable pay a sufficient amount to compensate the victims fully) but in order to reduce the burden of compensation.

And in the real world, there will be even more reason to use punishment in some cases. For the victims of some kinds of conduct are capable of being compensated in principle but are very unlikely to be compensated in practice. This will be so if those who are held civilly liable are unlikely to be able to afford to pay proportionate compensation on the model described above. That will be particularly true where it is difficult to discover who has perpetrated the relevant conduct, and so it is difficult to hold anyone civilly liable. The costs that each person who is held liable will face, in order to create a fund big enough to compensate people who are victims of the conduct, will be very large.

For example, suppose that we decriminalized theft. We might expect there to be a large number of thefts, since thieves are unlikely to be discovered. But the costs that each thief who is held liable would have to pay under the scheme of civil regulation outlined above will be very large. They will have to pay more in order to compensate victims of the large number of thefts that others perpetrate who have not been brought to justice. They are unlikely to be able to afford to do this.

This would present us with four choices. We could require thieves to work for their whole lives to provide compensation to those from whom they have stolen. That might not be effective, though, because even were we able to

[26] The significance of the opportunity to avoid a burden in determining questions of liability is explored in depth in Scanlon (ibid) ch 6.

enforce this in a reasonably humane way it would be likely to be more trouble than it is worth to force thieves to work to compensate victims.[27] Or we could shoulder the burden of compensation through taxation. Or we could require victims to shoulder some of the burden. Or we could punish thieves to reduce the instances of the conduct.

There are difficult moral and empirical questions to be addressed here, but my tentative view is that punishment has a role to play in the case of theft. We punish in order to reduce the burden that will otherwise be picked up by victims of theft and the taxpayer for the costs of theft. We will not be able to cancel out that burden entirely, but we will be able to reduce it. And it will be fair to reduce it if we give thieves a perfectly good opportunity to avoid being punished through a clearly formulated criminal law announced to them in advance. The criminalization of theft would be warranted, not because we want to condemn thieves (I see no greater reason to condemn thieves than to condemn those who breach contracts), but only in order to reduce the burden of compensation that has to be borne by those held liable for theft, taxpayers, and victims.

V   Conclusions

I have suggested that there may be good reason to use the criminal law to regulate some harmful conduct which, in principle, we could adequately compensate the victims for suffering. We criminalize in order to reduce the instances of harmful conduct. In doing that, we attempt to protect people as best we can, and in as fair a way as we can, from suffering either as victims, as perpetrators, or as taxpayers. This can be thought of as a question of proportionality. I wish to close this chapter with some more general thoughts about how we should understand proportionality on the model of punishment that I favour.

In the philosophy of punishment, the idea of proportionality has primarily figured in expressivist and retributivist thinking.[28] Expressivists think that punishments must be proportionate to the gravity of the wrongdoing to ensure that the degree of censure reflects the gravity of the wrong. Retributivists claim that the punishment must fit the crime; and that gives rise to a conception of proportionality as fittingness. On this view of proportionality, we

---

[27] Philosophers sometimes naively assume that forced labour of offenders will be economically effective: see eg, Boonin (n 22 above) 262.

[28] For a good overview, see A von Hirsch and A Ashworth, *Proportionate Sentencing: Exploring the Principles* (Oxford: Oxford University Press, 2005) ch 9.

aim to reflect, in some way, the wrongdoing that has been perpetrated in the punishment.

But the idea of proportionality, understood in a different way, has also been explored in other contexts, contexts where the expression of blame and desert have almost no significance at all. For example, we are warranted in defending ourselves only if the harm that we impose on others is proportionate to the threat that we will avert. And it is permissible to go to war with another country only if that is a proportionate response. On this second conception of proportionality, a proportionate response is not a fitting response. It is a response that takes seriously as a bad thing the harm that one party will cause, and requires a positive good to balance that harm.

This second conception of proportionality is familiar from classic utilitarian accounts of punishment, but it is also the one that is relevant, in a different way and with a different set of principles, to the instrumentalist but non-consequentialist approach to punishment that I favour. On this view, whether punishing a person is proportionate does not depend entirely on the consequences of punishment. It depends on a more complex set of principles about the significance of different harms and goods to the justification of punishment, as well as the way in which those harms and goods come about.

The distinction between non-consequentialist and consequentialist views of proportionality, in the sense I am considering here, has been explored in some depth in the context of war.[29] For example, for consequentialists all of the good consequences of going to war are significant in determining whether the decision is proportionate. For non-consequentialists some goods, such as any economic benefits that going to war might bring, may not be significant in rendering the decision proportionate. For consequentialists the lives of soldiers and civilians, insofar as those lives are valuable, count equally in determining whether the decision to go to war is proportionate. For non-consequentialists the lives of soldiers may count less than the lives of civilians. For consequentialists the lives of enemy soldiers count as much as the lives of our own soldiers in determining whether some action in the course of war is permissible. Non-consequentialists may hold, in contrast, that we are entitled to prefer the lives of our own soldiers to the lives of the enemy.

I do not say that any of these non-consequentialist principles is true. I refer to them merely to highlight the difference between consequentialist and non-consequentialist approaches to questions of proportionality. Whether it is fair

---

[29] For excellent contributions, see T Hurka, 'Proportionality in the Morality of War' (2005) 33 *Philosophy and Public Affairs* 34 and J McMahan, *Killing in War* (Oxford: Oxford University Press, 2009). I explore the significance of this conception of proportionality for punishment at greater length in *The Moral Foundations of Criminal Law* (n 13 above).

to impose punishment on people for committing some wrongful or harmful action also plausibly depends on a set of non-consequentialist principles of this kind. For example, the suffering of offenders may count less than collateral harms that are caused by punishment. In one way, it also counts less than the harms that would otherwise be suffered by victims of crime. Because offenders have made themselves liable to be harmed by offending we are entitled to give their suffering less weight in deciding whether punishing them is proportionate.

But in another way, the bad effects of punishment, on the offender and particularly on innocent people, count more than the harms that citizens would otherwise suffer as victims of crime. This is for the reason, endorsed by non-consequentialists but rejected by consequentialists, that it is worse to harm a person than it is to fail to prevent a person being harmed. Outlining a set of non-consequentialist principles to guide us in deciding whether punishment is proportionate has not been done in any depth, to my knowledge at least.

With this basic picture in mind, we can now consider two further issues that are of significance in determining whether punishment is proportionate. The first is moral and the second empirical. Whether punishment is justified for some conduct will depend in part on social justice. One way in which we protect people from being punished is by providing them with the education, opportunities, and social and economic circumstances in which they are unlikely to become criminals. It might be unjust to impose punishment on people where we have not done enough to improve the criminogenic circumstances in which the majority of offenders have grown up. In that case, it may be fair that the taxpayer bears a heavier part of the burden to compensate victims of theft, for example. The fairer the background social conditions in which we operate, the more likely we are to conclude that it is fair to punish people. For in providing fair social conditions to people we also protect them from becoming offenders.[30]

The difficult empirical question is how effective the criminal law is in preventing crime. Some scholars are very sceptical about the ability of the criminal law to deter at all. If they are right we have good reason to abolish most of the criminal law. We should retain it only to condemn a very narrow range of seriously wrongful conduct. But I doubt that it can be shown that the criminal law is altogether ineffective in deterring. We would need to compare a society with a criminal law to a similar society without one, and we do not have comparators of this kind. We should not conclude from the fact that differences in sentencing make little difference to the rate of offending, that the criminal

---

[30] For further discussion, see V Tadros, 'Poverty and Criminal Responsibility' (2009) 43 *Journal of Value Inquiry* 391.

law does not deter. We should rather conclude that there are decisive reasons to reduce sentences to a low level. High sentences probably harm offenders for no benefit.

Whether or not these things are true, we at least have arguments on the table that support the plausible idea that, in principle and probably also in practice, we can use the criminal law to regulate conduct beyond the narrow core of conduct for which we cannot compensate people. The criminal law harms some people to protect others. It is regrettable that we harm people, and that is true as much with respect to offenders as anyone else, but sometimes that might be the best option given the unpalatable alternatives that we face.

8

Criminal Law between Public and Private Law

*Markus D Dubber**

To criminalize something (not someone, ordinarily) means to bring it within the scope of criminal law; in this sense, crime is a legal phenomenon, as is punishment. This means that an account of criminalization needs an account not of crime *simpliciter*, but of law in general, and of criminal law within it. In this chapter, I approach this task equipped with two distinctions, one—between law and police—designed to illuminate the concept of law, and the other—between public and private law—meant to clarify that of criminal law.

Law is here understood as a mode of state governance that is usefully contrasted with police.[1] There are two ways to think about the state: as a normative concept or as a prudential one. As a normative concept, the state is the manifestation of the idea of right (*Recht*) in the political realm. It is that collection of individuals, institutions, animate and inanimate objects, practices, and so on that brings to life the idea, or if you like the ideal or promise, that all persons can be legitimately governed only as persons, which means they are fundamentally equal (as persons) and free (as persons). It would be nice if they were also brothers and sisters, but I do not think the idea of *fraternité* is essential to that of the state in quite the same way as are those of *liberté* and *égalité*, which might explain why the French Revolutionaries denied it the pride of first, or second, place on their shortlist of demands. This idea of the state is closely connected to the idea of democracy (or political self-government) and, more generally, to the fundamental concept of the political and moral thought of the enlightenment: autonomy (or self-government unmodified).

* Many thanks to David Dyzenhaus, Mary Ellison, Lindsay Farmer, Tatjana Hörnle, Peter Kasiske, Nicola Lacey, Sandra Marshall, Lorenzo Perilli, and Michel Troper for helpful suggestions.
[1] See generally MD Dubber, *The Police Power: Patriarchy and the Foundations of American Government* (New York, NY: Columbia University Press, 2005).

As a prudential concept, the state is the means by which the collectivity's welfare, well-being, commonweal(th), good, etc is advanced. Here the state does not differ qualitatively from any number of other collectivities, or groups, that are bound together, voluntarily or less so, by a common destiny or at least are treated, or treat themselves, as a unit of communal welfare, with each member's individual welfare being more or less closely related to the welfare of the entity as a whole. From this perspective, the state appears as a house-hold governed by what we used to call 'police' and what we now call 'political economy', defined by Rousseau as the government of the state as a giant (or, in the case of Geneva, not so giant) household.

The normative state, in contrast, is qualitatively different: it is unique in its essential connection to the concept of right, or justice. Other institutions, even individuals, can affect, minimize, or maximize others' or their own wel-fare, but only the normative state manifests the idea of right. There is a connec-tion between this feature of the normative state and what is often misleadingly called the state's monopoly on violence—misleading because it gives the false impression both that the use of state violence is a matter of (improper, or at least suspicious, if not simply inefficient) market domination with the attend-ant power over consumers (here is the only connection between monopoly and state violence—power), and that this monopoly is somehow accidental, in the sense of non-essential, so that it could (at least theoretically) be broken up (by distributing market power among other institutions or individuals) or transferred as a whole (onto another monopolist). The state's monopoly of violence, I think, is the state's exclusivity of (or exclusive right of) violence because 'violence' is only legitimate if it is used to manifest right, and the nor-mative state is the manifestation of right. Only the state can do right, in other words, and therefore only the state is entitled to use violence to do right (or to undo wrong).

Corresponding to these normative and prudential concepts of the state—or perhaps these are two aspects of the same concept, as I do not think this makes much difference—are two modes of governance: *law* (formal *Recht*) being the mode of governing the normative state, and *police* (or political economy, if you prefer) being that of governing the prudential state. Using more contem-porary terminology, one might substitute 'regulation' or even 'administration' for police and get pretty much the same picture.[2] Either way, in one mode the state manifests (or should manifest) right (substantive *Recht*), in the other it pursues (or should pursue) welfare.

---

[2] See, eg N Lacey, 'Criminalization as Regulation: The Role of Criminal Law' in C Parker *et al* (eds), *Regulating Law* (Oxford: Oxford University Press, 2004) 144; MD Dubber, 'Regulatory and Legal Aspects of Penality' in A Sarat and M Umphrey (eds), *Law as Punishment/Law as Regulation* (forthcoming).

Public law and private law are two species of law, rather than of police.[3] Initially, it is not obvious why one would need to give an account of the distinction between public law and private law; the concept of law as the mode of state governance *vis-à-vis* persons does not appear to call for it, and might in fact be hostile to it, depending on how it is fleshed out. Still, it is a distinction that is invoked and, more interestingly, attacked often enough to deserve our attention as we try to shed some light on criminal law's place within the realm of law. Its critics (most audibly among CLS historians and feminist scholars) may well be right that the distinction could be, and has been, abused for political/oppressive ends, something that arguably does not set it apart from other distinctions in legal rhetoric; whether it has theoretical purchase for our project is a separate question.

The concept 'civil law' is often used interchangeably with that of 'private law'. (Not helpfully, but relevantly, it is also often contrasted with that of 'criminal law'.) There are some good reasons for *not* treating the two terms as synonymous. First, they have not always been treated that way. Justinian's Digest, often cited as the first recognition of the distinction between public and private law, distinguishes public law (*ius publicum*) from private law (*ius privatum*), but then proceeds to divide private law into natural law, *ius gentium*, and civil law.[4] Interestingly, the Digest (or at least Ulpian) appears to think of civil law as characteristically private in one sense: civil law is local law, Roman law, 'a law of our own', that is distinct from, though 'not altogether independent of natural law or *ius gentium*'. Here civil law is formally distinguished from the other types of private law by its scope, and I suppose its origin, rather than in any substantive sense.

Second, using civil law and private law as synonyms and, at the same time, as antonyms of criminal law, classifies criminal law as a species of public law, rather than of private law. This would make quick definitional, but uninteresting, work of our task of regarding criminal law from the perspectives of public and private law.

I The Public/Private Distinction in Roman Law

If we stick with Ulpian for another moment, he distinguishes public law, which concerns 'the government of the Roman empire' (*ad statum rei Romanae*)

---

[3] There is an analogous distinction in the realm of police: that between the macro-household (or political household, state) and the micro-household (or domestic, familial household). See J-J Rousseau, JR Masters (trans), 'Discourse on Political Economy' in *On the Social Contract, with Geneva Manuscript and Political Economy* (New York, NY: St Martin's Press, 1978) 209, 209.

[4] Dig 1.1.1.2 (Ulpian); Inst 1.1.1.4.

from private law, which concerns 'the welfare of individuals' (*ad singulorum utilitatem*). Remarkably, this way of framing the distinction has remained essentially unchanged since then (if, for the Roman Empire we substitute the macro-household *du jour*, most recently the abstract 'state'). As remarkably, and perhaps not unrelatedly, this way of framing the distinction is not particularly illuminating, since it tells us nothing about what 'the government of the Roman Empire' (or of the state) might encompass and how it might differ from, and not involve, 'the welfare of individuals'.

The text does go on to say that public law is 'concerned with sacred rites, with priests, with public officers', which suggests a rather limited view of public law as a form of internal management (one might say, of matters concerning the micro-household), with the possible exception of the regulation of sacred rites, which one might view as being concerned with the interaction between members of the state's micro-household (state officials, 'bureaucrats') and other, less privileged, members of the macro-household, who might form the audience for, and consumers of, sacred rites, at least insofar as they are performed—or reported—in public. The definition of public law, then, like that of civil (private) law as Roman local law, is framed formally in terms of its addressees, or objects, rather than in terms of the substance of the rules governing their behaviour, or the nature of their interactions amongst each other, or with others, including the state itself.

In this light, Roman public law appears as the direct continuation and expansion of the original model of Roman governance, of the household by the householder, of the *familia* by the *pater familias*. Public law in this sense might be subject to various guidelines of prudence, and certainly to divine supervision if not control, but it was not subject to publicized rules and principles to be formulated, critiqued, revised, and interpreted in 'legal opinions' by jurists.

If we consider the distinction between law and police, Roman public law is better thought of as a species of police than of law. Put another way, Roman law is private law. Public law is not law properly speaking, but police, and as such subject to the sort of prudential considerations explored in Marcus Aurelius's *Meditations*, and later on in Machiavelli's *The Prince*.

The police, or shall we say domestic, character of public law reflects what is often speculated to be the origin of Roman state power in general, the power of the *pater familias* over his *familia*, which included human and non-human resources, and (among humans) spouse, children, servants, and slaves, and extended to the power over life and death within whatever limits custom and religion might impose. As the story goes, this familial governance was subjected to general rules with the growth of a Roman state, the accumulation and publication of the Twelve Tables marking an important early step in this process (despite, and through, their codification of the father's *vitae necisque potestas*, the power of life and death). The familial mode of governance, however, never disappeared entirely, either in the micro-*familia* or in the new and ever growing macro-*familia* of the Roman state, which eventually was governed by the emperor as a *pater familias* would govern his *familia* (under the non-publicized prudential norms labelled 'public law'). Indeed, the emperor was seen as governing the entire state, and not merely his officials, as a *familia*, a development symbolized early on in Augustus's assumption of the title *pater patriae*.[5]

It is often said that the Romans (or rather Roman jurists) did not pay much attention to the distinction between public law and private law, showed little interest in public law, and—being the 'pragmatic and casuistic' lot they are said to have been—kept adjusting the distinction between public and private law to suit their needs from case to case, and certainly from emperor to emperor. This may or may not have been the case, at one point or another in Roman history; we will never know. The distinction between public and private law, at any rate, is widely, if not universally, considered to be of Roman origin and the gist of the distinction, in all its vagueness, continues to resonate today. It therefore is not exclusively of historical interest to note that Roman law in practice (and in theory, though Roman jurists also apparently paid little attention to criminal law) at one point classified much behaviour that today falls under the heading of criminal law as private law, with the exception—as is often noted somewhat cryptically—of 'very serious' offences, which appear to have encompassed offences against the state itself, most notably treason and its various relations. Robbery, assault, theft, and other property offences were considered, to use the *Institutes'* distinction, as matters regarding 'the welfare of individuals' rather than the 'government of the Roman state'.[6]

Although the Roman classificatory system has proved difficult to reconstruct (because it was not laid out clearly, or where laid out clearly was

---

[5] See, eg OF Robinson, *Criminal Law of Ancient Rome* (London: Duckworth, 1995) 9; see also RA Bauman, *The* Crimen Maiestatis *in the Roman Republic and Augustan Principate* (Johannesburg: Witwatersrand University Press, 1967) 238. The significance of this title is contested: see, eg SI Oost, 'Review of Bauman' (1969) 64 *Classical Philology* 205, 206 fn 1 (citing Mommsen, and cautioning that '[o]ne should not be misled by the language of poetry or flattery,' which is true enough).

[6] For an interesting selection of cases and other resources on delictual liability, see BW Frier, *A Casebook on the Roman Law of Delict* (Atlanta, Ga: Scholars Press, 1989). Proceeding from a (narrow) definition of delict as a 'private wrong', ibid, xiii (or, more precisely, as 'a misdeed that is prosecuted through a private lawsuit brought by the offended individual and punished by a money penalty that the defendant must pay to the plaintiff', ibid, 1), Frier's collection includes cases of assault, murder, arson, robbery, adultery, and destruction of property.

not implemented and followed consistently, and, at any rate, evolved over time), historians appear to have settled generally on a distinction between private delicts (*delicta privata*) and public delicts (*delicta publica*), each triggering a different process and subject to different remedies or sanctions—compensation in the former case, and punishment in the latter, including fines, banishment, civil death, and death. This 'old Roman distinction', too, can claim contemporary significance, as 'revived' in Blackstone's still much-cited distinction between private and public wrongs.[7]

There may be something to the recognition of the delict as a general concept subject to further differentiation, though not necessarily along the public–private line.[8] We will return to this point a little later. For now, suffice it to say that German law (still?) distinguishes somewhat lazily between criminal delict (*Kriminaldelikt* or *Strafdelikt*) and civil delict (*Zivildelikt*). (*Zivildelikt* is often translated as tort, and *Deliktsrecht* as tort law.) Delict in general is unlawful culpable behavior, with the civil delict being compensable and the criminal delict being punishable. Very little effort, however, is expended to distinguish between civil and criminal delicts other than by the nature of the applicable remedy or sanction.

While it is difficult to reconstruct the distinction between *delicta publica* and *privata* (if not impossible, or futile, since 'the' distinction may never have been drawn *ex ante* or in general, as opposed to in a particular case, and where it is not even clear who drew the distinction and when) it is worth noting that Mommsen, whose monumental study of Roman criminal law remains the standard treatment of the subject today, over a century after its publication, located the origin of Roman criminal law in the *patria potestas*, that is the practically (if not religiously) limitless disciplinary power of the *pater familias* over his household.[9] If we eliminate *delicta privata* from the realm of Roman criminal law as public law, and, even in a slight sleight of hand, call the remainder public criminal law or Roman criminal law properly speaking, then Roman criminal law concerns itself with acts that affect the government, or perhaps slightly more broadly, the operation and administration of the Roman state. If that state in turn is based on the macro-household model itself (as suggested above), then (public) Roman criminal law properly speaking concerns itself with offences against the state and, most notably, against the head of the state and the officials charged with executing his sovereign commands. In this view

---

[7] H Mannheim, *Comparative Criminology* (London: Routledge, 1965) 27.

[8] Cf T Mommsen, *Römisches Strafrecht* (Leipzig: Duncker and Humblot, 1899) 10–11 (distinguishing the older term *delictum* from *crimen*, which came to be used primarily, though not exclusively, to refer to private delicts).

[9] Ibid, 16–17; see especially 16 ('The householder's limitless power over household members is essentially identical to the state's power over community members').

of (public) Roman criminal law, the most serious offence is an offence against the emperor as macro-householder (*laesae majestatis*), the macro-version of the traditional micro-offence against the *pater familias* at home.[10]

These familial offences of denial of respect and insubordination traditionally elicited the most brutal punishments, with punishments for parricide often involving sewing perpetrators in a sack, accompanied by a dog and perhaps other animals, including an ape, and then dumping them into the sea or, if that proved impracticable, exposing them to wild beasts or, later on, burning them.[11] Despite the colourful punishments for parricide, which bear an interesting resemblance to the punishment for petit (and high) treason and regicide in English (and American colonial) and French law,[12] it is somewhat misleading to focus on the punishment for the elimination of the *pater familias*, since, by definition, their execution requires the existence of a punitive power beyond the *pater familias* himself.[13] More significant is the regular exercise of the father's disciplinary power over family members *before* the catastrophic event of his death. It is this punitive power that Mommsen posited as the origin of Roman criminal law; crimes, in this view, are offences against patriarchal sovereignty and their punishment a discretionary reassertion of that sovereignty designed to affirm the (quasi-)householder's superior power *vis-à-vis* the offender. (Gustav Radbruch later on generalized the point and traced criminal law in general back to patriarchal discipline over members

[10] There is apparently some dispute about the nature of the *majestas* at issue (*populi Romani* or *dignitas*), at least in the Republic and early Empire, and relatedly about the precise timing of the transition to a macro-state household. See, eg Bauman (n 5 above) (arguing that, as late as Augustus, the relevant *majestas* was that of the Roman people, ie fundamentally republic, rather than quasi-patriarchal). There is little doubt that this development was well on its way out by the time of the *Institutes*, however, after some five centuries of imperial rule.

[11] Cicero makes much of the brutality, or rather the indignity, of the punishment for parricide in his oration in the case of Sextus Roscius: Cicero, 'The Defence of Sextus Roscius' in *Murder Trials* (Harmondsworth: Penguin, 1975) 27.

[12] See, eg W Blackstone, *Commentaries on the Laws of England,* vol 4 (Oxford: Clarendon Press, 1769) 75 (petit and high treason, which Blackstone treats as 'equivalent to the *crimen laesae majestatis* of the Romans'), 92 (high treason), 203–4 (petit treason); M Foucault, *Discipline and Punish: The Birth of the Prison* (New York, NY: Vintage Books, 1979) 3 (punishment of Damiens for regicide); AP Scott, *Criminal Law in Colonial Virginia* (Chicago, Ill: University of Chicago Press, 1930); R Semmes, *Crime and Punishment in Early Maryland* (Baltimore, Md: Johns Hopkins Press, 1938); see generally Dubber, *The Police Power* (n 1 above) 26–31. For a fascinating account of a petit treason case from late colonial Massachusetts, see AC Goodell, *The Trial and Execution for Petit Treason of Mark and Phillis, Slaves of Capt. John Codman, Who Murdered Their Master at Charlestown, Mass., in 1755; for Which the Man Was Hanged and Gibbeted, and the Woman Was Burned to Death* (1883), online at <http://www.archive.org/details/trialexecutionfo00good> and <http://www.gutenberg.org/etext/26446>.

[13] G Long, 'Leges Corneliae' in W Smith, *A Dictionary of Greek and Roman Antiquities* (London: J Murray, 1875) 686–687, online at <http://penelope.uchicago.edu/Thayer/E/Roman/Texts/secondary/SMIGRA*/Leges_Corneliae.html>.

of the household.[14]) This punitive power was discretionary in every sense—with respect to the fact, the quantity, and the quality of its exercise. It was an internal family matter, and in this sense could be classified, in Rome, as a species of public law, rather than of private law.

Roman (public) criminal law then appears, as all Roman public law, as a precursor of police regulations, eventually derived from norms of police science discovered by police scientists and taught at police academies to budding bureaucrats. Police science was eventually pushed out by administrative law, taught at faculties of law, rather than at police academies (which gave rise to a 'new' university, notably in eighteenth century Germany), a subject so closely associated with the notion of public law as today to have become virtually indistinguishable from it in many countries, notably those without a long tradition of positive constitutional law (for example, the UK). Administrative law, however, arose from the attempt to place public and formal constraints on the exercise of police power through police—that is, regulatory—agencies. While the line from the Roman view of public law, such as it was, to administrative law is direct, it is important to recall that Roman public law was not concerned with public control of administrative action, but rather with the internal norms governing that action itself, that is, not with limits on governmental power, but with its exercise.[15]

II   Public Police and Criminal Administration

From the—anachronistic—retrospective of the later distinction between police and law, then, Roman public law appears more policial (police-like) than legal. The police origins of administrative law are intriguing: while the emphasis in administrative law tends to be placed on the law-like aspect of administrative law (administrative *law*), its police-like aspect is easily forgotten (*administrative* law). Administrative law spends surprisingly little time studying its subject matter, administration, and instead focuses almost exclusively on a tiny fraction of this subject: that which is subject to formal legal review. This creates the impression of a state under the deep and wide control

---

[14]   G Radbruch, 'Der Ursprung des Strafrechts aus dem Stande der Unfreien' in *Elegantiae Iuris Criminalis*, 2nd edn (Basel: Verlag fur Recht und Gesellschaft, 1950) 1.

[15]   A similar distinction played a central role during the formative period of administrative law in the United States, when the study of police power (as exercise) morphed into the discipline of administrative law (as limit, constitutional or not). See O Kraines, *The World and Ideas of Ernst Freund: The Search for General Principles of Legislation and Administrative Law* (Tuscaloosa, Ala: University of Alabama Press, 1974); Comment, 'Ernst Freund: Pioneer of Administrative Law' (1962) 29 *University of Chicago Law Review* 755.

of 'the rule of law', which might misrepresent the actual operation of state government, the overwhelming bulk of which occurs beneath and beyond the limits of administrative law. Another way of putting this point is to say that administrative law favours process over substance; it is not generally concerned with analysing and testing the substantive scope of administrative power and instead attempts to subject that power to procedural rules at the margins.

The study and theory of modern criminal law resembles that of modern administrative law in many of these respects, though considerably more effort is expended on questions of substance in criminal law than in administrative law. Still, at least in so-called common law countries (that is, in countries with legal systems that are (still) heavily influenced by the British colonial experience), procedural criminal law, and indeed procedural law in general, continues to be viewed as a more appropriate subject of doctrinal attention than is substantive criminal law. Within substantive criminal law, in turn, very little effort goes into exploring the scope of the state's power to criminalize, as opposed to the sorts of rules that should govern the application of this so-called special part of criminal law to particular acts and individuals (the general part, which, in this sense, can be viewed as applicatory, and therefore procedural). Then there is the tendency of modern criminal law to focus on exceptional and traditional crimes—most notably murder—rather than on the huge and ever-growing mass of so-called regulatory (or police) offences that include, importantly, offences generated (or at least defined) by administrative agencies, generally acting under only the vaguest of guidelines set by the legislature.

More fundamentally, modern criminal law resembles administrative law in fact (rather than in study or theory) in that both bear traces of their origin in a conception of public law that, if only sketchily, can be seen in the Roman law of the *Institutes*. It is a view of criminal law that is state-centred—it is concerned with behaviour that affects the interests of the state, from the smooth operation of its administrative process to the existence of the macro-householder at its head.[16]

In this view of criminal law, the state is the ultimate victim of crime; the most serious—purest—crimes are offences against the state; all other offences

---

[16] 'Perhaps the parallel should not be forced too far, but it is impossible to escape the suggestion that the *potestas* of the master over the slaves and freedmen within his *dominium* was similar in kind to, though more limited in scope, to the *maiestas* of the prince over the subjects beneath his *regnum* or *imperium*': FS Lear, '*Crimen Laesae Maiestatis* in the *Lex Romana Wisigothorum*' (1929) 4 *Speculum* 73, 82–3. The author continues: 'This line of thought links up with parricide, which may originally have been punished as a violation of the *patria potestas* and so have constituted a rudimentary form of treason within the family-group in an age when the family-group fulfilled functions of a semi-public character'.

are watered-down versions of (splinters off)[17] the ultimate offence of interfering with the authority of the state, of acting beyond one's inferior status as a member of the state household. These inferior offences are indirect state offences insofar as they compromise the state's ability to govern, for instance, by depriving the state of a resource (human or otherwise)[18] or through disobedience of a state command. As already noted, the bulk of modern criminal law consists of regulatory offences that often bear a remote and, more importantly, generally unexamined relation to the welfare of the state household and are best understood as more or less explicit offences of disobedience that attach sanctions to the mere violation of a state command—many issued by regulatory agencies, rather than the legislature—without an inquiry into the actor's intention or, more relevant, the causing or even threatening of harm to another individual (though of course the mere violation of the command can be regarded as causing harm to the state's authority). The effective publication and dissemination of the incomprehensible, and constantly growing, array of criminal norms is impossible and, for that reason, considered unnecessary (which is perhaps surprising given the significance attached to the fact of disobedience); enforcement of criminal norms is essentially discretionary (which is no surprise given once again the sheer number of prohibitions and criminal regulations). In fact, the other ill-understood and ill-connected features of the rule of law (or, if you prefer, of the principle of *nulla poena sine lege*), including specificity, prospectivity, and legislativity, appear not as strict formal principles, but as flexible prudential guidelines, much like the norms of good human resource management one might find in a seminar for corporate executives or, once again, Marcus Aurelius's *Meditations.*[19]

III   The Publicness of Criminal Law

If the publicness of criminal law is explored—and it is taken so much for granted that the question rarely arises—the fact that it is a species of public *law* is, oddly, rarely mentioned. Instead, the inquiry proceeds straight to the publicness of criminal law itself, as if the publicness of other areas of law were beside the point (and as if criminal law were somehow *sui generis*). At the

---

[17] See H Brunner, 'Abspaltungen der Friedlosigkeit' in *Forschungen zur Geschichte des deutschen und französischen Rechtes* (Stuttgart: JG Cotta, 1894) 444.

[18] For a discussion of homicide and maiming as (human) resource deprivation, see Dubber, *The Police Power* (n 1 above).

[19] See MD Dubber, '*Commonwealth v Keller*: The Irrelevance of the Legality Principle in American Criminal Law' in R Weisberg and D Coker (eds), *Criminal Law Stories* (New York, NY: Foundation Press, forthcoming, 2010).

same time, general inquiries into the publicness of public law, generally speaking, rarely discuss the publicness of criminal law. By and large they are exercises in (English) administrative law and, more specifically yet, inquiries into the availability, scope, desirability, and justifiability of official immunity in English law, which is thought to be the more or less necessary consequence of the recognition of a separate process (with separate courts, judges, and doctrines) for the resolution of disputes thought to qualify as instances of administrative law, a procedural and institutional feature traditionally associated with French law, and for that reason condemned as inconsistent with the liberty of Englishmen, as notably suggested by AV Dicey.[20]

One—popular—possibility is to give formal answers of various kinds. One might say, for instance, that public law includes any and all disputes (or, more generally, interactions) that involve the state on one side or another. So, for instance, much ink has been spilt in American constitutional law on the matter of state action, ie whether the behaviour in question can be attributed to a state actor. This is crucial because, and only insofar as, American constitutional guarantees cover only 'official' conduct, rather than 'civilian' conduct. Similar attribution questions also occupy the attention of English public (read 'administrative') lawyers, with similarly disheartening results. In both cases, the doctrine is so Byzantine and abstractly yet unsystematically complex that it is not uncommon to hold it up as a prime example of the result-oriented manipulation of formal legal distinctions (which in turn is often said to characterize legal doctrinal rhetoric in general), if not of the uselessness of the distinction between public and private law in the first place.[21]

Although it is rarely mentioned in this context, commonsensical views of the criminal law as public law fit into this general formal approach, except that in the case of criminal law the state appears as the subject of the dispute, rather than its object, as the prosecutor/plaintiff/complainant, rather than the defendant. Even if formal distinctions of this type were considered helpful in any way, the state's role as a 'party' in a criminal case is not as straightforward as it might seem at first, and certainly not as it is in a civil case where the state (or some subdivision or department thereof) appears as a defendant. American jurisdictions frame criminal cases as 'People v X', 'State v X', and 'Commonwealth v X', and English (and Canadian etc) criminal cases bear the caption 'The Queen v X'. But—leaving aside the question of the connection between the state, the people, the commonwealth, and especially the

---

[20] See M Loughlin, *The Idea of Public Law* (Oxford: Oxford University Press, 2003) 3 (British 'constitutional lawyers . . . have concluded that public law does not exist').

[21] See C Harlow, '"Public" and "Private" Law: Definition without Distinction' (1980) 43 MLR 241; MJ Horwitz, 'The History of the Public/Private Distinction' (1982) 130 *University of Pennsylvania Law Review* 1423.

monarch, and even disregarding the long-standing practice of 'private prosecutions' (not just in English criminal law)[22]—these formal titles themselves
say nothing about the publicness of the dispute, though the designation of the
first (prosecuting) party may of course point to a substantive view of the dispute (that might regard the state, the people, the commonwealth, or—again
more interestingly—the monarch as the victim of the alleged offence).

The formal publicness reflected in the title of criminal cases instead reflects
the procedural and institutional framework for its resolution: on the basis of
one state official's investigation (the police officer), the case is brought by
another state official (the prosecutor) before yet another (the judge) who—
generally without, but very rarely with the assistance of another group whose
officialness is difficult to pin down (the jury, lay judges in a mixed court)—
disposes of the case and, in the event of a guilty verdict and sentence, passes
it on to another state official (bailiff, prison warden, parole officer, etc).
Certainly the reference to the state (or some more or less closely and obviously related thing) in the formal case title is not thought to be a prerequisite
for the publicness of a dispute. German cases, for instance, refer simply to
the 'Criminal Case against X'; a reference to 'the People' appears only in the
judgment disposing of the case ('in the name of the people'). This reference,
however, appears not only in criminal cases (before criminal courts), but
in civil cases (before civil courts) as well, once again highlighting the (non-
essentially) procedural and institutional nature of the publicness of criminal
law.[23]

Before we home in on views of the publicness, rather than the public lawness, of criminal law, it makes sense to consider briefly the distinction between
public law and private law in German jurisprudence, if only because it has
received more sustained attention there than elsewhere. Interestingly, the
'interest theory' (*Interessentheorie*) of the distinction, derived directly from
Ulpian's definition quoted above (public law 'regards the government of the
Roman empire' and private law 'the welfare of individuals'), prevailed until
the early twentieth century. It has since fallen into disfavour largely because
it was thought unable to accommodate those aspects of modern public law

---

[22] A Ashworth, 'Punishment and Compensation: Victims, Offenders and the State' (1986) 6
OJLS 86, 107–8. On German private prosecutions (which in title are distinguishable from public
prosecutions and in practice tend to be brought by large repeat victims of minor crimes, such as
department stores in shoplifting cases), see MD Dubber, 'American Plea Bargains, German Lay
Judges, and the Crisis of Criminal Procedure' (1997) 49 *Stanford Law Review* 547, 572.

[23] Andrew Ashworth makes a similar point when he concludes, after an exceptionally insightful discussion of various accounts of the ' "public element" in crimes', that it is 'the existence of
a machinery of enforcement (police, prosecutors, courts, prisons, etc.) which marks out the difference between criminal and civil liability': Ashworth (ibid) 89. Recall also that French law, on
procedural grounds, classifies criminal law as *private* law.

(for example, constitutional law) that (also) protect private interests rather than concern the operation of the state. The currently preferred account of the distinction, 'modified subject theory' (*modifizierte Subjektstheorie*) generally resembles the commonsensical view just outlined, with some further specification: a conflict, or relationship, falls under public law if the state (or one of its subdivisions) appears as a party in its capacity as sovereign, rather than as one juristic person among others.[24] This theory is thought to be more useful, though this increase in usefulness may well come at the price of emptiness—public law applies to the state when it acts as state.

More interestingly, this 'modified' theory is regarded as a compromise between 'subject theory' (*Subjektstheorie*) and the most intriguing theory of the lot, 'subordination theory' or 'subjection theory' (*Subordinationstheorie*, *Subjektionstheorie*). Subordination theory distinguishes public law from private law by looking to the power relationship between the parties to a dispute (or relationship); public law governs relationships among unequals, private law those among equals. This theory has been roundly dismissed not only as impracticable (since power relations may be difficult to decipher and public law—under some other, non-explicit, classification—also includes some relationships among equals), but also, and more interestingly, because it is incompatible with the very idea of a modern democratic state based on the principle of equality. (Note that modified subject theory likewise recognizes the uniqueness of state sovereignty, but does not rely on it exclusively to distinguish public from private law.)

The classification of criminal law as public law in German jurisprudence is less interesting than the various attempts to distinguish public law from private law. Suffice it to say that the consensus in German jurisprudence appears to be that criminal law 'technically' is a species of public law no matter which version of the public/private law distinction one prefers. At the same time, however, criminal law is treated, and taught, separately from public law because criminal law is said to have preceded public law, historically speaking.[25] Whether this makes any sense naturally depends on one's definition of criminal law and public law and on one's view of legal history, which might lead one to recognize the existence of criminal law as private law in, say, Roman law. But to say

---

[24] Compare a similar distinction in the American law of torts, which permits the state to sue in tort only in its capacity as property owner, not in its governmental capacity: W Prosser, *Handbook of the Law of Torts*, 4th edn (St Paul, Minn: West Publishing, 1971) ch 1 §2.

[25] One current manifestation of the distinction between the disciplines of public law and penal law is the dispute about the constitutional significance of supposedly pre-constitutional principles of criminal law, notably the *Rechtsgutstheorie*. See most recently BVerfG 2 BvR 392/07 (26 February 2008) (affirming constitutionality of criminal incest prohibition as applied to adult siblings).

that criminal law was not always public law would of course challenge the unexamined consensus that criminal law is a species of public law.

Subordination theory, or rather its critique from the standpoint of subject theory, raises the question whether public law is possible (or, if possible, desirable) in a modern liberal state.[26] Much of the English debate about the distinction between private and public law revolves around the related question of whether public law is consistent with the English Constitution, which is thought to guarantee an ever-changing (and presumably ever-expanding), unwritten slate of proto-Enlightenment equal rights of Englishmen. Here the very existence of public law is taken to reflect a deeply hierarchical and centralized (read 'French') system of government that accords special protections (immunities) to state officials jealously protected by pseudo-judicial administrative tribunals staffed by other state bureaucrats who have little regard for the rights of non-officials who dare challenge the expert discretion of their fellow bureaucrats. (In some ways, the English theoretical literature on the nature of public law—as opposed to the uninspiring doctrine—can be seen as still operating, and expressing discomfort, with Ulpian's approach to public law as pertaining to the administration of the state without any reference to public accountability or, for that matter, public norms.)

The very question of the possibility of English public law appears oddly insular, even if modern commentary has aimed to move beyond Dicey's ill-informed, and by now outdated, musings about French administrative law. For one, the institutional focus of the debate remains, as does the association between the questions of public law and of official immunity. Moreover, the comparative discussion, such as it is, retains Dicey's narrow focus on French administrative law and, more specifically, the institutional structure of French administrative adjudication. Broadening the comparative view to include other systems with an established public law tradition, such as Germany, might lead one to question the link between public law and state impunity. German law, for instance, recognizes, in theory if not in practice, serious criminal liability for officials who deviate from basic norms of state conduct. The German Criminal Code, for instance, has long included serious offences of official misconduct in a criminal case,[27] such as 'bending the law' in favour of one party

---

[26] While some argue that all law is (must be) private, others argue that all law is (must be) public. Cf A Ripstein, 'Private Order and Public Justice: Kant and Rawls' (2006) 92 *Virginia Law Review* 1391. A variation on the latter claim, that all law is (must be) *also* public, is also quite common and is often taken to support the general claim that the distinction between public and private (in general, and not only in law) is fatuous or, more specifically, borne of an attempt to shield 'private' (property) rights from 'public' control: see, eg Horwitz (n 20 above).

[27] Since its original version of 1871, which in turn was derived from the Prussian Criminal Code of 1851. Felonies for official misconduct already appear in Frederic I's Prussian *Allgemeines Landrecht* of 1794. See H Lüpkes, *Die Verbrechen der Diener des Staats im Allgemeinen Landrecht*

or another (*Rechtsbeugung*, punishable by up to five years' imprisonment[28]) and obstruction of punishment, including the failure to comply with the principle of legality (*Legalitätsprinzip*), or the principle of compulsory prosecution, which requires the investigation (by the police) and the prosecution (by the prosecutor) of all colourable criminal matters (punishable by up to five years' imprisonment[29]).

Still, the English literature on the possibility of public law as a distinct category (largely institutionally and personally, rather than substantively) reflects a broader tension between the idea of public law and the modern idea of law in general. The challenge of public law, in this context, is to find its place in a system of government under the rule of law that places the autonomous person at the centre, as governor and as governed. The Enlightenment's radical political notion of equality challenges any species of law—public law, private law, criminal law—that presumes a fundamental inequality of governed and governor, of state and individual. The challenge of modern law, then, is to legitimate the exercise of coercive power by one person (acting under the authority of the state) against another, with the power to punish as the most blatant example. Criminal law, in this light, appears as the sharp edge of public law, raising the legitimacy question of public law in its most acute form.

At bottom, then, the question of the definition of public law (and its distinction from private law) is the question of legitimate state power under the rule of law. To the extent that any exercise of state power over an individual implies (and requires) a relationship of subordination, in the sense of the final unavoidability of experiencing that power on one's person even in the absence of actual consent, then rejecting the very notion of public law as inconsistent with the modern idea of law goes too far. The question is not the existence of power (with its attendant hierarchy of subject and object), but its legitimacy. Similarly, in the case of criminal law—whether characterized as public law or private law—the Enlightenment's person-based concept of law does not, by itself, dispose of the state's power to punish, but (merely?) poses a difficult and entirely new challenge to its legitimacy in terms of right, rather than merely of (household) welfare.

---

für die preußischen Staaten von 1794 und ihre Entwicklung zu den Vergehen und Verbrechen im Amte im Strafgesetzbuch für die preußischen Staaten (Frankfurt: Peter Lang, 2004).

[28] StGB §339.

[29] StGB §§258, 258a. On the potential criminal liability under German law of police officers who engage in conduct that might amount to the defence of entrapment in Anglo-American law, see JE Ross, 'Tradeoffs in Undercover Investigations: A Comparative Perspective' (2002) 69 *University of Chicago Law Review* 1501.

IV   Crimes as Public Wrongs

It is one thing to consider the publicness of criminal law in abstraction from other areas of law, or of any broader category of public law. It is another to ignore the lawness of criminal law altogether and proceed straight to an inquiry into the publicness of *crime*, or the publicness of the criminal 'wrongs,' which presumably are distinct from the privateness of non-criminal (civil?) wrongs (where it remains unclear whether any or all other areas of law concern themselves with wrongs at all). The alegality of this inquiry (and the attendant tendency to ignore the political aspect of punishment as a state practice), which treats the lawness of criminal law as at best an incidental, or perhaps formal, characteristic precludes reference to foundational concepts such as 'the rule of law' or the *Rechtsstaatsprinzip* or any account of law, for that matter. This inquiry will generate a more or less coherent account of 'crime' and 'punishment' in an alegal realm occupied by wrongs, public and private, criminal and civil, that cannot hope to capture criminal law as a historical or current practice, institution, concept, or ideal.

It is often said that criminal law protects 'public interests'. It is not usually made clear just what these public interests are, nor what makes them public, but we can, with fairly little effort, assemble a list of these interests: for instance, the Model Penal Code recognizes the following categories of offence that make reference to what may be considered 'public interests': offences against the existence or stability of the state, offences against public administration, offences against public order and decency.

These categories use 'public' in (at least) two different senses. The first two are offences against 'the public' in the sense of the state and its instrumentalities. These might fit best with the traditional Roman conception of what makes a *delictum publicum*. The third category, however, appears to include offences against 'the public' standing alone, and apart from the state. There are difficulties with defining 'the public' in this category with sufficient specificity: the legitimacy of punishing offences against an ill-defined communal concept (or, if you prefer, collective interests), rather than against the persons that may or may not constitute it is also questionable. But these concerns are beside the point in this context. It is enough to note that the Model Penal Code also recognizes 'individual' (or private) interests as worthy of penal protection: as a criminal code, it concerns itself, in language that has been cited repeatedly in US criminal law and elsewhere, with 'conduct that unjustifiably and inexcusably inflicts or threatens substantial harm to individual or public interests'.[30]

---

[30]   §1.02(1)(a).

The categories of offence that refer to private interests include offences involving danger to the person and offences against property, with offences against the family occupying an uncertain intermediate position (depending on one's view of the family, as a collection of persons or as a smaller political community within 'the public'). Again, offences against property might well be seen as protecting public interests ('the property system'[31]) as well as (or in the case of the Model Penal Code even ahead of) private interests; the point is not the classification of an interest as public or private, but the recognition of offences that interfere with individual interests, rather than public ones.

The publicness of criminal law, then, cannot derive from the fact that it is concerned with the protection of 'public interests' since at least some offences are thought to interfere with 'individual interests' instead. Alternatively, and more ambitiously, it is often said that *all* crimes affect 'public interests', or rather 'the public interest' (or, simply, '(the) public welfare'). Public interest offences such as the ones listed in the Model Penal Code, then, are not the only public offences: they are *only* public offences, ie offences against the public, but not also against individuals. It is not always clear what it means to say that every crime (by definition?) offends the public; it cannot mean that all crimes harm, dull, disturb, or otherwise interfere with public sensibilities since most crimes require neither commission in public (or even in the presence of a single person other than the perpetrator and the victim, or the single perpetrator in one-person, 'victimless' crimes), nor, for that matter, subsequent publication or even detection, which might harm public sensibilities after the fact.

Alternatively, the essence of crime is often said to lie in its interference with, or threat to, not merely 'the public' but more specifically 'the public peace'. Initially, this way of putting things does not look any more promising, since the public peace, in the sense of the public's peace, is no more necessarily disturbed by (any or all) crime than is any other characteristic or interest of the public, such as, say, its sensibilities or its health, or wealth, or welfare. But its peace is not simply one characteristic of the public among others. After all, there is no offence of 'disturbance of the (public's) welfare' or 'disturbance of the (public's) sensibilities', while disturbance (or breach) of the (public) peace has been a staple of penal law for centuries.

The public peace is the modern manifestation of the traditional concept of the king's peace, which in turn is the centralized version of the householder's peace. Every householder had his peace, as Maitland and Pollock point out, from the most modest serf to the king. Breach of the householder's peace (or *mund*) challenged the householder's authority to maintain this peace, ie to guarantee the welfare of his or her household (human and otherwise).

---

[31] Model Penal Code 220.1–230.5 cmt at 157 (larceny as 'threat to the property system').

To maintain, or reassert, that authority, householders might respond to the breach by any means necessary, using their essentially unlimited discretionary authority against members of their household and, in other cases, according to a more or less formal, and eventually centralized, set of intercommunal customs covering the interaction among householders (such as the wergild system).[32] ('Lordless' men, that is individuals not under the peace of another householder, who breached a householder's peace were subject to any discipline the victim-householder might see fit to impose.[33])

The public peace, then, is not strictly speaking *the public's* peace. It is the peace of the sovereign who governs the public, much as the household peace (*Hausfrieden*, still the basis of a German crime, *Hausfriedensbruch*, breach of the *Haus* peace, as distinct from *Landfriedensbruch*, breach of the *Land* peace[34]) was not the household's or its members', alone or taken together, but the householder's. This point has become obscured in post-Revolutionary American criminal law, which replaced the concept of the king's peace with that of the public peace, as part of the general transfer of sovereignty from the English king to 'the people'. In England, as in Commonwealth countries, the criminal law's connection to the protection of the king's (or queen's) peace remains closer to the surface in the form of indictments, which allege an offence 'against the peace of our Lady the Queen [Lord the King], her [his] crown and dignity', as well as in the title of criminal cases, which are generally framed as the Queen [King] v X.[35]

If we now return to the distinction between police and law cited at the outset of this chapter, the view of crimes as violations of the public peace ultimately regards crimes as police offences. 'Police' was the early modern term for the ancient concept of 'peace' (or welfare, well-being, (common) wealth);[36] a police offence, ie an offence against the police, then, simply is an offence against the peace, as protected by the householder-sovereign and, later on in liberal democracies, by the abstract non-personal construct of the sovereign state.

---

[32] See generally Dubber, *The Police Power* (n 1 above) 9–10.   [33] Ibid, 15, 52.

[34] StGB §§ 123–125a. Then there's also the offence of disturbing the public peace (*Störung des öffentlichen Friedens*), §126. All three peace offences are classified as offences against public order (*Straftaten gegen die öffentliche Ordnung*).

[35] In the United States, see, eg US Constitution Art I §6 (members of both Houses of Congress immune from arrest except in cases of 'Treason, Felony, and Breach of the Peace'); Texas Code of Criminal Procedure §45.019(a)(7) (every criminal complaint 'must conclude with the words "Against the peace and dignity of the State"').

[36] Cf the continuing characterization of 'police officers' as 'peace officers,' even at a time when the concept of police in common usage has been radically reduced from its once all-encompassing scope. Cf *City of Chicago v Morales* 527 US 41 (1999), 107 (Thomas J, dissenting) ('In most American jurisdictions, police officers continue to be obligated, by law, to maintain the public peace').

Under this, the police model of penal power, the victim of crime is the state. The paradigmatic crime is an offence against the sovereignty of the state and its officials. The sovereign state literally takes offence at the violation of its commands backed up by the threat of penal sanction. Each sovereign is free, but not required, to reaffirm its authority for any violation of 'its' norms. As the dual sovereignty exception to the double jeopardy prohibition in US constitutional law makes clear, the victim of the 'offence' is not the individual who might have suffered harm but the sovereign state; if a single act harms a single person but violates two sovereigns' penal norms, each sovereign is free, but not required, to exercise its penal power against the offender.[37] At the same time, as the ultimate victim of crime, the sovereign is also free to refrain from penally disciplining someone who has harmed another person: the public peace is, once again, not the public's, but the state's.[38]

Insofar as it merely restates, in somewhat antiquated form, the police model of penality, the view of crime as an offence against the public peace amounts to a comprehensive view of crime, rather than a description of some crimes. Moreover, it captures the publicness of crime as such, not just in some instances.

The problem is that it does so at the expense of draining crime of any private aspect—since the police model is entirely public—and, more importantly, of draining criminal law of its lawness. An account of crime as an offence against the public peace is not an account of criminal law: it is an account of criminal police.

The problem with the police model, and its account of the public element of crimes, is not descriptive, but legitimatory. The police model, in this respect, resembles the now disfavoured German subordination theory of the distinction between public and private law, and faces similar objections. The critique of subordination theory overshot its aim insofar as it rejected any notion of unequal power relationships in a modern liberal state. The critique might more fairly be directed at the police model of penal power in particular, and of state governance in general, since it goes beyond capturing a necessary aspect of inequality in the threat and exercise of state power: the radical distinction between governor (householder) and governed (household) is not

---

[37] See MD Dubber, 'Toward a Constitutional Law of Crime and Punishment' (2004) 55 *Hastings Law Journal* 509 (discussing *Heath v Alabama* 474 US 82 (1985) (laying out dual sovereign exception to constitutional prohibition of putting a person twice in jeopardy 'for the same offence')).

[38] On limitless official discretion (to prosecute, as well as not to prosecute) in the US penal process, and the absence of a principle of compulsory prosecution (*Legalitätsprinzip*), see MD Dubber, 'The New Police Science and the Police Power Model of the Criminal Process' in MD Dubber and M Valverde (eds), *The New Police Science: Police Power in Domestic and International Governance* (Stanford, Cal: Stanford University Press, 2006).

incidental, but essential to police governance. Historically, the idea of modern law, and law governance (ie government under the rule of law) arose in explicit contradistinction to the idea of police; the equality of governor and governed was posited and pursued against the inequality of governor and governed in a police regime.

If we leave aside the general question of the legitimacy of police govern-ance in a modern liberal state, which since the very inception of the distinc-tion between police and law in the Enlightenment has been laden with basic conceptions of, and prejudices about, the nature and limits of state power, a more specific, and perhaps more manageable, question remains: what might constitute the public element of crime—the publicness of criminal law, the public law aspect of state penality—in a modern democracy? Put another way, it is worth considering whether recognizing crime as public commits one to a general endorsement of police governance, or whether another, non-policial (or at least apolicial) account of the publicness of criminal law is possible. Such an account, in turn, would inform an account of the scope of the state's penal power or, in other words, of the limits of legitimate criminalization.

The police model regards criminal law (or, rather, criminal police) as a pub-lic matter because the paradigmatic victim of crime is the public, or rather the state, which as macro-householder has unlimited ultimate discretionary authority to protect the public's 'police' (that is, welfare). Instead, one might think of the 'public interest in crime' in a different way, not as the 'public's interest' in its welfare—(re)defined, monitored, and protected by the state-householder—nor as various more specific 'public interests' protected by crim-inal law norms defining various means of interfering with these interests, and then threatening this interference with criminal punishment, but as the 'pub-lic interest in' crime as an interpersonal event. In this account, the paradig-matic victim of crime would not be the public (that is, the state, the sovereign, the king, the householder, etc) but the person. The paradigmatic perpetrator would not be the violator, or disturber, or offender, of the 'public' peace—a status that, historically, was not limited to humans but included animals (not infrequently pigs), plants (notably trees), and inanimate objects (swords)—but the person. Crime, then, would be an interpersonal event between one person (labelled 'offender' or 'perpetrator') and another (labelled 'victim'). The public's (state's) interest would not be in preserving its own welfare, peace, etc, but in protecting the personhood of both 'victim' and 'offender', which is threatened by crime and (the threat, imposition, and execution of) punish-ment, respectively.

From the perspective of law, regarding criminal law as law, the public would *take an interest in* crime, rather than crime directly violating the public's interest.[39] This recognition of the public (or superindividual) aspect of an interindividual matter is a crucial feature of a system of law that is easily overlooked. At bottom, this recognition is not a question of 'the state', or even 'the public', somehow taking an interest in the affairs of individuals, but is itself an interpersonal event. The key to understanding the nature of this interest, its source, its operation, and its continuous recreation (also) lies with the concept of *personhood*. One person (or group of persons), acting in an official capacity as authorized by the state, must recognize the fellow personhood of the parties to the conflict. By identifying herself with each party as persons (rather than on the basis of some other, more substantive, similarity—age, sex, ethnic origin, citizenship, favourite color), the person sitting in judgment *empathizes* with the object of her judgment and for that, and only that, reason, 'takes an interest in' the affairs of the persons involved in the dispute.[40] The jury captures this process of interpersonal empathy (interest taking through identification), but is neither necessary, nor sufficient, for the legitimacy of the legal process as a whole, as all state officials must 'take an interest in' the objects of their judgements in this way in order to legitimate the power wielded by the state.

Crime thus affects the public indirectly, with criminal law transforming a private matter (among persons) into a public one (that involves the state). Put another way, and drawing on our discussion of Roman law, crime is the public aspect of the interpersonal delict—*delictum publicum*. (Tort is its private aspect—*delictum privatum*.) Under this model, the delict becomes a public matter, not because it interferes with the operation of the state as a separate, superior, entity of government, but because the state's function is precisely to manifest and protect the personhood of its constituents, even and especially when they commit a delict against one another.

V   Criminalizing Delicts

To further develop this account with an eye towards generating more specific principles of legitimate criminalization, one might begin by recalling that the key to the public interest in crime, and therefore the ground for the state's taking an interest in an interpersonal delict, lies in the *personhood* of

---

[39] Cf G Lamond, 'What is a Crime?' (2007) 27 OJLS 609, 629 (crimes are 'public wrongs not because they are wrongs *to* the public, but because they are wrongs that the public is responsible for punishing'); RA Duff, *Answering for Crime: Responsibility and Liability in the Criminal Law* (Oxford: Hart Publishing, 2007) 141–2 (public wrong not a 'wrong that injures the public' but one that 'properly concerns the public').

[40] Cf MD Dubber, *The Sense of Justice: Empathy in Law and Punishment* (New York, NY: New York University Press, 2006).

the perpetrator and the victim of the delict. A delict is a state matter—as crime—if it puts into question the *victim's* personhood. At the same time, the response to a delict that is public in this sense is also a state matter—as (state) punishment—so that the *perpetrator's* personhood is not violated in the name of (re)affirming the victim's, but rather itself affirmed. (In this sense, the state has a 'monopoly' on punishment and the offender *qua* person has a right to be punished.[41]) A delict, then, is a public matter—a crime, *delictum publicum*—insofar as it requires state intervention to manifest and protect the personhood of its constituents (victims and perpetrators alike). It is a private matter—a tort, or *delictum privatum*—insofar as it does not.

This is one way of making sense of, and filling in, the vague notion that crimes are 'serious' violations of another's interest or, for that matter, that crimes which are not sufficiently 'serious' (so-called '*de minimis* infractions'[42]) do not warrant state intervention.[43] Seriousness (in general, and among crimes) would be measured in terms of the perpetrator's behaviour's effect on, or relation to, the victim's personhood; personhood, in turn, would be defined in terms of the capacity for autonomy. The greater the challenge to the victim's personhood, that is, his capacity for autonomy, the more serious the delict. Seriousness, then, would range from, at one extreme, the complete destruction of another's physical and mental faculties essential for the capacity for autonomy, through homicide or very serious assaults, to the threatened temporary interference with the exercise of that capacity, through remote threats of assault or physical restraint (at the other).

All law, including criminal law and tort law, is concerned with persons, understood as beings with the capacity for autonomy. All delicts are interpersonal events—as are all contractual transactions, which manifest both parties' capacity for autonomy, the exercise of which in the form of a 'promise' is reflected, and respected, through the imposition of liability in the event of a unilateral breach. (Property law, by contrast, is concerned with persons' control of, and exercise of their capacity for autonomy through, non-personal things, as objects only.[44]) Through criminal law (in its various aspects—from the definition of penal norms (in substantive criminal law), via the imposition of these norms in particular cases (criminal procedure, from investigation to trial), to the execution of threatened sanctions for their violation (execution law, prison law)), the state manifests and safeguards, *ex ante, ex post*, and in the

---

[41] See MD Dubber, 'The Right to Be Punished: Autonomy and Its Demise in Modern Penal Thought' (1998) 16 *Law and History Review* 113; H Morris, 'Persons and Punishment' (1968) 53 *Monist* 475.   [42] See, eg Model Penal Code §2.12 (judicial dismissal).

[43] See, eg StPO §153 ('no public interest in the prosecution').

[44] See, eg A Brudner, *The Unity of the Common Law: Studies in Hegelian Jurisprudence* (Berkeley, Cal: University of California Press, 1995).

moment, the personhood of both victims and offenders (so offenders have a right to be punished, as victims have a right to *have* offenders punished, rather than to punish offenders themselves).

The state's role in tort law (and contract and property law) is less (pro)active and more facilitative; by providing a mechanism for the resolution of conflicts, it assists persons in the direct assertion of their personhood through the pursuit of a private cause of action itself, rather than (re)asserting it through a public prosecution on their behalf (where, again, the state also represents the *offender's* personhood through empathic identification, an ideal and a process institutionalized by the jury). In criminal law, the process is (part of) the punishment; in tort law, the process is (part of) the compensation.

Tort compensation restores the victim, or rather the plaintiff, to his or her pre-delict state. Criminal punishment reasserts the victim's personhood in the face of its denial through the offender's criminal act. Punishment puts the offender 'in his place'; not, as some have suggested, by visiting upon him the humiliation he inflicted on the victim, but by confirming that he is no better, nor worse, than the victim, that they are equals as persons.[45] In this sense, crime is concerned not only with the victim's personhood, but also with the offender's. In the end, punishment reasserts the equal personhood of victim and offender (and judge) alike.

If one thinks of crimes and torts as public and private interpersonal delicts, respectively, the question of the complementarity of criminal law and tort law arises. From the perspective of law, tort law appears as the preferable response to the commission of a delict, since the act of 'prosecuting' of a tort suit by the victim/plaintiff reflects her personhood and the imposition of tort liability does not threaten the tortfeasor/defendant's personhood in the same way as would the imposition of criminal liability, and the infliction of criminal punishment. Criminal law, then, would be reserved for cases that threaten, and deny, the victim's personhood, rather than simply diminishing his resources for the exercise of his capacity for autonomy. In this account, the so-called *ultima ratio* principle would be linked to law's essential concern with persons as defined by the capacity for autonomy. The criminal law, as posing the greatest threat to the personhood of its objects (offenders), should be limited to 'serious' cases in which it is necessary to (re)assert the personhood of victims, not only in the abstract (as reflected in the scope of the substantive criminal law) but also in the particular case, so as not to violate the victim's autonomy in the name of manifesting it.

---

[45] Cf GP Fletcher, 'Domination in Wrongdoing' (1996) 76 *Boston University Law Review* 347, 353–4.

9

Criminal Wrongs in Historical Perspective[*]

Lindsay Farmer

I Introduction

A theory of criminalization—of the proper scope of the criminal law, and of the principles that might define, limit, and organize that law—conventionally begins with some attempt to specify a core principle (or principles) that are to provide the analytical framework through which particular types of behaviour or legislation might be assessed. These are typically concerned with the limits of state power and the maximizing of individual freedom. Thus, the most famous of these theories, though far from being conceived of as a theory of 'criminalization' as such, John Stuart Mill's 'harm principle', sought to specify the conditions under which certain sorts of behaviour might properly be regarded as permitting state intervention.[1] To a surprising degree, later writings more explicitly directed at the theme of criminalization have not advanced substantially beyond these early insights: most are conducted from within the framework of liberal political theory laid out by Mill, and more often than not take the form of critiques of current law or state practices. There have been refinements in the conceptual terminology—notably in the discussion of the concept of harm and the emergence of the distinction between harms and wrongs. However, to a remarkable extent, the parameters of these kinds of debate have not shifted much in the period since the publication of Mill's *On Liberty*.

Discussion of criminalization has largely focused on the concept of 'harm', which seemed to offer a value-neutral basis for the criminal law which could

[*] My thanks to Sarah Armstrong, Stuart Green, Niki Lacey, Peter Ramsay, my co-researchers, and the workshop participants for their ideas and comments.
[1] JS Mill, *On Liberty* (Oxford: Oxford University Press, 1991) 14.

act as a bulwark against the enforcement of particular moral and political values. Here, however, increasing theoretical sophistication has been undercut by the breadth of the underlying concept. Joel Feinberg's four-volume work on the moral limits of the criminal law developed a sophisticated account of the harm principle that was directed specifically at the theme of criminalization.[2] However, even Feinberg had to concede that the principle had some limits, as he struggled to deal with the problems of paternalism (harm to self) and behaviour that was offensive (but not harmful) to others. Later critics have stressed the essential indeterminacy of the concept of harm, and its potential to be under or overinclusive.[3] In spite of these criticisms, the harm principle has continued to generate extensive academic discussion, and has also come to be an attractive resource to those arguing for transformations of the criminal law. This is in part a matter of its political appeal. Critical criminologists, for example, while favouring decriminalization of consensual behaviour on the grounds that there can be no harm, have argued in favour of criminalization of a range of activities on the basis of an expanded notion of 'social' harm.[4] Likewise, because harm concerns the effect of conduct rather than being a property of that conduct, it is straightforward for individuals or groups that feel themselves to be victimized to claim legal protection on the basis of the harm they have suffered. The problem here, as Harcourt has pointed out, is that the harm principle ultimately collapses into itself once all claims have been translated in terms of the concept of harm.[5] It is ironic, and also telling about its weakness as a theoretical position, that a principle initially formulated as a means of thinking about the limits of state power should be called in aid of manifold claims to extend the scope of the criminal law and thus the power of the state.

Accordingly, much recent attention has been directed at the associated concept of the 'wrong', either as a means of correcting for some of the weaknesses of the harm principle,[6] or as the basis for a discrete theory of criminalization.

---

[2] J Feinberg, *The Moral Limits of the Criminal Law* (4 vols, Oxford: Oxford University Press, 1984–8). See the useful review and analysis in J Stanton-Ife, 'The Limits of Law' *Stanford Encyclopedia of Philosophy,* <http://plato.stanford.edu/entries/law-limits/>.

[3] See RA Duff, *Answering for Crime: Responsibility and Liability in the Criminal Law* (Oxford: Hart Publishing, 2007) ch 6.

[4] See, eg essays in P Hillyard *et al* (eds) *Beyond Criminology: Taking Harm Seriously* (London: Pluto Press, 2004); *Criminal Justice Matters* special issue on Criminalization (vol 74, issue 1, 2008).

[5] B Harcourt, 'The Collapse of the Harm Principle' (1999) 90 *Journal of Criminal Law and Criminology* 109

[6] Notably J Feinberg, *Harm to Others* (Oxford: Oxford University Press, 1984) 31 suggesting that a legally relevant harm is a setback to interests which also wrongs those whose interests are set back. See also Duff (n 3 above) 128: criminal law is concerned not just with harm but with *wrongful* harm.

Of course, it is clearly the case that the idea of the wrong has a long history in criminal law, with recent discussions frequently taking as a starting point Blackstone's conception of the criminal law as 'public wrongs'.[7] However, what is distinctive about recent contributions is that they have developed out of the revival of interest in theories of retributive punishment—that punishment must be for the commission of a wrongful act—and seek to use this insight to say something about the content of the criminal law. At one extreme this can lead to a new kind of legal moralism—that there is good reason to criminalize all morally wrongful actions—which assumes that criminal law is straightforwardly a species of moral theory.[8] More often, though, it seeks to temper such an extreme position with the acknowledgement that it is necessary to distinguish between different levels and types of wrongdoing in making the decision to criminalize. This position thus seeks to strike a balance between the strong demands of the legal moralist, on one hand, and the harm principle on the other, through a recognition that certain conditions, such as that wrongs will normally have brought about harm, must be met before wrongs can be legally relevant. However, the problem here is that of specifying which other conditions should be met: how can we identify and agree on a list of legally relevant wrongs? It is not enough here to rely on moral theory, for even if we could agree on an account of wrongs, this would not tell us which of these should be enforced by law in general, by criminal law in particular, or what the appropriate mode of definition and enforcement should be.[9] What is crucial, then, if this approach is to be taken, is that we have some account of how we should move from the concept of a moral wrong to an account of legal wrongs, that is to say from moral theory to criminalization. And if this is something that is not easily done then it raises serious questions about the plausibility of an approach that takes 'wrongs' as its starting point.[10]

In this chapter I shall look at three different (if overlapping) ways this gap has been approached in recent criminal law theory in order to challenge what seems to me to be a rather unreflective account of the relationship between crime and wrongs in much of the literature on criminalization. In doing this, I should stress that the aim of this chapter is not, in the first instance, that of developing an account of wrongs, but of looking at the way that the idea of

---

[7] *Commentaries on the Laws of England* (1765–9) vol IV, ch 1.

[8] M Moore, *Placing Blame: A General Theory of the Criminal Law* (Oxford: Oxford University Press, 1997) 33–5.

[9] J Elster, 'Non-Criminalisation of Harmful and Immoral Acts' (unpublished manuscript) 8, distinguishing between 'deep' morality and principles of regulation.

[10] Cf N Christie, *A Suitable Amount of Crime* (London: Routledge, 2004) 3, listing 'crime' among other forms of what he calls 'badness'—irritations, unpleasantness, disgust, sin. He argues that the category crime (and hence, presumably, wrong) has no fixed meaning, but only acquires it in any given social framework.

the wrong has been used. One of my contentions here is that there is no easy or straightforward translation between moral theory and criminal law, and that insufficient attention has been paid to the gap between the two. In more positive terms the chapter will use historical examples to address the questions of whether criminal offences are conceived around a preconceived idea of moral wrong, whether and how the content of this idea might change over time, and whether, if this is the case, the concept of a wrong can provide a firm enough basis for a theory of criminalization.

II 'Wrongs' in Criminal Law Theory

A 'Conventionalist' account

One of the most influential recent accounts of criminalization is that provided by Husak in his book *Overcriminalization*.[11] While the book has much to say about the topic of criminalization in general, I want to focus here on what is quite a small part of his argument, that concerning the nature of a wrong.

Husak's starting point is that the phenomenon of overcriminalization leads to too much punishment—in the sense that the infliction of punishment will be unjust because sentences are excessive, or imposed following convictions for crimes that do not reflect the underlying wrong, or more generally because they are inflicted for conduct that should not have been criminalized at all.[12] This leads him to identify what he sees as a series of possible internal and external constraints on criminalization. Amongst the internal constraints are what he terms the 'wrongfulness constraint': that 'criminal liability may not be imposed unless the defendant's conduct is (in some sense) wrongful'.[13] This constraint, Husak claims, is internal because of the existence in the general part of the criminal law of the requirement that criminal liability can only be imposed where there has been wrongdoing. This is illustrated by reference to the theory of excuses, which requires that we first establish that there has been wrongdoing, and then consider whether or not liability should be imposed.[14] Without this presupposition of a requirement of wrongdoing, it is suggested that a theory of excuses would not make sense. This claim about defences is then called in aid of

---

[11] *Overcriminalization: The Limits of the Criminal Law* (Oxford: Oxford University Press, 2008).   [12] Ibid, 3.

[13] Ibid, 66. The others are the non-trivial harm or evil constraint, the desert constraint, and the burden of proof constraint: see ch 2.

[14] Ibid, 72–3 citing J Horder, *Excusing Crime* (Oxford: Oxford University Press, 2004). See also G Fletcher, *Rethinking Criminal Law* (Boston, Mass: Little, Brown and Co, 1978) ch 6, on the distinction between wrongdoing and attribution.

the more general claim, made in the context of strict liability offences, that the
mens rea requirement in the general part should be understood as requiring that
conduct criminalized in substantive offences should be wrongful.[15]

While this gives some indication as to how the constraint might work, little
is said about the content of the constraint—what makes conduct wrongful.
For some indication of Husak's views on this, and thus on how the concept of
a crime should be understood, we must turn to his discussion of the distinction between *mala in se* and *mala prohibita*.[16] He argues that something is a
malum prohibitum when 'the conduct proscribed is not wrongful prior to or
independent of law'.[17] Here Husak suggests that the wrongfulness of *mala in
se* is obvious,[18] before going on to discuss various categories of *mala prohibita*,
which are by definition not wrongful. While all criminal laws should be subject to the constraints that he identifies, it seems to be assumed that this will be
more straightforward in the case of 'core' crimes because their 'wrongness' will
be more readily identified. Implicit in this are two factors that are made explicit
earlier in the book and in some of his other writings: that there is a distinction
between the core and the periphery of criminal law; and that certain crimes
are paradigmatic.[19] Core offences are offences which are wrong prior to and
independently of law, and that 'share whatever features are important from the
standpoint of justice';[20] peripheral offences are those, primarily new offences,
which are not and do not. To understand which features are important from
the standpoint of justice we must turn to the idea of the paradigmatic crime.
This is a crime which can provide the basis for generalization in thinking about
the relevant normative characteristics of criminal law, that is as a model for
the proper understanding of the criminal law as a body of rules. The criteria
for selection of a paradigmatic crime are normative, which is to say that they
should not just be based on features such as frequency of prosecution but on
features which are important from the standpoint of justice.[21] And returning us to our starting point, their function is that of locating restrictions on
the structure of crimes in the special part, and hence to be capable of acting
as a constraint on the conduct that can be criminalized.[22] Thus the notion

---

[15] Ibid, 74.   [16] Ibid, 103–19.

[17] Ibid, 105. Thus, implicitly, that a *mala in se is* wrongful prior to and independently of law.

[18] Ibid, 104.

[19] Ibid, 33–6. See also D Husak, 'Crimes outside the Core' (2003–4) 39 *Tulsa Law Review*
755. G Fletcher (n 14 above) refers to core offences (234), but sees these as containing 'a polycentric body of principles' (xxii); W Stuntz, 'The Pathological Politics of Criminal Law' (2001) 100
Michigan Law Review 506.   [20] Husak, *Overcriminalization*, ibid, 34.

[21] Presumably features such as the requirement of *mens rea*, that this should extend to all material elements of the offence etc.

[22] D Husak, 'Limitations on Criminalization and the General Part of the Criminal Law' in
S Shute and AP Simester (eds), *Criminal Law Theory: Doctrines of the General Part* (Oxford: Oxford

of a core supports the claim that there is an area of settled moral agreement, while the 'paradigmatic' crime guides us on how the wrong is to be appropriately institutionalized in law. This account can be described as conventionalist because it assumes that the already existing criminal law both reflects and supports our settled moral intuitions and can guide us in our understanding of the proper scope of criminalization.[23]

What is troubling about this is that there is a certain evasiveness: that the basis for his constraint is never fully articulated, but is instead deferred to another set of distinctions. While Husak can justifiably respond that his project concerns the phenomenon of *over*criminalization and hence the proliferation of *mala prohibita*, and that it is not his aim in the book to provide a definition of wrongful conduct, the project nonetheless seems to be resting on certain key assumptions: that there are *mala in se* that are wrongful prior to and independently of law, that the institutionalization of these wrongs in law is straightforward and unproblematic, and that there is a settled core of *mala in se* which can provide the foundation for his critique of overcriminalization.

Why does this matter? After all, Husak might reasonably object that there is in fact settled moral agreement around certain wrongs (such as murder and rape) which are treated as serious crimes in all systems of criminal law, and that analysis of these wrongs is therefore an appropriate place for a theory of criminalization to begin. While the initial part of this claim can be conceded, I want to contest the idea that it necessarily leads to any conclusions about the significance of these wrongs for a system of criminal law, such as how they might define core offences or how this core might be of wider significance to the structure or content of the law. This point can be developed through three more specific objections.

First, there is a kind of implicit history embedded in this analysis, whether or not this is deliberate. On this account peripheral offences are those that are ancillary, overlapping, statutory, and new (and which, by definition, do not have features which are important from the standpoint of justice); while the settled (and older) core comprises established common law crimes (those on the basis of which the existing general part has been constructed).[24] Now, I do not wish

University Press 2002) 17–18. Cf G Fletcher, 'Blackmail: The Paradigmatic Crime' (1993) 141 *University of Pennsylvania Law Review* 1617. For a different account of blackmail see P Alldridge, ' "Attempted Murder of the Soul": Blackmail, Privacy and Secrets' (1993) 13 OJLS 368.

[23] Cf G Lamond, 'What is a Crime?' (2007) 27 OJLS 609, suggesting that a theory must provide an 'intelligible rationale' for settled instances of crime based on certain general characteristics of these settled instances.

[24] Husak, 'Crimes outside the Core' (n 19 above) argues that the core is normative rather than historical (756–7), and thus that the identification of core crimes depends on their normative significance.

to imply that this distinction is applied in a crude or uncritical way, but more that the critical analysis does not extend to the meaning of wrongs or non-trivial harms—and that, at the very least, there is a risk of reproducing a rather unhelpful common law ideology which uncritically privileges that which is old and customary. Second, there is a lot more at stake in the claim that there can be paradigmatic crimes. We might plausibly claim that, just as different historical periods had distinctive ways of thinking about the nature of the criminal law, they also had distinctive or paradigmatic crimes. Here we might think of the paradigmatic in two further (and possibly overlapping) senses: structurally (that which has generalizable features for the criminal law, whether or not these also comply with the requirements of justice); and substantively (that which reflects the concerns or fears of the particular age).[25] And just as, historically, a structuring crime might not meet with the requirements of justice as we understand them now, so we should recognize that our own understanding of the way that the requirements of justice are articulated in law may itself be historically contingent. For example, while the requirement of *mens rea* has long been recognized as a precondition of punishment, it is only comparatively recently that it has taken on its contemporary 'subjective' form.[26] In either case it is necessary to say a great deal more about how the crime has been shaped and how it might structure the criminal law. Moreover, if we recognize that there are different patterns of liability across the criminal law, there may be no single set of generalizable features.[27] The idea of a 'paradigmatic crime' might thus be expressed at such a level of generality as to be of little assistance in thinking about criminal law.[28] Finally, this raises the question of whether it makes sense to talk about a core of the criminal law, even where this is defined in stipulative terms as containing those crimes which have features which are important from the standpoint of justice. On the one hand, we might contend, the core is in fact always changing, either because crimes which were regarded as central or paradigmatic are no longer treated as such (eg treason, blasphemy[29]) or because central features of

---

[25] For a different analysis of how murder has been the perfect, and therefore 'paradigmatic', crime for the modern criminal law, see L Farmer, *Criminal Law, Tradition and Legal Order* (Cambridge: Cambridge University Press, 1997) ch 5.

[26] See essays by Lacey and Farmer in MD Dubber and L Farmer, *Modern Histories of Crime and Punishment* (Stanford, Cal: Stanford University Press, 2007). See also Hildebrandt, in this volume.

[27] Fletcher (*Rethinking Criminal Law* (n 14 above) pt I) analyses 'paradigm' shifts within the pattern of liability for the crimes of larceny and homicide. Husak refers to this, in his discussion of Fletcher, as a polycentric model: 'Crimes outside the Core' (n 19 above), 759.

[28] Fletcher ('Blackmail: the Paradigmatic Crime' (n 22 above), for example, suggests that blackmail is paradigmatic because of its focus on the morally unjust relation of dominion. While this may be regarded as a feature of all crimes, it would almost certainly not capture what is specifically wrong about certain crimes.

[29] Abolished by Criminal Justice and Immigration Act 2008, s 79: R Sandberg and N Doe, 'The Strange Death of Blasphemy' (2008) 71 MLR 971. See also D Nash, 'Blasphemy and the

'core' crimes change in ways which shift the meaning and social significance of the crime.[30] Even if we fall back on the stipulative definition that the core at any given time should contain only those crimes which do in fact meet the requirements of justice, the content of the idea of non-trivial harm or wrong is going to be highly dependent on the temporally contingent social meaning of certain actions. That is to say, it simply might not be possible to determine whether something is a public wrong prior to and independently of law.

B   Proceduralist account

A second kind of approach can be found in the work of Antony Duff, whose argument has focused on the role that the idea of wrongdoing might play in the public definition and condemnation of criminal behaviour, at the expense of detailed examination of the content of the wrong of any particular crime or group of crimes.[31] Like Husak, he begins from the intuition that individuals can only be answerable (and therefore liable) for wrongdoing, but that since not all wrongs can, or should, be crimes there must be some means of distinguishing between different wrongs. However, for Duff there can be no central or organizing 'master principle', such as the harm principle, for such principles will either be underinclusive (if they are determinate) or too broad or general in scope to play any useful role in determining the scope of the law.[32] His argument about the relationship between wrongs and the criminal law thus rests on a different kind of claim, one that is not primarily related to substantive content.

Central to Duff's account of the criminal law is the idea that crimes are 'public wrongs'.[33] This, he argues should be understood not just in terms of being a wrong to the public, since the criminal law should also include laws protecting private individuals against wrongs committed against them. Crimes

Anti-Civilizing Process' in KD Watson, *Assaulting the Past: Violence and Civilization in Historical Context* (Newcastle: Cambridge Scholars Publishing, 2007) and E Visconsi, 'The Invention of Criminal Blasphemy: *Rex v. Taylor* (1676)' (2008) 103 *Representations* 30.

[30] For example, in theft the shift from trespass to taking to dishonesty; in assault the expansion of the personal sphere to include identity and psychic harm and modes of commission to include silence and non-presence. See Part III B below.

[31] See *Answering for Crime* (n 3 above), especially chs 4 and 6. See also SE Marshall and RA Duff, 'Criminalization and Sharing Wrongs' (1998) 11 *Canadian Journal of Law & Jurisprudence* 7; RA Duff and SE Marshall, 'Public and Private Wrongs' in J Chalmers, F Leverick, and L Farmer (eds), *Essays in Criminal Law in Honour of Sir Gerald Gordon* (Edinburgh: Edinburgh University Press, forthcoming, 2010). [32] *Answering for Crime*, ibid, 135.

[33] Ibid, 140–6. And such wrongs should properly be understood as wrongs against private individuals in which the public takes an interest, rather than as merely being derivative of the public interest. Cf Husak (*Overcriminalization* (n 11 above), 199), who shares this view of public wrongs in arguing against 'legal moralism'.

should be understood as wrongs which concern us all as members of the community, and can thus be distinguished from private wrongs which concern
only those individuals directly involved. These are wrongs for which 'we are
criminally responsible as citizens to our fellow citizens'.[34] This is an important
and persuasive account of answerability but, as Duff notes, it cannot in itself
answer the question of why something should be criminalized, or which kinds
of wrongs we, as citizens, share in a common interest. Duff's answer to these
questions is that public wrongs should be understood as those wrongs which
could be seen as violating the values that define us as a community. Thus:

> A justification of criminalisation will need to begin by specifying some value(s)
> that can be claimed to be public, as part of the polity's self-definition; show how
> the conduct in question violates that value or threatens the goods that it protects;
> and argue that that violation or threat is such as to require or demand a public
> condemnation.[35]

The important point here is that Duff is seeking to found the legitimacy of
the criminal law in the process of norm-formation. To this extent, the value of
his account rests on its recognition that there is a gap between an account of
moral wrongs and one of criminalization, and that the political legitimacy of
the criminal law cannot depend solely or even mainly on an account of moral
wrongs.[36] Indeed, to the extent that Duff locates the question of legitimacy in
the political process of norm-formation and denies moral theory any proscrip-
tive role, his account can be understood as a proceduralization of the issue of
criminalization.[37] That said, even this minimalist account might be capable
of producing some substantive content for the criminal law. If a key role of
the criminal law in calling individuals to account is to recognize and address
them as individuals who are members of the community, it is arguable that the
criminal law must at least contain norms which criminalize conduct directed
against individuals as valued and respected members of the community.[38]
More significantly, perhaps, Duff's argument is centrally based on the claim
that actions cannot be understood solely in terms of their outcomes, but in
terms of their meaning—the character of the practice in question to the actor,
the victim, and the community. Thus, in discussing whether consent might
be a defence to certain forms of assault (such as sado masochistic sexual conduct), he contends that a better approach is to understand the meaning of the

---

[34] Ibid, 142.   [35] Ibid, 143.

[36] Though it is only fair to note that earlier in the book Duff defends an idea of *mala in se* as
declaratory of pre-legal wrongs: ibid, 82–9. It is not clear whether he sees this as an independent
constraint on the formulation of a public wrong.

[37] Ibid, 86–7. Cf J Habermas, *Between Facts and Norms* (Cambridge: Polity, 1997) chs 3 and 4.

[38] And Duff suggests that this might even go so far as to support the criminalization of various
mala in se: ibid, 87.

act in context, and whether it fulfils the interests of those involved.[39] Equally, in his discussion of whether or not offensive behaviour should be criminalized, he contends that 'some behaviour is wrong... because it is offensive', a claim which requires more specific elaboration of how, and in what context, certain forms of behaviour are understood to be offensive to others.[40] What becomes clear here is that, for an account which relies heavily on claims about the meaning of actions, we need to know more about how this meaning is acquired and recognized in law.

C   Particular wrongs?

A third type of approach focuses on the wrong or wrongs which are central to a particular offence or group of offences.[41] These types of account seek to move beyond the assertion that something is obviously a wrong, or discussions of wrongs in general, to discussions of specific instances of wrongness. While these analyses look only at the content of the specific wrong discussed and do not claim to be developing a 'master principle' that would be good for the whole of the criminal law, the approach is of broader significance as it points towards a more general account of wrongs and their relation to the criminal law as a whole. These analyses are clearly focused on the idea that there is a central moral 'wrong', independent of any harm, which can be identified in relation to specific crimes and that understanding this wrong will then elucidate central features of the legal offence. (Indeed it has become a trope of these analyses to explore the 'harmless' instance of the crime in order to elucidate the nature of the wrong.) There is no necessary claim that the qualities of any individual wrong should be shared by the wrongs of other crimes, or as to the public or shared quality of the wrong. This type of approach can be exemplified by Gardner and Shute's influential account of the 'wrongness' of rape.[42]

The central claim in their paper is that the wrongness of rape consists in the 'sheer use' of another person, treating them as an object and denying their

---

[39] Ibid, 131. Discussing the case of *R v Brown* [1994] 1 AC 212, Duff considers that we should look at whether the conduct attains morally legitimate ends (mutual sexual pleasure) or morally admirable values (love and respect).   [40] Ibid, 133.

[41] See, eg SP Green, *Lying, Cheating and Stealing: A Moral Theory of White-Collar Crime* (Oxford: Oxford University Press, 2006) especially 39–47; J Gardner, 'Rationality and the Rule of Law in Offences against the Person' (1994) 53 CLJ 502; AP Simester and GR Sullivan, 'On the Nature and Rationale of Property Offences' in RA Duff and SP Green (eds), *Defining Crimes: Essays on the Special Part of the Criminal Law* (Oxford: Oxford University Press, 2005).

[42] 'The Wrongness of Rape' in J Horder (ed), *Oxford Essays in Jurisprudence*, 4th series (Oxford: Oxford University Press, 2000) 193–217, reprinted with a short response to critics in J Gardner, *Offences and Defences* (Oxford: Oxford University Press, 2007). For discussion of the original paper see also J Stanton-Ife in this volume.

personhood.[43] This conclusion is based on the Kantian idea that the wrong should be understood as the treatment of the victim as a means or an object. Thus, they contend that rape should not be understood in terms of harm or an interference with the right to self-ownership of the body, and that this account of the wrongness of rape further allows the differentiation of rape from other forms of wrong.[44] Thus, they contend that '[a]ll sheer use of human beings, all treatment of them merely as means, is *ab*use; and rape is the central case of such abuse'—even while conceding that this need not lead to the conclusion that any specific instances of this wrong should be criminalized.[45] While they might have concluded at this point, the argument goes on to consider how this general account might further illuminate specific features of the crime of rape—notably the focus on lack of consent, on penetrative sexual abuse, and on mistakes as to consent. Taking the second of these, sexual penetration, they argue that the centrality of this requirement cannot be explained solely in terms of the Kantian argument but must depend on the social meaning of certain acts.[46] This, they suggest, depends on the 'special symbolism of penetrative sexual activity' and its subversion in rape.[47] Thus, 'the elevation of penetrative non-consensual sexual violation to the status of special paradigm is a longstanding, but culturally conditioned application [of the more general principle].'[48]

What we have here then is an approach that seeks to marry an attention to general philosophical principles to the social meaning of certain acts as reflected in the existing law. It is important because, while still dealing with the core of the criminal law, it goes beyond the assertion of the self-evidence of the general category of wrong to look more deeply at the question of how specific conduct might legitimately be criminalized. It is ostensibly more limited— attending only to the wrong of rape and not criminal law in general—and not claiming 'master principle' status.[49] That said, Gardner and Shute leave significant questions unanswered. First, as Stanton-Ife points out, their definition is somewhat loaded in the use of the terms 'sheer' use and 'mere' means.[50] These adjectives are no doubt intended to add something, a certain weight or emphasis, to the bare (or 'mere') Kantian formula, but it is never really made clear what this is. As Stanton-Ife's discussion makes clear, in accounting for the seriousness of rape compared to other offences, this seems to introduce a

---

[43] Ibid, 205. Cf Ripstein's idea of the sovereignty principle: A Ripstein, 'Beyond the Harm Principle' (2006) 34 *Philosophy and Public Affairs* 215.

[44] Or, at least, allows this differentiation in the case of the 'pure' rape: ibid, 197.

[45] Ibid, 205; emphasis in original.   [46] Ibid, 210.   [47] Ibid.   [48] Ibid, 211.

[49] Though they do suggest (ibid, 205) that the Kantian argument may be central to the explication of the wrongs in other crimes, and that rape is the central case of the Kantian argument.

[50] This volume, Chapter 6, Part II.

particular kind of attitude into the formulation something that makes *this* use or *that* action worse than others. However, once this concession is made it is no longer clear why some actions involving sheer use are worse than others, or why rape is a special case, or what is to account for the particular wrong of rape, without having a more detailed account of the social meaning of the acts in question. And here I would argue that the claim as to the special symbolism of penetrative sex, and in particular the question of how it might elucidate analogous wrongs, is simply too thin to be of much use. If it is to provide such elucidation, this account would surely need both to demonstrate why penetration should have such a special symbolism, as well as to explain how ideas of consent and sexual autonomy relate to the idea of penetration—in ways which have unquestionably led to the expansion of the scope of the legal wrong.[51]

This analysis of the wrongness of rape thus demonstrates some of the strengths and weaknesses of this type of approach. The general pattern here is to begin from existing law and then to identify a 'pure' case as a means of analysing a central aspect of moral wrongdoing at a level of generality. This general approach of identifying the particular values and attitudes that different wrongs reflect is a plausible way of beginning to think about why and how particular conduct should be criminalized, but I would argue that it is unable to explain specific aspects of seriousness, nor even necessarily why we should see particular forms of conduct as distinct wrongs, without reference to the social meaning of that conduct. There is still, that is to say, a significant gap between the identification of the moral wrong and an account of criminalization. Moreover, where this approach attempts to fill the gap by looking at the existing criminal law (taken as the basis of our understanding of social meaning), this can come close to the conventionalist approach (and thus be open to the same criticisms), or alternatively might close off the exploration of other options or understandings of conduct.

* * *

A number of more general conclusions can be drawn from this far from exhaustive survey. First, like Duff, we should be sceptical about the possibility of identifying a 'master principle', both for the reasons that he advances, and because even this limited discussion suggests that when we seek to move from moral theory to a discussion of legal wrongs the picture becomes too complex

---

[51] See, eg Sexual Offences Act 2003, s 1 and Sexual Offences (S) Act 2009, s 1, both of which extend the definition of rape to include penile penetration of the vagina, anus, or mouth of another person. We can see that non-consensual sexual penetration is treated as especially serious, but it is not obvious why actions other than vaginal penetration should amount to rape unless we also understand the crime in terms of a distinct value in protecting sexual autonomy.

to rely on any single principle. Second, given the precariousness of positing a theory of criminalization on the existence of a core of wrongs, it is necessary to begin with the analysis of particular crimes to see if it is possible to discern patterns of liability in the development of legal wrongs and how they relate to the body of criminal law as a whole.[52] And third, if we are to pursue this approach, we cannot take social meaning as something that is unproblematically represented in the criminal law, but must explore how meanings develop and change over time in particular areas of social life. In other words, if we are to begin from existing offences or understandings of the criminal law as a whole, it is necessary to unpick the historical assumptions around cores and paradigms. More generally, then, this would support Macintyre's assertion that a moral philosophy presupposes an underlying sociology.[53] In the following part I shall set out three possible ways in which the kind of historical approach that I am advocating can illuminate our understanding of these core criminal wrongs.

III   Criminalization and Wrongs in Historical Perspective

A   Public wrongs and juridification

The distinction of public wrongs from private, of crimes and misdemeanours from civil injuries, seems principally to consist in this: that private, or civil injuries, are an infringement or privation of the civil rights which belong to individuals, considered merely as individuals; wrongs, or crime and misdemeanours, are breach and violation of the public rights and duties, due to the whole community, considered as community, in its social aggregate capacity... [T]reason, murder, and robbery are properly ranked among crimes; since, besides the injury done to individuals, they strike at the very being of society; which cannot possibly subsist, where actions of this sort are suffered to escape with impunity.[54]

As I noted above, Blackstone is often cited in support of the idea that crimes must be understood as 'public wrongs'. However, while he unquestionably uses this phrase, it is not obvious that the phrase 'public wrong' carried the same meaning then as in present-day legal theory. For Blackstone the idea of the public wrong striking at the very being of society consisted primarily in the

---

[52] Indeed, even if we want to accept that there is a core, I would argue that we still need to do a lot more work in terms of justifying why these wrongs in these particular legal forms should be taken as the core offences, as well as explicating their relationship to the criminal law as a whole.

[53] A Macintyre, *After Virtue: A Study in Moral Theory*, 2nd edn (London: Duckworth, 1985) 23.

[54] Sir William Blackstone, *Commentaries on the Laws of England* (1765–9) vol IV, 5.

breach of the king's peace, or the realm understood as an extension of the royal household.[55] This, it should be noted, was further reflected in his categorization of crimes which reflected a roughly descending order of seriousness from crimes against god and religion, to treason and lesser felonies against the king's prerogative, to offences against the public peace, trade, and public health, before only then coming to a discussion of homicide and other crimes against the person. There is, to be sure, an emerging awareness of the importance of wrongs against the individual as public wrongs in something like the modern sense, reflecting changing conceptions of liberty and personhood, but this represents a tension in Blackstone's conception of crime rather than the fully-fledged emergence of the modern view of the person. Indeed, to the extent that eighteenth-century criminal law was organized around an idea of public interest in the protection of private right at all it was the concept of private property that was seen as foundational to legal and political authority.[56] More generally, this points to something important about the relationship between moral wrong and legal and political forms—that legal wrongs and conceptions of seriousness are closely related to the institutions and forms of legal and political authority. This, it should be clear, is not to suggest that 'wrongs' can be reduced to political forms, but that legal conceptions of wrong in particular must be understood in this context.

This can have a bearing on consideration of the distinction between *mala in se* and *mala prohibita* discussed above. Criminal law theorists have struggled with this distinction, with the status of *mala prohibita* in general, and with specific kinds of *mala prohibita* such as strict liability offences, precisely because they do not seem to criminalize 'wrongs', or because the nature of the wrong and the associated form of culpability is at best unclear.[57] However, an alternative approach would be to trace the changes in the conception of the legal idea of a public wrong and its relation to the changing form of the legal subject and the state. This, to be sure, will not directly answer the question of whether punishment is justifiable in any given instance, but it can provide a

---

[55] See MD Dubber, *The Police Power: Patriarchy and the Foundations of American Government* (New York, NY: Columbia University Press, 2005) ch 2, linking this to the feudal origins of the modern police power.

[56] See D Hay, 'Property, Authority and the Criminal Law' in D Hay *et al* (eds), *Albion's Fatal Tree* (Harmondsworth: Penguin, 1977).

[57] See, eg the essays in AP Simester (ed), *Appraising Strict Liability* (Oxford: Oxford University Press, 2005). It is now generally accepted that not all statutory offences should be understood as *mala prohibita*: the term should be reserved for those offences which are not wrong in themselves, but only made wrong by prohibition. Likewise, the objection to strict liability offences is that some involve serious wrongs (and thus are not *mala prohibita* as traditionally conceived), but without corresponding fault requirements.

more subtle and nuanced account of the nature of a legal wrong and of the appropriate legal or political response.[58]

Over the course of the nineteenth and twentieth centuries the criminal law was extended to regulate a large number of otherwise lawful forms of conduct.[59] In the creation of these new offences the law was typically concerned less with punishing wilful wrongdoing than with distributing the burden of avoiding the risk of harm. While this is normally understood as involving the recognition of a new range of social harms involved in the production and distribution of goods and services in a capitalist industrial society, we should not overlook the fact that it also entailed a change in the concept of public wrong. This expanded to capture the full range of offences which 'in some way interfere with the conditions which ensure [a] person's integration into the political system, with their "rights" as a full member of the community, with their citizenship'.[60] In the welfare state, Ramsay argues, this principally reflected the central idea of democratic citizenship, comprising civil, political, and social aspects, since this alone could legitimize 'the apparently diverse and contradictory forms and functions of modern criminal law'.[61] The idea of civil rights as the rights necessary for individual freedom could justify the existence of laws protecting the individual's right to dispose of their own person and property, irrespective of the occurrence of harm—precisely those offences which are taken to be the core of the criminal law; formal equality and a de-moralized form of fault were only taken up by the criminal law following the recognition of ideas of universal political citizenship. However, as Ramsay points out, it is the idea of social citizenship that both drives the development of regulatory criminal law—aimed at addressing practical or substantive limitations on civil and political citizenship—and which seeks to legitimate this broader idea of public wrong, socializing the burdens of risk.[62] The state, in other words, is both the guarantor and the provider of freedom. These social offences, including the numbers of 'regulatory' offences of strict liability introduced with the expansion of the state, were integral to the modern criminal law. More importantly they cannot be seen as 'merely technical' or morally neutral since they protected important legal goods. The changed understanding of 'public wrong' reflected the delicate balance between the different functions of the criminal law and roles of the state, so that it does

---

[58] See M Hildebrandt, 'Justice and Police: Regulatory Offences and the Criminal Law' (2009) 12 *New Criminal Law Review* 43, pointing out that for medieval jurists the distinction had an ontological status and discussing the evolution of the distinction in European legal thought.

[59] P Ramsay, 'The Responsible Subject as Citizen: Criminal Law, Democracy and the Welfare State' (2006) 69 MLR 29. [60] Ibid, 39.

[61] Ibid, 40, discussing TH Marshall's concept of modern democratic citizenship.

[62] Ibid, 48–52.

not make sense to treat certain specific forms of wrong as having either historical or normative priority. This is not to say that we should treat all such norms uncritically, nor that they do not give rise to problems of justification or legitimation, but that our conception of public wrong, as it refers to a body of norms, is linked to a particular kind of view of the criminal law and particular institutional forms.

This argument is also relevant to understanding the recent scholarly interest in the phenomenon of overcriminalization.[63] A broader context for understanding these types of argument is the decline in the legitimacy of the modernist criminal law project described above, as the broad project of social citizenship (and related ideas such as rehabilitation in punishment) have been abandoned in favour of a neo-liberal project which prioritizes state security and individual responsibility.[64] There is not space to explore the ramifications of this development here, but it is interesting to note that there is a school of sociological writing about law which understands the recent growth in legislation as part of a more general regulatory crisis in the post-welfare state.[65] This raises two important issues for the criminal law. First, the question is how we might understand the phenomenon of overcriminalization in the context of juridification (as over-regulation) or regulation in response to a legitimation crisis of the state. Second, it should lead us to ask whether there is anything distinctive about the criminal law that would require us to see it as a special case of juridification. It is a striking comment on the isolation of much criminal law theory that there has been so little engagement with this important theme of sociological thought.

---

[63] For some prominent examples see variously Husak, *Overcriminalization* (n 11 above); A Ashworth, 'Is the Criminal Law a Lost Cause?' (2000) 116 LQR 225; MD Dubber, *Victims in the War Against Crime* (New York, NY: NYU Press, 2002); N Lacey, *The Prisoners' Dilemma: Political Economy and Punishment in Contemporary Societies* (Cambridge: Cambridge University Press, 2008); Stuntz (n 19 above); N Christie, 'Conflicts as Property' (1977) 17 *British Journal of Criminology* 1.

[64] A theme developed by Dubber in his writings on the Modern Penal Code: see MD Dubber, 'Reforming American Penal Law' (1999) 90 *Journal of Criminal Law and Criminology* 49. See also N Lacey, 'In Search of the Responsible Subject: History, Philosophy and Social Science in Criminal Law Theory' (2001) 64 MLR 350, on coordination and legitimation problems in the criminal law.

[65] J Habermas, *A Theory of Communicative Action*, vol 2 (Cambridge: Polity, 1987) 357–73; G Teubner (ed), *Juridification of Social Spheres* (Berlin: de Gruyter, 1987); see also L Friedman, *Total Justice* (New York, NY: Russell Sage Foundation, 1985). For an introduction see S Veitch *et al*, *Jurisprudence: Themes and Concepts* (London: Routledge–Cavendish, 2007) 216–26. N Lacey, 'Criminal Law as Regulation' in J Braithwaite *et al* (eds), *Regulating Law* (Oxford: Oxford University Press, 2004) makes an initial attempt to understand contemporary criminal law in this context.

B   Changing content of particular wrongs

I want to turn now to the question whether or not it is possible to specify certain moral wrongs *a priori* (or as existing prior to and independently of the criminal law), or whether the fact of the continually changing content and structure of wrongs can actually undermine these kinds of claim at a fundamental level. This also requires that we return to the question of whether or not (and in what sense) there can be paradigmatic wrongs or crimes.

My starting point here is the claim that an understanding that something is wrongful depends on our understanding that there is in fact a relation in time and space between conduct and outcome or, less abstractly, between the persons involved.[66] Judgements of wrongfulness cannot be made in abstract terms but always depend on some account of particular ways of acting against another person or thing. This is also reflected in crime definitions. In basic terms, typically the definition of any crime will contain two or more of the following three elements: an account of the object to be protected; an account of modes of commission, or the ways that this object may be interfered with or harmed, or of the prohibited conduct; and an account of the relevant form of agency.[67] However, our understandings of the content and meaning of each of these elements will be shaped by a number of other factors. Both the objects of the criminal law (property, person, and so on) and the means of wrongdoing (how the wrong may be inflicted or caused) are relational—that is to say that they depend on social understandings of the proper extent of either objects or actions in time and space. Thus, as part of any judgement of wrongfulness, we are making decisions about the extent of the object in space and time (where does my body end? What is my property? etc), as well as understanding the extent of any harmful action—not in terms of its consequences but in terms of how harm or wrongdoing is brought about. Our understanding of agency, moreover, is also embedded in social understandings. This might include judgements of who does or does not have agency (for example, an insane person or automaton), but also extends more widely to understandings of how a person might act through time and space, for example in attempting to bring about a certain future outcome in a certain place. An account of criminalization must attend to these temporal and social relations. And these social understandings also raise historical questions: in the words of one eminent historian of crime, an understanding of how crime modernized must 'set the

---

[66] This argument is developed more fully in L Farmer, 'Time and Space in the Criminal Law' (2010) *New Criminal Law Review*, 333.

[67] See, eg J Horder, 'Rethinking Non-Fatal Offences against the Person' (1994) OJLS 335, 341. This account is not intended to be exhaustive—it should also contain an account of the name of the crime etc.

question in the wider context of how the personal comportment, psychological framework, and expectations about interpersonal interactions of individuals altered'.[68]

We can explore the significance of these issues in relation to offences of violence against the person. While this would normally be regarded as a core area of the criminal law, protecting a fundamental interest in the body or personhood, even a brief historical survey suggests that it is not easy to determine either that there is a central or consistent object that is being protected or any clear or central meaning of key concepts such as violence. This raises questions about whether what we take to be central features of this area of crimes have any centrality beyond their immediate historical context, and thus suggests that we should be wary of attaching too much normative weight to our own local conceptions.

In the late eighteenth century, it seems, many assaults were rarely prosecuted, either because they were viewed as private wrongs or because private individuals lacked either the will or the resources to prosecute.[69] This changed as organized police forces were established, enabling the more systematic prosecution and punishment of certain forms of interpersonal violence as public wrongs. This development has been linked to broader arguments about the overall decline of violence in British society since the Middle Ages and changing social attitudes towards violence evidenced both in the disapproval of overt acts of aggression and in the decline in the use of public physical punishments.[70] Yet while much of the effort in this civilizing process was directed at the eradication of forms of public interpersonal violence—thus transforming what were seen as private into public wrongs—this was accompanied by a subtle transformation in the understanding of violence and the person.

This had a huge impact on the scope and structure of the criminal law. Liability for an assault or battery was originally organized around the idea of a personal attack: the kind of direct assault on the body of another person that could only be inflicted intentionally.[71] However, as the modern law developed central aspects of this definition were reformed to cover a wide range of different behaviours, subtly altering the object of the law. These in turn reflected

---

[68] JA Sharpe, 'Crime in England: Long-Term Trends and the Problem of Modernization' in EA Johnson and EH Monkkonen (eds), *The Civilization of Crime: Violence in Town and Country Since the Middle Ages* (Urbana, Ill: University of Illinois Press, 1996) 30.

[69] Blackstone, *Commentaries* (n 54 above) vol IV, 356–7 quoted in P King, 'Punishing Assault: The Transformation of Attitudes in the English Courts' (1996) *Journal of Interdisciplinary History* 43, 58.

[70] See J Carter Wood, *Violence and Crime in Nineteenth-Century England: The Shadow of Our Refinement* (London: Routledge, 2004); Watson (n 29 above).

[71] Cf G Binder, 'The Meaning of Killing' in Dubber and Farmer (n 26 above), on conceptions of killing in the early modern law of homicide.

changes in expectations of interpersonal relations and personal behaviour. First, the transformation of criminal liability enabled the identification and protection of an extended range of legal objects, specifically in the transformation of the sphere of personhood. If the object of the law of assault was originally the protection of the corporeal body, this is now understood to extend to a fuller sense of personhood: the body is protected less as an object in its own right than as a means to develop a sense of personhood or autonomy. Building on this, recent developments in English and Scottish law have seen the protection of the person against 'psychic harm' as well as the protection of forms of racial and religious identity in the limited recognition of 'hate crimes'.[72] The concept of the person here is one which extends beyond the body to include a kind of personal space in which an individual is able to exercise or develop their autonomy and sense of self.[73] In addition, this allows for an extended range of modes of commission, reflecting a change in the understanding of violence. Liability was originally based on the paradigm of direct interpersonal violence, with one person attacking or inflicting injury on a person who is in their immediate vicinity. The new form of liability, by contrast, extends to cover a range of other modes of causing harm or inflicting injury on another person.[74] As a consequence liability could be imposed for actions that brought about consequences in a different place or at a later point in time if they interfered with the personhood of the victim. This is dramatically illustrated by a recent English case in which liability was imposed for the making of silent phone calls which caused psychic harm to their victims where there was no suggestion that the defendant was in the proximity of the victim.[75]

On the basis of even this schematic account it is not easy to see how it might make sense to talk about an *a priori* 'wrong' in offences against the person. We see a shift from a law which is organized around the central case of directly, and intentionally, inflicted physical violence, to one in which the central, or organizing, case is arguably that of an intentional interference with the person. This includes all the cases that fell within the older conception, but also allows

---

[72] *Rv Ireland; Rv Burstow* [1998] AC 147; Crime and Disorder Act 1998 ss 28–33; Criminal Justice (S) Act 2003, s 74.

[73] Cf D Cornell, *The Imaginary Domain: Abortion, Pornography and Sexual Harassment* (London: Routledge, 1995). It is worth noting that this is subtly different from traditional ideas of honour (as something which might be attacked or defended) or status—both of which have at times been protected by the criminal law.

[74] See, eg Lord Ellenborough's Act 1803 (43 Geo III ch 58): 'An Act for the further Prevention of malicious shooting, and attempting to discharge loaded Fire-Arms, stabbing, cutting, wounding, poisoning, and the malicious using of Means to procure the Miscarriage of Women'. See also provisions of Offences Against the Person Act 1861 discussed in P Handler, 'The Law of Felonious Assault in England, 1803–61' (2007) 28 *Journal of Legal History* 183.

[75] *Rv Ireland; Rv Burstow* [1998] AC 147.

the law a more flexible and extended reach. While a case might be made for seeing either one of these as the central or paradigmatic form of wrong in this area of law, the more fundamental point is surely that each one reflects and is linked to particular social meanings of acts, and that these change over time. At the same time, it is possible to argue that assault has been paradigmatic for modern criminal law, though less in the sense of providing a normative model than because by the mid-nineteenth century violent offences had come to be seen as a greater threat to society than property offences.[76] The central point here is that the criminal offences are not necessarily formed around, or do not reflect, a preconceived idea of moral wrong, but are articulated through changing practices of policing and transformations in the social order of modernity. Even a normative account of criminal wrongs must address the social and historical context in which the criminal law is developing in a more sophisticated way than it does at the moment.

C   New crimes and new wrongs?

We come finally to the question of whether there can be 'new' wrongs or whether any new crime must inevitably be reduced to being a form of an existing wrong.[77] This question can raise complex issues of the identity of wrongs and how we might specify criteria for determining whether something is actually new or merely an old wrong committed in a new way. However, fascinating as these questions might be, my main focus here is to raise some questions about whether it makes sense to think in terms of a determinate set of existing wrongs or to think more flexibly about an open-ended set of wrongs, where changes in kind might emerge from the changing contours of already-existing rights and wrongs in an ongoing process of reproducing the social and moral order.

Let me begin by introducing two examples from recent news reports. In the first example, a large number (1,300) of sexually explicit digital photographs showing Chinese-Canadian actor, Edison Chen, with a variety of different women were released onto different websites.[78] He claimed that the pictures had been taken in consensual situations and for his private use only, but that they had been accessed by staff at a computer repair shop and uploaded to a number of different websites. He described the episode as a 'well-planned attack', as the images were not released all at once, but over a period of time, thereby gaining more attention. The incident led him to flee China and to

---

[76]   Handler (n 74 above) 197.
[77]   Or indeed the question whether an 'old' form of wrong might become obsolete, eg sodomy and offences against nature.
[78]   <http://news.bbc.co.uk/1/hi/entertainment/7256657.stm>.

announce that he was giving up his music and acting career; the perpetrators were arrested and prosecuted for obtaining access to a computer with illegal intent.[79] The second example concerns the phenomenon of so-called 'upskirt' photography.[80] This practice, which has been enabled by the wide availability of mobile phones with cameras, involves men surreptitiously taking photographs pointing up the skirts of women who are in public places and then posting them on the internet. This is usually done without identifying the woman—who is normally a stranger to the photographer.[81] This is leading to calls for criminalization of the conduct in the UK.[82]

These examples raise a number of interesting issues. First, in both cases the fact that the images are digital means that they can be distributed instantly to huge numbers of people, in ways that would not have been possible with older forms of technology; the wrong therefore might not consist just in the trespass, but in the rapid and irrecoverable public dissemination of the images.[83] Second, in the case of 'upskirting' in particular, the victim is unaware of the infringement and indeed might never become aware of it nor be an identifiable victim. Third, while both apparently involve some sort of infringement of (at least) the privacy of the victim, this also seems to cut across traditional conceptions of public and private. 'Upskirt photography' is a violation of privacy but in a public place, requiring the protection of private parts as well as private acts.[84] In the case of Chen, the photographs compromised not only the actor (a public figure), but also the women involved, who had presumably initially consented to the photography for private use. It is arguable that some sort of greater wrong is involved, that there is in fact some kind of an 'attack' or assault on his character or reputation rather than his privacy, but here it becomes harder to articulate what it is that is being attacked. If this is an attack on reputation (in the former case) or privacy (in the latter) these would involve extensions to our understanding of the idea of an assault; if the infringement of privacy is the central wrong, then it might be that, as a result of technological development, this is developing a new and paradigmatic importance for the criminal law.

---

[79] <http://www.guardian.co.uk/world/2009/feb/24/edison-chen-court-testimony-sex -scandal>.   [80] <http://www.guardian.co.uk/lifeandstyle/2009/feb/25/women-upskirting>.

[81] Though not in all cases: there is also the phenomenon of 'celebrity upskirt photographs' which are apparently much prized by tabloid newspapers and magazines.

[82] See now Criminal Justice and Licensing (Scotland) Bill (Stage 2, Amendment 110) amending the offence of voyeurism in the Sexual Offences (S) Act 2009.

[83] In the case of Chen it was claimed that the websites received more than 25 million hits in China alone and crashed several servers.

[84] There have been some prosecutions under the Sexual Offences Act 2003, s 67 (sexual voyeurism), though this arguably stretches the meaning of the definition: 'observing another person doing a private act'.

Consider, finally, two examples from recent legislation, both of which have a meaning or significance which cannot necessarily be reduced to other crimes: sexual grooming of a child,[85] and possession of extreme pornography.[86] I do not want to defend these specific crimes here because the provisions outlining them are unquestionably poorly drafted and broader in scope than necessary, but again they challenge us to think seriously about the kinds of assumption that underpin our thinking about legal and moral wrongs.[87]

The first offence, sexual grooming, is defined as meeting or communicating with a child on at least two occasions and travelling to meet them in any part of the world with the intention of committing a relevant offence (under the Sexual Offences Act 2003). The first point to note about this offence is that it is extremely inchoate. In terms of a traditional conception of attempted crime, it is not clear that two communications are sufficient to establish evidence of an intent to commit the more serious offence, nor that merely travelling would mark the move from preparation to perpetration of the crime. To the extent that either does, the new offence merely recriminalizes existing criminal behaviour.[88] The creation of this crime in response to a moral panic about online sexual predators has been controversial and has been much criticized by criminal lawyers—for responding to fears which are not as real or widespread as is claimed and for criminalizing conduct where there is no harm or underlying wrong which cannot be reduced to an existing crime.[89] However, we might ask whether the law is raising a more fundamental set of issues. On the one hand, it addresses a distinctive contemporary concern about the vulnerability of the individual, something that is exacerbated by communication over the internet.[90] On the other, it reflects a collapse of ideas of proximity and trust, which have underpinned social interaction and, in turn, the law of criminal attempts.

---

[85] Sexual Offences Act 2003, s 15 as amended by Criminal Justice and Immigration Act 2008, s 73 and Sch 15.

[86] Criminal Justice and Immigration Act 2008, ss 63–7; Criminal Justice and Licensing (S) Bill, s 34. The law was the outcome of a campaign by the mother of a woman murdered by a consumer of such extreme pornography. For a commentary on the legislation see AD Murray, 'The Reclassification of Extreme Pornographic Images' (2009) 72 MLR 73–90; C McGlynn and E Rackley, 'Criminalising Extreme Pornography: A Lost Opportunity' [2009] Crim LR 245.

[87] Both would fall foul, say, of the external constraints identified by Husak, *Overcriminalization* (n 11 above) ch 3.

[88] That is, the attempt to commit the sexual offence, though with a penalty under the Act of up to ten years' imprisonment.

[89] In Husak's terms this seems to be an ancillary offence (surrogates for the prosecution of core crimes): *Overcriminalization*, n 11 above, 40–44; but might it be the case that the wrong is the grooming and, say, the psychological impact it might have on the development of the child?

[90] This is something that has been most fully addressed by Peter Ramsay in the context of the ASBO. See 'Vulnerability, Sovereignty and Police Power in the ASBO' in MD Dubber and M Valverde, *Police and the Liberal State* (Stanford: Stanford University Press, 2008).

The second offence, possession of extreme pornography, is defined as possession of an image which is both pornographic and extreme. The latter term is defined as either an act which 'portrays, in an explicit and realistic way' acts which threaten life, serious injury, interference with a corpse, or sexual acts with an animal where 'a reasonable person looking at the image would think that any such person or animal was real',[91] or an image which is 'grossly offensive, disgusting or otherwise of an obscene character'.[92] That the law is defined in this way—directed at possession, rather than supply or distribution—reflects the impact of the internet on criminal laws controlling pornography. It is much harder to regulate the internet, to trace supply or distribution, or to enforce such laws as do exist as a result of digitization and network communication. In addition, where laws against such practices traditionally aimed at preventing harm to the victims (ie those portrayed in the photographs, treated as a record of the criminal act), the new law does not require that any harm have taken place at all—demonstrating the undermining of the stability of representation by the internet.[93] It might of course be contended that such 'pseudo'-images create an indirect harm, supporting, encouraging, and facilitating further sexual offences, but there is little evidence to support such a claim.[94] It is also hard, in the absence of actual commission of a sexual offence, to see what the wrong might be, given that the crime is the possession of the image.[95] That said, it is arguable that the impact of the internet is such that there is a problem here that must be dealt with (preventing exposure of minors to such material; protection of those involved in the production of such material), and that this legislation demonstrates precisely the difficulties in trying to address this through traditional categories of harm (direct or indirect) and wrong.

All these examples raise issues of the impact of technology on the criminal law, leading to questions of whether the technology creates new objects to value, and thus potentially new wrongs, or just facilitates new modes of committing existing wrongs.[96] All are arguably situations in which there is

---

[91] Section 63(7). There is a defence that the defendant participated in the acts and that they did not involve the infliction of non-consensual harm, or that what was portrayed in the image as a corpse was not in fact a corpse.

[92] Section 63(6). The offence carries a penalty of up to three years' imprisonment or a fine or both (s 67).

[93] That is, that an image/representation need not represent something or somebody real: see M McGuire, *Hypercrime* (London: Routledge–Cavendish, 2007) 28–31.

[94] By analogy with child pornography. See Murray (n 86 above) 77, discussing the empirical evidence.

[95] For a critique of possession offences see Dubber, *Victims in the War Against Crime* (n 63 above) ch 2.

[96] See the chapter by M Hildebrandt in this volume, on the 'affordances' of technology. See also C Reed, 'Why Must You Be Mean to Me? Crime and the Online Persona' (2011) *New Criminal Law Review*, forthcoming.

no harm, but all challenge us to think about the meaning of violence, of an 'attack', and of the object that is to be protected. Part of the answer to these sorts of question might require us to think about the extent to which technology might afford new forms of wrongdoing, and more radically to consider whether the existing conceptual framework for thinking about these issues is going to continue to be adequate.

IV Conclusion

In this chapter I have tried to challenge those approaches to criminal wrongs which have been too distant from the criminal law. I have tried to show how these approaches rely on certain assumptions about the criminal law, which at the very least need to be brought into the open, and through the use of historical and contemporary examples to raise some questions that must be addressed by a theory of criminalization. Broadly speaking there are two alternative positions, which arguably have the same implications for thinking about criminalization. First, we could accept the contention that there is some sort of unchanging moral concept of wrong, but that its legal content is continually changing.[97] However, this concession is not something minor or incidental—a detail to be filled in once the major issues of wrong have been clarified—but lies at the very heart of the issue. As I hope I have shown, the moral wrong is too remote and general to be of much assistance in developing an account of criminalization. It is, to be sure, important to bear it in mind, but what has been absent is an account of how legal wrongs are generated by and productive of social order. The more radical conclusion is that particular moral concepts of wrong themselves change over time, and if this is the case, then we need to understand more about how our own conceptions have been produced. I am not arguing, it should be clear, against the importance of normative theory in thinking about criminalization; what I have tried to do is to show how this normative theory needs to address some unexplored assumptions as well as responding to transformations in social and political relations. In so doing, I am well aware that the chapter presents many more questions than answers, but the challenge for a normative theory as I see it is to begin to develop a richer account not only of what count as legal wrongs but of how these legal wrongs are linked to social, political, and legal order.

---

[97] This is not unlike the suggestion in Gardner and Shute (n 42 above) 210: 'Much is left to lawmakers and law-interpreters in deciding how best to embody and reflect such symbolic values in a given legal system'.

10

Theories of Criminalization and the Limits of Criminal Law: A Legal Cultural Approach

Kimmo Nuotio*

I   A Theory of Criminalization with a Continental Mindset?

In criminal law theorizing, a theory of criminalization has played only a marginal role compared to many other issues, such as the theory of punishment. Why is this the case? Do we need a specific theory of criminalization and if so, for what purpose? And on what premises should such a theory stand?

I do not claim to be able to fully answer these questions here, but in the following I wish to advance our understanding of these matters. My aim is to show that, if we understand the theory of criminalization in a broad sense, more progress has already been made than might be thought. Continental criminal law theorizing, on which I mainly draw here, has significant resources for thinking about what and how to criminalize. Criminal law theorizing, for two centuries now, has been informed by philosophical points of view, but equally important have been the practice of codification, the practice of law reform, and constitutional debates concerning the proper scope of the criminal law. The distinction between genuine criminal law and police law as well as administrative law has received significant attention. All of this has left its traces in our understanding of the principles guiding criminalization.

In contemporary theory, several approaches and views are in evidence. Whilst they do not amount to a strict theory of criminalization, they can be brought together under an umbrella that could be called the 'European

* Professor of Criminal Law, Centre of Excellence in Foundations of European Law and Polity Research, University of Helsinki.

culture of criminalization'. This more open definition has the advantage that it does not aim to provide a general theory of criminalization, but rather draws on the historical experience of criminalization both in theory and in practice; placing the full range of approaches in their proper context. The historical and social context of theorizing about criminalization would accordingly be taken as part of our study, and in consequence we would better understand the difficulties in constructing a theory of criminalization that remains formal, rational, and scientific while simultaneously reflecting the broader contemporary debates about what sort of criminal law we have and what we think about it. Only a narrow, technical, and output-oriented approach could avoid engaging in issues of justice—issues of the values that lie behind criminalization decisions. My approach in the following is principled rather than functionalist.

The word criminalization itself is ambiguous, referring both to the actual norms that place certain conduct under the threat of punishment and to the legal (often legislative) action of introducing these norms. In the continental European context particularly, talk about criminalization often involves this duality of meaning. Generally speaking, criminalization means the legally binding decision to put a certain form of conduct under the threat of punishment. More specifically, it may also refer to the resulting individual norms of criminal law defining specific forms of conduct as criminal offences. Provisions concerning statutory offences describe certain types of action and define these legally as offences.

The word 'criminalization' gets part of its meaning from its relation to some other concepts. Criminalization is the opposite of *decriminalization*, a practice much talked about but seldom practised. Decriminalization means a deliberate legislative action to remove a particular form of conduct from the list of offences. We probably would not view the effects of judicial decisions as decriminalizing even if they might have the same legal effect as legislative decisions. For instance, the well known phenomenon of the non-application of a criminal law for a significant period of time (desuetude) has a similar legal effect to legislative decriminalization and, if the legislature desires it, requires a legislative act of *recriminalization* to render the relevant conduct criminal.

In a certain sense, the essentials of the criminal law are the sum total of the individual norms of criminalization. In continental systems, the core area of the criminal law has usually been codified, meaning that a penal code has been enacted which contains provisions outlining both the general principles of criminal liability and particular criminal offences. In academic scholarship, the section of the criminal law containing the definition of particular crimes is called the Special Part. Today, the legal positivist presumption is usually that the statutory offences are presented in the light of the legal provisions determining them. In earlier times this was not always the case.[1]

Usually, also, the code covers criminal law fairly holistically, in a somewhat similar fashion to a written constitution. It sets out the law's material contents systematically. The opening chapters of the special part of a criminal code are often highlighted and are more significant than those that follow. The entirety is seen to mirror particularities in a meaningful manner. All this depends on how systematic an enterprise the particular penal code is. Then, criminal law commentators will seek to look at the various offences with a systematic eye, placing them into some sort of order. Thus, a theory of criminalization should also be able to deal with the holistic aspects of fit.

The nineteenth century was marked by this modern emphasis on codification, and this idea has largely prevailed since. The codes of that era have already been reformed at least once. The modern history of criminalization deals with the questions of how, and following what principles, legislatures have treated particular offences in criminal codes; what has been criminalized; what offences have been abolished; and what conduct has been left out, as well as what kind of system the offences constitute when looked at as a whole.

Even in those jurisdictions whose criminal law is mostly contained in a single penal code, other legislation may include additional provisions on offences, albeit usually those which are less serious. The borderline between criminalization and other proscriptions of conduct might no longer be completely clear, especially as far as lesser offences are concerned, since different kinds of administrative sanction share some of the characteristics of punishment. For example, tax authorities may impose additional tax demands where taxation rules are breached. This is not intended as a fine, but for the person required to pay the difference might seem semantic.

True criminalization, in a formal sense, lies in the fact that a defined form of conduct is assigned punishment rather than some other sanction. This has implications for the nature and meaning of decriminalization. Decriminalization could mean removing a prohibition altogether, but it could also mean regulating the conduct in some other way.

It is commonplace that the scope of the criminal law has expanded considerably since the nineteenth century. This growth reflects the regulatory needs of modern societies. Instead of dying out, as perhaps a Durkheimian view would have suggested, criminal law is more important than ever. Criminal codes are increasingly amended by new provisions covering economic and

---

[1] For instance, PJA Feuerbach builds his textbook on criminal law on an abstract typology of various offences, some of which were not recognized as offences in earlier law books: Feuerbach, *Lehrbuch des peinlichen Rechts* (Giessen: Heyer, 1832).

environmental offences, organized crime, trafficking offences, sexual offences, terrorism, and many other forms of criminality. Only very few areas that are regulated seem not to attract some criminal prohibitions. This flood of legislation certainly explains the need to rethink the boundaries of criminal law, and to assess the risks and merits of this trend critically.

II   A Descriptive or a Normative Account? Defining Offences as Public Wrongs?

Academic theories about the special part rules on offences may adopt one of two different approaches: an analytical or a normative one. The difference between the approaches goes back to different interests of knowledge.[2]

The analytical-descriptive approach tries to develop a theory which explains the scope and content of the criminal law by analysing some of its general features, thus revealing the general characteristics of various particular offences and collating them into some broader categories. This approach might also be called systematic.

A normative approach would state the requirements for criminalization. Such an approach seeks to establish normative principles that can serve as critical yardsticks to determine whether criminalization is appropriate. We might also call this approach critical. Under modern conditions decisions whether to criminalize or not are political matters. Even normative scrutiny of the guiding principles cannot provide us with full answers to the political questions, but it would frame the margins of political decision-making. Actual politics might at times drive policy outside such normative frames, which accounts for surprises and exceptions that might be found in the contents of particular criminal codes.

Criminalization could also be understood as defining certain public wrongs and declaring that these wrongs are blameworthy. Offences might be regarded as instances of particular wrongs. But this invites the question: what makes a wrong truly wrong?

We might develop either a material or a formal understanding of the wrongness or wrongfulness of criminal offences. Under the material conception, there are wrongs and harms that qualify as criminal wrongs through the process of criminalization. A formal conception would also stress the constitutive aspect of the process of criminalization. Probably a formal conception would

---

[2] Here I draw loosely on the discussion in W Hassemer, *Theorie und Soziologie des Verbrechens* (Frankfurt: Europäische Verlagsanstalt, 1973) 17–56.

tend to the descriptive, whereas a material conception would also include a normatively critical function.

The idea of a public wrong as the 'substance' of every offence might deliver the same basic insights as the German doctrine of *Rechtsgut*, which we will discuss later. Its merit is that by means of the concept of a wrong the 'general aspect' of a crime committed can be highlighted without downplaying the role of the victim. The wrong of a wrongdoing is public, but in addition an individual may be wronged.[3] The challenge, however, is to explain what this wrong is, in the last instance, if it is something more than just violation of a norm. Further, the concept of a public wrong might need to be connected with that of public goods. Offences directed at the privacy of individuals, for instance, could be characterized as public wrongs, despite protecting something very private.[4] I cannot pursue this issue any further here.

Obviously, any normative account would seek to formulate its results one way or another in terms of reasons underlying criminalizations. The decision to render some form of action punishable must certainly be backed up by reasons, and these reasons obviously relate the offence to some broader context. These reasons certainly continue to be relevant after an action has been criminalized, as they continue to support the criminalization in some substantial sense. If none of the original reasons any longer count as valid, and if no new reasons have emerged, that particular criminalization would look suspect and outdated.

Reasons for making a form of conduct an offence are also likely to be somehow related to the reasons for considering it as wrong (unless we adopt a rather formalistic view of crimes). These reasons could even be the same. Criminalizing careless driving in traffic makes sense as one of the ways to promote traffic safety and save lives. Labelling a particular form of conduct an offence renders it a special instance of reproach, which label could be helpful in shaping the actual ways people drive in traffic.

A theory of criminalization could be constructed on a variety of theoretical and methodological insights. A legal theory or normative theory approach might focus on the special structures of the norms defining offences. A sociological theory of criminalization might look at the social practices that are regarded as offences or, of course, at the practices of legislation. Moral philosophy might theorize about the values to be protected through criminalization. A theory of punishment is also highly important, because labelling an action

---

[3] SE Marshall and RA Duff, 'Criminalization and Sharing Wrongs' (1998) 11 *Canadian Journal of Law and Jurisprudence* 7.

[4] Marshall and Duff move towards communitarian political thinking in explaining that ultimately individual goods turn out to be goods shared with others who are part of the same political community: ibid, 21.

a crime must of course be shown to be a legitimate purpose for law. Political philosophy might look at the democratic debates and procedures that ought to guide legislation.

A relativist theory of criminalization indicates that the law develops, or should develop, at the same pace as society more generally. Society defines itself through criminalization. This view regards the historical and comparative analysis of criminalization and its underlying values as the most important tasks, ahead of the development of universal and generally valid criteria about criminalization that are intended to apply regardless of time and place. We can contrast this view with more normative views. Liberals might believe, for example, that criminalization for paternalistic reasons is never warranted regardless of social circumstances.

Behind these options, such as the relativist/universalist choice, we will find the ranges of approach that we also find in moral and political philosophy. There is always a kind of pre-legal normativity or pre-legal rationality involved. Interestingly, criminalization manifests forbidden forms of conduct, thus representing a kind of negative social imagery. The powerful imagery of the criminal law highlights and even scandalizes prohibited conduct. The related condemnatory role of the criminal law is undoubtedly crucial to understanding criminalization.

Generally in all legal systems offences are harmful forms of conduct which have been forbidden and placed under the threat of punishment and which also constitute something wrong. John Stuart Mill introduced the famous harm principle, a principle that has been explored by Joel Feinberg. Certainly the harm principle is important, and criminal offences could be ordered and ranked according to the type of harm involved. The harm principle also brings in the need to investigate the consequences of various social practices that could be defined as crimes.

Crimes of violence, for instance, not only disturb the general social peace, but also threaten the most important rights and liberties of the individual. Economic crimes may be very harmful both to the state budget and the individual creditors who have invested in this economic activity. One tax fraud does not significantly affect the state budget, but fraudulent general practices do.

Any convincing view on the decision to criminalize will need to be informed by sociological insights. The problem though is that often sociological knowledge does not deliver the answers we seek. It is easier to generate statistics about the rate of domestic violence than it is to estimate what difference introducing new criminal offences in that area would make.

Criminal codes may also contain offences that do not satisfy any reasonable criteria of social harmfulness. This leftover group could be called offences of morality. Many of these are relics of earlier times. They include offences of incest, sodomy, homosexuality, and perhaps blasphemy as well.

Today, it is often argued that balance of utility needs to be clearly positive before criminalization should be resorted to. Not only are the benefits of the protection of value, but the price to be paid needs to be taken into account. Konstantinos A Papageorgiou has developed the principles of criminalization to account for both the primordial nature of the normative harm principle for criminalization, and the normatively restricting principles of autonomy and anti-moralism.[5]

III   *Rechtsgutslehre*

In continental legal thought, the concept of *Rechtsgut*, literally 'legal good', has played an important role in the theory of criminalization. The idea of a *Rechtsgut* is in itself not that far from the harm principle.[6] It also has a utilitarian tone. However, conceptual history also indicates that this approach has some distinctive characteristics of its own.

The idea is that all offences are there to defend specific *Rechtsgüter*, legally protected interests, which denote the substantial sphere of protection that penal provisions represent. The doctrine has been popular in German legal science since the late nineteenth century and has a connection with the jurisprudence of interests (*Interessenjurisprudenz*) of that time. This line of thought started as a follow-up to the work of PJA Feuerbach, who had wanted to define the limits of true criminal law by requiring that a violation of law (*Rechtsverletzung*) always had to have taken place. Mere endangerment would not be enough to found an offence.

Historically, the doctrine of the *Rechtsgüter* was developed as a critique of the Kantian view that a crime is always a violation of law. Feuerbach followed the Kantian line. For Feuerbach, legislation is first and foremost a product of reason.[7] Philosophy of law imposes on positive criminal law certain structures and principles. In the German context, codifying criminal law was of central importance, and idealistic philosophy suggested a critical stance. Codifying was not just a matter of collecting together the existing

---

[5]   KA Papageorgiou, *Schaden und Strafe: Auf dem Weg zu einer Theorie der strafrechtlichen Moralität* (Baden-Baden: Nomos, 1994).

[6]   Cf T Hörnle, 'Offensive Behaviour and German Penal Law' (2002) 5 *Buffalo Criminal Law Review* 255, especially 257ff. Interestingly, Hörnle believes that German penal theory would profit from taking a closer look at Feinberg's work.

[7]   On Kant, see EJ Weinrib, 'Law as a Kantian Idea of Reason' (1987) 87 *Columbia Law Review* 472. Feuerbach dealt extensively with issues of penal legislation.

positive laws, but also of casting light on the law in general, which was regarded as rough, unorganized, and problematic. Accordingly, positive law was thought to be subordinate to philosophically enlightened criminal law thinking. The requirement of a *Rechtsverletzung* was a critical concept and an expression of that link.

Importantly, the concept of criminal law required that conduct could be criminal only if it violated the law. Feuerbach did not suggest that *Rechtsverletzung* be narrowed down simply to infringements of rights of the individual. For instance, blasphemy was still regarded as a proper offence, since it meant an infringement on the social honour of the church.[8] However, he objected particularly to the mixing of punishment with sanctions based on security or defence of society. The first and foremost substantial requirement of an offence was that it unlawfully infringed the system of mutually compatible freedoms in a society.[9] The significant point is that the entirety of critical criminal law theorizing aimed at drawing the boundaries of the criminal law. In a sense it entailed a theory of criminalization even if that term was not used.

For Feuerbach, law was about freedom. The freedom of individuals is the starting point, and we should be granted the greatest amount of freedom compatible with the freedom of the others. In substantial terms, conduct is criminal if it is directed against this system of legally organized freedoms. This rationalistic premise explains why in this view the individual is our focus, and not the interests of society. The crucial thing was that criminal law should be distinguished from *Polizei*, that is, from regulation mainly meant to preserve order in a society.[10] Criminal law differed from *Polizei* in all of its characteristics, since the *Polizei* could legitimately address people from a security and prevention point of view. Criminal law was, however, supposed to require substantial limitations. The doctrine of *Rechtsverletzung* was meant to serve this specific aim.

The positive laws and legislators, however, did not easily adjust to such requirements. Even Feuerbach himself had to admit that many offences, although not being offences proper, still deserved to be held punishable as so-called police offences (*Polizei-Vergehen*). The philosophical programme of the Enlightenment was too rigid to be followed consistently.

---

[8] PJA Feuerbach, *Kritik des Kleinschrodischen Entwurfs zu einem peinlichen Gesetzbuch für die Churpfalz–Bayrischen Staaten* (Giessen: Heyer, 1804) 34–5.

[9] PJA Feuerbach, *Revision der Grundsätze* (Erfurt: Erster Theil, 1799) 39, 49–50.

[10] K Amelung, *Rechtsgüterschutz und Schutz der Gesellschaft* (Frankfurt: Athenaeum, 1972) 24, stresses the point that, in the philosophy of the Enlightenment, the main critical effort was to exclude police offences from the realm of criminal law. Police offences were regarded as striking against the humanistic conception of the value of individual human beings.

This call for a more pragmatic account of criminal law led to the elaboration of a new concept for clarifying what criminal law norms were to protect, if not individual rights. JMF Birnbaum was the first to describe these objects as 'goods'.[11] This view captured better the essence of the existing offences.

The doctrine of *Rechtsgüter*, by introducing a mediating concept between the offence and the actual harm, clarified the substance of the protected interest as something valuable and rendered the 'bad' in the offence understandable as threatening a positive value, the good. The Hegelian criminal law philosophy did not need any theory of the *Rechtsgüter*, but since these premises had been abandoned and theorists of Roman Law, such as Rudolph von Ihering, had developed an objective view on wrongfulness, the route was clear for the development of this concept. The point of view shifted from elements of volition to the material consequences of criminal acts.[12]

The obvious merit of this approach was that offences could be classified according to the interests that they were intended to preserve. The offence of treason protects interests that are very different from those protected by the offence of theft, and the offence of counterfeiting money protects an interest that is very different from that protected by the offence of fraud. Some protected interests are very close to the rights of individuals, such as the right to life, health, and property, whereas other interests are societal and public, such as the operation of traffic or the functioning of the economy, while others again could be state interests. The *Rechtsgut* approach suited a regulatory state because it had a functionalist tone. Various branches of social life could be addressed by means of criminalization. All social life potentially needs some criminal sanctions, and all interests might be endangered and in need of some protection. This move from retribution on the basis of an infringement of right to prevention of crime and protection of interests marks a move towards a profoundly social and relativist conception of criminal law.[13]

Proponents of what became called the classical school, such as Karl Binding, adopted this terminology, but interpreted it rather descriptively. The tension between analytical-descriptive and ethical-normative theories that I mentioned earlier can be seen here as well.[14] According to Binding, the idea of a *Rechtsverletzung* was inadequate, because an individual right cannot really be

---

[11] JMF Birnbaum, 'Über das Erforderniss einer Rechtsverletzung zum Begriffe des Verbrechens' (1834) 15 *Archiv des Criminalrechts (Neue Folge)* 149.   [12] Amelung (n 10 above) 52.

[13] On the difference between liberal and social law, see F Ewald, *L'État Providence* (Paris: Grasset, 1986).

[14] According to Amelung, had not Binding taken up the work of Birnbaum, the whole story of *Rechtsgüter* might have ended: (n 10 above) 45.

violated. The idea of a good explains better what is at stake, since a protected good is negatively influenced when an offence is committed.[15]

Franz von Liszt, the renowned proponent of a sociological school, heavily criticized the views of Binding because, in von Liszt's view, he was too interested in the logical analysis of the concept of norms in criminal law. This, von Liszt argued, led him to leave the concept of *Rechtsgut* unanalysed and consequently did not allow the distinct nature of criminal law to be expressed. Also, von Liszt claimed, Binding presupposed almost an essence of the *Rechtsgut*, which was simply too much. And finally, there was too much variation in the definition of *Rechtsgut*. For von Liszt himself, the *Rechtsgut* was a central concept that connected the content of the criminal law to its policy purposes: a general legal concept not confined to the sphere of penal law. He referred to the views of Carl Gareis, who had defined *Rechtsgut* as an interest protected by a norm.[16]

Slowly but steadily this concept, which had been elaborated by both of the main schools of criminal law thought, became part of the standard vocabulary. It could be adapted to be used by all possible theoretical models. The concept *Rechtsgut* could be used analytically, because it allowed one to suggest that every offence must have a reason, which only has to be brought to light. The criminal law scholar should do this, and thus reconstruct criminal law in a rational manner from a policy perspective. The purpose of protection would then be useful when applying the provision, because of course only cases which advance the purpose should qualify. However, even this approach suffers from some obvious shortcomings. Despite its powerful ability to render provisions on offences understandable and to bring them into systematic contexts, the world of interests is simply too enormous and diffuse to explain the criminal law in any sensible manner. Criminal law might simply take on any social task whatsoever.

Over time, the concept *Rechtsgut* has been defined in a number of different ways,[17] but we need not be diverted by the differences. Legally protected interests encompass not only the interests of the individual (life, health, etc), but also those of society (trust in the currency, trust in documents, functioning of the economy, trust in civil servants), and even the interests of the state (fair elections, defence, protection of state secrets, etc). In the German-speaking world the concept is both profound and familiar. As noted by Markus Dirk Dubber, it could, together with the theory of positive general

---

[15] K Binding, *Handbuch des Strafrechts,* Erster Band (vol 1) (Leipzig: Duncker & Humblot, 1885).

[16] F von Liszt, 'Der Begriff des Rechtsgutes im Strafrecht und in der Encyklopädie der Rechtswissenschaft' (1888) 8 *Zeitschrift für die gesamte Strafrechtswissenschaft* 133.

[17] See, eg C Roxin, *Strafrecht, Allgemeiner Teil I,* 4th edn (München: CH Beck, 2006) 14–15.

prevention, be regarded as one of the great achievements in German criminal law scholarship.[18]

The rich German scholarship on *Rechtgutslehre* could be regarded as an effort to reflect on the limits of the criminal law. Interestingly, academic writing on the history and significance of *Rechtsgutslehre* started mainly in the 1960s. Peter Sina's study, with a classical tone, was the first to reconstruct the emergence and development of these ideas.[19] Knut Amelung continued this investigation a few years later with an extensive examination, also taking into account the functioning of various social systems.[20] Michael Marx contributed his proposal for a hermeneutically inspired normative definition. For him, the law's ultimate goal is to enhance the self-fulfilment of human beings, and the *Rechtsgüter* are those things needed for this.[21] It is fairly clear that such a positive determination of what deserves to be classed as *Rechtsgut* is not very convincing.

Winfried Hassemer followed quickly with his influential study of the theory and sociology of criminal law, focusing particularly on issues of *Rechtsgut*. Hassemer understood the necessity to introduce a social theoretical perspective on criminal law while at the same time being critical of a too functionalist understanding of this area.[22] The stage was set for an active debate, aiming at also identifying the current stage of criminal law's development. Some authors welcomed the modernization of criminal law, and wanted to make criminal law more responsive *vis-à-vis* the emerging regulatory interests, whereas others defended the traditional structures and virtues of criminal law. Hassemer sought a mediating position.

A lot of effort has been made to work on a concept that would serve both descriptive and normative purposes. During the 1990s, the discussion began to relate the *Rechtsgut* to constitutional rights. These efforts proved that the concept of *Rechtsgut* simply could not deliver all the good things it seemed to promise. A very important summary of the debates is a collection of articles from 2003. Andrew von Hirsch, writing about the relationship between the harm principle and the concept *Rechtsgut*, concluded that the concept of a *Rechtsgut* 'cannot alone carry an adequate theory of criminalization'.[23]

---

[18] MD Dubber, 'Theories of Crime and Punishment in German Criminal Law' (2005) 53 AJCL 679.

[19] P Sina, *Die Dogmengeschichte des strafrechtlichen Begriffs 'Rechtsgut'* (Basel: Helbing & Lichtenhahn, 1962).   [20] Amelung (n 10 above).

[21] M Marx, *Zur Definition des Begriffs 'Rechtsgut': Prolegomena einer materialen Verbrechenslehre* (Köln: Heymans, 1972) 60–62.   [22] Hassemer (n 2 above).

[23] 'Der Rechtsgutsbegriff und das "Harm Principle"' in R Hefendehl *et al* (eds), *Die Rechtsgutstheorie: Legitimationsbasis des Strafrechts oder dogmatisches Glasperlenspiel?* (Baden-Baden: Nomos, 2003) 25.

Something more is thus needed. But this, in turn, is the part which has been less systematically developed.

Since the *Rechtsgut* approach has allowed for a certain instrumentalization of criminal law, promoting functionalist understandings, the more critical approaches seek progress towards more profound normative yardsticks, adding new dimensions to the *Rechtsgut* approach. One of the critics of functionalist thinking in criminal law, Winfried Hassemer, has stressed the necessity to underline the importance of person-related *Rechtsgüter*. According to Hassemer we should always try to preserve the link to personal rights and interests, even when we talk about functions and about systems in action.[24] This brings back an aspect of the original idea that Feuerbach put forward in the early days. Furthermore, Arthur Kaufmann constantly stressed the need to preserve a normative link to the concept of a person in all legal theory, to ensure that the legal tradition is not too flexible or output-oriented.[25]

The *Rechtsgut* approach works on teleological premises. The purpose of the rule is part of the penal law norm itself. If every norm has a purpose, this is an analytical truth. It does not say anything about the interests themselves. The same goes for the idea that the protected legal interest could guide the application of these provisions. Since the purpose could be regarded as a perspective on the provisions rather than a separate entity, arguments based on the protected interest tend to be circular. The protected interest could first be interpreted out of the provision, and then with its help, the provision can be interpreted. In order to avoid circularity, the interests should be recognizable separately; independently of the norms of the penal law and the interpretation thereof.[26] The doctrine of *Rechtsgüter* mediates between social practices and legal matters, and has the potential to serve as a point of reference.

The circularity problem could be solved, however, for instance by resorting to a broader doctrine of legal sources. *Travaux préparatoires* could describe what is meant by the provision in terms of the protected interest. Systematic arguments could also be used, especially if the protected interests are reflected in the way the criminal law order has been organized.

There is thus some merit in the notion of *Rechtsgutslehre*. I would put it in the following way. The regulatory interests that call for criminalization are

---

[24] W Hassemer, 'Grundlinien einer personalen Rechtsgutslehre' in L Philipps and H Scholler (eds), *Jenseits des Funktionalismus: Festschrift für Arthur Kaufmann* (Heidelberg: Decker & Müller, 1989) 85–94.

[25] See, eg A Kaufmann, *Rechtsphilosophie in der Nach-Neuzeit* (Heidelberg: Decker & Müller, 1992).

[26] B Schünemann, 'The System of Criminal Wrongs: The Concept of Legal Goods and Victim-Based Jurisprudence as a Bridge between the General and Special Parts of the Criminal Code' (2004) 7 *Buffalo Criminal Law Review* 551, 552–3.

often diffuse and societal. The *Rechtsgutslehre* allows us to recognize this context in a relatively flexible and insightful manner. The purpose in protecting an interest goes beyond protecting particular specific objects. Criminalizing theft gives protection to all property, not just what was stolen. *Rechtsgüter* are a species of generalized social interest, which are usually no longer solely social interests. The level of abstraction is higher than is typical in a consequentialist analysis directly addressing the social merits or harmfulness of a form of conduct. The concept of *Rechtsgut* is flexible enough not only to be applied in modernizing law and an instrumentalist reading, but also to mediate connections to law's ultimate non-functionalist purposes.

The decision to criminalize a particular form of conduct usually takes place within an established legal context. The stage is already set. Theft is not just the particular action of 'taking and removing of personal property with intent to deprive the rightful owner of it', it is an essential interference with a legally recognized system of rights. Whether to criminalize theft or not is a decision situated in the legal context of existing mutual legal obligations.

Many theories of criminalization lend themselves to various types of use. They could be used in an analytical sense, but other uses are equally possible. The *Rechtsgutslehre*, for instance, may be used to classify various offences according to the type of interest they represent. This use might be quite helpful, enabling a systematic approach to the special part of the criminal law.

A more normatively critical approach would stress the fact that the requirement for a legally protected interest establishes a critical yardstick by which to judge all criminal offences. Even the various possible categories of legally protected interest could be looked at critically in order to see whether they deserve the protection of the criminal law. The *Rechtsgutslehre* is meant to provide such normative yardsticks.[27] One might also try to make this doctrine fit various contexts, such as protection of individual autonomy, avoiding paternalistic criminalization (not using a safety belt might be made punishable, because when I sit in a car, what more could I do were I given more freedom?).

The *Rechtsgutslehre* recognizes that certain diffuse protected interests are not enough to justify criminal law norms. We might imagine, for instance, that a parking infringement can be annoying, but it cannot be regarded as an offence worthy of punishment unless it amounts to a breach of a *Rechtsgut*. Of course, drawing limits between the penal law sphere and the sphere of administrative sanctions is to a degree a matter of convention. It might even be that we need to resort to the question of punishment in order to define the core area of criminal law. We could perhaps accept the view that those offences for which a custodial sentence is threatened require more substantial

---

[27] This is often called the 'system-critical' function: see Roxin (n 17 above) 16–18.

justification than lesser offences that might even be comparable to administratively sanctioned conduct. This would be a judgement of proportionality. Such thresholds are important if we hope to be able to draw borderlines for the legitimate use of punishment as part of criminal law in particular. This is very much the sort of debate in which scholars were engaged when *Rechtsgüter* were first discussed.

Especially suspect on this approach are offences that only serve to uphold general morality, because accepting such a diffuse interest would mark the end of all efforts to limit the sphere of criminal laws.[28] Adding a historical dimension, we might even see the advance of principles of criminalization that are able to censure practices of criminalization. Quite clearly these will be based on human rights and notions of fundamental rights. I have in mind the criminalization of homosexuality or of engaging in sex with an animal. Today, the right to express one's sexuality is backed by constitutional provisions. The only ground for regarding bestiality as worth being criminalized would be to consider it as a violation of the interests of the animals—an argument that probably has not been influential.

Other offences that do not truly serve the legitimate interest of protection are also threatened when this normative censure is applied. For instance, blasphemy laws probably do not serve any legitimate interest any longer, unless a new intermediate level of protected interests could be identified. The gods themselves are not in need of, nor entitled to, protection by the criminal law. Obviously enough, human blasphemous action cannot harm the gods themselves. In order to defend criminalization of blasphemy, something else needs to be present. For many decades the reason given for the criminalization of blasphemy, in jurisdictions where this is still done, has been upholding the religious peace and the religious feelings of believers. But it is doubtful that a belief system can be protected by the criminal law. Believers have a right to practise their belief and not be confronted by insults and disturbance. Should belief systems as such be protected? Freedom of speech would then have to be limited accordingly. The matter is rather complicated, as belief systems operate both collectively, in churches, and individually, at the level of individual believers practising their beliefs. I do not wish to pursue this question, but merely hint that a careful analysis of the rights and interests involved is necessary, and that the clear tendency is for such protection of collective belief interests no longer to seem rational and well founded. If upholding such belief

---

[28] In her extensive habilitation study Tatjana Hörnle concludes that criminalizations which only aim to protect morals, sentiments, or taboos, should be removed: Hörnle, *Grob Anstössiges Verhalten: Strafrechtlicher Schutz von Moral, Gefühlen und Tabus* (Frankfurt: Vittorio Klostermann, 2005) 483.

systems is no longer in the interests of society as a whole, blasphemy should be decriminalized.[29]

Religious insults have the potential to trigger severe and violent conflicts if believers start defending the primary values of their beliefs against intentional offence. The legal context is partly formed by the right to exercise religious freedom and establish a church. The modern state grants rights to religious groups, and in some national legal systems protection of these core beliefs against blasphemous action is still granted, not only internally under church laws, but also externally, in the larger community. Blasphemy laws seem to have been reduced and partly removed without severe consequences. They seem to be more a source of the problem than its solution. Curiously enough, hate crime regulations have emerged almost at the same time. It seems better grounded today to protect individuals, including believers, against severely discriminatory practices, than to protect the church as a collective. The *Rechtsgut* approach is not decisive in itself, but it helps us analyse the various directions of protection separately.

IV   Criminalizations as Restrictions on Constitutional Rights

In the German context we see certain continuity from Feuerbach to modern constitutional theories about the limits of criminal law. The idealistic 'Subject philosophy' of Kant and Hegel has over the course of time given way to constitutional law, constitutional theory, and philosophy. Both share the sense of humanism placing the individual at the heart of the legal system. Even the *Rechtsgut* theory preserves a connection both to Feuerbach's ideas and to constitutional theory.

The classical heritage of liberal individualism led to a primacy of the *Rechtsgüter* of the individual *vis-à-vis* the 'collective' *Rechtsgüter*. A modern system of constitutional rights entails both rights and freedoms of the individual, and thus the core values of liberal individualism, but at the same time increasingly recognizes collective interests and societal goals and values as well. The constitution mediates these philosophical ideas into the domain of law. We could even say that a theory of *Rechtsgüter* is actually a way of speaking about these constitutional commitments in the field of criminal law.

---

[29] See R Sandberg and N Doe, 'The Strange Death of Blasphemy' (2008) 71 MLR 971. See also Council of Europe, *Recommendation 1805 (2007): Blasphemy, religious insults and hate speech against persons on grounds of their religion*.

The development of constitutional laws parallels that of the doctrine of the *Rechtsgüter*.[30]

The constitutional setting has a great impact on how these issues are framed in constitutional practice. Constitutional judicial review could deal with matters of criminalization. In constitutional jurisprudence the matter at issue is often a proper balancing of constitutional rights. This brings the discussion close to the legal theory debates about basic rights as legal principles.[31]

In German scholarship, Otto Lagodny has produced an extensive study of the mutual relationship between criminal law and constitutional law.[32] The study proves the usefulness of a constitutional law analysis in various areas of criminal law. Constitutional law provisions are able to some extent to back up the principles of criminal law and also to limit the scope of the criminal law by requiring a substantial argument in support of every decision to criminalize. Fundamental rights guide the legislator to regard criminal law as a scarce resource.[33]

In his study on collective *Rechtsgüter* Roland Hefendehl seeks to establish the ways in which the constitution frames the substantial construction of collective *Rechtsgüter* in criminal law. According to him, constitutional law provisions are not identical to how criminal law legitimately sees collective *Rechtsgüter*, but the constitution is nevertheless able to set limits to what may count as protected interests. The best way of proceeding towards collective *Rechtsgüter*, according to him, must go via the constitution.[34]

The question of how criminalization relates to constitutional rights and principles is also a very practical matter. In modern continental constitutional practice every offence needs to be justified as a restriction of fundamental rights, since all restrictions of basic liberties need to be so justified.

This normative theory of criminalization stresses the legal effects of a decision to criminalize. It raises the issue of legal costs and burdens, and these in turn call for substantial justification. It is clear that the weightiest case for creating a new offence is that criminalization is necessary to protect another important right, such as another fundamental right. Criminalizing theft may be necessary to protect respect for the property rights in society effectively. In

---

[30] MD Dubber has pointed out that in the US context the formalism and proceduralism of constitutional law has marginalized the search for limitations to criminal law, thus contributing to a subordination of the individual to social and state interests in the field of criminal law: see 'Toward a Constitutional Law of Crime and Punishment' (2004) 55 *Hastings Law Journal* 509.

[31] R Alexy, *A Theory of Constitutional Rights* (Oxford: Oxford University Press, 2002).

[32] O Lagodny, *Strafrecht vor den Schranken der Grundrechte* (Tübingen: JCB Mohr, 1996) (Criminal law barred by the constitution).   [33] Ibid, 535.

[34] R Hefendehl, *Kollektive Rechtsgüter im Strafrecht* (Köln: Carl Heymanns Verlag, 2002) 379–80.

some cases criminalizing pollution might be necessary in order to grant suffi-cient respect for environmental interests, and so on.

A normative theory of criminalization typically involves two lines of argu-ment. The first looks at the restrictions on criminalization, whereas the second requires positive policy-type reasoning. The first is mainly of a legal quality, whereas the second requires a sufficiently weighty social need. These criteria may of course be legislated. Other criteria could also be developed, such as that the proposed legislation under scrutiny must satisfy certain criteria of fairness. Criminalization should not be used in a discriminatory fashion, for instance, or allocate burdens unfairly. Jonathan Schonsheck has raised such issues as regards drugs criminalization.[35]

As I have already suggested, the important idea in the fundamental rights approach to decision making about criminalization is that this decision itself is regarded as imposing a burden that requires justification. Therefore, we might say, the legislator is in fact far from free in deciding what to criminalize and how.

I think we see the various competing logics here. A constitutional, funda-mental-rights-oriented, normative theory seeks to define a legitimate sphere for the criminal law by resorting to fundamental rights specifically and the system of rights more generally. As a result, the democratic legitimacy of crim-inalization is pushed into the background. A theory of criminalization that is anchored in constitutional norms works more on the restraints part than on the constitutive part. It leaves it to the political debate to come up with reason-able solutions, but it imposes its principles as part of the requirements of the legal system on this political reasoning.

A substantial normative constitutional theory provides a context for the leg-islator to work within. The same indeed could be said of human rights as both arguments for and factors limiting the scope of the criminal law.

There is certainly a margin for action, and internal changes in the system of rights especially may call for change and adaptation. The development towards new types of fundamental rights, such as environmental rights, has been paralleled by a corresponding growth in legislation concerning environ-mental offences. The fundamental rights approach also manages to preserve some idea of how the reasoning concerning decisions to criminalize should be formulated.

The main problem with a fundamental-rights-based approach is that it usu-ally remains at a rather general level, especially when compared with a *Rechtsgut* approach. It is thus usually a constitutional court or some similar body that

---

[35] J Schonsheck, *On Criminalization: An Essay in the Philosophy of Criminal Law* (Dordrecht: Kluwer, 1994) ch 6.

will control the legal quality of a decision to criminalize. Constitutional law cannot encompass all the nuances of criminal law. Many topics, however, are shared ones, with the principle of legality, for instance, belonging in both of these spheres. The provisions need to be clear and well formulated, they may not be applied retroactively, and so on. Constitutional law on its own cannot bear the whole project of a theory of punishment, but obviously it sets out some of the legal framework within which such a theory must operate.[36]

In a case before the German Federal Constitutional Court the issue was whether the criminal law provision on incest, valid in itself, could be applied, now that it no longer serves any legitimate purpose.[37] The ruling was that it could still be applied. One judge, Winfried Hassemer, a well known scholar, was of a dissenting opinion.

The reasoning of the court is very deep and revealing. It was clearly the case that the court only tested the constitutionality of the relevant norm, that is, whether the penal law norm was contrary to the constitutional norms. The court referred to various limiting principles, such as the *ultima ratio* principle and the principle of proportionality. The court also referred to the fact that the cultural history of the prohibition of incest between siblings showed a very deep societal conviction that such conduct is worth being held punishable. It was ultimately for the legislature to make decisions on such issues. The analysis by Hassemer was more critical, as he saw no sufficient reason to support the punishability of the conduct in question, and gave this deficit a direct legal effect. He regarded the application of this provision as failing the general proportionality test, and believed that the norm prohibiting incest no longer serves any legitimate purpose. It seems that sometimes even the lack of a clear reason backing the relevant criminalization does not lead to non-application, which shows that a theory with more normative bite would be needed.

V   Criminal Law as *Ultima Ratio*

The principle that criminalization should be a last resort, and hence be governed by a principle of *ultima ratio*, might be seen as an important moral and legal obligation.[38] This principle has been much stressed, especially in continental models. The *ultima ratio* principle means very much the same as the subsidiarity principle: all other options need to be resorted to first.

---

[36] Lagodny (n 32 above) 511.

[37] *Beschluss des Zweiten Senats* vom 26 February 2008 – 2 BvR 392/07 (26 February 2008).

[38] See, eg P Minkkinen, ' "If Taken in Earnest": Criminal Law Doctrine and the Last Resort' (2006) 45 *Howard Journal of Criminal Justice* 521.

Criminal law should not be considered *prima ratio* or *sola ratio*, but *ultima ratio*. According to Hassemer, the universalistic *Rechtsgüter* are a part of the problem as these tend to limit the possibilities of defending the subsidiarity principle. The broader the protected interests, the weaker the link between the offence and that interest.[39]

The moral character of this principle can be seen in the specific marking of the sphere of criminal law as something that should basically be avoided. This has to do with legitimacy requirements, and the fundamental legitimacy deficit that criminal law always faces. The *ultima ratio* principle emphasizes the difference between criminal law and other law involving sanctions. *Ultima ratio* is also connected with the ethical and moral nature of the entire enterprise of the criminal law.

A theoretical model of criminalization that does not recognize the role of *ultima ratio* as a powerful limiting principle could be accused of not understanding the fundamental character of criminal law and its distinguishing feature.[40] The moral nature of the enterprise is also expressed in that blaming people for what they have done, which is a crucial general component of criminal liability, requires that the sphere of criminal law be limited and restricted in order to safeguard the weight of blame against inflationary routine use. The *ultima ratio* principle has been stressed in normative criminalization theories, and it goes nicely together with limiting constitutional principles, such as the protection of human dignity.[41] Indirectly it further underlines the point that people should not be treated as objects but rather as subjects, and that criminal law must be constructed according to principles sharing this view.

Doug Husak is one of the few who have seriously tried to assess the significance of the *ultima ratio* principle as part of criminalization theory. He defends the principle on the ground that criminal law is different and 'must be evaluated by a higher standard of justification because it burdens interests not implicated when other modes of social control are employed'. At the same time he, realistically, stresses that this principle alone cannot effectively stop the current flood of new criminalization.[42] Still, I would regard this principle as important because it expresses something about the identity of criminal law. For this particular reason this principle is important today, when instrumentalists often see the criminal law as just one of many sanctioning mechanisms. The entire tradition of critical criminal law scholarship defends the necessity to think about criminal law as different. In contrast with other principles, such

---

[39] Hassemer (n 2 above) 93–4.

[40] The particular nature of criminal law has been discussed by the German Federal Constitutional Court, in its judgment on the ratification of the Lisbon Treaty: Judgment of 30 June 2009.   [41] See, eg N Jareborg, *Scraps of Penal Theory* (Uppsala: Iustus, 2002) 107–22.

[42] D Husak, 'The Criminal Law as Last Resort' (2004) 24 OJLS 207, 234.

as the principle of proportionality, *ultima ratio* is a principle which governs the criminal law in particular and is not merely a principle of good legislation. For example, the principle of proportionality does not express the particular nature of criminal law in the same way.

Ultima ratio as subsidiarity organizes a priority of order. *Rechtgüter* mainly cover a great variety of less significant interests. This is why we have administrative fines and the like. Although we might be concerned with the flood of administrative laws, these are not governed by the *ultima ratio* requirement.

VI   The Nordic Theoretical Approaches

In recent Nordic study theories of criminalization have increasingly received attention. For example, Claes Lernestedt's 2003 book aimed to provide a critical analysis of the various discourses concerning principles of criminalization.[43] Although learned in both German and Anglo-American traditions, his critical aim to prove the insufficiency of both the *Rechtsgut* approach and the harm principle dominates so heavily that the results are relatively meagre.[44] The study, however, showed the theoretical and practical significance of looking at criminalization issues.

The other comprehensive study focusing on these issues is Sakari Melander's study from 2008,[45] which offers a general analysis of the legal rules and principles limiting legislative decisions to make a form of behaviour punishable. The study is both theoretical and pragmatic, because it aims at developing and systematizing the legal constraints, but it does this with the specific intention of contributing to a more structured legislative practice in the domestic legal setting; in this case Finnish law. The focus in Melander's study is almost exclusively on legislative decision-making, which may be problematically narrow. We ought not to underestimate the importance of court decisions in a theory of criminalization.

The study is helpful and learned, but perhaps the limitation to specifically legal constraints together with the pragmatic aims narrows the perspective a bit when regarded as a full theory of criminalization. The normative approach

---

[43] C Lernestedt, *Kriminalisering—Problem och principer* (Uppsala: Iustus, 2003) (Criminalization—Problems and Principles).

[44] See the review by K Nuotio, 'En kritik av kritiken—möjligheten till begränsande sållningsargument vid kriminaliseringsbeslut. En diskussion kring Claes Lernestedts doktorsavhandling' (2004) 91 *Nordisk Tidsskrift for Kriminalvidenskab* 1.

[45] *Kriminalisointiteoria—rangaistavaksi säätämisen oikeudelliset rajoitukset* (Helsinki: Suomalainen Lakimiesyhdistys, 2008) (Theory of Criminalization—On the Legal Constraints on Making an Act Punishable).

has much in common with Husak's approach, manifesting uneasiness about criminalization in practice and seeking improvement through a systematic normative approach. Such an effort is also in line with the *Zeitgeist*, as in Finland both constitutional legal practice and constitutional law theories have been feeding this kind of normative approach. In criminal law scholarship constitutional limits to criminal law were discussed by, for instance, Raimo Lahti[46] and Ari-Matti Nuutila.[47] Since the 1995 reform of the basic rights provisions in the Finnish constitution the constitutional committee of the Parliament has dealt actively with such issues and even developed a doctrine to test the constitutionality of legislation.[48] In the Nordic context, the Finnish approach, both in theory and in practice, has perhaps given the most room for elaborating the restricting principles as part of the legal order itself, thus granting them more actual influence on legislative decisions.

VII   Bringing Reason to Politics

The constitutionally-framed theory of criminalization is legal, as it searches for legal limits and aims to control legal change, in this case the creation of new offences. In a general setting, we see law setting itself above politics, thus resulting in law controlling law. Law often presents itself as a level of reason above politics, which is the raw power to be tamed.

Law as reason is not enough, however. A criminal law theory may not even hope to fully determine the sphere of criminal law. Instead it must understand its own limitations. The constitutive political aspect of criminalization should also be accounted for and there is at least some potential for reason in politics itself. In a democratic political system, the sovereign will of the people is supposed to give the ultimate justification for political decisions. The quality of the political debate is certainly influential if we consider actual political developments. It is a commonplace that we have a lot of criminal law today, much more than is needed, perhaps, and this might have to do not only with deficient legal controls but also with deficient political constraints. Douglas Husak's *Overcriminalization* is a reaction to this situation.

We should distinguish between the ethical and the moral in speaking about legislation. By the ethical I mean the specific conception of good that the political system of a political community seeks to define in its everyday workings

---

[46] R Lahti, 'Constitutional Rights and Finnish Criminal Law and Criminal Procedure' (1999) 33 *Israel Law Review* 592.

[47] A-M Nuutila, 'Crime, Punishment and Fundamental Rights' (2000) 2 *Turku Law Journal* 1.

[48] As concerns constitutional law theory, see V-P Viljanen, *Perusoikeuksien rajoitusedellytykset* (Helsinki: WSLT, 2001).

and struggles. The moral, in contrast, is made up of general and abstract moral principles.

The actual criminal law is one of the markers of a good and decent polity. Issues of criminal law also require special treatment in political handling. I would stress the need to adopt what we might call a 'we perspective' on proposed legal regulations. Political argument should be structured accordingly. The we perspective is normatively binding in the sense that even affected groups and people, even the potential perpetrator, need to be addressed and involved in this debate. Arguments need to be generalized in order to overcome the perspective of individual and private interests only. Criminal law requires that normative moral-ethical language be adopted at the stage of political debate. The previous remarks on the potential risks of democratic processes could be related to these ideas. Too often the models that criminal policy produces are being approached offensively, in terms of conflict, as if the 'enemy' is internal rather than external, and as if the targeted group were not moved by reason and were not part of the legal and political community. In democratic theory, deliberative models express these links between the political and the legal roles better than do aggregative models, which in turn focus on voting and majorities.

If we look at current criminal policy battles in multicultural societies, the we perspective forces a move beyond one's own community, which might be based on strong shared values. Unless the whole political community can share such strong values, the criminal law should not be used to enforce them. In multicultural and multireligious issues, such as blasphemy laws or when regulating the circumcision of boys, often the only wise solution is to withdraw these issues from the sphere of criminal law, because of a lack of consensus on the issue in the ethical community, and because such laws would have problematic effects in censuring normatively social practices and burdening some social groups more than others. It is not obvious how a political community might learn to become sensitive enough *vis-à-vis* the particular traditions of minority groups, and not simply censure them normatively.

VIII   Towards a Decent Culture of Criminalization

Drawing on what has been said earlier, I would like to outline some important elements of a decent and responsible way of dealing with criminalization. What we should aim at, I suggest, is a decent culture of criminalization rather than a narrow and scholarly theory of criminalization. If we wish to call this a theory model, it could have the name 'ethical-normative theory of criminalization', since it takes seriously the legitimacy challenges a criminal law has to face, and seeks to elaborate on the restricting principles contributing both to the legitimacy of criminal law and to its limits. Such a theory is rich in that it unites various sources of inspiration. It could somehow even present itself as a general model of thinking about criminal law in the context of a constitutional democratic state. Furthermore, the links to the Enlightenment tradition of liberal humanism are visible.

The conditions for legitimacy of the criminal law, then, are partly built into the rules and principles of the criminal law itself, and partly into the larger setting of accounting for the legitimacy of law more generally. The principles marking the specific character of criminal law are all expressions of the fundamental moral dilemma, the fundamental legitimacy deficit, mentioned earlier. Criminalization principles could and should be elaborated within the context of a criminal law that is being looked at from the viewpoint of its legitimacy conditions; and the principles themselves are intended to be expressions of such culture.

The *ultima ratio* principle, for instance, requires that criminalization be resorted to only when there is no other way to deal with the problem. Human dignity and proportionality of action should be respected so that the punishments are not cruel, nor humiliating, nor too severe. All these principles mark a criminal law culture that should be cherished in order to preserve the moral nature of the whole enterprise. Bringing a particular issue up as a penal issue brings it simultaneously into this circle of penal law with its special character. Criminalizing a form of conduct by a legislative decision and the abolition of an offence are the clearest examples of how this border is crossed in one direction or the other.

Principles of legality and proportionality are certainly general constitutional principles, and mainly the criminal law context just adds more strictness and emphasis to them. Human dignity is a constitutional principle *par excellence*, but the criminal law context is crucial for it. The *ultima ratio* principle, for instance, really marks the distinction between the criminal law and other laws, by requiring every effort to be made not to resort to criminal law in the first place. The principle of individual guilt is a criminal law principle, but its non-observance would put citizens' enjoyment of their constitutional rights and liberties severely at risk, because criminal liability could hit them unexpectedly.

In my eclecticism I would build an ethical-normative theory of criminalization on the various criteria that are relevant for restoring and safeguarding the legitimacy of criminal law. The harm principle is certainly valuable, because a pressing need to intervene via the criminal law must involve harm that has to be minimized and prevented. The *Rechtsgutslehre* provides us with similar tools. We need to analyse the sphere of protection that a provision is thought to cover.[49] Moral criminalization and similar cases in which the *Rechtsgut* test fails should not be resorted to.

Collective goods cannot warrant protection through the criminal law if they are too general and diffuse. Preservation of law and order, for instance, would not pass that threshold. One should take seriously the challenge of seeking alternatives presented by the *ultima ratio* principle.

We should also work more with the relationship between political thinking and a theory or view of criminalization. We see that different assumptions lead us in different directions. A liberal position has the strength of delivering a powerful normative theory as regards the limits of criminal law. On the other hand, it also operates with a pre-political conception of rights that serves as the ultimate source of normative censure. A more republican or a more communitarian view would indicate that many of the yardsticks also need to be developed and agreed on, and that the development of a society forces us to strike new balances. With something else in mind than just a liberal critique, we will encounter the most perplexing questions. The German debates concerning doctrines of *Rechtsgut* have taught us that we are in a situation in which we can no longer reduce the criminal law to clear-cut categories. Developments in the practice of criminalization have been too dynamic to be understood in simple terms only. These developments further underline the need to elaborate critical and normatively restricting principles. But these principles also need to be backed further by some deeper-level normative principles. In the last instance, we need to refer back to our basic conceptions of criminal law.

---

[49] We need to keep in mind the observation by Nils Jareborg that we need something better articulated, more rational, and less abstract than *Rechtsgutslehre*, in order to develop a theory of reasons for and against criminalization: Jareborg (n 41 above) 78–9. He has summarized his own principles for criminalizations: 94–5.

Index